Al-Jazeera's "Double Standards" in the Arab Spring

Zainab Abdul-Nabi

Al-Jazeera's "Double Standards" in the Arab Spring

A Peace Journalism Analysis (2011–2021)

Zainab Abdul-Nabi
The University of Sydney
Sydney, Australia

ISBN 978-3-031-14278-9   ISBN 978-3-031-14279-6   (eBook)
https://doi.org/10.1007/978-3-031-14279-6

© The Editor(s) (if applicable) and The Author(s), under exclusive licence to Springer Nature Switzerland AG 2022
This work is subject to copyright. All rights are solely and exclusively licensed by the Publisher, whether the whole or part of the material is concerned, specifically the rights of translation, reprinting, reuse of illustrations, recitation, broadcasting, reproduction on microfilms or in any other physical way, and transmission or information storage and retrieval, electronic adaptation, computer software, or by similar or dissimilar methodology now known or hereafter developed.
The use of general descriptive names, registered names, trademarks, service marks, etc. in this publication does not imply, even in the absence of a specific statement, that such names are exempt from the relevant protective laws and regulations and therefore free for general use.
The publisher, the authors, and the editors are safe to assume that the advice and information in this book are believed to be true and accurate at the date of publication. Neither the publisher nor the authors or the editors give a warranty, expressed or implied, with respect to the material contained herein or for any errors or omissions that may have been made. The publisher remains neutral with regard to jurisdictional claims in published maps and institutional affiliations.

Cover illustration: Fadhi Muhammed / EyeEm / Getty Images

This Palgrave Macmillan imprint is published by the registered company Springer Nature Switzerland AG.
The registered company address is: Gewerbestrasse 11, 6330 Cham, Switzerland

Foreword

Annabel McGoldrick and I defined Peace Journalism in terms of editors and reporters making "choices, of what to report and how to report it", which prompt and enable audiences to "consider and value non-violent responses to conflict" (2005: 5). This has always presented difficulties of implementation. How far, after all, are journalists—in any media, at any time—free to choose?

The way in which this question is answered underpins the divide between two approaches to consideration of the societal role of news and its significance in wider relations of cause and effect. Relevant scholarship tends to attribute the chief influences on news content to the political economy of media, including the interests of owners, advertisers and political sponsors. On this view, the extent of journalistic agency is unavoidably limited by the economic, organisational and ideological structures within which it is exercised.

The carefully cultivated public image of Al Jazeera has always seemed to draw heavily on the alternative approach, which emphasises the social responsibility of journalism and the fealty of its exponents to ethical standards and values, which should be applied without fear or favour. Following its launch in the 1990s, it appeared as a standard-bearer of dauntless objectivity, with the impertinence to put candid questions to Gulf rulers more accustomed to fawning servility. Later, the channel's English-language service set out to distinguish itself from Western-owned rivals by promising to show what happens when US missiles land on urban centres (in the 2003 invasion of Iraq, for instance) rather than merely when they are launched.

In this book, Zainab Abdul-Nabi shows that Al Jazeera's journalism was by no means immune, however, from those behind-the-scenes compromises that have become so familiar from studies of Western media. At the very point when some of its most famous coverage—of the "Arab Spring" uprisings in 2011—seemed to endorse its reputation as a catalyst of liberal reform, it was, in truth, applying distinctions in line with the foreign policy goals of its paymasters in the Qatari royal family.

So, those opposing the rule of Bashar Al-Assad in Syria were routinely presented as plucky rebels and freedom fighters, whereas pro-democracy protesters in Bahrain—who went to some lengths, in their messaging, to unite Sunnis and Shias in one movement—were characterised as following a mere "sectarian" agenda, echoing the smears of the country's autocratic rulers. When they were quelled in a security crackdown, backed by Saudi troops deployed through the Gulf Cooperation Council (of which both Qatar and Bahrain are fellow members), it was, therefore, made to seem a more acceptable and understandable response.

Later, Abdul-Nabi shows, AJ executed an abrupt "reverse ferret"—a manoeuvre familiar to watchers of Britain's tabloid press, as targets for attack are suddenly deemed worthy of applause instead. During the so-called Gulf crisis from 2017, which saw Doha at loggerheads with both Riyadh and Manama, the Bahrain protesters straightaway began to enjoy a more sympathetic portrayal by the channel.

Among the more than 700 online articles analysed in this study are some that concern chemical weapons attacks in Syria—an apparently unconnected story, except for the common denominator, that Qatari foreign policy interests were implicated. Here, too, Abdul-Nabi finds, these were faithfully reflected in the coverage offered.

The most significant distinctions here are those of framing. Portraying regime opponents as concerned chiefly with political freedom, on the one hand, or sectarian division and strife, on the other, leads us to expect strong effects in a category that Robert Entman, in a landmark study, calls "moral evaluation" (1993: 52). (Are they "goodies" or "baddies"?) There is then a logical sequence, Entman continues, through "problem definition" and "causal interpretation", whereby audiences can be cognitively primed for "treatment recommendations" to match.

This is where Abdul-Nabi's use and interpretation of her data overlap with the Peace Journalism model, which develops these basic framing concepts to identify those that predicate violent or non-violent conflict responses, respectively. Al Jazeera employed predominantly War Journalism

FOREWORD   vii

frames, she finds: oriented towards violent events, and the propaganda transmitted from official sources, reproducing the definitions and perspectives endorsed by them—all within an overall narrative structure leading, apparently, towards either victory or defeat.

There were, on the other hand, pockets of resistance to these trends. The content analysis is supplemented by interviews with current and former Al Jazeera journalists, including some who quit in protest over the channel's original editorial response to Bahrain's Arab Spring. And there were varying minority amounts of Peace Journalism, testifying to continuing efforts, by at least some AJ editors and reporters, to disclose key issues of background and context, showing process as well as event, to reach out to alternative sources and engage audience critical thinking and even to enable debate over possible policy solutions for the unmet needs and interests of parties to these interlocking issues of conflict.

The result is a rich tapestry of research, highly innovative in its combination of methods and materials, allowing us to trace relations of influence, both on and from media, in a sequence of political events whose interpretation remains vital to any comprehensive critical engagement with the forces and dynamics shaping our modern world. "The History Channel is broadcasting live"—it spread virally as a laconic quip about the Russian invasion of Ukraine in 2022, but it could equally have applied to Al Jazeera's reporting, from its unique ringside seat, on the upheavals of the previous decade throughout southwest Asia.

I am inescapably reminded of the occasion when, as a BBC newsreader and reporter, I applied unsuccessfully for a job with Al Jazeera. It was more of an informal chat, with a former colleague who was preparing, at that stage, for the imminent launch of a London bureau for the AJ English service.

There need be no qualms over its objectivity, I was assured. Problems might arise over stories about Qatar itself, but that was of, at most, marginal concern, because "Qatar is never in the news".

Since then, Qatar has, instead, found itself all too frequently in the news, whether as the result of the country's own vigorous campaigns of public diplomacy or through its manifold connections with developments throughout its region and beyond. Al Jazeera is one of its signature "brands". Zainab Abdul-Nabi gives us, in this volume, the means to develop a nuanced and sophisticated understanding of its significance. As such, the book represents a substantial contribution to scholarly literature not only about Al Jazeera itself, nor even "just" about the Arab Spring uprisings—but both, and also to the study of media-political relations in general.

Chair of the Department of Peace
and Conflict Studies (DPACS)
University of Sydney,
Sydney, Australia

Jake Lynch

REFERENCES

Entman, R. M. (1993). Framing: Toward clarification of a fractured paradigm. *Journal of Communication, 43*(4), 51–58.

Lynch, J., & McGoldrick, A. (2005a). *Peace journalism*. Hawthorn Press.

The author owes a debt of heartfelt gratitude and appreciation to Associate Professor Jake Lynch, Chair of Department of Peace and Conflict Studies at the University of Sydney and a leading scholar in Peace Journalism, for his generous and tireless feedback and critique during the journey of writing this book.

PREFACE

Abbas Al-Samea, a young physical education teacher, was executed by the firing squad on January 15, 2017, for taking part in Bahrain's uprising. The Bahraini authorities charged the 27-year-old activist with conducting a bombing attack in March 2014, as a result of which a police officer was allegedly killed. Although Abbas had an alibi as he was teaching in the Al-Rawabi Private School when the alleged "bombing" took place, he was still sentenced to death. The authorities threatened both Abbas' lawyer and the school's headmaster who testified during his trial. Having attempted to prove his innocence in his own way, Abbas had smuggled a smartphone to his cell, filming himself and refuting the regime's accusation: "I am innocent... I am not afraid, rather completely calm and confident, that the path that I have embarked on is the path of peaceful struggle". This video which brought him more torture had been distributed among social media accounts and posted on YouTube but that was about it. No prominent news media outlet deemed it worthy to mention his story.

Abbas' mother, along with the families of other activists, desperately appealed to the entire world to exert pressure on the Bahraini regime to stop the execution. Yet, no news media outlet knew, listened or reported anything. Abbas, Ali and Sami were all executed on the same day.

Without any delay, most news wires and mainstream media outlets, including the likes of Al-Jazeera Network, covered the story: "Three men executed in Bahrain". That was it. End of the story. On the next day, nothing was reported as nothing was "new" anymore. That is a typical practice of what "War Journalism" or put differently, conventional media routines are all about. What "news values" do this story intersect with? The event is not a major one, the victims are not prominent, the number of victims is not high and the death itself was not that "dramatic".

According to professional, journalistic standards, such stories do not make headlines. At best, the names of Abbas and other activists will be stated in the annual reports of human rights organisations.

Being a journalist myself, I was appalled at journalists' blind obsequiousness to these conventions. That is why, I was fascinated by the "Peace Journalism" approach which, according to its founders Johan Galtung and Jake Lynch, still applies the principles of professional journalism while focusing on prioritising "ordinary people", "creative solutions", "conflict formations" and "history and background" and not shying away of naming the "perpetrators". An approach that deals with the conflict as a "process" that needs to be analysed, understood and explored instead of an "event" that depends temporarily on "here and now".

When the Arab Spring uprisings swept the Middle East in 2011, Al-Jazeera, especially the Arabic channel, was proactive in conveying the voice of those ordinary people. In the aftermath of the downfall of the Tunisian regime, Al-Jazeera's reporters were among the people and even seemed more excited than the protesters themselves. Their stories mattered and made headlines. Even though the channel was banned and restricted in Egypt, it managed to keep its cameras 24/7 in the Tahrir Square. Similar attention was given to the Libyan and Syrian protesters. Though, these cameras and that enthusiasm were not seen in the Pearl Roundabout, the focal point of Bahraini protesters in Manama.

This book utilises the Peace Journalism model as an analytical tool to examine the Al-Jazeera coverage as well as to explore how Qatar's politics, an ally of Bahrain's regime at the beginning of the uprising in 2011, have determined which revolution was "newsworthy" and which revolution was not.

Sydney, Australia   Zainab Abdul-Nabi

CONTENTS

1 Why "Peace Journalism" and Why Al-Jazeera's Coverage of Bahrain and Syria? — 1
  1.1 Introduction — 1
  1.2 Peace Journalism Model — 3
  1.3 Research Design — 4
    1.3.1 Case Studies — 4
  1.4 Theoretical Framework and Methodology — 10
    1.4.1 Peace Journalism Orientations — 10
    1.4.2 Peace Journalism Frames — 12
    1.4.3 Evaluative Criteria of Peace Journalism Frames — 13
  1.5 Research Questions — 14
  1.6 Book's Significance — 15
  1.7 Outline of Book Chapters — 16
  References — 19

2 Al-Jazeera's Relationship with Qatar Before, During and After the Arab Spring (1996–2021) — 25
  2.1 Introduction — 25
  2.2 Al-Jazeera's Sponsor — 27
  2.3 Al-Jazeera's Independence — 28
  2.4 Why Was Al-Jazeera Founded? — 30
  2.5 Al-Jazeera's Coverage of Conflicts — 32
  2.6 Foundation of Al-Jazeera English — 33
  2.7 Differences Between Al-Jazeera Arabic and English — 36

xii CONTENTS

2.8	Al-Jazeera's Role Before the Arab Spring: Qatar's Public Diplomacy	37
	2.8.1 New Public Diplomacy	39
	2.8.2 Hybrid Diplomacy	40
2.9	Al-Jazeera's Role After the Arab Spring: Qatar's Propaganda	41
2.10	Conclusion	44
References		46

3 Peace Journalism Model: Characteristics, Misconceptions and Challenges 53

3.1	Introduction	53
3.2	Definition of Peace Journalism	54
3.3	Evolving of Peace Journalism Characteristics	55
	3.3.1 Galtung's Table	55
	3.3.2 Two-Stage Strategy	56
	3.3.3 Shinar's Five Headings	56
	3.3.4 Good Journalism	56
3.4	Critics of Galtung's Peace Journalism Model	57
	3.4.1 Gilboa's Three-Dimensional Framework	57
	3.4.2 Actor-Event Framework	59
	3.4.3 Reconciliatory Function Characteristics	60
3.5	Expanding Peace Journalism Model	61
	3.5.1 Gender Awareness	61
	3.5.2 Human Rights Journalism	62
3.6	Epistemology of Peace Journalism	62
	3.6.1 Critical Realism	62
	3.6.2 Critical Pragmatism	64
3.7	"Which Facts Are Allowed Through the Gate?"	66
3.8	Peace Journalism and Objectivity	68
	3.8.1 Feedback Loop	68
	3.8.2 Objectivity Regime	70
	3.8.3 Objectivity and Propaganda	71
3.9	Peace Journalism and Advocacy Role	72
	3.9.1 Good Journalism or Advocacy Journalism?	72
	3.9.2 Advocacy Frameworks	74
3.10	Challenges Facing Peace Journalism	75
	3.10.1 News Values	75

| | | CONTENTS | xiii |

| | 3.10.2 | *Media Structure* | 76 |

| | 3.10.3 | *Journalists* | 79 |

| 3.11 | *Possibility of Practising Peace Journalism* | | 80 |

| 3.12 | *Audience Responses* | | 82 |

| 3.13 | *Conclusion* | | 83 |

| *References* | | | 85 |

4 Theoretical Framework and Research Questions — 91

| 4.1 | *Introduction* | | 91 |

| 4.2 | *Theoretical Framework* | | 92 |

| | 4.2.1 | *Peace Journalism Frames* | 92 |

| | 4.2.2 | *Evaluative Criteria of Peace Journalism Frames* | 95 |

| 4.3 | *Time Frame of Selected Online Articles* | | 97 |

| | 4.3.1 | *Data Collection* | 98 |

| 4.4 | *RQ1 and 6: Peace Journalism Framing in Bahrain's and Syria's Conflicts* | | 98 |

| | 4.4.1 | *Peace Journalism Frames and Evaluative Criteria in Bahrain and Syria Coverage* | 98 |

| | 4.4.2 | *Significance of Context in Founding Evaluative Criteria of PJ Frames* | 100 |

| | 4.4.3 | *Context of Bahrain's Uprising* | 101 |

| | 4.4.4 | *Proposed Evaluative Criteria of PJ Frames in Bahrain's Coverage* | 109 |

| | 4.4.5 | *Context of the Al-Ghouta Attack* | 117 |

| | 4.4.6 | *Proposed Evaluative Criteria of PJ Frames in Syria's Coverage* | 122 |

| 4.5 | *RQ 2 and 7: Influence of "Here and Now" on Absence and Presence of PJ Frames* | | 129 |

| 4.6 | *RQ 3 and 8: Dominant Sources in the Bahrain and Syria Coverage* | | 130 |

| 4.7 | *RQ 4 and 9: Framing of Syrian and Bahraini Conflicts* | | 131 |

| 4.8 | *RQ 5 and 10: Pro- and Anti-Qatar Framing in the Bahrain and Syria Coverage* | | 132 |

| 4.9 | *RQ11: Estimation of the Number of Syrian Victims* | | 135 |

| 4.10 | *RQ12: Extent of Depending on News Wires in the Coverage of Bahrain and Syria* | | 135 |

| 4.11 | *Conclusion* | | 136 |

| *References* | | | 137 |

xiv CONTENTS

5 Bahrain's Uprising: Pro-democracy Protests or Sectarian Movement? 143

5.1 Introduction 143

5.2 Key Findings 144

5.3 AJA Coverage of Bahrain's Protests (March–June 2011): A Quantitative Analysis 145

    5.3.1 AJA: Sectarian Framing of Bahrain's Protests and Protesters 145

    5.3.2 Implications of Excluding the Peace/Conflict-Orientated Frames in AJA 146

    5.3.3 AJA: Implications of Excluding the Truth- and Solution-Orientated Frames 155

    5.3.4 AJA: Implications of Including Official Sources and Excluding the Marginalised 159

    5.3.5 AJA: Pro-Qatar and GCC Framing 164

    5.3.6 Can PJ Still Be Implemented in AJA? 167

5.4 AJE Coverage of Bahrain's Protests: Quantitative Analysis 168

    5.4.1 AJE: Implications of Applying the Peace-, Solution- and Truth-Orientated Frames 168

    5.4.2 AJE: Implications of Applying the People-Orientated Frame 172

    5.4.3 AJE: Anti-Qatar Framing 175

    5.4.4 AJE's Shouting in the Dark: An Ideal Example of Peace Journalism 175

5.5 Differences Between AJA and AJE 179

5.6 Conclusion 181

References 182

6 Syria's CWs Coverage (2013): Peace Deal or Military Action to "Punish" the Perpetrator? 191

6.1 Introduction 191

6.2 Key Findings 192

6.3 Implications of Not Displaying Peace Journalism Framing in AJA and AJE 193

6.4 Omission of Significant Facts 194

    6.4.1 Geopolitics of the Syrian Conflict 194

    6.4.2 Omission of the Context of Previous CW Attacks 196

	6.4.3	Omission of Al-Qaeda-Affiliated Groups as Potential Suspects	201
	6.4.4	Omission of Alternative Accounts	209
6.5	Favouring Opposition Sources over the Regime		212
	6.5.1	Double Standard Coverage of the Syrian Regime and Opposition	214
	6.5.2	Double Standards Between Al-Nusra's Captive and Leader	216
6.6	Pro-Qatar Framing in AJA and AJE		222
6.7	Reporting Claims as Facts		224
	6.7.1	Launching Point and Range of Rockets Fired at Al-Ghouta Claims	224
	6.7.2	Intelligence Claims	227
	6.7.3	Number of Victims Claim	229
6.8	AJA and AJE: Differences and Similarities		231
	6.8.1	Significant Application of Solution Frame in AJA and AJE	231
	6.8.2	AJE Is More People-Orientated than AJA	232
	6.8.3	AJA Uses More Emotive Language than AJE	234
6.9	Conclusion		239
References			240

7 Al-Jazeera's (2011–2013) "Double Standards" Coverage of the Bahraini and Syrian Conflicts

		249
7.1	Introduction	249
7.2	Comparison Between the Findings of Bahrain's Uprising in 2011 and Syria's Second CW Attack in 2013	250
7.3	Politics of Media Ownership	251
7.4	Double Standards of Qatar's Foreign Policy in Bahrain and Syria	253
7.5	AJA and AJE: Journalism Culture, Journalists and Target Audience	256
7.6	Developments of Events: Here and Now	259
7.7	News Wires	265
7.8	Conclusion	265
References		267

xvi CONTENTS

8 Gulf Crisis (2014–2021): Al-Jazeera's Dramatic Shift from Pro- to Anti-Bahraini Regime   271
  8.1   *Introduction*   271
  8.2   *Key Findings*   273
  8.3   *Truth Frame in AJA and AJE*   274
        8.3.1   *AJA: Intensive Focus on "Human Rights Violations" After 2017 Gulf Crisis*   274
        8.3.2   *AJE: Consistent Focus on "Human Rights Violations" During All Research Periods*   276
        8.3.3   *AJA and AJE: Reporting "Protesters' Violence" as a "Fact"*   277
  8.4   *AJA and AJE: More Reporting on "Torture" and "Sexual Assaults" After 2017 Crisis*   278
  8.5   *AJA and AJE: More Dependence on Human Rights Sources After 2017 Gulf Crisis*   280
  8.6   *Possible Reasons Behind the Increase of "Human Rights" Coverage*   282
        8.6.1   *AJA: Delegitimising the Bahraini Regime to Serve Qatar's Interest*   282
        8.6.2   *AJE: Less Influenced by Qatar's Foreign Policy*   284
  8.7   *Framing of Saudi Military Intervention and Israeli-Bahraini "Normalisation Deal"*   285
        8.7.1   *AJA: Critical Coverage of Saudi Troops After the 2017 Gulf Crisis*   285
        8.7.2   *AJE: Critical Coverage of Saudi Troops Before and After 2017 Gulf Crisis*   286
        8.7.3   *AJA: Critical Coverage of "Normalisation Deal"*   287
        8.7.4   *AJE: Critical Coverage of "Normalisation Deals"*   290
  8.8   *Domination of "Al-Jazeera" as the Main Source of News After 2017 Gulf Crisis*   291
  8.9   *AJA and AJE: Peace Frame and Representation of "Protests" and "Protesters"*   292
        8.9.1   *AJA: Sectarian Framing of Bahrain's Uprising During All Research Periods*   292
        8.9.2   *AJE: Less Sectarian Framing of Bahrain's Uprising During All Research Periods*   298
  8.10 *AJA and AJE: Limited Application of People Frame*   301
  8.11 *AJA and AJE: Increase in Solution Frame After the 2017 Gulf Crisis*   303

8.12	Overall Peace Journalism Framing in AJA and AJE	305
8.13	Conclusion	306
References		309

9 Conclusion 315

9.1	Introduction	315
9.2	Quantitative Findings	316
9.3	Analytical Findings	317
	9.3.1 Implications of Not Including PJ Frames in 2011 Bahrain's Uprising Coverage	317
	9.3.2 Implications of Not Including PJ Frames in the Al-Ghouta CW Attack Coverage	318
	9.3.3 Double Standard Coverage of Bahrain's (2011) and Syria's (2013) Conflicts	319
	9.3.4 Al-Jazeera After 2017 Gulf Crisis: Legitimisation of Bahrain's Uprising	319
	9.3.5 AJA and AJE: Similarities and Differences	320
	9.3.6 Factors Behind Inclusion and Exclusion of PJ Frames	321
9.4	Suggestions and Limitations	322
References		325

Index 329

ABOUT THE AUTHOR

Zainab Abdul-Nabi received her PhD from the University of Sydney in 2017, and has taught Media and Middle East-related courses at the Universities of Sydney and New South Wales in Australia. Her latest research articles have been published in the journals *New Media & Society*, *Global Media and Communication*, *Peace Review* and *Arab Media & Society*.

List of Tables

Table 3.1	Peace Journalism vs. War Journalism (Galtung, 1998)	55
Table 4.1	Peace Journalism model of Johan Galtung (1986, 1998)	93
Table 4.2	Time frames and number of selected articles for each conflict during a specific research period	99
Table 5.1	Framing of Bahrain's conflict in AJA's coverage	145
Table 5.2	Framing of the protesters in AJA's coverage of Bahrain's uprising	146
Table 5.3	Percentage of including/mentioning the Peace/Conflict-Orientated criteria in AJA's coverage of Bahrain's uprising	147
Table 5.4	Percentage of including/mentioning the Truth-Orientated criteria in AJA's coverage of Bahrain's uprising	156
Table 5.5	Percentage of including/mentioning the Solution-Orientated criteria in AJA's coverage of Bahrain's uprising	158
Table 5.6	Percentage of including/mentioning the People-Orientated criteria in AJA's coverage of Bahrain's uprising	160
Table 5.7	Quoted sources in AJA's coverage of Bahrain's uprising	163
Table 5.8	Pro- and anti-Qatar framing in AJA's coverage of Bahrain's uprising	165
Table 5.9	Framing of Bahrain's conflict in AJE's coverage	169
Table 5.10	Framing of the protesters in AJE's coverage of Bahrain's uprising	169
Table 5.11	Percentage of including/mentioning the Peace/Conflict-Orientated criteria in AJE's coverage of Bahrain's uprising	170
Table 5.12	Percentage of including/mentioning the Truth-Orientated criteria in AJE's coverage of Bahrain's uprising	172
Table 5.13	Percentage of including/mentioning the Solution-Orientated criteria in AJE's coverage of Bahrain's uprising	172

xxi

xxii LIST OF TABLES

Table 5.14	Quoted sources in AJE's coverage of Bahrain's uprising	173
Table 5.15	Percentage of including/mentioning People-Orientated criteria in AJE's coverage of Bahrain's uprising	173
Table 5.16	Pro- and anti-Qatar framing in AJE's coverage of Bahrain's uprising	174
Table 5.17	Percentages of PJ frames in Shouting in the Dark documentary film aired by AJE	176
Table 5.18	Framing of Bahrain's conflict in Shouting in the Dark documentary	177
Table 5.19	Percentages of quoted sources in Shouting in the Dark documentary	177
Table 5.20	Percentage of Peace Journalism frames in AJA's and AJE's coverage of Bahrain's uprising	179
Table 6.1	Percentage of Peace Journalism frames in AJA's and AJE's coverage of Syria's chemical attack	193
Table 6.2	Percentage of including/mentioning the Peace/Conflict-Orientated criteria in AJA's and AJE's coverage of Syria's chemical attack	195
Table 6.3	Percentage of including/mentioning the Truth-Orientated criteria in AJA's and AJE's coverage of Syria's chemical attack	201
Table 6.4	Dominant sources in AJA's and AJE's coverage of Syria's chemical attack	210
Table 6.5	Pro- and anti-Qatar framing in AJA's and AJE's coverage of Syria's chemical attack	223
Table 6.6	Estimation of the number of the victims in AJA and AJE news and features	229
Table 6.7	Percentage of including/mentioning the Solution-Orientated criteria in AJA's and AJE's coverage of Syria's CW attack	231
Table 6.8	Percentage of including/mentioning the People-Orientated criteria in AJA's and AJE's coverage of Syria's chemical attack	232
Table 6.9	Framing of Al-Ghouta's attack in AJA's and AJA's coverage	234
Table 6.10	Framing of the Syrian conflict in AJA and AJE	235
Table 7.1	Frequencies (F) of the PJ frames displayed in AJA during the three months that followed the deployment of GCC troops in Manama	260
Table 7.2	Frequencies (F) of the PJ frame displayed in AJE during the three months that followed the deployment of GCC troops in Manama	261
Table 7.3	Frequencies (F) of the PJ criteria mentioned in AJA during the first three weeks of Syria's CW attack	262
Table 7.4	Frequencies (F) of the PJ criteria mentioned in AJE during the first three weeks of Syria's CW attack	263

Table 7.5	The extent of Al-Jazeera's dependence on news wires while covering Bahrain's uprising and Syria's CW attack	265
Table 8.1	Percentages of including/mentioning the Truth-Orientated criteria in AJA's coverage of Bahrain's uprising in three research periods, from March 5, 2014, to September 28, 2021	275
Table 8.2	Percentages of including/mentioning the Truth-Orientated criteria in AJE's coverage of Bahrain's uprising in three research periods, from March 5, 2014, to September 1, 2021	276
Table 8.3	Frequency of including lexical choices that legitimise the Bahraini protesters in AJA in three research periods, from March 5, 2014, to September 28, 2021	278
Table 8.4	Frequency of including lexical choices that legitimise the Bahraini protesters in AJE in three research periods, from March 5, 2014, to September 1, 2021	280
Table 8.5	Quoted sources in AJA's coverage of Bahrain's uprising in three research periods, from March 5, 2014, to September 28, 2021	281
Table 8.6	Quoted sources in AJE's coverage of Bahrain's uprising in three research periods, from March 5, 2014, to September 1, 2021	281
Table 8.7	The framing of the Saudi military intervention in AJA's coverage of Bahrain's uprising in three research periods, from March 5, 2014, to September 28, 2021	286
Table 8.8	The framing of the Saudi military intervention in AJE's coverage of Bahrain's uprising in three research periods, from March 5, 2014, to September 1, 2021	287
Table 8.9	The extent of critical framing in AJA's coverage of the normalisation deal between Israel and Bahrain	288
Table 8.10	Framing of the normalisation deal signed between Israel and Bahrain in AJA's coverage	288
Table 8.11	The extent of critical framing in AJE's coverage of the normalisation deal between Israel and Bahrain	290
Table 8.12	Framing of the normalisation deal signed between Israel and Bahrain in AJE's coverage	291
Table 8.13	News sources in AJA's coverage of Bahrain's uprising in three research periods, from March 5, 2014, to September 28, 2021	292
Table 8.14	News sources in AJE's coverage of Bahrain's uprising in three research periods, from March 5, 2014, to September 1, 2021	293
Table 8.15	Percentages of including/mentioning the Peace/Conflict-Orientated criteria in AJA's coverage of Bahrain's uprising in three research periods, from March 5, 2014, to September 28, 2021	294

xxiv   LIST OF TABLES

Table 8.16   Framing of Bahrain's conflict in AJA's coverage in three
research periods, from March 5, 2014, to September 28, 2021   296

Table 8.17   Framing of the protesters in AJA's coverage of Bahrain's
uprising in three research periods, from March 5, 2014, to
September 28, 2021   297

Table 8.18   Percentages of including/mentioning the Peace/Conflict-
Orientated criteria in AJE's coverage of Bahrain's uprising in
three research periods, from March 5, 2014, to September 1,
2021   299

Table 8.19   Framing of Bahrain's conflict in AJE's coverage in three
research periods, from March 5, 2014, to September 1, 2021   300

Table 8.20   Framing of the protesters in AJE's coverage of Bahrain's
uprising in three research periods, from March 5, 2014, to
September 1, 2021   301

Table 8.21   Percentages of including/mentioning the People-Orientated
criteria in AJA's coverage of Bahrain's uprising in three
periods from March 5, 2014, to September 28, 2021   302

Table 8.22   Percentages of including/mentioning the People-Orientated
criteria in AJE's coverage of Bahrain's uprising in three
periods from March 5, 2014, to September 1, 2021   302

Table 8.23   Percentage of including/mentioning the Solution-Orientated
criteria in AJA's coverage of Bahrain's uprising in three
periods from March 5, 2014, to September 28, 2021   303

Table 8.24   Percentages of including/mentioning the Solution-
Orientated criteria in AJE's coverage of Bahrain's uprising in
three periods from March 5, 2014, to September 1, 2021   304

Table 8.25   Percentages of PJ frames in AJA's coverage of Bahrain's
uprising in three periods from March 5, 2014, to September
28, 2021   305

Table 8.26   Percentages of Peace Journalism frames in AJE's coverage of
Bahrain's uprising in three periods from March 5, 2014, to
September 1, 2021   306

CHAPTER 1

Why "Peace Journalism" and Why Al-Jazeera's Coverage of Bahrain and Syria?

1.1 INTRODUCTION

The former Qatari Emir Sheikh Hamad bin Khalifa Al-Thani might not have expected the amount of success that Al-Jazeera has achieved, as well as the political troubles it has caused since its foundation in 1996. One year of toppling his father in 1995, Sheikh Hamad initiated sophisticated public diplomacy and state branding strategies. Sheikh Hamad carried out political and economic reforms, dissolved the Ministry of Information and founded Al-Jazeera in 1996. The Al-Thani royal family has tried to put Doha on the global map by funding as well as hosting high ranked, Western-based universities and international sport events. Qatar's public diplomacy was at its height when Sheikh Hamad, along with the former Foreign Minister, Hamad bin Jasim, played a mediating role in the region, especially in Sudan and Lebanon before the Arab Spring.

In Al-Jazeera's early days, nearly all Arab ambassadors in Doha complained to the Qatari authorities about the channel's blunt criticisms to their regimes (El-Nawawy & Iskander, 2003). It was unprecedentedly the first news outlet in the Middle East that challenged the monopoly, manipulation and propaganda of the one-sided Arab state media found throughout the region (Miles, 2010; El-Nawawy & Iskander, 2003; Zayani, 2005; Seib, 2008; M. Lynch, 2006b; Sakr, 2007). This "phenomenal channel" (Zayani, 2005) not only transformed Arabic media, but became a

© The Author(s), under exclusive license to Springer Nature Switzerland AG 2022
Z. Abdul-Nabi, *Al-Jazeera's "Double Standards" in the Arab Spring*,
https://doi.org/10.1007/978-3-031-14279-6_1

1

"powerful non-state actor" (Powers & Gilboa, 2007) and an effective "pan-Arab and pan-Islamist public diplomacy tool" (Seib, 2008, 2010).

Al-Jazeera was the most watched TV channel when the Arab Spring uprisings swept the Middle East in 2011. Its viewership included heads of state such as former President of the United States (US) Barack Obama and Secretary of State Hillary Clinton who praised the coverage of Al-Jazeera English (AJE) during the Egyptian revolution. Al-Jazeera's role during the Arab uprisings has been compared to the "CNN effect" in the first Gulf War. Both Al-Jazeera Arabic (AJA) and AJE intensively covered, facilitated and mobilised pro-democracy protests acting as an "instrument of democratisation" (Bebawi, 2016; Abdelmoula, 2015). While Al-Jazeera enthusiastically covered the revolutions in Tunisia, Egypt, Syria, Libya and Yemen in 2011, it downplayed the uprisings in Qatar's neighbourhood including uprisings in Bahrain and Saudi Arabia—allies of Doha at the time.

In protest to the channel's selectivity in amplifying the voices of Syrian activists over the pro-democracy movement in Bahrain, prominent reporters and journalists resigned from the network in 2011. The main contention of this book is that Al-Jazeera has legitimised the protests in Syria by framing it as a "revolution", yet represented the opposition movement in Bahrain as a mere "sectarian conflict". This book argues that when diplomatic ties were severed between the rulers of Qatar and Bahrain amid what has been known as the "Gulf crisis" in 2017, Al-Jazeera, especially AJA, dramatically shifted its editorial policy. This dramatic shift in policy has now seen it supporting the Bahraini protesters and opposition and shaming and naming human rights violations in the country.

Although scholars who specialise in the politics of Gulf states have widely criticised Qatar's influence on the Al-Jazeera coverage of the Bahrain and Syria uprisings (Kamrava, 2013; Ulrichsen, 2014; Khatib, 2013), Arab media academics and Al-Jazeera scholars have rarely tested these criticisms from a media research perspective (M. Lynch, 2013b, 2015, 2016; Kraidy, 2014).

This book examines Al-Jazeera's "double standards" in Bahrain and Syria during the early stages of the Arab uprisings (2011–2013) using quantitative and qualitative content analysis methods. Utilising framing theory (Entman, 1993) and the Peace Journalism Model (PJM) (Galtung, 1986, 1998), this monograph measures the extent of Al-Jazeera's conformity with Qatar's foreign policy in both conflicts. The study moves beyond the Arab Spring and analyses how the deterioration of ties between Qatar and its neighbours during and after the Gulf crisis in 2017 has affected Al-Jazeera's representation of the Bahraini uprising.

The findings were extracted after analysing a total of 713 online stories from AJA and AJE, as well as conducting interviews with the channels' journalists. The data of the AJA and AJE coverage of the Bahrain uprising was collected from two main periods: (1) the Saudi military intervention from March 14 to June 1, 2011, and (b) the periods before and after the 2017 Gulf crisis from March 5, 2014, to September 28, 2021. The articles on the Syrian conflict, with a focus on the Al-Ghouta CW attack, were collected from August 21 to September 14, 2013.

1.2 Peace Journalism Model

There are a significant number of studies about media coverage on the conflicts in the Middle East, but a very limited number of them have been analysed through the lens of the PJM (Fahmy & Eakin, 2014). This is also the first study that used PJ characteristics to examine both AJA and AJE coverage together.

Galtung (2015, p. 321) states, "to say something about Peace Journalism, something has to be said about peace. To say something about peace, something has to be said about conflict and its resolution". J. Lynch and McGoldrick (2000) describe PJ as a "broader, fairer and more accurate way of framing stories". According to the PJ approach, a balanced coverage can be accomplished by (1) focusing on all conflict phases, before, during and after, (2) explaining conflict formation and (3) giving voice to elites as well as ordinary people (J. Lynch & Galtung, 2010). J. Lynch and McGoldrick (2005a, p. 5) who developed this model on theoretical and empirical levels define it as "when editors and reporters make choices—of what stories to report, and how to report them—that create opportunities for society at large to consider and value non-violent responses to conflict".

The model was founded as a response to the hegemony of news values, traditional media practices and objectivity conventions which are biased in favour of official sources, events and dualism. PJ, therefore, can be considered as an "insurgent form" (J. Lynch, 2014) and "internal reform movement" that aims at revising the professional norms of conventional journalism (Hackett, 2011).

Galtung (1986, 1998) classifies PJ and War Journalism (WJ) based on four orientations: (1) Peace/Conflict vs. War, (2) Truth vs. Propaganda,

4   Z. ABDUL-NABI

(3) People vs. Elites and (4) Solution vs. Victory. PJ scholars argue that displaying PJ orientations in media coverage can create sympathy and better understanding of conflicts, encourage audiences to "consider non-violent responses" and enable viewers to de-code propaganda and distinguish between "facts and claims" (J. Lynch & McGoldrick, 2005a, 2013, 2016; J. Lynch, 2014).

This study further examines to what extent Al-Jazeera has implemented the above orientations of the PJM in its coverage of the Bahrain and Syria conflicts. It also measures the consequences of including and excluding these orientations in both cases. More specifically, it explores whether the application of PJ frames can help de-code officials' allegations, challenge elites' manipulations and create a more accurate image of reality.

1.3   RESEARCH DESIGN

1.3.1   Case Studies

This study explores whether Al-Jazeera's coverage of two case studies, (1) Bahrain's uprising during the Arab Spring in 2011 and during the periods before and after the Gulf crisis from 2014 to 2021 and (2) Syria's second CW attack in 2013, reflects Qatar's foreign policy. The following section of this chapter introduces the context of both conflicts briefly as Chap. 4 dissects the historical background of Bahrain's uprising and Syria's CW attacks in more depth.

Bahrain's Uprising
The people of Bahrain took to the streets on February 14, 2011, demanding democracy and political reforms. Shias, who made up the majority of the protestors and also 65% of the population of Bahrain, have been systematically discriminated against by the Sunni minority rulers, the Al-Khalifa regime. Bahrainis protested peacefully, chanting the slogan that brought down the dictatorships of Egypt and Tunisia: *Al-Sha`ab yurid isqat Al-Nidham* النظام يريد إسقاط الشعب (the people want the downfall of the regime). Both Shias and Sunnis gathered in the Pearl Roundabout, the focal point of the sit-in protest, carrying Bahraini national flags and chanting together "No Shias, no Sunnis, we are all brothers".

Despite the peaceful nature of the pro-democracy protests, the Al-Khalifa regime conducted a violent crackdown on the protestors and portrayed the movement as having a "sectarian" agenda. The Bahraini authorities blamed Iran for "plotting" against its regime and accused the protesters of being "Iranian agents". On March 14, 2011, the regime invited Peninsula Shield Forces (PSF)[1] to quell the uprising. In tandem with deploying 2000 Saudi-led troops (Qatari and Emirati officers were among them) in the capital Manama, King Hamad bin Isa bin Salman Al-Khalifa declared martial law.

On March 15, 2011 (one day after the deployment of PSF troops), the Qatari Prime Minister and Foreign Minister at the time, Sheikh Hamad bin Jasim bin Jaber Al-Thani, told AJA in an interview:

> There are common responsibilities and obligations within the GCC countries, the arrival of Saudi and UAE troops in Bahrain is in line with a GCC defence agreement that calls for all members to oblige when needed and to fully co-operate. We are committed to adhering to the GCC agreement. At the moment, we have peacekeeping troops. We don't have a full force there, but this is up for discussion. (AJE, March 15, 2011)

Days after this interview, a senior Qatari military official told the Qatar News Agency, "the duty of the Qatari force participating in the PSF is to contribute in restoring order and security..., as a Qatari force we are receiving our orders from the head of the joint PSF" (Ulrichsen, 2011).

While Qatar backed a UN resolution to impose a no-fly zone on Al-Gaddafi's forces on March 18, 2011, just four days earlier the PSF were being deployed in neighbouring Bahrain to crack down on the pro-democracy protesters (Mabon, 2012). Qatar's support for democracy in Libya and dictatorship in Bahrain shows how "intervention" has completely different meanings (Ulrichsen, 2014). To Qatar, the uprisings in North Africa did not pose any threats or challenges to the interests of the Emirate, whereas allowing a revolution against an ally and neighbouring country (only 25 miles away from its western shore) could encourage others to protest in the GCC countries (Ulrichsen, 2014). Reports disclose that Saudi Arabia put pressure on Qatar to be part of the Saudi-led troops into Bahrain (Kamrava, 2013). Despite Qatar's continuous attempts to be perceived as independent from Saudi Arabia (Friedman, 2012), Qatari

---

[1] While the Iraq-Iran war was escalating in 1984, the Gulf Cooperation Council (GCC) established the Peninsula Shield Force (PSF) to protect and defend the GCC states from any external threats or attack. The PSF was not deployed during the Iraqi invasion of Kuwait in 1990. It was, however, deployed for the first time since its foundation against the domestic population in Bahrain to quell the uprising in 2011.

authorities made the decision not to oppose the Al-Saud's decision to quell the Bahrain uprising (Khatib, 2013). The uprising in Bahrain brought Saudi Arabia and Qatar closer together, as the success of the pro-democracy movement could mean a rise of a Shia power in the region and a potential ally to Iran (Kamrava, 2013).

Consistent with Qatar's policy at the time, AJA did not cover what was known locally as "Bloody Thursday" in which four protesters were killed and around 300 injured (Matthiesen, 2013). On that day, February 17, 2011, Bahraini security forces raided the Pearl Roundabout at 3 am and opened fire while most protesters were asleep in their tents (Matthiesen, 2013). During the violent crackdown by GCC troops, Al-Jazeera was, in Kamrava's (2013) words, "tongue-tied".

Al-Jazeera from the outset of Arab Spring uprisings framed Libya's and Egypt's protests as "revolutions" (El-Nawawy & El-Masry, 2015; Al-Nahed, 2015). Bahrain's pro-democracy movement, however, has never been referred to as a "revolution" (Abdul-Nabi, 2015). The Bahrain protests were instead reported either as routine events (Noueihed & Warren, 2012) or a sectarian conflict (M. Lynch, 2013b). A study that analysed 94 opinion articles on AJA states that two articles only were about the protests in Bahrain; both of them were "guardedly critical" (Lo & Frkovich, 2013). Furthermore, 60% of AJE's online coverage of the Egyptian and Tunisian uprisings in 2011 quoted ordinary people and citizens (Bashri et al., 2012), whereas only 30% of AJE's coverage of Bahrain's uprising gave voice to the voiceless (Abdul-Nabi, 2015).

On June 5, 2017, Saudi Arabia, Bahrain, the United Arab Emirates (UAE) and Egypt cut off diplomatic ties with Doha over its alleged "support to terrorism, Muslim Brotherhood and Al-Jazeera". Relations between Qatar and Bahrain have deteriorated significantly since the blockade began. What has followed, though, is critical coverage by AJA's channel towards Bahrain with a strong focus on the violent crackdown and systematic torture of opposition figures and protestors by the Bahraini regime. Al-Jazeera has subsequently legitimised the demands of the Shia majority for the first time since 2011 by representing them through a "pro-democracy" lens rather than a "sectarian" one. This study contends that the official shift of Qatar's foreign policy towards Bahrain and Saudi Arabia from 2017 to 2021 has led to a similar shift in Al-Jazeera's editorial policy.

Syria's Second CW Attack

The Syrian uprising started in March 2011, when students were arrested and tortured after writing graffiti calling for the downfall of the regime on the walls of their school in the southern town *Deraa* (where Sunnis make up the majority) (McHugo, 2014). The protests began as a peaceful movement that demanded democracy and real reform. In return, the protesters were met by live ammunition and an excessive use of force. M. Lynch (2013b) says that the violence was indiscriminate and created more anger than deterrence. As a result of the killings, arrests and torture, thousands of Syrians took up arms and many soldiers defected from the regime's army, founding the Free Syrian Army (FSA) which would later be backed and armed by the West and Gulf states (Hughes, 2014).

Carpenter (2013) argues that the Syrian and Bahraini conflicts are only "one theatre in the geopolitical rivalry between Saudi Arabia and Iran". Like the Bahrain protests, Syria's uprising put the interests of Qatar and Saudi Arabia together despite a long history of tense relations (Colombo, 2013). The rivalry between the two countries is still seen in Syria, as both sides have armed conflicting rebel groups. Ulrichsen (2014) and Kamrava (2013) state that Saudi support to Salafis and Qatar's funding to the Muslim Brotherhood (MB) have widened the gap between Syrian groups, making it difficult to form a unified Syrian opposition.

Saudi Arabia and Qatar were quick to condemn Al-Assad's "brutality", calling for international intervention to protect the Syrian people. It is difficult to argue that Saudi Arabia was concerned about Syrian civilians, while its troops were quelling the peaceful pro-democracy movement in its neighbour, Bahrain (Dabashi, 2012; M. Lynch, 2013b). The GCC and Western powers wanted to rid Syria of the Al-Assad regime, not because of his corruption or ruthlessness towards his own people, but because of his strong alliance with Iran (Carpenter, 2013). Even if Al-Assad is not toppled, imposing comprehensive sanctions and international isolation would still affect Syria's value to Iran (M. Lynch, 2013b).

Qatar was the first Arab country that withdrew its ambassador from Damascus in July 2011 (Colombo, 2013). It was leaked that, when the Algerian Foreign Minister Mourad Medelci asked to review the decision of suspending Syria's Arab League membership during the Arab League emergency meeting in November 2011, the Qatari Foreign Minister (at the time) Hamad Bin Jasim (HBJ) warned Medelci to "stop defending Syria because your turn will come, and perhaps you will need us [Qatar]" (Ulrichsen, 2014). One year later, Qatar took a more aggressive stance, calling to arm Syrian rebel groups (Blanchard, 2012). In March 2012, the Qatari authorities provided USD100 million as a "donation" to Syrian rebel groups (Ulrichsen, 2014).

The *Khan Al-Assal* CW attack that occurred on March 19, 2013, was considered an escalation that "crossed Obama's red line".[2] The Syrian Observatory for Human Rights, an organisation based in London and close to the opposition, stated that "16 government soldiers and 10 civilians were killed, and more than 86 were injured" in the CW attack (Barnard, 2013). Syria's allies (Iran and Russia) and the antagonists in the Syrian conflict (the United States, the United Kingdom [UK], France, Turkey, Saudi Arabia and Qatar) traded accusations over the responsibility of using CW. The Syrian regime asked the United Nations (UN) Secretary-General Ban Ki-moon to create an inquiry to investigate the incident. This prompted France and the United Kingdom to demand the UN expand the investigative team's mandate to include incidents that occurred in 2012 (Zanders & Trapp, 2013).

After months of delay, UN inspectors were able to enter Syria to investigate the use of CW in March and April 2013. On August 21, 2013, two days after their arrival, Eastern *Ghouta* in the south-eastern outskirts of Damascus, which was an area controlled by rebels, was struck by rockets containing sarin gas. Hundreds were killed in the attack, including women and children. The United States estimates the number of deaths at 1429, while Médecins Sans Frontières (MSF) (who had medical personnel on the ground in *Al-Ghouta*) estimated that 355 were killed (Erlich, 2014).

Before any investigation was conducted, the Obama administration blamed Syria's Al-Assad regime for the *Al-Ghouta* attack and threatened to launch a limited military action against the country. An agreement was reached on September 14, 2013, between Washington and Moscow over eliminating Syria's CW arsenal. This last-minute agreement saved the country from a possible imminent military strike.

Two months before the Al-Ghouta attack, the Independent International Commission of Inquiry on the Syrian Arab Republic (IICISAR) (2013, p. 21) stated that both sides could use and might have

---

[2] On August 20, 2012, the former US president Barack Obama declared that CW in Syria is a "red line" that—if used—would change his calculations. He said, "We have been very clear to the Assad regime, but also to other players on the ground, that a 'red line' for us is we start seeing a whole bunch of chemical weapons moving around or being utilized. That would change my calculus. That would change my equation" (CNN, 2012).

access to CW. Reports released by the UN and Human Rights Watch in 2014 concluded that the Al-Assad regime as well as the Islamic State in Iraq and Levant (ISIL) used sarin gas during the civil war.

On April 4, 2017, another major CW attack was carried out in *Khan Shaykhun,* killing 74 and injuring 557, with a majority of causalities being civilians. Similar to the *Al-Ghouta* attack, the mainstream media and the United States, the United Kingdom, France, Turkey, Saudi Arabia and Israel were quick to attribute the responsibility to the Al-Assad regime. Three days later, the Trump administration launched 59 cruise missiles, targeting the *Shayrat* Syrian regime Air Base.

Unlike Al-Jazeera's coverage of Bahrain during the early days of its uprising, its coverage of the second CW attack in Syria favoured the opposition. In its coverage of this attack, Syrian regime's sources and views were hardly presented (Ayaad, 2014). What was similar to the Bahrain coverage was that AJA was dominated by Islamist sources that used "sectarian terminologies" (Ayaad, 2014). Ayaad (2014) argues that Al-Jazeera's correspondents appeared to be supportive of military intervention in Syria after the *Al-Ghouta* attack. Salama (2012) (who went to Syria to cover the revolution when it began) criticised the network's reporting and concluded that Qatar's foreign policy has shaped its coverage. M. Lynch (2013b) says, "Al-Jazeera has become a major weapon in Qatar's arsenal, allowing that tiny state to play an outsized role in shaping the Arab agenda".

One might ask why two incompatible cases (Bahrain's uprising and Syria's second CW attack) that have more differences than similarities were selected to be analysed in this book. Selecting two conflicts in which Qatar is politically involved can aid in testing the extent of agreement and disagreement between Qatar's policy in both conflicts and Al-Jazeera coverage. While Qatar participated with Saudi-led troops to suppress Bahraini pro-democracy protesters, it aggressively called for military intervention in Syria to remove "the Al-Assad's dictatorship". Choosing these two conflicts can determine whether Qatar's changing foreign policy in Bahrain and Syria has resulted in inconsistent reporting or "dual standard coverage" of both conflicts. In other words, this study aims to examine if Qatar as Al-Jazeera's sponsor has used the channel as a conduit to its own foreign policy aims, politics and propaganda.

The second reason of selecting these incompatible conflicts is to find out to what degree the differences in these two conflicts' intensity, proximity and political involvement will affect the percentages of applying PJ and WJ orientations/frames.

1.4 Theoretical Framework and Methodology

As mentioned in the introduction of this chapter, this study depends mainly on Entman's (1993) framing theory and Galtung's (1986, 1998) PJM.

Determining frames depends on the presence as well as the absence of certain keywords, phrases, ideas, context, sources and sentences "that provide thematically reinforcing clusters of facts or judgments" (Entman, 1993, p. 52). PJ framing in this study is determined based on the including and excluding of PJ characteristics/orientations.

1.4.1 Peace Journalism Orientations

The PJ schema is inspired by the field of peace research and conflict analysis. According to the peace research field, eliminating direct violence requires acknowledging and dissecting the other main forms of violence: structural and cultural. A peace journalist will not only report on a war, explosions or the number of the injured/victims in a certain conflict but also will have to dig deeper by analysing the roots and history of that conflict.

J. Lynch and McGoldrick (2005a, p. 5) further explain:

> Peace Journalism uses the insights of conflict analysis and transformation to update the concepts of balance, fairness, and accuracy in reporting, provides a new route map tracing the connections between journalists, their sources, the stories they cover, and the consequences of their journalism—the ethics of journalistic intervention, and builds an awareness of non-violence and creativity into the practical job of everyday editing and reporting.

If a conventional journalist has to answer six questions in a news story (what, who, where, when, why and how), a peace journalist will have to answer the questions of "conflict dynamics" which—according to Francis (2002)—includes history, background, causes and views of all parties and the nature of their involvement, the relationship between them and their interests and goals (J. Lynch, 2007).

Galtung (2003) argues that including a broad range of parties and causes makes coverage of conflicts transparent, while omitting these factors conveys a "distorted image of reality".[3] J. Lynch and Galtung (2010) consider PJ to be analogous to "health journalism", which draws attention to disease. Such an approach also explores causes of the disease and highlights possible preventative as well as curative measures. In contrast, they describe WJ as "sports journalism", where "winning is not everything, it is the only thing" (J. Lynch & Galtung, 2010). They also liken PJ to "the high road" where conflicts are seen as a challenge as well as an opportunity to find a creative solution that can transform them. In contrast to PJ, they describe WJ as "the low road" in which conflicts are portrayed as battles between two rivalries.

The only questions WJ asks are: Who is advancing and how many people were killed or injured? While J. Lynch and Galtung (2010) emphasise the significance of reporting peace initiatives and stimulating a dialogue between conflicting parties, they also insist on the necessity of asking the hard questions and revealing "deficits". They say, "No peace proposal, or proposer, is a sacred cow". Moreover, J. Lynch and McGoldrick (2005a) state that reporting peace does not mean overlooking violence. It means, however, emphasising distinctions in the context and in the framing of violent episodes. In short, "it ain't what you do, it's the way that you do it" (J. Lynch & McGoldrick, 2005a, p. 57).

Galtung (1986, 1998) classifies PJ and WJ through four orientations: (1) Peace/War, (2) Truth/Propaganda, (3) People/Elites and (4) Solutions/Victory.

- **Peace-Orientation** can be displayed in media coverage by giving open space and time and explaining history, roots, background, context, causes, parties and goals of all involved sides. **War-Orientation** includes giving restricted time and space, narrowing down the conflict to two parties only, focusing only on visible violence, dehumanising of the "other" and looking for reasons and solution to conflicts in the battlefield.
- **Truth-Orientation** or what J. Lynch (2014, p. 38) calls the "insurgent approach" can be implemented by uncovering propaganda,

---

[3] Johan Galtung uses the terms "reality" and "truth", whereas Jake Lynch uses the term "social reality". J. Lynch (2006a) argues that PJ's epistemology is based on "critical realism". According to this approach, the world cannot be represented "as it is". However, it can be represented "as-agreed" (social reality) (J. Lynch, 2014). This will be explained thoroughly in the epistemology section in Chap. 3.

exposing all wrongdoing of all sides (not only "their sides") and naming abusers. **Propaganda-Orientation** dominates media coverage if officials' allegations/agenda/lies are taken at face value without exposing their wrongdoings.

- **People-Orientation** gives a voice to the marginalised, women, old people, children and civilians caught in conflicts and stresses "peace tendencies in the population". In contrast, **Elite-Orientation** gives space only for elites' initiatives and quotations. It focuses on officials, spokespeople and representatives of known organisations.
- **Solution-Orientation** of Galtung's table requires journalists to give peace proposals (whoever they come from) a chance, voice and space. It invites journalists to be creative and try to find such initiatives. It focuses on implications, effects and the aftermath of conflicts. The **Victory-Orientation** is the exact opposite. It neglects peace proposals (especially if they are not introduced by elites or winners), focuses on winning, condones the effects of conflicts and moves immediately to covering another conflict if there is no more drama in the current one.

1.4.2 Peace Journalism Frames

The PJM is theoretically supported by framing theory (Lee et al. 2006a, 2006b). Gamson and Modigliani (1989, p. 143) define a media frame as "a central organising idea or story line that provides meaning to an unfolding strip of events". According to Entman (1993, p. 52), "to frame is to select some aspects of a perceived reality and make them more salient in a communicating text, in such a way as to promote a particular problem definition, causal interpretation, moral evaluation, and/or treatment recommendation for the item described". Entman (1991, 1993) further states that repeating, placing and reinforcing a text or an image could make a certain interpretation more convincing and salient than other interpretations. Entman (1993, p. 52) says that frames can be determined by including/presence of and excluding/absence of "certain keywords, stock phrases, stereotyped images, sources of information, and sentences that provide thematically reinforcing clusters of facts or judgments".

Mentioning certain facts/frames in a media coverage is as significant as excluding them, especially in political communication, as frames can draw attention to certain aspects of reality and obscure others (Entman, 1993).

Gamson (1989, p. 158) says, "Some facts are emphasised only by certain frames and not others; hence their presence or absence reveals the implicit story line. A frame analysis of news content calls our attention to omission as well as inclusions". *Peace/Conflict, Truth, People* and *Solution* frames will be determined based on (1) what PJ characteristics are included as well as excluded and (2) the frequency of the inclusions and exclusions of these orientations.

A significant number of quantitative studies that operationalised the PJM used framing theory to distinguish between PJ frames and WJ frames (see Lee et al., 2006a, 2006b, Lee & Maslog, 2005; J. Lynch, 2008; Siraj & Hussain, 2012; Hussain & Munawar, 2017). In these studies, the inclusions of PJ orientations were accounted as points for PJ framing. The exclusions of PJ orientations, however, were considered in favour of WJ framing. Youngblood (2017) says that framing and word choice are the key elements of PJ.

Youngblood (2017) further explains, "framing theory is significant for all journalists, but especially so for peace journalists, who often speak of narratives, which can be defined as the interpretation and presentation of a story". These interpretations and presentations are significantly powerful due to their role in creating meaning and thus structuring societal discourses (Youngblood, 2017). This "power" is likely to be misused by "traditional journalists" who create superficial narratives that lack context and strengthen stereotypes (Youngblood, 2017). Conversely, PJ "seeks to offer counter-narratives, and to frame stories in such a way as to encourage a more nuanced, thorough, and constructive societal conversation" (Youngblood, 2017).

1.4.3 Evaluative Criteria of Peace Journalism Frames

Since framing is all about (1) "selection" and (2) "salience" (Entman, 1993), PJ framing requires (1) including/selecting certain facts or "analytical criteria" and (2) mentioning them repeatedly in media content. In this study, these facts (evaluative criteria) are selected and proposed based on two major factors: (1) the context of both conflicts[4] and (2) the orientations/characteristics of the PJM. For instance, an article about Bahrain (analysis unit) will be framed as Truth-Orientated if it (1) exposed human rights violations committed by the Al-Khalifa regime, (2) revealed

---

[4] The contexts of both conflicts are explained thoroughly in Chap. 4.

violations of Saudi troops and (3) uncovered sectarian measures committed by the Bahraini and Saudi authorities. The extent of mentioning and repeating these three criteria will determine the percentage of applying the Truth frame in Bahrain's coverage/articles. Likewise, Peace/Conflict, Solution and People frames will be measured based on the presence and absence of certain criteria.

1.5   RESEARCH QUESTIONS

RQ 1: To what extent did AJE and AJA display PJ frames in their coverage of Bahrain's uprising during the Saudi military intervention (from March 14 to June 1, 2011) and during the periods before and after the 2017 Gulf crisis (from March 5 2014 to September 28, 2021)?

RQ 2: To what extent did the developments of events (here and now) impact on including or excluding PJ frames in Al-Jazeera's coverage of Bahrain's uprising during the Saudi military intervention in 2011?

RQ 3: What were the dominant (quoted) sources in AJA's and AJE's coverage of Bahrain's uprising during all research periods?

RQ 4: How did AJA and AJE frame the conflict and the protesters in Bahrain during all research periods?

RQ 5: To what extent did the framing of the AJA and AJE coverage of Bahrain's conflict during all research periods conform to Qatar's foreign policy?

RQ 6: To what extent did AJE and AJA display PJ frames in their coverage of the *Al-Ghouta* attack in Syria?

RQ 7: To what extent did the developments of the events (here and now) impact on including or excluding PJ frames in Al-Jazeera's coverage of Syria's second CW attack?

RQ 8: What were the dominant sources in AJA's and AJE's coverage of Syria's CW attack?

RQ 9: How did AJA and AJE frame the Al-Ghouta attack and the Syrian conflict?

RQ10: How did AJA and AJE frame the responsibility of using CW in Syria and to what extent did this framing conform to Qatar's foreign policy?

RQ 11: As the estimated number of the victims killed in the CW attack varied widely from one source to another (from 100 to 1600), which estimation dominated the coverage of AJA and AJE?

RQ 12: To what extent did AJA and AJE depend on news wires in its coverage of Bahrain's uprising during all research periods and Syria's second CW attack?

1.6 Book's Significance

Despite the fact that a significant number of studies examined Al-Jazeera's representations of the Arab Spring uprisings, only a few of them have focused on the extent of conformity between the editorial policy of the channel and Qatar's foreign policy (Ayaad, 2014; Al-Nahed, 2015; Abunajela, 2015). None of these rare studies examined the Al-Jazeera coverage of Bahrain, although it triggered wide criticisms from Gulf and Middle East scholars (Ulrichsen, 2014; Kamrava, 2013; Khatib, 2013; Roberts, 2012; M. Lynch 2013b, 2015, 2016). This study aims at filling this gap.

Moreover, most literature that criticised the Al-Jazeera coverage of Bahrain did not distinctively differentiate between the coverage of AJA and AJE. Unlike the majority of the existing literature (Kraidy, 2008; Fakhri, 2011; Fahmy & Al-Emad, 2011; Al-Nahed, 2015), this monograph found major differences between the coverage of AJA and AJE in relation to their commitment to the conventions and standards of objective reporting and journalistic writing.

This is the first comprehensive book that makes a comparison between Al-Jazeera's reporting of the Bahraini and Syrian conflicts and highlights Al-Jazeera's systematic "double standards" in the framing of oppositional movements as well as regimes. This book delves deeper than other similar texts by observing and dissecting the sudden shift in Al-Jazeera's coverage (especially AJA) of Bahrain during the periods before and after the 2017 Gulf crisis from 2014 to 2021. Due to the developing and dramatic nature of Qatar's imposed blockade, this analysis can quench the thirst of the Middle East researchers and analysts.

AJE coverage was previously examined based on the PJM (Ozohu-Suleiman, 2014); this is the first quantitative study, however, that uses the model to analyse the coverage of AJA. Since it was founded two decades ago, many studies have operationalised the PJ theory (see Ross, 2009; Hackett & Schroeder, 2009; Ozohu-Suleiman, 2014; Shinar, 2009; Lee & Maslog, 2005; Lee et al., 2006a, 2006b; Lee, 2010; Shaw et al., 2011; Fahmy & Neumann, 2012a, 2012b; Siraj, 2008, 2010). Very few of these studies focus on the consequences of the absence of PJ frames in representing conflicts (J. Lynch & McGoldrick, 2005b, J. Lynch, 2006a; Nohrstedt & Ottosen, 2011, 2015).

Four chapters of this book (Chaps. 5, 6, 7 and 8) explain thoroughly how excluding certain facts or what Nash (2016) calls a "production of silence" can make coverage vulnerable to propaganda and misrepresentation. For instance, the book found that the absence of the PJ evaluative criteria in the coverage of both conflicts has resulted in promoting the regime's sectarian framing of Bahrain's uprising and legitimising a military action against Syria. This study shows very clearly the value of implementing the PJ characteristics and the extent of distortion that WJ can cause.

Media structure, traditional news values and a "regime of objectivity" can significantly hinder putting PJ into practice (McGoldrick, 2006; Hackett, 2011; Tehranian, 2002; J. Lynch & McGoldrick, 2005a). The findings of this monograph, however, conclude that AJE's adherence to the standards of objective reporting resulted in using less emotive language than AJA. The results also demonstrate that covering the developments of both conflicts (here and now) led to saliently increase the frequency of the Solution-Orientated frame in certain periods. This research is, therefore, evidence that PJ is not a full "departure from professional journalism" and is still "feasible" despite restrictions and challenges (J. Lynch, 2013a, 2014).

Measuring the percentage of PJ frames in the media content of (1) two incompatible conflicts and (2) two channels funded by the same sponsor but still differ in their languages, journalists, media culture, target audiences and competitors can help explore the factors that can increase and decrease the application of PJ criteria.

1.7   Outline of Book Chapters

Chapter 2 sheds lights on the regional and geopolitical reasons behind the founding of AJA and AJE. It comprehensively explains the nature of the relationship between Al-Jazeera and its founder, Qatar. It concludes that before the Arab Spring uprisings, Al-Jazeera was effectively acting as a public diplomacy tool due to its high popularity, credibility and unprecedented criticisms towards Arab regimes. The chapter argues that the sudden change in Qatar's foreign policy from a cordial state to an aggressive interventionist actor in Syria, Libya and Egypt during and after the Arab Spring has been followed by a similar shift in Al-Jazeera's coverage. The chapter demonstrates how this transformation has altered the channel from effective public diplomacy to blatant propaganda serving Qatar and its agenda.

As PJ is utilised in this book as the backbone tool for examining Al-Jazeera's coverage of the Bahraini and Syrian conflicts, Chap. 3 details the characteristics and evolvement of the model since 1965. It presents the main criticisms and limitations of the model from media scholars' perspectives. It then highlights the major misconceptions of the PJ approach regarding its epistemology, advocacy role and [its] stance towards objectivity. This chapter also focuses on the most serious difficulties and challenges that hinder the use of PJ orientations in real-life applications. Moreover, it discusses the impact of the model on audiences and whether journalists can have a role in increasing its potential.

Chapter 4 presents the theoretical framework of the study: framing theory and Galtung's PJM. It thoroughly explains the frames of PJ as well as WJ approaches. This chapter demonstrates how the evaluative/analytical criteria of PJ frames are proposed and suggested. Since the analytical criteria of PJ frames are built based on the context of the Bahraini uprising and Syria's second CW attack, the chapter details the history, background, roots and geopolitics of both conflicts. Chapter 4 then presents the fundamental questions of the book and its quantitative methods.

Chapter 5 demonstrates the findings of the Al-Jazeera network coverage of the 2011 Bahrain uprising. The results show that the differences between the coverage of AJA and AJE were significantly notable. The chapter explains how the lack of PJ frames in AJA has helped downplay the Bahrain pro-democracy protests, instead viewing it as a "sectarian conflict" between the Shia majority and Sunni regime. The empirical analysis also found that the AJA coverage was dominated by regime accounts and pro-Qatar framing. In other words, the Arabic channel sided with the deployment of the Saudi troops in Manama, attributing their presence to "restoring order", and not quelling unarmed protesters. On the contrary, the presence of significant percentages of PJ in the English section aided in countering the Al-Khalifa's sectarian narrative, unveiling Saudi troops' violations, naming all wrongdoers and giving voice to the marginalised.

Unlike the previous chapter, Chap. 6 shows that the coverage of the Arabic and English channels of the second CW attack in Syria did not differ substantially. They were both dominated by WJ and pro-Qatar frames. However, they were notably contrasting in the language usage and adherence to the standards of professional journalism. For instance, AJA adopted more sectarian, emotive and polarising terms/language than AJE in

18   Z. ABDUL-NABI

referring to the Syrian regime and its allies. Chapter 6 argues that the high proportion of WJ in both channels has legitimised military action in Syria in 2013. The main contention of this chapter is that by not implementing PJ into practice, coverage resulted in the justification of a violent response against Syria and focused only on the wrongdoings of one side (Al-Assad regime) while exonerating Al-Qaeda-affiliated groups and ruling out any possibility of their involvement in the Al-Ghouta CW attack.

Chapter 7 argues that Qatar's support to the Al-Khalifa royal family in Manama in 2011 and vocal condemnation of Al-Assad in Damascus has been reflected in Al-Jazeera's coverage, especially AJA's channel. The chapter demonstrates how AJA's coverage favoured the Al-Khalifa regime over Bahraini protesters and Syrian opposition groups over the Al-Assad regime. The findings further reveal that the armed conflict in Syria in 2013 was still framed as a "revolution" by AJA, while the same term was never mentioned during the 2011 peaceful protests in Bahrain. This book defines this as "double standard" coverage which has made AJA a propaganda instrument and mouthpiece of Qatar's foreign policy.

Chapter 8 reveals that the "double standard" representation of the Bahraini and Syrian oppositions by Al-Jazeera has now changed since the Gulf crisis in 2017 when Bahrain, the UAE and Egypt, led by Saudi Arabia, imposed blockade on Qatar. From June 2017 to September 2021, Al-Jazeera reported on the Al-Khalifa regimes through a highly critical lens. Unlike AJA's inclination towards the Bahraini regime in 2011, the channel's coverage during the 2017 Gulf crisis has given legitimacy to Bahraini protesters and disclosed the systematic human rights violations practised by the Bahraini regime against activists. This chapter concludes that the major change in AJA's representation from pro- to anti-Bahraini regime following the 2017 Gulf crisis is in tandem with Qatar's foreign policy changes.

Chapter 9 summarises the main quantitative results of the 713 analysed articles and the implications of the presence, as well as absence, of PJ frames in the coverage of the Bahraini and Syrian conflicts. The chapter argues that media ownership, the degree of conflict intensity, the type of genres, the developments on the ground, the amount of drama, journalism culture, journalists' ideologies and the target audience can decrease as well as at times increase the percentage of PJ content in media coverage. The chapter then presents the limitations of this study and recommendations for future research.

REFERENCES

Abdelmoula, E. (2015). *Al Jazeera and democratization: The rise of the Arab public sphere.* Routledge.

Abdul-Nabi, Z. (2015). Based on the peace journalism model: Analysis of Al-Jazeera's coverage of Bahrain's uprising and Syria's chemical attack. *Global Media and Communication, 11*(3), 271–302.

Abunajela, M. A. (2015). *Al-Jazeera (Arabic) satellite television: A platform for the Muslim Brotherhood in Egypt.* (Doctoral Thesis, University of Bedfordshire). Accessed May 2, 2016, from http://uobrep.openrepository.com/uobrep/handle/10547/601085

Al-Jazeera English. (2011, March 15). *Saudi soldiers sent into Bahrain.* https://www.aljazeera.com/news/2011/3/15/saudisoldiers-sent-into-bahrain

Al-Nahed, S. (2015). Covering Libya: A framing analysis of Al Jazeera and BBC coverage of the 2011 Libyan uprising and NATO intervention. *Middle East Critique, 24*(3), 251–267.

Ayaad, S. W. (2014). *Qatari Foreign Policy, Al-Jazeera, and Revolution in the Middle East and North Africa* (Doctoral dissertation, Communication, Art & Technology: Communication). Accessed March 24, 2016, from http://summit.sfu.ca/item/14739

Barnard, A. (2013, March 19). Syria and activists trade charges on chemical weapons. *The New York Times.* https://www.nytimes.com/2013/03/20/world/middleeast/syria-developments.html?pagewanted=all

Bashri, M., Netzley, S., & Greiner, A. (2012). Facebook revolutions: Transitions in the Arab world, transitions in media coverage? A comparative analysis of CNN and Al Jazeera English's online coverage of the Tunisian and Egyptian revolutions. *Journal of Arab & Muslim Media Research, 5*(1), 19–29.

Bebawi, S. (2016). *Media power and global television news: The role of Al Jazeera English.* IB Tauris.

Blanchard, C. M. (2012). *Qatar: Background and U.S. relations.* Diane Publishing.

Carpenter, T. G. (2013). Tangled web: The Syrian civil war and its implications. *Mediterranean Quarterly, 24*(1), 1–11.

CNN. (2012, August 21). *Obama warns Syria not to cross 'red line'.* https://www.cnn.com/2012/08/20/world/meast/syriaunrest/index.html

Colombo, S. (2013). The GCC Countries and the Arab Spring. In D. John (Ed.), *Arab Spring and Arab thaw: Unfinished revolutions and the Quest for democracy* (pp. 163–179). Ashgate.

Dabashi, H. (2012). *The Arab Spring: The end of postcolonialism.* Zed Books.

El-Nawawy, M., & El-Masry, M. H. (2015). Revolution or crisis? Framing the 2011 Tahrir Square protests in two pan-Arab satellite news networks. *Journal of Applied Journalism & Media Studies, 4*(2), 239–258.

El-Nawawy, M., & Iskander, A. (2003). *Al-Jazeera: The story of the network that is rattling governments and redefining modern journalism.* Westview.

Entman, R. M. (1991). Framing US coverage of international news: Contrasts in narratives of the KAL and Iran Air incidents. *Journal of Communication, 41*(4), 6–27.

Entman, R. M. (1993). Framing: Toward clarification of a fractured paradigm. *Journal of Communication, 43*(4), 51–58.

Erlich, R. (2014). *Inside Syria: The backstory of their civil war and what the world can expect.* Prometheus Books.

Fahmy, S., & Al Emad, M. (2011). Al-Jazeera vs Al-Jazeera: A comparison of the network's English and Arabic online coverage of the US/Al Qaeda conflict. *The International Communication Gazette, 73*(3), 216–232.

Fahmy, S., & Neumann, R. (2012a). Shooting war or peace photographs? An examination of newswires' coverage of the conflict in Gaza (2008–2009). *American Behavioral Scientist, 56*(2), NP1–NP26.

Fahmy, S., & Neumann, R. (2012b). Analyzing the spell of war: A war/peace framing analysis of the 2009 visual coverage of the Sri Lankan civil war in Western newswires. *Mass Communication and Society, 15*(2), 169–200.

Fahmy, S., & Eakin, B. (2014). High drama on the high seas Peace versus war journalism framing of an Israeli/Palestinian-related incident. *International Communication Gazette, 76*(1), 86–105.

Fakhri, F. (2011). *Content analysis of how Al-Jazeera English and Arabic channels framed the war on Gaza* (Master's thesis). Retrieved from ProQuest Dissertations and Theses. Accession Order No. 1496764

Francis, D. (2002). *People, peace, and power: Conflict transformation in action.* Pluto Press.

Friedman, B. (2012). Battle for Bahrain: What one uprising meant for the Gulf states and Iran. *World Affairs, 174*(6), 74–84.

Galtung, J. (1986). On the role of the media in worldwide security and peace. In T. Varis (Ed.), *Peace and communication* (pp. 249–266). Universidad para La Paz.ed.

Galtung, J. (1998). High road, low road – Charting the course for peace journalism. *Track Two 7*(4). Accessed September 14, 2015, from http://reference.sabinet.co.za/webx/access/electronic_journals/track2/track2_v7_n4_a4.htm

Galtung, J. (2003). Peace Journalism. *Media Asia, 30*(3), 177–180.

Galtung, J. (2015). Peace journalism and reporting on the United States. *Brown Journal of World Affairs, XXII*(1), 321–333.

Gamson, W. A. (1989). News as framing: Comments on Graber. *American Behavioral Scientist, 33*(2), 157–161.

Gamson, W. A., & Modigliani, A. (1989). Media discourse and public opinion on nuclear power: A constructionist approach. *American Journal of Sociology, 95*(1), 1–37.

Hackett, R. A., & Schroeder, B. (2009). Does anybody practice Peace Journalism? A cross-national comparison of press coverage of the Afghanistan and Israeli–Hezbollah wars. *Peace and Policy, 13*(1), 26–47.

Hackett, R. A. (2011). New vistas for peace journalism: Alternative media and communication rights. In I. S. Shaw, J. Lynch, & R. A. Hackett (Eds.), *Expanding peace journalism: Comparative and critical approaches* (pp. 35–69). Sydney University Press.

Hughes, G. A. (2014). Syria and the perils of proxy warfare. *Small Wars & Insurgencies, 25*(3), 522–538.

Hussain, S., & Munawar, A. (2017). Analysis of Pakistan print media narrative on the war on terror. *International Journal of Crisis Communication, 1*(1), 38–47.

Independent International Commission of Inquiry on the Syrian Arab Republic. (2013). *Report of independent international commission of inquiry on the Syrian Arab Republic.* Accessed September 14, 2014, from http://www.ohchr.org/Documents/HRBodies/HRCouncil/CoISyria/A-HRC-23-58_en.pdf

Kamrava, M. (2013). *Qatar: Small state, big politics.* Cornell University Press.

Khatib, L. (2013). Qatar's foreign policy: The limits of pragmatism. *International Affairs, 89*(2), 417–431.

Kraidy, M. M. (2008). *Al-Jazeera and Al-Jazeera English: A comparative institutional analysis* (pp. 23–30). Woodrow Wilson International Center for Scholars. Accessed July 30, 2012, from http://repository.upenn.edu/cgi/viewcontent.cgi?article=1282&context=asc_papers

Kraidy, M. M. (2014). Media industries in revolutionary times. *Media Industries, 1*(2), 16–21. Accessed January 20, 2016, from http://www.mediaindustries-journal.org/index.php/mij/article/view/45

Lee, S. T., & Maslog, C. C. (2005). War or peace journalism? Asian newspaper coverage of conflicts. *Journal of Communication, 55*(2), 311–329.

Lee, S. T., Maslog, C. C., & Kim, H. S. (2006a). Framing analysis of a conflict: How newspapers in five Asian countries covered the Iraq War. *Asian Journal of Communication, 16*(1), 19–39.

Lee, S. T., Maslog, C. C., & Kim, H. S. (2006b). Asian Conflicts and the Iraq War: A comparative framing analysis. *International Communication Gazette, 68*(5–6), 499–518.

Lee, S. T. (2010). Peace journalism: Principles and structural limitations in the news coverage of three conflicts. *Mass Communication and Society, 13*(4), 361–384.

Lo, M., & Frkovich, A. (2013). Challenging authority in cyberspace: Evaluating Al Jazeera Arabic writers. *Journal of Religion and Popular Culture, 25*(3), 388–402.

Lynch, J., & Galtung, J. (2010). *Reporting conflict: New directions in peace journalism.* St. Lucia: University of Queensland Press.

Lynch, J., & McGoldrick, A. (2000). Peace journalism – How to do it? *Transcend Website (Peace Journalism)*. https://www.transcend.org/tri/downloads/McGoldrick_Lynch_Peace-Journalism.pdf

Lynch, J., & McGoldrick, A. (2005a). *Peace journalism*. Hawthorn Press.

Lynch, J., & McGoldrick, A. (2005b). War and Peace Journalism in the holy land. *Social Alternatives, 24*(1), 11–15.

Lynch, J. (2006a). What's so great about Peace Journalism. *Global Media Journal, Mediterranean Edition, 1*(1), 74–87.

Lynch, J. (2007). Peace journalism and its discontents. *Conflict and Communication Online, 6*(2), 1–13. http://www.cco.regeneronline.de/2007_2/pdf/lynch.pdf.

Lynch, J. (2008). *Debates in Peace journalism*. Sydney University Press.

Lynch, J., & McGoldrick, A. (2013). Responses to peace journalism. *Journalism, 14*(8), 1041–1058.

Lynch, J. (2013a). Is Peace Journalism feasible? Pointers for research and media development. *Ethical Space: The International Journal of Communication Ethics, 10*(2/3), 15–24.

Lynch, J. (2014). *A global standard for reporting conflict*. Routledge.

Lynch, J., & McGoldrick, A. (2016). Audience Responses to Peace Journalism: Merging results from a four-country research study. *Journalism Studies, 17*(5), 628–646.

Lynch, M. (2006b). *Voices of the new Arab public: Iraq, Al-Jazeera, and Middle East politics today*. Columbia University Press.

Lynch, M. (2013b). *The Arab uprising: The unfinished revolutions of the new Middle East*. PublicAffairs.

Lynch, M. (2015). How the media trashed the transitions. *Journal of Democracy, 26*(4), 90–99.

Lynch, M. (2016). *The new Arab wars: Uprisings and anarchy in the Middle East*. Public Affairs.

Mabon, S. (2012). The battle for Bahrain: Iranian – Saudi rivalry. *Middle East Policy, 19*(2), 84–97.

Matthiesen, T. (2013). *Sectarian gulf: Bahrain, Saudi Arabia, and the Arab Spring that wasn't*. Stanford University Press.

McGoldrick, A. (2006). War journalism and "objectivity." *Conflict and Communication Online, 5*(2), 1–7. Accessed June 14, 2016, from http://cco.regener-online.de/2006_2/pdf/mcgoldrick.pdf

McHugo, J. (2014). *Syria: From the great war to civil war*. Saqi.

Miles, H. (2010). *Al-Jazeera: How Arab TV news challenged the world*. Abacus.

Nash, C. (2016). *What is journalism? The art and politics of a rupture*. Palgrave Macmillan.

Nohrstedt, S. A., & Ottosen, R. (2011). Peace journalism–critical discourse case study: Media and the plan for Swedish and Norwegian defence cooperation. In I. S. Shaw, J. Lynch, & R. A. Hackett (Eds.), *Expanding peace journalism: Comparative and critical approaches* (pp. 217–238). Sydney University Press.

Nohrstedt, S. A., & Ottosen, R. (2015). Peace journalism: A proposition for conceptual and methodological improvements. *Global Media and Communication, 11*(3), 219–235.

Noueihed, L., & Warren, A. (2012). *The battle for the Arab spring: Revolution, counter-revolution and the making of a new era.* Yale University Press.

Ozohu-Suleiman, Y. (2014). War journalism on Israel/Palestine: Does contra-flow really make a difference? *Media, War & Conflict, 7*(1), 85–103.

Powers, S., & Gilboa, E. (2007). The public diplomacy of Al Jazeera. In *New media and the new Middle East* (pp. 53–80). Palgrave Macmillan US.

Roberts, D. (2012). Understanding Qatar's foreign policy objectives. *Mediterranean Politics, 17*(2), 233–239.

Ross, S. D. (2009). A Summer's pastime: Strategic construction of the 2006 war in Lebanon. In S. D. Ross & M. Tehranian (Eds.), *Peace journalism in times of war* (pp. 59–78). Transaction Publishers.

Sakr, N. (2007). *Arab television today.* IB Tauris.

Salama, V. (2012). Covering Syria. *The International Journal of Press/Politics, 17*(4), 516–526.

Seib, P. M. (2008). *The "Al Jazeera effect": How the new global media are reshaping world politics.* Potamac Books.

Seib, P. M. (2010). Transnational journalism, public diplomacy, and virtual states. *Journalism Studies, 11*(5), 734–744.

Shaw, I. S., Lynch, J., & Hackett, R. A. (Eds.). (2011). *Expanding peace journalism: Comparative and critical approaches.* Sydney University Press.

Shinar, D. (2009). Can Peace Journalism make progress? The coverage of the 2006 Lebanon War in Canadian and Israeli media. *International Communication Gazette, 71*(6), 451–471.

Siraj, S. A. (2008, May). *War or Peace Journalism in elite US newspapers: Exploring news framing in Pakistan-India conflict.* Paper presented at the annual meeting of the International Communication Association, Montreal, Quebec. Accessed June 14, 2016, from http://www.issi.org.pk/wp-content/uploads/2014/06/1303370133_44311323.pdf

Siraj, S. A. (2010). Framing War and Peace Journalism on the perspective of tali-banisation in Pakistan. *Media Asia, 37*(1), 13.

Siraj, S. A., & Hussain, S. (2012). War media galore in Pakistan: A perspective on Taliban conflict. *Global Media Journal: Pakistan Edition, 5*(1), 2–18.

Tehranian, M. (2002). Peace Journalism negotiating global media ethics. *The Harvard International Journal of Press/Politics, 7*(2), 58–83.

Ulrichsen, K. C. (2011). Qatar and the Arab Spring. *Open Democracy.* https://www.opendemocracy.net/kristian-coatesulrichsen/qatar-and-arab-spring

Ulrichsen, K. C. (2014). *Qatar and the Arab Spring.* Oxford University Press.

Youngblood, S. (2017). *Peace journalism principles and practices: Responsibly reporting conflicts, reconciliation, and solutions.* Routledge.

Zanders, J. P., & Trapp, R. (2013). Ridding Syria of chemical weapons: Next steps. *Arms Control Today, 43*(9), 8–14.

Zayani, M. (2005). *The Al Jazeera phenomenon: Critical perspectives on new Arab media.* Paradigm Publishers.

CHAPTER 2

Al-Jazeera's Relationship with Qatar Before, During and After the Arab Spring (1996–2021)

2.1 Introduction

Since its foundation in 1996, Al-Jazeera has revolutionised Arabic media, broken political taboos and challenged the immunity of Arab regimes that monopolised the media in the region for decades (Miles, 2010; El-Nawawy & Iskander, 2003; M. Lynch, 2005, 2006; Zayani, 2005; Seib, 2008; Sakr, 2007). Sakr (2007) says that the news bulletins in many Arab states' public broadcasters were full of stories about "leaders sitting together, talking together, and [saying] everything is fine; there is no news. But behind the scenes, everything is not fine" (cited in Ayish, 2002, p. 141). Al-Jazeera (known as the "phenomenal channel") was seen as an "agent of change" that elevated the expectations of its Arab viewers (Zayani, 2005). Within a few years, it became a global media outlet and source of exclusive footage from the frontlines of conflict zones (Miles, 2010).

In 2001, Al-Jazeera was the only broadcasting network that was allowed to report from Kabul during the war in Afghanistan, while Western journalists were ordered to leave by the Taliban regime (Miles, 2010). The White House described the channel as "Osama bin Laden's mouthpiece" and accused it of inciting the Arab people against United States' (US) foreign policy in the region (Mackinlay, 2006; Miles, 2010; El-Nawawy & Iskander, 2003; Zayani, 2005; Fandy, 2007; Fahmy & Al-Emad, 2011). Despite the fact that the most prominent news networks in the United

© The Author(s), under exclusive license to Springer Nature
Switzerland AG 2022
Z. Abdul-Nabi, *Al-Jazeera's "Double Standards" in the Arab Spring*,
https://doi.org/10.1007/978-3-031-14279-6_2

States like CNN, ABC, NBC and Fox News criticised Al-Jazeera's coverage heavily, all of them had "footage sharing agreements" with the channel (Rushing, 2007). M. Lynch (2006) suggests that the period from 1997 to 2002 should be described as the "Al-Jazeera's Era" due to its successful coverage of the Second Palestinian Intifada and the war in Afghanistan. During the Arab Spring uprisings that engulfed the region in 2011, the whole world was watching Al-Jazeera (Ulrichsen, 2014). Former US Secretary of State Hillary Clinton stated that, "You may not agree with it [Al-Jazeera], but you feel like you are getting real news around the clock" (Sultan, 2013, p. 254). Western news outlets such as CNN and MSNBC turned to American political analysts to comment on the developments in Egypt during the Arab Spring; however, AJE was at the time conducting live interviews with Egyptian opposition leaders and providing 24/7 news coverage even in the most dangerous locations (Howard & Hussain, 2013). Plunkett and Halliday (2011) argue that Egypt's uprising has done for AJE what the first Gulf War did for CNN.

The spread of the protest wave from Tunisia to Egypt, and then to the rest of the Arab world, is difficult to imagine without the facilitative role of Al-Jazeera (M. Lynch, 2015). However, "the transnational media soon degenerated into an arena for regional power struggles, with Al-Jazeera serving the interests of the Qatari regime" (M. Lynch, 2015, p. 93). While the revolutions in Tunisia, Egypt, Libya, Syria and Yemen have dominated the coverage of the Qatari channel, pro-democracy movements in neighbouring countries like Bahrain and Saudi Arabia have been given relatively little attention (Blanchard, 2012).

This chapter[1] sheds light on the independence of Al-Jazeera's editorial policy, reasons behind its foundation, Al-Jazeera's coverage of the conflicts in the Middle East and similarities and differences between AJA and AJE. In addition, it aims to explore the nature of the relationship between Qatar and Al-Jazeera before and after the Arab Spring.

---

[1] Sections from this chapter were published by the author and reproduced (from the article: Al-Jazeera's relationship with Qatar before and after Arab Spring: Effective public diplomacy or blatant propaganda?) with permission from the *Arab Media & Society* journal.

2.2 Al-Jazeera's Sponsor

Qatar is an oil-rich microstate, located in the Persian Gulf and caught between two main geopolitical rivals in the region: Iran and Saudi Arabia. As one of the largest exporters of the liquefied natural gas (LNG) in the world, Qatar's per capita income is over US$100,000 per year (Peterson, 2013). According to the national census, Qatari citizens make up only 15% of the 1.74 million population, while expatriates make up the remaining 85% (Kamrava, 2013). Like other Gulf states, Qatar is a close ally of the United States and hosts one of the biggest American military bases in the world (Da Lage, 2005). The Al-Udeid Air Base gained a prominent role in 2002 when the United States transferred its equipment and personnel from the Prince Sultan Air Base in Saudi Arabia to the Qatari base after Saudi conservative Wahhabis expressed their anger over the presence of foreign troops (Powers, 2009). The military base facilitated the US wars in Iraq and Afghanistan to the extent that the former President George Bush told the Qatari Emir, "You made some promises to America, and you kept your promises. We are honoured to call you [a] friend" (Cooper & Momani, 2011, p. 123).

Sheikh Hamad bin Khalifa Al-Thani, the ruling Emir from 1995 to 2013, had toppled his father Khalifa Al-Thani overnight and declared himself the new Emir. This, however, was not unusual among the largest and most argumentative ruling dynasty in the Middle East (Miles, 2010). A British administrator named them the "thugs of the Gulf" who have come to power either by a coup or shedding blood (Miles, 2010). Boyce (2013), a former British diplomat that served as an ambassador to Qatar, Kuwait and Egypt, says that the Emir moved against his father because he was frustrated with the slow pace of change and lack of development of the country's huge gas reserves. Without any warning, Sheikh Hamad, whose policies and proactive public diplomacy transformed Qatar from a hardly known state to an influential player on the global stage, stepped down in 2013 and appointed his fourth son as the new Emir (Kamrava, 2013). It is difficult to understand the real reasons behind this decision or other policies due to the absence of transparency and official explanation from the Qatari establishment (Roberts, 2012).

2.3   Al-Jazeera's Independence

Once Sheikh Hamad came to power in 1995, he dissolved the ministry of information and founded Al-Jazeera in what appeared as a move to democratise the country (Rugh, 2004). The notion of establishing the channel had emerged for the first time in 1994 when the former Emir (a crown prince at the time) decided to found a media outlet that could compete with Saudi-funded BBC Arabic (BBCA) (Bahry, 2001). Yet, the Saudi sponsors shut BBCA down after it broadcasted a critical documentary film on the Saudi royal family (Bahry, 2001).

Taking advantage of the collapse of the Saudi channel, the Emir launched Al-Jazeera in 1996 (Da Lage, 2005). Sheikh Hamad was supposed to finance Al-Jazeera for the first five years only, but failing to cover its expenses (along with the Saudi pressure on the advertisers not to deal with the channel) made it difficult to continue without Qatar's support (Bahry, 2001). The former Emir gave Al-Jazeera US$137 million at the outset (Miles, 2010). Al-Jazeera's board of directors is also chaired by a member of the Qatari royal family (Kasmani, 2014).

Qatar's generous financial support and direct involvement in the management of Al-Jazeera have raised doubts about the editorial independence of the news network (Fandy, 2007; Kasmani, 2014). However, Zayani and Sahraoui (2007) (who consider Al-Jazeera as an "alternative brand of journalism") argue that the Qatari channel is somehow similar to CNN and the BBC as it is "publicly-funded, but independent-minded" (cited in Kraidy, 2008, p. 25). Fandy (2007, p. 8) criticises the comparison between the Arabic channel and the well-known international broadcasters. According to him, if a comparative study were conducted, Al-Jazeera would be similar to the American Christian Broadcasting Network (CBN), "not the BBC and not CNN for sure". Moreover, the BBC is funded by licence fees based on clear rules and regulations, whereas the Qatari channel is financed directly by the Emir himself (El-Ibiary, 2011; Fandy, 2007). Adding to this, the long history of democracy and free press in the United Kingdom (UK) is incomparable to the nature of the political system in the Sheikhdom (Da Lage, 2005). While it seems that Al-Jazeera operates freely, Qatar's state media has always been under restrictions and censorship (El-Nawawy & Iskander, 2003; Figenschou, 2011).

Prominent human rights organisations have condemned Qatar over the lack of freedom of speech, press and assembly (Blanchard, 2012; Davidson, 2013). Despite the fact that most of the Arab ambassadors in Doha complained about Al-Jazeera's critical reporting (M. Lynch, 2006), there was no "serious coverage" of Qatar's politics (El-Nawawy & Iskander, 2003). El-Ibiary (2011) infers that Al-Jazeera's content is restricted to what he calls "anywhere but here phenomenon". This means that any state can be covered and criticised by the network except Qatar. Doha, however, attributes the limited proportion of Al-Jazeera's coverage to its small population and insignificant internal affairs in comparison to other states and conflicts in the region (Sakr, 2007).

However, some argue that Al-Jazeera has turned a blind eye to crucial and controversial developments in Qatar (Fandy, 2007; M. Lynch, 2006). For instance, the channel avoided shedding light on opening an Israeli commercial office in Doha, inviting the former Israeli Prime Minister, Ariel Sharon (Fandy, 2007), and postponing parliamentary elections in 2001 (M. Lynch, 2006). A study found that the opinion piece writers of AJA's website did not challenge or criticise Qatar or Saudi Arabia's politics openly (when the two countries were allies) (Lo & Frkovich, 2013). Moreover, the arrest of the Qatari poet who had condemned the former Emir received no coverage on the channel (Davidson, 2013).

Al-Jazeera does not always take a passive stance towards its sponsor, though. For instance, some shows gave space to critical voices that revealed the shortcomings of Qatar's judicial system and criticised the role of the US military base in the 2003 Iraq War (Sakr, 2007). Moreover, AJE has reported on Qatar's violations of foreign workers' rights and regulations (Bigalke, 2013). Nye (2008) says that giving airtime to "self-criticisms" is one of the best strategies to create credibility. Qatari leaders have always denied their involvement in the editorial policy (Bahry, 2001). Miles (2010) states that when the US administration asked Qatar's Emir to "tone down Al-Jazeera reporting" during the war in Afghanistan, Sheikh Hamad said that Qatar does not intervene in the channel:

> The network had given both US and Afghan officials equal airtime since the attacks. We are balanced and objective and never interfere in the news. We give all opposing views. Bin Laden is a party to the conflict, and his opinions must be heard. (Miles, 2010)

However, leaked reports disclosed that the Al-Thani's intervened to "tone down Al-Jazeera's coverage" of the war in Iraq in 2003 (Sakr, 2007; Powers, 2012) and Saudi affairs in 2007 (Samuel-Azran, 2013). Furthermore, Sakr (2007) argues that Al-Jazeera's Code of Ethics was introduced in 2004 as a response to US resentment over Al-Jazeera's coverage of the 2003 war in Iraq. The code came after Colin Powell, the US Secretary of State at the time, announced that Al-Jazeera had "clouded" the US-Qatari relationship (Sakr, 2007). Not long after that, Sheikh Hamad bin Jasim (the former Qatari foreign minister, known as HBJ in the West) told US Vice-President Dick Cheney and Defence Secretary Donald Rumsfeld that he "would tell Al-Jazeera to review its coverage, to be more professional and not to disseminate 'wrong information'" (Sakr, 2007, p. 70).

A Qatari official said, "Pressure from the Emirate had contributed to lessened hostility toward the US-led coalition in the later stages of its Iraq war coverage" (Powers, 2012, p. 14). Wikileaks cables revealed that Wadah Khanfar, the former managing director of the channel, ordered the Al-Jazeera website to remove images of wounded Iraqi civilians in acquiescence to a request from the US embassy in Qatar. In 2011, Khanfar was replaced with a member of the Qatari ruling family, a move which inevitably raised more questions about the independence of the Qatari news network (Ulrichsen, 2014).

2.4 WHY WAS AL-JAZEERA FOUNDED?

Given the long history of the rivalry between Saudi Arabia and Qatar, media scholars argue that Al-Jazeera was founded partially to challenge Saudi Arabia and weaken its influence in the region (Rugh, 2004; Sakr, 2007; Powers, 2009, 2012; Da Lage, 2005; Fandy, 2007; Samuel-Azran, 2013; El-Ibiary, 2011):

> In 1995, the new Emir was confronted with attacks in the Saudi and Egyptian press questioning his legitimacy as the rightful ruler of Qatar. Al-Jazeera was launched, in part, to give the Qatari Emir a megaphone to challenge the Egyptian and Saudi governments by broadcasting programmes featuring popular Egyptian and Saudi political dissidents. (Powers, 2012, p. 10)

A Qatari official said that Sheikh Hamad Al-Thani founded Al-Jazeera to use it as "political self-defence" against Saudi Arabia which already owns MBC, ART and Orbit channels and controls the main media outlets in the Arab world (Rugh, 2004). It is even argued that the reason behind broadcasting the speeches of Osama bin Laden (a critical Saudi citizen of

Al-Saud's dynasty) on Al-Jazeera was to undermine the rulers of Riyadh (Fandy, 2007). Thus, to Qatar, the Saudi regime was the target, not the Arabic audience (El-Ibiary, 2011).

The Al-Saud regime considers itself the "supervisor" of the Gulf Cooperation Council (GCC) countries (Miles, 2010). For example, in the 1970s, the Saudi royal family forced Kuwait and Bahrain to dissolve their parliaments because "such forms of governance were antithetical to the Wahhabi principles of Islam" (Da Lage, 2005, cited in Powers, 2009). The conflict between Qatar and Saudi Arabia escalated in the early 1990s when Saudi Arabia put restrictions on the exportation of Qatari gas supplies to Bahrain, Kuwait, the United Arab Emirates (UAE) and Oman (Roberts, 2012). Deterioration between the two states continued when the Qatari-Saudi border dispute turned into violent clashes in 1992 (Rabi, 2009).

In an attempt to challenge the Al-Saud family's hegemony over the region, Sheikh Hamad tried to improve relations with Iran, the main rival of Saudi Arabia (Rabi, 2009). Qatar was the only member of the United Nations Security Council (UNSC) that voted against a resolution that set "a deadline for Tehran to halt its uranium enrichment" in 2006 (Rabi, 2009, p. 447). The former Qatari Foreign Minister HBJ visited Tehran in 2007 and called for a diplomatic solution to the nuclear issue (Rabi, 2009). Haykel (2013) infers that relations with the United States and Saudi Arabia are what matter most in Qatar's foreign policy and the Emir's calculations.

Although Qatar follows the strict Wahhabi doctrine officially, it has embraced the Muslim Brotherhood's (MB) ideology to avoid relying on the Saudi Wahhabi scholars and jurists (Roberts, 2014). Both Qatar and Saudi Arabia welcomed members of the MB when they were oppressed and targeted by the Abdul-Nasser regime in Egypt and Baath party in Syria (Haykel, 2013). However, Qatar was more successful than Saudi in confining their influence and directing their energies "outside" the country (Haykel, 2013). There was a "tacit understanding" between Qatar and the MB that they could criticise and express their opinions freely on the regional level but not on the local one (Ulrichsen, 2014). Unlike their relations with Qatar, the ties between the MB and Saudi worsened in 1991 when the former supported Saddam Hussain's regime during the Iraqi invasion of Kuwait (Roberts, 2014).

Qatar's "open door policy" encouraged prominent dissidents such as the spiritual leader of the global MB movement, Yusuf Al-Qaradawi, to seek refuge in Doha (Ulrichsen, 2014). Zayani (2013) argues that in 2010, Al-Jazeera aired leaked official Palestinian documents that disclosed the corruption of the Palestinian Authority (PA) in order to empower Hamas (an offshoot of the MB movement) and weaken the PA and its allies, Saudi Arabia and Egypt.

2.5   AL-JAZEERA'S COVERAGE OF CONFLICTS

Many studies have analysed Al-Jazeera's coverage of numerous conflicts in the Middle East (see Fahmy & Al-Emad, 2011; El-Nawawy & Iskander, 2004; Barkho, 2010; Seib, 2008; M. Lynch, 2005; Al-Najjar, 2009; Rinnawi, 2003). A comparative study of Al-Jazeera's and CNN's coverage of the war in Afghanistan states that Al-Jazeera focused on the humanitarian side of the conflict more than CNN (Fahmy & Al-Emad, 2011). However, Fandy (2007) criticises Al-Jazeera's coverage of the war because, according to him, it portrayed Osama bin Laden and Ayman Al-Zawahiri as "victims" and Al-Jazeera avoided any mention of bin Laden's "history of terror" and the Taliban's wrongdoings.

Similarly, Powers and Gilboa (2007) argue that the network failed to document the horrors, torture and mass killings of innocent citizens by the Taliban and Saddam Hussein's regime. On the contrary, El-Nawawy and Iskander (2004) state that although the Arab street and public opinion were against the war in Iraq, Al-Jazeera presented "the other opinion" as it hosted members of the Iraqi opposition who welcomed the overthrow of Saddam's regime.

El-Nawawy and Iskander (2003) argue that Al-Jazeera was targeted, bombed by the United States in Baghdad and accused of being anti-American because its coverage focused on showing the causalities of the wars in Afghanistan and Iraq. At the same time, CNN and other US networks were not accused of being anti-Arab in their coverage although they did not show any images of Iraqi and Afghani victims (El-Nawawy & Iskander, 2003). The authors ask, "How much is too much for Al-Jazeera, and how little is too little for American networks?" While Fahmy and Al-Emad (2011) conclude that Al-Jazeera and CNN aired "propagandistic messages" during the war on Iraq, El-Nawawy and Iskander (2004, p. 323) have a different point of view:

> While the American media showcased US state-of-the-art military machines in action and the high morale of the US troops in what was described as a

'war of liberation,' Al-Jazeera focused on Iraqi civilian casualties and damage to Iraqi cities in a 'war of occupation.'

Miles (2010) says that during the invasion of Iraq, Al-Jazeera "had broken the hegemony of the Western networks and, for the first time in hundreds of years, reversed the flow of information, historically from West to East". Kellner (2004) says that the main media outlets in the United States such as Fox, NBC and CNN cable networks lost their objectivity after the one-sided coverage of the 2003 war in Iraq. Likewise, Finney (2007) argues that CNN's coverage of the war was "pro-America and pro-Bush". The elimination of Weapons of Mass Destruction (WMD) was framed as the main reason for invading Iraq by the mainstream media. The then US Deputy Defence Secretary told an interviewer that "this line was chosen for public consumption for bureaucratic reasons, as the lowest common denominator among proponents of war" (J. Lynch & McGoldrick, 2005, p. 8). Thompson (2003) argues that the major American media conduits undermined the possibility that Iraq's oil was the major motive behind invading Baghdad.

In relation to Al-Jazeera's coverage of the Israeli-Palestinian conflict, Rinnawi (2003) states that Al-Jazeera interviews Palestinian leaders more than Israeli officials who are, according to Barkho (2010), presented negatively on the network. However, Rushing (2007) argues that Al-Jazeera conducts interviews with Israeli administrators regularly and gives them airtime more than any other channel outside Israel. The most popular Palestinian reporter of Al-Jazeera Walid Al-Omary says, "We are not interested in officials, we are interested in people [and] there is no denying that the Palestinians are under occupation and that they are suffering. That is what we show" (Miles, 2010). More about Al-Jazeera's coverage of the Second Palestinian Intifada and the Gaza War is discussed in the following sections of this chapter.

2.6   Foundation of Al-Jazeera English

In 2006, ten years after the foundation of the Qatari channel, the former Emir launched AJE (Kraidy, 2008). According to Powers (2012), AJE was mainly founded to clear Al-Jazeera's name in the West after being heavily criticised by the US administration over its controversial coverage of the wars in Afghanistan and Iraq. It was reported that the US President at the time George W. Bush warned the Qatari leaders that "if Al-Jazeera failed to reconsider its news content, the US would, in turn, have to reconsider its relations with Qatar" (Powers, 2012, p. 16).

The United States cancelled a scheduled meeting between Sheikh Hamad's wife, Sheikha Mozah bint Nasser Al-Missned, and the First Lady Laura Bush, as well as several official meetings between HBJ and the Department of Defence and State Department (Powers, 2012). Steve Clark, "AJE's architect", reveals that these cancelled high-profile meetings upset Sheikh Hamad and drove him to think of founding a project that could generate "goodwill" towards Qatar (Powers, 2012). The name of the new channel was changed from "Al-Jazeera International" to "Al-Jazeera English" because, according to Kraidy (2008), the staff of AJA felt that the new brand would threaten the popularity of the original one. AJE has been fully financed by Sheikh Hamad Al-Thani himself as he gave it US$1 billion at the outset of its foundation (El-Nawawy & Powers, 2008).

AJE opened 21 offices and four centres in Qatar, the United Kingdom, Malaysia and the United States (El-Nawawy & Powers, 2008). The founders expected to reach 100 million households in 60 countries, but it was able to reach 110 million households in less than two years (Al-Najjar, 2009). AJE was the first English-speaking channel that had the resources and journalistic capacity to reach ignored and isolated audiences in the world (El-Nawawy & Powers, 2008). A study found out that AJE gives airtime to the "global south" more than "global north" (Figenschou, 2011). Furthermore, Josh Rushing (2007), AJE's reporter in the United States, stated that the channel focuses on the "underreported places" that have usually been neglected by its Western competitors. Figenschou (2011, p. 362) says, "AJE's management and staff aim to redress the elite domination in international news, by consciously redirecting attention from the 'corridors of power' to the margins". Likewise, Al-Najjar (2009) states that AJE was founded to break "the Western monopoly on the telling of history". El-Nawawy and Powers (2008) say that unlike the mainstream media, AJE has been able to bring diverse audiences together and encourage dialogue, empathy, responsibility as well as reconciliation. More specifically, a survey conducted in six countries by El-Nawawy and Powers (2008) shows that the journalists, presenters and reporters of AJE focus on "providing a voice to the voiceless". It further found out that AJE's audiences in Asia, the Middle East, Europe and North America believe that the channel works towards a "conciliatory function" (El-Nawawy & Powers, 2008). It also infers that "the longer viewers had been tuning into

AJE, the less dogmatic they were in their cognitive thought" (El-Nawawy & Powers, 2008, p. 50).

AJE was the only channel that reported from the ground during the Gaza War in 2009 as many media outlets were not able to enter the Strip due to the Israeli blockade (Firdous, 2009). Firdous (2009) concludes that AJE stood by Gaza's people and exposed the humanitarian side of the conflict. In addition, a comparative study between AJE, the BBC and CNN's coverage of the Gaza War stated that AJE "reversed the systematic source imbalance in international coverage of the Israeli–Palestinian conflict" (Figenschou, 2010). For instance, based on content analysis of the BBC and ITV during different periods of the Second Intifada, Philo and Berry (2004) conclude that Israeli views and perspective dominated the coverage of the event on British television news.

AJE's coverage, on the other hand, undermined the Israeli media campaign by asking hard questions and providing critical contextualisation of the Israeli side (Figenschou, 2010). AJE did not use unfavourable language or negative terms such as "militias" or "terrorists" when referring to Hamas, and unlike CNN, it critically reported on US support to Tel Aviv during the 2009 Gaza War (Firdous, 2009). Furthermore, a content analysis study conducted by Loomis (2009) found out that AJE has the least number of positive news stories about the United States comparing to the BBC, CBS and CNN (cited in Fornaciari, 2011). Furthermore, AJE viewers were found to be more critical of US foreign policy towards the Palestinian–Israeli conflict compared with CNN viewers (El-Nawawy & Powers, 2009). Rushing (2007, p. 194) speaks about his own experience with AJE:

> In our editorial meetings, I have never heard mention of our marketing strategy, or even who our audience is meant to be. Even the competition—which for us is first and foremost the BBC World and CNN International—does not come up unless we're discussing how they are handling a story we're also covering, and how we can do it differently. The questions we ask ourselves are, "What can we add to the coverage that exists?" And especially, "Who does not have a voice in this story?" That is a question that comes up often.

Powers (2012, p. 25) argues that AJE can be classified as a "hybrid model" that is a "quasi-governmental international broadcaster" on one hand and "quasi-voice of the voiceless" on the other. Kraidy (2008) states that AJE is even more advantaged than the BBC and CNN because it does not have to worry about the source of funding. Zayani and Sahraoui (2007) reveal that an Al-Jazeera producer told them the word "budget" is not heard at Al-Jazeera's building at all (cited in Kraidy, 2008).

2.7 Differences Between Al-Jazeera Arabic and English

Although AJA and AJE carry the same logo, belong to the same family, operate in the same building and report to Wadah Khanfar, the former managing director, they are still "dissimilar" (Kraidy, 2008). They can be described as "cousins who hate each other but have to learn to live together" (Kraidy, 2008, p. 24). Despite the fact that there are several studies comparing the coverage between AJA and AJE (Fakhri, 2011; Al-Najjar, 2009; Fahmy & Al-Emad, 2011), others argue that it is hard to compare between them because they target different audiences, markets, competitors as well as languages (Kraidy, 2008). For example, Fahmy and Al-Emad (2011) found out that 81.4% of AJE website's users are from the United States and other Western countries, whereas 98% of the AJA website's users are from the Arab world. In addition, the main broadcasting centre of AJA is based in Qatar, while AJE alone broadcasts from four centres in four different countries (Kraidy, 2008). AJA was the first channel of its kind in the Arab world (M. Lynch, 2005; Sakr, 2007; Rinnawi, 2003); however, AJE has had to compete with already well-founded and powerful English-language news networks while at the same time trying to meet the standards of Western audiences (Kraidy, 2008).

Some studies, however, did not find major differences between the coverage of the English and Arabic channels (Fakhri, 2011; Al-Nahed, 2015; Fahmy & Al-Emad, 2011). For instance, Fahmy and Al-Emad (2011) argue that their comparative study proves that AJA and AJE did not avoid representing Al-Qaeda and the United States negatively during the war in Afghanistan. Moreover, Fakhri (2011) states that both channels shed light on the necessity of saving the people of Gaza during Israel's war in 2008–2009. Furthermore, according to Al-Najjar (2009), AJE's news focuses on nongovernmental attacks, internal clashes, civil wars and human rights, whereas AJA focuses more on combat and military actions, domestic governments, internal politics, external diplomacy and political conflicts.

Kraidy (2008) concludes that AJA and AJE are similar in their coverage of the Middle East, but the tone of AJA sounds "harsher" than AJE. Al-Nahed (2015) argues that the main reason behind recording minor differences between AJA and AJE is that they are mainly influenced by Qatar's foreign policy. Other studies and analysis found serious differences between both channels especially when it comes to reporting on Bahrain's uprising (Kamrava, 2013; Abdul-Nabi, 2015) and Saudi Arabian external and internal affairs (Samuel-Azran, 2013).

2.8 Al-Jazeera's Role Before the Arab Spring: Qatar's Public Diplomacy

Several media scholars have focused on the role of Al-Jazeera in transforming the reality of the Arabic media and challenging dictatorships in the region (El-Nawawy & Iskander, 2003; Zayani, 2005; M. Lynch, 2006; Miles, 2010; Sakr, 2007); however, politics scholars refer to Al-Jazeera as part of Qatar's public diplomacy and state branding efforts (Ulrichsen, 2014; Kamrava, 2013; Peterson, 2013; Khatib, 2013; Da Lage, 2005; Roberts, 2012). Despite the fact that its influence on Arab public opinion was undeniably unprecedented (M. Lynch, 2006; Seib, 2008), the former Emir founded Al-Jazeera to portray Qatar as a "progressive state" to the world (Ulrichsen, 2014). Qatar's strategic interests of founding the network are therefore "multifaceted, ranging from the global level, regional level, and intra-Gulf rivalry" (Figenschou, 2011, p. 368). Along with founding Al-Jazeera, scholars argue that the other ingredients of Qatar's sophisticated public diplomacy include promoting Doha as an educational and cultural hub, hosting international sporting events, developing luxury travel and tourism markets, investing in clean energy (Ulrichsen, 2014), mediation efforts (Kamrava, 2013) and supplying humanitarian aid (Khatib, 2013). Manheim (1994, p. 4) defines public diplomacy as "efforts by the government of one nation to influence public or elite opinion in a second nation for the purpose of turning the foreign policy of the target nation to advantage" (cited in Samuel-Azran, 2013, p. 1293).

Zayani (2005) and El-Nawawi and Iskander (2003) acknowledge the role of Al-Jazeera in putting Qatar on the international map; however, at the same time, they argue that the channel was not used to promote Doha's foreign policy. They constructed their argument based on the inconsistency between Al-Jazeera's critical coverage and Qatar's "cordial" diplomatic policy. For instance, Al-Jazeera's critical coverage of Israel during the Palestinian Intifada in 2000 mobilised Arabs and united them for the first time since the 1970s (M. Lynch, 2006; Miles, 2010; Zayani, 2005; Seib, 2008). At the same time, Qatar maintained unique diplomatic relations with Israel (Da Lage, 2005). In 2003, Sheikh Hamad met with his Israeli counterpart, Silvan Shalom, and expressed his readiness "to seriously consider the possibility of increasing the level of diplomatic relations" (Da Lage, 2005, p. 57).

This contradiction between "playing-all-sides" policy (Haykel, 2013) and Al-Jazeera's "critical" coverage of Qatar's ally was calculatedly part of Qatar's public diplomacy (Khatib, 2013; Sakr, 2007; Da Lage, 2005). Despite the significant role that the Al-Udeid Air Base (Qatari military base) played during Afghanistan and 2003 Iraq wars, Al-Jazeera was critical of the United States to the extent that the White House called it "Osama bin Laden's mouthpiece" (Powers & Gilboa, 2007; Da Lage, 2005). At the first glance, it seems that such coverage would not serve Qatar's "cordial" foreign policy, as it could serve to cause embarrassment to the microstate and worsen its relations with the United States. Giving the "airwaves" (Al-Jazeera) to the Al-Qaeda Islamists and the "airstrip" (military base) to the Americans (Fandy, 2007) however aimed at appeasing Arab public opinion on one hand and maintaining good relations with its Western allies on the other (Khatib, 2013).

Furthermore, allowing Arab viewers to express their resentment against the US foreign policy would, by default, portray Qatar as a "defender of Arab nationalist interests" (Sakr, 2007, p. 144). Adopting this tactic has proved that the microstate is a shrewd political player that has been able to gain friends on both sides (Khatib, 2013). Da Lage (2005) argues that Doha's alliance with Washington was the "original sin" that Arabs forgave, thanks to Al-Jazeera's aggressive coverage. According to Nye (2008), broadcasting non-propagandistic content that is attractive to the target audience can transform a media outlet to a productive public diplomacy tool. It can be inferred that what appeared to some scholars (Zayani, 2005; El-Nawawi & Iskander, 2003) as a contradiction or distance between Al-Jazeera's critical coverage and Qatar's foreign policy helped make the channel a successful tool of Qatar's public diplomacy.

2.8.1   New Public Diplomacy

Powers and Gilboa (2007) argue that Al-Jazeera proved to be more than a transnational media outlet, as regional and international powers treated it as a political player. Almost all Arab countries complained about the channel to its founder, Sheikh Hamad, while some withdrew their ambassadors from the Gulf state (El-Nawawy & Iskander, 2003). Miles (2010) says, "Arab ambassadors in Doha spent so much time complaining about Al-Jazeera that they felt more like ambassadors to a TV channel than ambassadors to a country". Jordan closed down Al-Jazeera's office after an American academic interviewee criticised and "ridiculed" the Hashemite monarch (M. Lynch, 2006). Morocco did the same when the channel discussed its occupation of Western Sahara (M. Lynch, 2006). The Algerian regime cut power to the whole city of Algiers to prevent people from watching a show that was supposed to shed light on the political situation in Algeria (Bahry, 2001).

Al-Jazeera has also created tension between Qatar and powerful states like the United States (Powers & Gilboa, 2007). For instance, the State Department and Department of Defence founded a dedicated working group to monitor the network's programmes 24-hours a day, seven days a week (Powers & Gilboa, 2007). In addition, Seib (2010, p. 739) argues that the channel was able to unite Arabs and serve as a "pan-Arab and perhaps pan-Islamist public diplomacy tool". Its live, vivid coverage, accompanied with graphic imagery and supportive commentaries during the Second Palestinian Intifada and war in Afghanistan, made sure that Al-Jazeera dominated the Arab public discourse (M. Lynch, 2006).

Zayani (2005, p. 8) says, "Al-Jazeera has reinvigorated a sense of common destiny in the Arab world and is even encouraging Arab unity, so much so that pan-Arabism is being reinvented on this channel" (cited in Seib, 2010, p. 739). Additionally, Al-Jazeera's criticisms of Arab regimes' lack of action during the Gaza War in 2008–2009 triggered protests across the Arab world against Arab authoritarian rulers (Seib, 2010). Therefore, Seib (2008, p. 175) who is the first scholar that used the term "the Al-Jazeera effect" argues that the news channel is more important than CNN and the BBC because it has changed the relationship between those "who govern and those who are governed". Unlike traditional public diplomacy that is led and implemented by states (Nye, 2008), Al-Jazeera can be classified as a successful example of "new public diplomacy" in

40 Z. ABDUL-NABI

which non-state actors employ tactics to "influence attitudes and behaviours of others" (Powers & Gilboa, 2007).

Seib (2010, p. 743) says that the "rise of Al-Jazeera and similar news organisations is changing the nature of public diplomacy by not acting as merely an arm of a state but rather devising and advancing its own political perspective". The success of Al-Jazeera can be attributed to its adherence to journalistic standards (Seib, 2010), its effectiveness, accomplishments, talented journalists and organisational system (Zayani & Sahraoui, 2007). A survey conducted by the UAE's University of Sharjah in several Arab countries found that Al-Jazeera is "the most credible out of all the Arab news channels during the [Iraq war], followed by Abu Dhabi TV, with Al-Arabiya third" (Miles, 2010). Another study shows that Al-Jazeera's viewers believe that their channel is more credible than the BBC and CNN (Fahmy & Johnson, 2008). This popularity enabled Al-Jazeera to be more influential than the state of Qatar itself (Powers & Gilboa, 2007). Seib (2010, p. 741) goes even further and suggests that the channel "should be regarded as a virtual state for Arabs and Muslims, in itself not on the map but real in a virtual sense".

2.8.2 Hybrid Diplomacy

Based on an eight-year-long examination of Al-Jazeera's coverage of the Saudi affairs, Samuel-Azran (2013) theorised what he called "the hybrid model". Samuel-Azran (2013, p. 1294) defines the model as a new type of media public diplomacy in which "a state-sponsored station operates independently in routine affairs, which gives it the credibility of a privately owned station, and reverts to state-sponsored-style broadcasting only during a crisis involving the state". The study that analysed Al-Jazeera's coverage of the Saudi politics from 2001 to 2008 found out that there was a strong consistency between AJA coverage and Qatari interests (Samuel-Azran, 2013; Samuel-Azran & Pecht, 2014). Samuel-Azran and Pecht (2014) observed a dramatic rise in negative news about Saudi Arabia during the Saudi-Qatari conflict (from 2001 to 2007), while there was an absence of criticisms in the year that followed the historic Saudi-Qatari resolution in 2007.

According to a WikiLeaks cable, the US Ambassador of Qatar Joseph Lebron revealed that the "toning down" of Al-Jazeera's coverage of Saudi Arabia was part of that resolution (Samuel-Azran, 2013). A news editor of Al-Jazeera said to *The New York Times*:

The top management sometimes used to force-feed the reluctant news staff negative material about Saudi Arabia, apparently to placate the Qatari leadership, however, after the agreement, orders were given not to tackle any Saudi issue without referring to the higher management. All dissident voices disappeared from our screens. (Worth, 2008)

In another WikiLeaks document, Lebron says, "Qatar will continue to use Al-Jazeera as a bargaining tool to repair relationships with other countries particularly those soured by Al-Jazeera's broadcasts" (Figenschou, 2013, p. 27). Samuel-Azran (2013) concludes that Al-Jazeera's credibility (which was gained during its coverage of issues where Qatar's interests were not directly involved) has made Al-Jazeera a "potent public diplomacy tool" that can effectively influence the public opinion on one hand and put pressure on Sheikh Hamad's rivals on the other. Samuel-Azran (2013, p. 1308) further argues that his hybrid model is more likely to sustain simply because "Qatar is a peripheral player in international politics and, therefore, most viewers are indifferent to Qatar's political affairs or interests". However, this model along with the previous arguments that regard Al-Jazeera as a successful public diplomacy tool can be profoundly challenged after the uprisings in the Middle East.

2.9   Al-Jazeera's Role After the Arab Spring: Qatar's Propaganda

Al-Jazeera is attributed with an essential catalytic role during the Arab Spring uprisings at the beginning of 2011 (Khatib, 2013). M. Lynch (2013) states that even the then President of the United States, Barack Obama, was watching AJE to follow the latest developments of Egypt's revolution. M. Lynch (2013) adds that the success of Al-Jazeera in Egypt has reinforced its role as a "useful weapon" in regional politics. Despite the fact that very few media studies examined to what extent Al-Jazeera's coverage conformed to Qatar's foreign policy during the Arab Spring (Al-Nahed, 2015; Ayaad, 2014; Lo & Frkovich, 2013; Abdul-Nabi, 2015), Arab media academics (M. Lynch, 2013, 2015; Kraidy, 2014) and politics' scholars (Ulrichsen, 2011, 2013, 2014; Haykel, 2013; Kamrava, 2013; Davidson, 2013; Roberts, 2012; Stephens, 2012; Dabashi, 2012; Colombo, 2013; Matthiesen, 2013; Cooper & Momani, 2011; Khatib, 2013) argue that Al-Jazeera's coverage has been serving Qatar's policy, interests and agenda.

Having just secured hosting the 2022 FIFA World Cup in 2010, the Arab Spring was a timely opportunity for Qatar to distinguish itself from the authoritarian regimes in the region and present itself as a champion of human rights and democracy (Ulrichsen, 2014). Once Qatar realised what was going on in Egypt, it changed its foreign policy from an impartial regional broker to a direct interventionist (especially in Syria and Libya) (Roberts, 2012; Kamrava, 2013; Ulrichsen, 2014; Khatib, 2013). This sudden and swift change in Qatar's foreign policy can be attributed to the lack of large-scale strategic planning (Roberts, 2012) and institutional depth (Ulrichsen, 2013), Doha's dependence on "pragmatic opportunism" (Khatib, 2013), absence of domestic accountability (Ulrichsen, 2014) and the personalised nature of the decision-making process (Ulrichsen, 2014; Roberts, 2012). The authors add that leaving the design of Qatar's local and foreign policy is in the hands of four people from the royal family: (1) the former Emir; (2) his second wife, Mozah bint Nasser Al-Missned; (3) the current Emir [Mozah's son], Sheikh Tamim bin Hamad; and (4) HBJ. Whatever these four "decide will be done, for good or for ill" (Roberts, 2012).

In Libya, Doha was the first Arab country that recognised and legitimised the Libyan opposition body, the Transitional National Council (TNC) (Ulrichsen, 2014; Colombo, 2013; Roberts, 2012). Along with being an "enthusiastic partner" in the NATO-led mission (Colombo, 2013), Qatar provided political, economic and militarily support to the Libyan rebels. More specifically, it supplied combat jets, cruise missiles, military advisers, ground troops and US$400 million worth of financial aid (Ulrichsen, 2014; Peterson, 2013). Al-Gaddafi himself did not expect the extent of Qatar's reversal due to his consideration of Qatar as a regional ally (Ulrichsen, 2014). There were reports claiming that Qatar granted Egyptians Qatari citizenship on the condition of fighting with the rebels (Cooper & Momani, 2011). Ulrichsen (2014, p. 2) points out that:

> The sight of Qatar's distinctive maroon and white flag flying atop the ruins of Al-Gaddafi's Bab al-Aziziya compound was as rich in symbolism as it was reflective of the country's outsized role in engineering regime change in Tripoli.

In parallel with Qatar's military intervention in Libya and its unlimited support to the Libyan rebels, an empirical content analysis study found out that Al-Jazeera's coverage was in favour of the Libyan opposition and military intervention (Al-Nahed, 2015). Some claim that Al-Jazeera aired fabricated stories and images in order to gain support for a particular point of view during the Libyan uprising (Khatib, 2013; Ulrichsen, 2014). For example, Al-Jazeera reported on February 21, 2011, that the Al-Gaddafi regime was using its air force to attack unarmed civilians in Tripoli and other cities (Ulrichsen, 2014). After months of investigation, Hugh Roberts, the director of the International Crisis Group's North Africa Project, says that the story was baseless:

> The story was untrue, just as the story that went around the world in August 1990, that Iraqi troops were slaughtering Kuwaiti babies by turning off their incubators, was [found to be] untrue and the claims in the sexed-up dossier on Saddam's weapons of mass destruction were [also] untrue. (Ulrichsen, 2014, p. 125)

Colombo (2013) argues that Qatar has "skilfully exploited" Al-Jazeera, to rally Arab public opinion in supporting foreign military intervention in Libya.

Similarly, in his quantitative content analysis study, Ayaad (2014), found that Al-Jazeera's reporters appeared to support a military intervention in Syria after the second chemical weapons (CW) attack in Eastern Al-Ghouta in 2013. Paradoxically, AJA legitimised the Saudi military intervention in 2011 in Bahrain, to (unlike in Syria and Libya) help the regime quell the growing protest movement (Abdul-Nabi, 2015). Additionally, during the violent crackdown of the Saudi-led Peninsula Shield Forces (PSF) against protesters in Bahrain, Al-Jazeera was, as Kamrava (2013) puts it, "tongue-tied".

Indeed, the channel represented the protests in Libya and Egypt as "revolutions" (El-Nawawy & El-Masry, 2015; Al-Nahed, 2015), yet refrained from ever framing Bahrain's uprising as such (Abdul-Nabi, 2015). One of the rare studies to critically examine Al-Jazeera coverage of Bahrain's protests found that AJA posted only two opinion pieces about the uprising among 94 articles available on its website (Lo & Frkovich, 2013). The channel downplayed the significance of Bahrain's protests by framing it as sectarian tension between the country's Shia and Sunni populations (M. Lynch, 2013). At the same time, Al-Jazeera's enthusiasm towards covering Syria's uprising led the network to "broadcast inaccurate reports and unverified or fake footage" (Khatib, 2013, p. 428).

44 Z. ABDUL-NABI

More studies have examined the influence of Qatar's foreign policy on AJA and AJE after the 2017 Gulf crisis when Saudi Arabia, the UAE, Egypt and Bahrain imposed a blockade on Qatar for allegedly supporting "terrorism" and MB movements in the region. Alshabnan (2018) and Mejalli (2019) found that AJA framed the war on Yemen, and the Saudi-led coalition that involved Qatar, in a "positive tone" before the deterioration of Saudi-Qatari ties in 2017. Conversely, the channel presented the war in a "negative tone" after the 2017 crisis (Alshabnan, 2018; Mejalli, 2019). Consistently, Ajaoud and Elmasry (2020) argue that AJA's coverage was inclined towards supporting Qatar and that it framed the country as a "victim" that was being attacked by an "oppressor" (Saudi Arabia) during the 2017 Gulf crisis.

As indicated earlier in this chapter, although AJE has been assessed as more moderate than AJA (likely due to targeting a different audience and competitors, and the difference in language), the most recent studies found that AJE's coverage has also been used as a "political instrument" by Qatar's politics, especially during the 2017 Gulf crisis (Gasim, 2018; Alhendyani, 2019; Kharbach, 2020; Kosárová, 2020).

2.10 Conclusion

To conclude, scholars of Al-Jazeera (El-Nawawy & Iskander, 2003; Fandy, 2007; M. Lynch, 2013; Miles, 2010; Powers, 2012; Seib, 2008; Zayani, 2005) acknowledge that the Qatari network cannot be fully independent of its founder, Qatar's royal family. Before the Arab uprisings in 2011, Al-Jazeera succeeded to a great extent in acting as an effective tool of Qatar's public diplomacy (Seib, 2008, 2010; Powers & Gilboa, 2007; Da Lage, 2005; Khatib, 2013; Samuel-Azran, 2013) as it helped the microstate gain a political niche that exceeds its actual size (Da Lage, 2005; Rugh, 2004; El-Nawawy & Iskander, 2003).

The channel, additionally, acted as a "pan-Arab and pan-Islamist public diplomacy tool" that united Arabs, triggered protests, changed relations between those "who govern and who is governed" and transformed the nature of public diplomacy (Seib, 2008, 2010). Some went even further and described Al-Jazeera as a powerful non-state player that is even more influential than the State of Qatar itself (Powers & Gilboa, 2007).

The main reasons behind Al-Jazeera's success as a traditional and new public diplomacy tool before the Arab Spring can be attributed to its popularity, credibility (Powers & Gilboa, 2007), critical coverage of Arab regimes (El-Nawawy & Iskander, 2003), high journalism standards (Seib, 2010) and most importantly its relative independence from Qatar's foreign policy (Da Lage, 2005; Zayani, 2005; El-Nawawi & Iskander, 2003; Khatib, 2013). Since the Arab Spring however, Al-Jazeera's coverage has reflected and promoted Qatari foreign policy in the region (Barakat, 2011; M. Lynch, 2013, 2015; Kraidy, 2014; Al-Nahed, 2015; Ayaad, 2014; Abdul-Nabi, 2015).

It can be concluded that the dramatic change in Qatar's foreign policy from a neutral mediator to an "aggressive" military interventionist at the outset of the revolutions has been followed by a similar shift in Al-Jazeera's editorial policy. Legitimising a protest movement by framing it as a revolution in an "enemy state [Libya, Syria, Egypt, Tunisia, Yemen]" while delegitimising another by presenting it as a sectarian protest in a "client state [Bahrain]" is an ideal application of what Herman and Chomsky (2010) called "dual standard" or propaganda-orientated coverage.

According to Nye (2008), broadcasting information that "appears to be propaganda" will not only be mocked by the target audience, but it will be fully counterproductive as a public diplomacy instrument. In addition, the narrow gap between Qatar's foreign policy and Al-Jazeera's coverage during the uprisings made the channel "lose its lustre" as an effective public diplomacy tool (Khatib, 2013). Critics who consider the term public diplomacy as a synonym for propaganda have totally "missed the point" as "good public diplomacy has to go beyond propaganda" (Nye, 2008). If not, it will fail to convince the audience (Nye, 2008). As an illustration, Al-Hurra channel, an Arabic channel financed by the US administration, has not been able to compete with other media outlets in the region, simply because it has been widely looked at as a tool of US propaganda (Nye, 2008). Some even suggest that the United States could get a better result on its investment if Al-Hurra was turned into an international C-SPAN that airs seminars, town meetings and congressional debates (Nye, 2008). If Qatar wants to bring back the impressive diplomatic role of Al-Jazeera, it should distance itself from Al-Jazeera's management and keep its hands off the editorial policy.

This book will utilise quantitative content analysis methods, framing theory and the PJM to measure the extent of Qatar's influence on Al-Jazeera's coverage of Bahrain's uprising and Syria's second CW attack. It will also look at whether Al-Jazeera was used as a propaganda tool in serving Qatar and the GCC's foreign policy in the region.

Previous studies that examined the coverage of AJE (Al-Najjar, 2009; El-Nawawy & Powers, 2008; Firdous, 2009; Figenschou, 2011) showed that the channel has a tendency to give a "voice to the voiceless" (one of the PJ orientations). This tendency however was not observed in AJA. There has been a relatively small amount of media coverage of conflicts in the Middle East that have been examined based on the PJM (Fahmy & Eakin, 2014). That is why this study analyses Al-Jazeera's coverage of Bahrain and Syria's conflicts based on this unconventional framework (PJM). The next chapter introduces the model, its orientations, evolvement, misconceptions, challenges and significance while covering conflicts.

REFERENCES

Abdul-Nabi, Z. (2015). Based on the peace journalism model: Analysis of Al-Jazeera's coverage of Bahrain's uprising and Syria's chemical attack. *Global Media and Communication, 11*(3), 271–302.

Ajaoud, S., & Elmasry, M. H. (2020). When news is the crisis: Al Jazeera and Al Arabiya framing of the 2017 Gulf conflict. *Global Media and Communication, 16*(2), 227–242.

Alhendyani, A. (2019). *The cost of truth in a world of politics: How Al-Jazeera and Al-Arabiya are influenced by Qatar and Saudi Arabia* (Master's thesis, California State University). https://scholarworks.calstate.edu/downloads/t722hd103

Al-Nahed, S. (2015). Covering Libya: A framing analysis of Al Jazeera and BBC coverage of the 2011 Libyan uprising and NATO intervention. *Middle East Critique, 24*(3), 251–267.

Al-Najjar, A. (2009). How Arab is Al-Jazeera English? Comparative study of Al-Jazeera Arabic and Al-Jazeera English news channel. *Global Media Journal, 8*(14), 1–35.

Alshabnan, A. (2018). The politicization of Arab Gulf media outlets in the Gulf Crisis: A content analysis. *Global Media Journal, 16*(30), 1–6.

Ayaad, S. W. (2014). *Qatari Foreign Policy, Al-Jazeera, and Revolution in the Middle East and North Africa* (Doctoral dissertation, Communication, Art & Technology: Communication). Accessed March 24, 2016, from http://summit.sfu.ca/item/14739

Ayish, M. I. (2002). Political communication on Arab world television: Evolving patterns. *Political Communication, 19*(2), 137–154.

Bahry, L. Y. (2001). The new Arab media phenomenon: Qatar's Al-Jazeera. *Middle East Policy, 8*(2), 88–99.

Barakat, R. (2011). *New media in the Arab world: A tool for redesigning geopolitical realities* (Master's Thesis, Lebanese American University, Lebanon). Accessed November 11, 2013, from http://laur.lau.edulb:7080/xmlui/handle/10725/1047

Barkho, L. (2010). *News from the BBC, CNN, and Al-Jazeera: How the three broadcasters cover the Middle East.* Hampton Press.

Bigalke, N. (2013). *Al Jazeera English: Margins of difference in international English-language news broadcasting* (Doctoral dissertation, The London School of Economics and Political Science (LSE)). Accessed November 11, 2015, from http://etheses.lse.ac.uk/901/

Blanchard, C. M. (2012). *Qatar: Background and U.S. relations.* Diane Publishing.

Boyce, S. G. (2013). Qatar's foreign policy. *Asian Affairs, 44*(3), 365–377.

Colombo, S. (2013). The GCC Countries and the Arab Spring. In D. John (Ed.), *Arab Spring and Arab thaw: Unfinished revolutions and the Quest for democracy* (pp. 163–179). Ashgate.

Cooper, A. F., & Momani, B. (2011). Qatar and expanded contours of small state diplomacy. *The International Spectator, 46*(3), 113–128.

Dabashi, H. (2012). *The Arab Spring: The end of postcolonialism.* Zed Books.

Da Lage, O. (2005). The politics of Al Jazeera or the diplomacy of Doha. In *The Al Jazeera phenomenon: Critical perspectives on new Arab media* (pp. 49–65). Paradigm Publishers.

Davidson, C. M. (2013). *After the Sheikhs: The coming collapse of the Gulf monarchies.* Hurst & Company.

El-Ibiary, R. (2011). Questioning the Al-Jazeera effect: Analysis of Al-Qaeda's media strategy and its relationship with Al-Jazeera. *Global Media and Communication, 7*(3), 199–204.

El-Nawawy, M., & Iskander, A. (2003). *Al-Jazeera: The story of the network that is rattling governments and redefining modern journalism.* Westview.

El-Nawawy, M., & Iskander, A. (2004). Al-Jazeera and war coverage in Iraq: The media's quest for contextual objectivity. In S. Allan & B. Zalizer (Eds.), *Reporting war: Journalism in wartime* (pp. 315–332). Routledge.

El-Nawawy, M., & Powers, S. (2008). *Mediating conflict: Al-Jazeera English and the possibility of a conciliatory media.* Figueroa Press.

El-Nawawy, M., & Powers, S. (2009). Al-Jazeera English and global news networks: Clash of civilizations or cross-cultural dialogue? *Media, War & Conflict, 2*(3), 263–284.

El-Nawawy, M., & El-Masry, M. H. (2015). Revolution or crisis? Framing the 2011 Tahrir Square protests in two pan-Arab satellite news networks. *Journal of Applied Journalism & Media Studies, 4*(2), 239–258.

Fahmy, S., & Johnson, T. J. (2008). How support for press freedom and political ideology predict credibility of Al-Jazeera among its audience. *The International Communication Gazette, 70*(5), 338–360.

Fahmy, S., & Al Emad, M. (2011). Al-Jazeera vs Al-Jazeera: A comparison of the network's English and Arabic online coverage of the US/Al Qaeda conflict. *The International Communication Gazette, 73*(3), 216–232.

Fahmy, S., & Eakin, B. (2014). High drama on the high seas Peace versus war journalism framing of an Israeli/Palestinian-related incident. *International Communication Gazette, 76*(1), 86–105.

Fakhri, F. (2011). *Content analysis of how Al-Jazeera English and Arabic channels framed the war on Gaza* (Master's thesis). Retrieved from ProQuest Dissertations and Theses (Accession Order No. 1496764).

Fandy, M. (2007). *(Un)civil war of words: Media and politics in the Arab world.* Praeger Security International.

Figenschou, T. U. (2010). A voice for the voiceless? A quantitative content analysis of Al Jazeera English's flagship news. *Global Media and Communication, 6*(1), 85–107.

Figenschou, T. U. (2011). The south is talking back: With a white face and a British accent – editorial dilemmas in Al Jazeera English. *Journalism, 13*(3), 354–370.

Figenschou, T. U. (2013). *Al Jazeera and the global media landscape: The South is talking Back.* Routledge.

Finney, M. L. (2007). *And knowing is half the battle: How endorsements for war were hidden in CNN's coverage of the conflict with Iraq* (Doctoral thesis). Retrieved from ProQuest Dissertations and Theses (Accession Order No. 3273673).

Firdous, T. (2009). *Al Jazeera English presenting a non-western viewpoint and contesting western media dominance during the Gaza crisis* (Master's thesis). Retrieved from ProQuest Dissertations and Theses (Accession Order No. 1507250).

Fornaciari, F. (2011). Framing the Egyptian revolution: A content analysis of Al Jazeera English and the BBC. *Journal of Arab & Muslim Media Research, 4*(2+4), 223–235.

Gasim, G. (2018). The Qatari crisis and Al Jazeera's coverage of the war in Yemen. *Arab Media & Society, 25,* 1–9.

Haykel, B. (2013). *Qatar and Islamism.* Norwegian Peacebuilding Resource Centre. Accessed November 25, 2015, from www.peacebuilding.no

Herman, E. S., & Chomsky, N. (2010). *Manufacturing consent: The political economy of the mass media.* Random House eBooks.

Howard, P. N., & Hussain, M. M. (2013). *Democracy's fourth wave? Digital media and the Arab Spring.* Oxford University Press.

Kamrava, M. (2013). *Qatar: Small state, big politics.* Cornell University Press.

Kasmani, M. F. (2014). The nation-state factor in global news reporting: A study of the BBC World News and Al Jazeera English coverage. *International Communication Gazette, 76*(7), 594–614.

2 AL-JAZEERA'S RELATIONSHIP WITH QATAR BEFORE... 49

Kellner, D. (2004). Spectacle and media propaganda in the war on Iraq: A critique of US broadcasting networks. In *War, media, and propaganda: A global perspective* (pp. 69–77). Rowan and Littlefield.

Kharbach, M. (2020). Understanding the ideological construction of the Gulf crisis in Arab media discourse: A critical discourse analytic study of the headlines of Al Arabiya English and Al Jazeera English. *Discourse & Communication, 14*(5), 447–465.

Khatib, L. (2013). Qatar's foreign policy: The limits of pragmatism. *International Affairs, 89*(2), 417–431.

Kosárová, D. (2020). Al Jazeera and Al Arabiya: Understanding media bias. *Politické vedy, 23*(4), 87–108.

Kraidy, M. M. (2008). *Al-Jazeera and Al-Jazeera English: A Comparative institutional analysis* (pp. 23–30). Woodrow Wilson International Center for Scholars. Accessed July 30, 2012, from http://repository.upenn.edu/cgi/viewcontent. cgi?article=1282&context=asc_papers

Kraidy, M. M. (2014). Media industries in revolutionary times. *Media Industries, 1*(2), 16–21. Accessed January20, 2016, from http://www.mediaindustriesjournal.org/index.php/mij/article/view/45

Lo, M., & Frkovich, A. (2013). Challenging authority in cyberspace: Evaluating Al Jazeera Arabic writers. *Journal of Religion and Popular Culture, 25*(3), 388–402.

Loomis, K. D. (2009), A comparison of broadcast world news web pages: Al Jazeera English, BBC, CBS, and CNN', Electronic News, 3 (3), pp. 143–60.

Lynch, M. (2005). Watching Al-Jazeera. *The Wilson Quarterly, 29*(3), 36–45.

Lynch, M. (2006). *Voices of the new Arab public: Iraq, Al-Jazeera, and Middle East politics today.* Columbia University Press.

Lynch, J., & McGoldrick, A. (2005). Peace journalism. Stroud: Hawthorn Press.

Lynch, M. (2013). *The Arab uprising: The unfinished revolutions of the new Middle East.* PublicAffairs.

Lynch, M. (2015). How the media trashed the transitions. *Journal of Democracy, 26*(4), 90–99.

Mackinlay, J. (2006). Losing Arab hearts and minds: The coalition, Al Jazeera and Muslim public opinion. RUSI Journal, 151(4), 86–87.

Manheim, J. B. (1994). *Strategic public diplomacy and American foreign policy: The evolution of influence.* Oxford University Press.

Matthiesen, T. (2013). *Sectarian gulf: Bahrain, Saudi Arabia, and the Arab Spring that wasn't.* Stanford University Press.

Mejalli, W. H. A. (2019). *Analyzing Al-Jazeera Arabic online news articles during the development of war in Yemen* (Master's Thesis, University of Oslo). https://www.duo.uio.no/handle/10852/70323

Miles, H. (2010). *Al-Jazeera: How Arab TV news challenged the world.* Abacus.

Nye, J. S. (2008). Public diplomacy and soft power. *The Annals of the American Academy of Political and Social Science, 616*(1), 94–109.

Peterson, J. E. (2013). *Qatar's international role: Branding, investment and policy projection.* Policy Brief, Norwegian Peacebuilding Resource Centre. Accessed December 2, 2015, from www.peacebuilding.no

Philo, G., & Berry, M. (2004). *Bad news from Israel.* Pluto Press.

Plunkett, J., & Halliday, J. (2011, February 7). Al-Jazeera's coverage of Egypt protests may hasten revolution in world news. *The Guardian.* Retrieved from: https://www.theguardian.com/media/2011/feb/07/al-jazeera-television-egypt-protests

Powers, S., & Gilboa, E. (2007). The public diplomacy of Al Jazeera. In *New media and the new Middle East* (pp. 53–80). New York, NY.

Powers, S. (2009). *The geopolitics of the news: The case of the Al-Jazeera network* (Doctoral Thesis, University of Southern California). Retrieved from ProQuest Dissertations and Theses (Order No. 3389538)

Powers, S. (2012). The origins of Al Jazeera English. In *Al Jazeera English: Global news in a changing world* (pp. 5–28). Palgrave Macmillan.

Rabi, U. (2009). Qatar's relations with Israel: Challenging Arab and gulf norms. *The Middle East Journal, 63*(3), 443–459. Accessed February 4, 2013, from http://ezproxy.library.usyd.edu.au/login?url=http://search.proquest.com/docview/218504444?accountid=14757

Rinnawi, K. (2003). Intifadas live: Arab satellite TV coverage of the Al-Aqsa Intifada. *Palestine Israel Journal, 10*(2), 1–5. Accessed August, 2011, from http://www.pij.org/details.php?id=42

Roberts, D. (2012). Understanding Qatar's foreign policy objectives. *Mediterranean Politics, 17*(2), 233–239.

Roberts, D. (2014). Qatar and the Muslim brotherhood: Pragmatism or preference? *Middle East Policy, 21*(3), 84–94.

Rugh, W. A. (2004). *Arab mass media: Newspapers, radio, and television in Arab politics.* Greenwood Publishing Group.

Rushing, J. (2007). *Mission Al Jazeera.* Palgrave Macmillan.

Sakr, N. (2007). *Arab television today.* IB Tauris.

Samuel-Azran, T. (2013). Al-Jazeera, Qatar, and new tactics in state-sponsored media diplomacy. *American Behavioral Scientist, 57*(9), 1293–1311.

Samuel-Azran, T., & Pecht, N. (2014). Is there an Al-Jazeera–Qatari nexus? A study of Al-Jazeera's online reporting throughout the Qatari–Saudi conflict. *Media, War & Conflict, 7*(2), 218–232.

Seib, P. M. (2008). *The "Al Jazeera effect": How the new global media are reshaping world politics.* Potamac Books.

Seib, P. M. (2010). Transnational journalism, public diplomacy, and virtual states. *Journalism Studies, 11*(5), 734–744.

Stephens, M. (2012). Qatar's Plan B for Syria: A wise choice?. Open Democracy, 1. Retrieved from: https://www.opendemocracy.net/michael-stephens/qatar%e2%80%99s-plan-b-for-syria-wise-choice (accessed 20 March 2016)

Sultan, N. (2013). Al Jazeera: Reflections on the Arab Spring. *Journal of Arabian Studies, 3*(2), 249–264.

Thompson, J. (2003). *Crisis and regime change: The nuclear nonproliferation regime and the challenge from nuclear terrorism* (Master's Thesis). Retrieved from ProQuest Dissertations and Theses (Order No. EC53324)

Ulrichsen, K. C. (2011, April 12). Qatar and the Arab Spring. *Open Democracy*. Accessed July 3, 2013, from https://www.opendemocracy.net/kristian-coates-ulrichsen/qatar-and-arab-spring

Ulrichsen, K. C. (2013). *Foreign policy implications of the new emir's succession in Qatar*. Policy Brief. Accessed November 1, 2015, from https://www.peace-building.no/Regions/Middle-East-and-North-Africa/The-Gulf/Publications/Foreign-policy-implications-of-the-new-emir-s-succession-in-Qatar

Ulrichsen, K. C. (2014). *Qatar and the Arab Spring*. Oxford University Press.

Worth, R. F. (2008, January 4). Al-Jazeera no longer nips at Saudis. *The New York Times Online*. http://www.nytimes.com/2008/01/04/world/middleeast/04jazeera.html?pagewanted=all

Zayani, M. (2005). *The Al Jazeera phenomenon: Critical perspectives on new Arab media*. Paradigm Publishers.

Zayani, M., & Sahraoui, S. (2007). *The culture of Al Jazeera: Inside an Arab media giant*. McFarland & Co.

Zayani, M. (2013). Al Jazeera's Palestine papers: Middle East media politics in the post-WikiLeaks era. *Media, War & Conflict, 6*(1), 21–35.

CHAPTER 3

Peace Journalism Model: Characteristics, Misconceptions and Challenges

3.1 INTRODUCTION

Many studies have analysed the media coverage of conflicts and their negative role in escalating violence. A few of them however have focused on its contributing role in conflict resolution (Gilboa, 2009). In a comprehensive review of the literature, Ross (2006) found that the media can facilitate mediation, reconciliation and peacekeeping processes. It also helps parties exchange information and creates public pressure that can bring differing parties into dialogue (Ross, 2006). This role though is rarely practised by the mainstream media which mainly cover violence (Wolfsfeld, 2004), display war frames [even when it covers peace] and portray negotiations as a "verbal battle" (Galtung & Fischer, 2013). Johan Galtung (1993) [a prominent scholar and the father of peace studies] says, "As the media work, they amplify the sound of guns rather than uniting them" (cited in Cottle, 2006).

The literature demonstrates that mainstream media coverage was propagandistic, nationalistic and blatantly served the interests of powerful and aggressor states [during the First and Second World Wars and invasions of the Middle Eastern, Asian, African and South American states] (Lynch & McGoldrick, 2005a; Spencer, 2004; Ross, 2006; Wolsfeld, 2004 cited in Hussain, 2016). Galtung (1998) describes this type of coverage as "War Journalism" (WJ) that does "not only legitimise violence but it is violent

---

© The Author(s), under exclusive license to Springer Nature Switzerland AG 2022

Z. Abdul-Nabi, *Al-Jazeera's "Double Standards" in the Arab Spring*, https://doi.org/10.1007/978-3-031-14279-6_3

53

54   Z. ABDUL-NABI

in and of itself". In one of the most cited and critical articles of war reporting and conventional news values of media, Galtung and Ruge (1965) conclude that the major five factors of newsworthiness in the Norwegian newspapers' coverage of the Congo, Cuba and Cyprus crises are as follows: "threshold, frequency, negativity, unexpectedness and unambiguity".

As a response to these values and the reality of the mainstream media, Galtung (1986, 1998) coined the model of Peace Journalism (PJ). This concept emerged as a trans-disciplinary field in the mid-1990s [not long after the first Gulf War in 1991] when journalists were "caught up, whether they like[d] it or not, in the loops and coils of conflict and political process" (Lynch, 2008, p. 193). Since this book analyses Al-Jazeera's coverage of Bahrain's uprising and Syria's second chemical weapons attack on the basis of Galtung's (1986, 1998) orientations of PJ, this chapter focuses on the characteristics of the PJ Model (PJM), its developments and main criticisms against it. This chapter also discusses the misconceptions of PJ among media scholars and practitioners in respect to its epistemological approach, advocacy role and position towards objectivity. Furthermore, it sheds lights on the professional and political challenges the concept faces, the possibility of practising it on the ground and how audiences have perceived it so far.

3.2   Definition of Peace Journalism

Lynch and McGoldrick (2000) [who have developed the PJM and expanded its indicatives] describe it as a "broader, fairer and more accurate way of framing stories". They define PJ as "when editors and reporters make choices—of what stories to report, and how to report them—that create opportunities for society at large to consider and value non-violent responses to conflict" (Lynch & McGoldrick, 2005a, p. 5). Shinar (2007, p. 2) considers PJ as "a normative mode of responsible and conscientious media coverage of conflict, that aims at contributing to peace-making, peacekeeping, and changing the attitudes of media owners, advertisers, professionals, and audiences towards war and peace". Lynch and McGoldrick (2005a) state that the PJ approach has been inspired by the field of peace research and conflict analysis. Therefore, a peace journalist will focus on the three forms of violence [structural, cultural and direct violence] while reporting.

3.3 Evolving of Peace Journalism Characteristics

As explained in the introduction, Galtung and Ruge's (1965) article sowed the seeds of the PJ orientations. The authors proposed 12-point suggestions [or what they called "policy implications"] in an attempt to reform the media and counter the dominance of the aforementioned five news values [threshold, frequency, negativity, unexpectedness and unambiguity]. They suggest more emphasis and reporting on (1) background and context, (2) complex and ambiguous events, (3) culturally distant zones, (4) irregular events, (5) the predictable and frequent, (6) "composition factors in order not to create news artefacts", (7) non-elite nations, (8) non-elite people, (9) non-personal causes of events, (10) positive events, (11) non-dramatic events and (12) a "continuity factor", by following up events even if there are no significant developments.

3.3.1 Galtung's Table

During a forum in 1997 in the United Kingdom, these 12 points were shortened to four orientations, when Johan Galtung, the principle speaker, "drew up a table to go into the delegates' packs: a single side of A4, divided into two columns, setting out the respective characteristics of WJ and PJ" (Lynch, 2013, p. 15). As shown in Table 3.1, PJ and WJ classifications are divided into "Peace, Truth, People and Solution" vs. "War, Propaganda, Elite and Victory". According to Galtung's (1998) table, Peace or Conflict-Orientated coverage will have to explore conflict formation, present all different parties not only two parties, explain goals, causes and history, give open time and space, focus on structural and cultural aspects of a conflict and adopt a win-win approach. Truth-Orientated coverage will have to expose propaganda and "untruths" of all sides and

Table 3.1 Peace Journalism vs. War Journalism (Galtung, 1998)[a]

Peace and/or Conflict Journalism	War and/or Violence Journalism
I. Peace and/or conflict oriented	I. War and/or violence oriented
II. Truth orientated	II. Propaganda oriented
III. People oriented	III. Elite oriented
IV. Solution orientated	IV. Victory orientated

[a]The detailed table of Galtung's (1998) peace orientations is quoted/cited in the methodology chapter (Chap. 4)

56   Z. ABDUL-NABI

"uncover all cover-ups". People-Orientated coverage will have to give voice to the voiceless, the vulnerable, victims, women, peacemakers and ordinary people. Solution-Orientated coverage will have to shed lights on peace initiatives; focus on resolution, reconstructions as well as reconciliations; and present the aftermath and implications of conflicts.

3.3.2   Two-Stage Strategy

In order to combat the dominant, escalation-orientated reporting, Kempf (2003) suggests a two-step strategy. The first phase is described as "de-escalation-orientated coverage" or "quality journalism", in which coverage is required to focus on the win-win approach, question violence and militarily means and examine the processes of conflict formation. The second step or what Kempf (2003) calls the "solution-orientated coverage" is required to cover the peace-making and reconciliation initiatives.

3.3.3   Shinar's Five Headings

Shinar (2007) proposes five headings extracted from Galtung's model and utilised as evaluative criteria for PJ content analysis studies (Lynch, 2014a). Shinar (2007, p. 200) states that PJ coverage:

> Explores backgrounds and contexts of conflict formation, and presenting causes and options on every side so as to portray conflict in realistic terms, transparent to the audience.
> Gives voice to the views of all rival parties, not merely the leaders of two antagonistic 'sides.'
> Airs creative ideas, from any source, for conflict resolution, development, peacemaking and peacekeeping.
> Exposes lies, cover-up attempts and culprits on all sides, and revealing excesses committed by, and suffering inflicted on, peoples of all parties.
> Pays attention to peace stories and post war developments.

3.3.4   Good Journalism

On the basis of "critical realism"[1] epistemology, Lynch (2014a) considers PJ as "good journalism" or an "insurgent form" that works against the

---

[1] Lynch (2007) suggests "critical realism" as epistemology of PJ. Therefore good journalism depends on representing social truth and representing the world "as agreed not as it is". This will be explained further in the epistemology section of this chapter.

mainstream and "journalism-as-usual". This approach uncovers the manipulation of reality and asks questions, rather than repeating already considered answers (Lynch, 2014a). He further elaborates:

[Good journalism] is that which stands out from the mainstream. Put another way, journalism is only 'any good,' in the sense of being worth having, insofar as it contains the potential for, and supports the practice of, insurgent forms. The insurgent forms are the 'good thing' about journalism and the 'good bit' of it. It need not promote particular accounts and perspectives, but where they are unjustly excluded, it should enable them to be seen and heard. (Lynch, 2014a, p. 34)

Lynch (2014a, p. 33) proposes six characteristics that can enable media to discharge its responsibility. Therefore, good journalism will:

Dissolve boundaries between 'us' and 'them,' including in affective public responses.
Devise creative ways to bring background into foreground, reach out from centre to periphery and reconfigure processes as events.
Include a wide range of accounts of power and political process, avoiding stenography of dualistic 'jousts' between leaders of parties contesting government in its own country (who won the debate?)
Provide readers and audiences with cues and clues to prompt and equip them to develop critical awareness of attempts to pass off claims as facts, or 'social truths' as merely interpersonal.
Contribute to the construction of discursive truth by explaining new phenomena with reference to underlying causes and patterns.
Inspire by remitting into public spheres the hopes, dreams, aspirations and actions of those experimenting with and advocating new visions. (Lynch 2014a, p. 33)

3.4 Critics of Galtung's Peace Journalism Model

3.4.1 Gilboa's Three-Dimensional Framework

Gilboa (2009) attributes the lack of research in the role of media in conflict resolution to the deficiency of analysing tools and frameworks, challenges of multidisciplinary research and gaps between academics and practitioners in the fields of conflict resolution, communication and journalism. He argues that the PJM is not adequate to fill this gap due to its simplicity and "unrealistic approach" regarding the media effects. He also criticises the model for being in disagreement with the theory of mass communication (Hanitzsch, 2004). Therefore, he proposes a "three-dimensional framework", based on the combination and integration of components derived from the fields of international relations, conflict studies, communication and journalism.

Unlike other models, this "comprehensive framework" can be operationalised on different phases and levels of conflicts [low-intensity conflict (LIC) and high-intensity conflict (HIC)] (Gilboa, 2009). The framework depends mainly on a modified version of the conflict life cycle theory and the "functional approach of communication" (Gilboa, 2009). It aims to help understand how the media influences the beginning, evolution and termination of existing and future conflicts. It also enables researchers as well as practitioners to explore the positive and negative effects of contributions by the media through analysing and focusing on (1) the types [interstate and internal] and phases of conflicts [prevention, management, resolution and reconciliation], (2) the types [traditional media and new media] and levels of media [local, national, regional, international and global] and (3) the functions and dysfunctions of the media [news, interpretation, cultural transmission, entertainment and mobilisation] (Gilboa, 2009).

Despite the inclusiveness of the framework, it still allows researchers to select or implement certain parts only. For instance, a researcher can examine the five functions of the media during one phase of a conflict only or they can focus on just one function during the four conflict phases (Gilboa, 2009). In relation to utilising the framework for analysis, Gilboa (2009) suggests to (1) prioritise investigating the functions and dysfunctions of the local media due to its direct influence on people, (2) analyse the media coverage during the reconciliation phase, (3) explore the roles and functions of the new media and (4) focus more on analysing the LIC.

Nohrstedt and Ottosen (2015) consider Galtung's model as a significant "checklist tool" for journalists and peace researchers. At the same time, however, they state that the model is "generalised", limited and not relevant to different situations and stages of conflicts. For instance, the necessity of presenting potential conflict risks and possible military actions in the future is not emphasised in Galtung's model (Nohrstedt & Ottosen, 2015). Failing to mention these risks or what Bourdieu's theory calls "Doxa" can facilitate military involvement and escalate conflicts (Nohrstedt & Ottosen, 2015). For example, if media coverage focused only on the proposal of the Nordic Military Collaboration [between Finland, Norway and Sweden in 2001] and at the same time did not mention the possibility that this coalition could take part in the "global war on terror", then the coverage would be categorised as PJ-orientated. Not mentioning the coalition's participation in the "global war on terror" makes the coverage "opaque", "secret" and—hence—War Journalism-orientated (Nohrstedt & Ottosen, 2015). Therefore, in order to overcome this particular weakness of Galtung's model, Nohrstedt and Ottosen (2015) suggest equipping it with a critical awareness of this "silence (Doxa)".

3.4.2   Actor-Event Framework

Hanitzsch et al. (2016) criticise the "dualism" in Galtung's (1998) table, which, as explained earlier, divides conflict coverage into Peace-Orientated vs. War-Orientated, Truth-Orientated vs. Propaganda-Orientated, People-Orientated vs. Elite-Orientated and Solution-Orientated vs. Victory-Orientated. They argue that while PJ offers significant framing distinctions, it disregards relevant sub-distinctions, the positioning of certain elements in content and most importantly the interaction between these elements (Hanitzsch et al., 2016). Therefore, as a critical response to the dualistic approach of PJ, Hanitzsch et al. (2016) propose the "actor-event framework" which—according to them—aims to comprehensively deconstruct "news narratives" by adding more distinctions and analysing the representations of the two pillars of any narrative: actors and events of conflicts.

Their framework depends on the conceptualisation of news stories as "narratives[2]" and conflict research in social and political psychology, political communication and journalism studies. The main purpose of the actor-event model is not to focus on whether specific content, elements or sides of conflicts are mentioned or not, but how all these dimensions are represented, positioned, connected and grouped together within a certain narrative (Hanitzsch et al., 2016).

According to the framework, a conflict news narrative is divided into (1) conflict actors and (2) event actors. The actors are classified into (1) in-group actors, (2) out-group actors and (3) sub-group actors. All these different actors are evaluated and framed based on their (1) diversity and

---

[2] A narrative is defined as "discursive representations of sequences of events, which commonly focus on the actions of specific actors" (Abbott, 2008; Rimmon-Kenan, 2002 cited in Hanitzsch et al., 2016).

visibility, (2) characterisation and (3) the level of information about victims (Hanitzsch et al., 2016). While the PJM focuses only on two types of events [violence and war versus peace initiatives and processes], Hanitzsch et al.'s (2016) framework classifies events as (1) violence and military action; (2) economic, political and media measures; (3) ceasefires and avoidance of violence; and (4) gestures, dialogue and peace negotiations. Each event is assessed based on its (1) salience in the narrative, (2) supporting the course of action and (3) attribution of responsibility.

Hanitzsch et al. (2016) have applied this framework on the Israeli coverage [Haaretz, Israel Hayom and Ynet] of the Israeli-Palestinian conflict, Iran's nuclear programme and the Syrian civil war. The results of their quantitative content analysis agree with PJ scholars that elites and military actions dominate the media coverage (Hanitzsch et al., 2016). However, the findings show that the majority of official actors were quoted in Peace-Orientated narratives (Hanitzsch et al., 2016) which is inconsistent with PJ literature. The study also found that the visibility of the "other side" is not necessarily associated with an empathetic framing. Hanitzsch et al. (2016) argue that this reflects the significance of adding salience, characterisation and tone to the analysing frameworks of conflict coverage.

Nohrstedt and Ottosen (2015) acknowledge that many quantitative studies have proved that the mainstream media coverage is in line with Galtung's "polarised model". However, they argue that the model is still "rigid" and "does not contain any recipes in any other way". In agreement with Hanitzsch et al.'s (2016) criticisms of PJ's dualism, Nohrstedt and Ottosen (2015) contend that the diversity of public opinions and positions cannot always fit into PJ or WJ columns of Galtung's framework. Therefore, they propose a Critical Discourse Analysis (CDA) approach as a complementary tool that can be useful in explaining meanings, context and relationships between different actors.

3.4.3 Reconciliatory Function Characteristics

El-Nawawy and Powers (2008) criticise the PJM for not considering the role of collective identity of groups [religious, ethnic, national and transnational identities] in accepting or refusing non-violent responses to conflicts. It is argued that "mediatised recognition" in which media recognises the oppressed, isolated and marginalised (Cottle, 2006) can facilitate reconciliation, provide equal recognition to all social and political groups and "contribute to the peaceful integration of these groups" (Howard, 2002, cited in El-Nawawy & Powers, 2008). Based on this "mediatised recognition" concept (Cottle, 2006; Howard, 2003) and PJM (Lynch & McGoldrick, 2005a), El-Nawawy and Powers (2008) propose 11 characteristics of media coverage that can carry out a "conciliatory function".

They include (1) giving a voice to politically underrepresented groups, (2) demonstrating different perspectives, (3) focusing on the international public interests in general, (4) presenting "firsthand observation form eyewitnesses", (5) focusing on the injustice in the world, (6) unveiling journalists' mistakes whenever possible, (7) showing a tendency towards solutions rather than escalation, (8) avoiding victimising language, (9) avoiding demonising language, (10) avoiding presenting opinions that are not supported by "credible evidence" and (11) providing context and background. El-Nawawy and Powers (2008) argue that their 11-point typology can effectively challenge cross-cultural stereotypes, generate tolerance and pave the way for reconciliation among cultural rivals. As mentioned in Chap. 2, the authors proved empirically that AJE had adopted the majority of the above characteristics.

3.5 Expanding Peace Journalism Model

3.5.1 Gender Awareness

While some researchers criticise Galtung's model, proposing alternatives and more comprehensive frameworks (El-Nawawy & Powers, 2008; Hanitzsch et al., 2016; Gilboa, 2009), others suggest adding more classifications to the model (Jacobson, 2010; Shaw, 2011; Benn, 2015; Aslam, 2016). For instance, Jacobson (2010) suggests adding gender awareness and gender blindness distinctions to Galtung's table. Jacobson's (2010) proposal comes as a response to the systematic negligence of women's voice in the mainstream media. For instance, 85% and 89% of the coverage of Swedish media favour male subjects and sources, respectively (Jacobson, 2010).

Some argue that "gender awareness" is not necessary, as the model has already emphasised giving voice to the voiceless. However, Jacobson (2010) responds that including gender theory will not give the model credibility in academic spheres only, but it will make it appealing to women journalists and feminists as well. Benn (2015) agrees that gender addition is needed and suggests adding racial/ethnic awareness/blindness as well. Interestingly, Allan (2011) calls for including "peace photography" to reimagine the traditional photographic form, practice and epistemology that have prevailed through the dominant binary framing [good vs. evil and us vs. them].

3.5.2   *Human Rights Journalism*

Shaw et al. (2011) propose Human Rights Journalism (HRJ) as a complementary element of PJ. Shaw (2011, p. 107) defines HRJ as a "diagnostic style of reporting which offers a critical reflection of the experiences and needs of the victims and perpetrators of [physical, cultural and structural] human rights violations". Moreover, Shaw (2011, pp. 36–37) describes it as "journalism with a human face, a journalism that cares for the people, one that prioritises them over capitalism and, above all, over the whims and caprices of political demagogues".

The tenets of HRJ or "journalism without borders" were derived from the fields of human rights and global justice. It aims to solve the reasons behind violations and challenge the imbalances in politics, economy and culture on the local and global levels (Shaw, 2011). Shaw's (2011) framework of HRJ and Human Wrong Journalism (HWJ) is divided into five classifications: PJ vs. WJ, Global reporting vs. Selective reporting, Proactive reporting style vs. Reactive reporting style, Attachment vs. Detachment from victims of violence and Diagnostic orientation vs. Evocative orientation.

3.6   Epistemology of Peace Journalism

3.6.1   *Critical Realism*

Despite the fact that peace scholars have welcomed and considered the PJM as a "system of global media ethics" (Tehranian, 2002), it has not gained a wide acceptance among journalists and media researchers (Hanitzsch, 2004; Hanitzsch et al., 2016; Loyn, 2007, El-Nawawy & Powers, 2008; Gilboa, 2009). Hanitzsch (2004) criticises PJ's epistemological approach by arguing that it relies on "Naïve Realism". According to "Naïve Realists", reality can be seen and described "as it is" and, the observer [the knower] and the observed [the thing known] are two independent categories (Hanitzsch, 2004). Hanitzsch's (2004) criticisms of PJ epistemology were based on Galtung's (2002) statement, when he said that the mainstream media represents a distorted image of "reality".

Hanitzsch (2007, p. 5) says that Galtung missed the point as media can never be a "mirror of reality... every representation is inevitably biased, and any 'correspondence' between an objective reality and its representation(s) is hardly possible".

In response to Hanitzsch (2007), Peleg (2007) argues that while news cannot "mirror reality", it does not mean that it is not able to represent a "more considerate and fair-minded one". In line with Hanitzsch's (2007) criticisms, Shinar (2007) [a PJ advocate] considers the "Truth orientation" of Galtung's model "problematic". He says, "Even Galtung's loyal disciples Jake Lynch and Annabel McGoldrick (2005a) are cautious in dealing with the word 'Truth'". Interestingly, in a later article, Hanitzsch (2007) did not mention the "Naïve Realism" approach, assuming that PJ does not have an epistemology and as such asking its founders to find one. Even more interestingly, Peleg (2007), a proponent of PJ, agreed with Hanitzsch (2007) that PJ needs to be established on a solid theoretical base, despite the fact that Lynch (2006) had already suggested and considered "critical realism" as the foundation of PJ's epistemology in an article published earlier. Critical realism according to Wright (1996, pp. 35–36) is defined as:

A way of describing the process of 'knowing' that acknowledges the reality of the thing known, as something other than the knower (hence 'realism,') while also acknowledging that the only access we have to this reality lies along the spiralling path of appropriate dialogue or conversation between the knower and the thing known (hence 'critical'). (cited in Lynch, 2007, p. 6)

Thus, critical realism "acknowledges that reality exists independently of our knowledge of it", and because we do not live in a transparent world, "this knowledge is always fallible" (Danermark et al., 2002, p. 17). However, it is possible to obtain a "less fallible knowledge" by conducting a "dialogue" between the observer and the thing observed (Wright, 1996 cited in Lynch, 2007) or by applying what Lynch and McGoldrick (2005a) call "reflexivity". According to the authors, if this "reflexivity" is founded on the basis of the conflict analysis and peace research fields, it will be able to help journalists assess and determine what is important and what is missing in coverage (Lynch, 2007, p. 7).

As journalists "de-code texts and images and re-encode them" to the audience as argued by "Reception theory" (Hall, 1980), media coverage that challenges dominant, official narratives and gives voice to the marginalised can encourage reviewers and audiences to "de-code propaganda and produce their own 'negotiated reading'" (Hall, 1980 cited in Lynch, 2006). By reviewing news [press releases or dominant perspectives, for instance] critically and including well-grounded accounts, in coverage, Lynch (2014b, p. 32) infers that this might not represent the world "as it is", but it can assemble it "as agreed". In this sense, PJ considers facts as an "ongoing, reviewable social consensus" (Lynch, 2014a, p. 159). Lynch (2014b, p. 31) states that this is consistent with Calcutt's and Hammond's (2011, p. 8) insistence on journalists and academics "not to give up on the pursuit of 'social truths' and leave journalism with only 'truth-lite,' little better than 'interpersonal relations,' as an offering to its publics". In other words, journalists should practise "reflexivity" to avoid reporting claims [such as the existence of Weapons of Mass Destructions (WMDs) in Iraq] as facts and reporting facts [such as the climate change] as claims (Lynch, 2014b). Therefore, based on the critical realist foundation of PJ, Lynch (2014a, p. 33) has reconceptualised the second orientation of Gatung's table (Table 3.1) from "Truth" to providing "cues and clues to prompt and equip them [audience] to develop critical awareness of attempts to pass off claims as facts, or 'social truths' as merely interpersonal".

To conclude, PJ scholars have not agreed on an ideal philosophical basis for the concept. Depending on social theory, Lynch and Hussain (2015) conclude that the PJ literature can be classified based on four theoretical approaches. As explained earlier, Hanitzsch (2004) considers PJ as a (1) normative and idealist concept, whereas Lynch (2006, 2007, 2014a) suggests that (2) "critical realism" lies at its [PJ's] epistemological foundation. Some were inspired by the (3) "critical approach" which argues that PJ can only be implemented if the media profession and structure were comprehensively reformed (Galtung, 2000; Tehranian, 2002; Fawcett, 2002; Ross, 2006; Peleg, 2007 cited in Lynch & Hussain, 2015). Others, however, adopt the (4) "post-positivism approach" in which the PJM has been operationalised and utilised as a source of evaluative criteria (Kempf, 2003; Lee & Maslog, 2005; Lee, 2010; Siraj & Hussain, 2012, cited in Lynch & Hussain, 2015).

3.6.2   *Critical Pragmatism*

Given the impracticality of adopting "critical realism" and the "critical approach" [both described as radical by Lynch and Hussain (2015) especially in "semi-democratic countries" like Pakistan, where PJ is most needed], Lynch and Hussain (2015) propose "critical pragmatism" as a more flexible, "philosophical mooring" for PJ. Unlike post-positivism, critical pragmatism does not claim that it can reach "absolute knowledge", but, at the same time, it believes that "maximum possible knowledge" [which might be still fallible] can be gained through reliable means (Dewey, 1938). It is basically a compromising concept between the critical approaches and post-positivism (Lynch & Hussain, 2015).

Devoted specifically to areas engulfed by conflicts and risks, Lynch and Hussain (2015) designed the "Critical Pragmatic Model for Peace Journalism". The framework is structured on PJ's scholarship on "critical pragmatism literature" (Dewey, 1938; Habermas & Cooke, 2000) and detailed semi-structured interviews with 35 prominent conflict reporters, six editors, 12 conflict stakeholders, six media analysts and five peace and conflict resolution experts. Lynch and Hussain (2015) interviewed all these experts about five conflicts in Pakistan: the Taliban's actions, sectarianism, the crisis in Baluchistan, ethnic tension and the political conflict between the Pakistani government and the judiciary.

According to this framework, the task of peace journalists varies from one conflict to another. Due to restrictions and threats in some areas, it can be possible to practise "passive Peace Journalism;"[3] however, if the risks are lower, journalists might be able to display "active Peace Journalism."[4] The critical pragmatism approach assumes that journalists are fully aware of the threats and challenges that can affect their professionalism. At the same time, however, they have to find a creative way—whenever it is possible—to give a voice to the marginalised, neglected views of all victims, and focus on peace initiatives and implications of conflicts.

According to the model, two factors can determine which aspect of PJ can be implemented. The first one is the "perception" of the level of the threat to national security and the second one is the subsequent flak, generated by the media coverage of conflicts. Thus:

---

[3] Passive Peace Journalism indicatives include avoiding emotive or demonising language, using non-partisan language and framing and avoiding labelling as "good and bad" (Lynch, 2008).

[4] Active Peace Journalism indicatives include exploring context, challenging propaganda and making peace visible (Lynch, 2008).

1) If the level of national security threat is high, the media would be faced with "institutional flak" in which journalists might be accused of being foreign spies, traitors and unpatriotic. At this stage, media coverage would be dominated by patriotic discourse. Therefore, the best alternative would be to practise "passive Peace Journalism" that highlights humanitarian suffering, contextualises the conflict and gives history and background.

2) If the level of the national security threat is medium, the media would be encountered with "elite security flak" in which journalists might be fired from their jobs, threatened and even killed. At this level, media coverage would be dominated by the elite discourse. Hence, the best alternative would be to "oscillate between passive and active Peace Journalism". The task of a peace journalist would be to provide different perspectives, focus on the efforts of peace-makers, humanise and depoliticise the victims and initiate Solution-Orientated coverage.

3) If the level of the threat were low, the media would be met with "commercial/ethical flak" in which journalists might be pressured to bring interesting and dramatic news. At this stage, media coverage would be dominated by sensationalist discourse. Thus, the best way to improve the coverage would be to display active Peace Journalism. The role of a peace journalist would be to provide different perspectives; engage all parties; sponsor "harmony debates", seminars and conferences between conflicted parties; initiate Solution-Orientated coverage; reveal motives of parties and create critical awareness.

3.7 "WHICH FACTS ARE ALLOWED THROUGH THE GATE?"

Regardless of the epistemological approach of PJ, to Lynch (2007), the main dispute between PJ advocates and its critics (Loyn, 2007) is not over "reporting facts" and journalism's commitment towards "truthfulness" but is mainly about how and why certain facts are included in a coverage and others are not. What is meant by this is how "some facts are allowed through the gate, [while] others kept out?" Lynch (2007, p. 3) further asks:

How these particular facts, as distinct from a practically infinite number of others 'out there,' come to meet them; and how they, the reporters, come to meet these particular facts. If it's always the same facts, or the same kinds of facts, what consequences follow, for the nature of representation produced? How does that representation affect the understanding developed by readers and audiences, and their responses? And how do those responses, or assumptions about them, feed in to the actions and motivations of parties to conflict? These are the real questions in the Peace Journalism debate.

A few studies have focused on the absence of certain facts in the media coverage and how such exclusion can affect the framing of conflicts. For instance, Fahmy and Eakin (2014) analysed three international newspapers' coverage [*Haaretz, The Guardian* and *The New York Times*] of the Israeli attack on a Turkish ship[5] when it was on its way to Gaza during the strip's blockade. The results demonstrate that the most prevailed WJ indicative was "focus on here and now" at the expense of the background and context of the conflict. The coverage failed to highlight the main reasons behind the blockade and its humanitarian impacts on the people of Gaza (Fahmy & Eakin, 2014).

In addition, Lynch and McGoldrick (2005b) illustrate in their journal article "War and Peace Journalism in the Holy Land" the significance of mentioning the context and the Palestinian narrative while covering the Israeli-Palestinian conflict. For instance, the suicide bombing in *Shmuel Hanavi* which killed 20 Israelis in 2003 was portrayed by the mainstream media as an "unilateral Palestinian infraction, putting an end to the peace plan, road map" at the time (Lynch, 2008, p. 184). Twenty-one Palestinians were killed during that period according to the Red Crescent, and despite this there was no coverage of the daily Israeli violations that occurred (Lynch, 2008). Lynch and McGoldrick (2005b) state that "these incidents [facts] remained below the radar of many news desks and reporters". In his examination of the coverage of the UK press of Iran's nuclear crisis, Lynch (2006) found that none of the 211 analysed articles

---

[5] In 2010, the Turkish ship *Mavi Marmara* was shot at by commandos of the Israeli Defence Force (IDF) when it attempted to break the blockade of the Gaza Strip (Fahmy& Eakin, 2014).

68   Z. ABDUL-NABI

from different newspapers focused on the history and the context of the tense ties between the West and Iran which goes back to 1953.[6]

In another critical analysis of the mainstream media in the United Kingdom, Lynch and McGoldrick (2005a) indicate that while the media welcomed the official allegations over the existence of WMDs in Iraq, it disregarded the assessment of backbench Labour MP, Alan Simpson, and the Cambridge academic, Glen Rangwala. They said, "There is no case for a war on Iraq. It has not threatened to attack the US or Europe. It is not connected to Al-Qaeda. There is no evidence that it has new WMDs, or that it possesses the means of delivering them" (Lynch, 2006, p. 80).

Ottosen (2010) explores the impact of the absence of PJ orientations in the Norwegian media during the beginning of the war in Afghanistan. He states that although the presence of Norwegian soldiers in Kabul has been considered by the Norwegians as a crucial and controversial political problem in 2009, the coverage of the main newspapers in Oslo of the military intervention in 2001 was dominated by US-friendly framing and Western sources. Ottosen (2010) concludes that if the PJM were applied and certain facts were revealed at the time, Norway's responsibility for killing and injuring civilians would have been highlighted.

3.8   Peace Journalism and Objectivity

3.8.1   Feedback Loop

David Loyn (2007), a prominent correspondent for the BBC, criticises PJ heavily for being inconsistent with the elements of objectivity which—according to Hammond (2002)—includes the practices of truthfulness, accuracy, neutrality and emotional detachment. Ross (2006) wonders why PJ's calls to end violence are regarded as "anti-objectivity", whereas other media outlets that campaign against crimes, drugs and drinking and driving are not. Likewise, no one asks the media to be objective when it reports on rape and genocide, for instance (Ross, 2006). According to Lynch (1998, 2014a), PJ is not a full "departure" from journalism practice.

It is instead a "shift" in the way the news is seen, narrated and financed. It is a shift from spokespeople towards citizens and from following

---

[6] This date is particularly important as 1953 is when the CIA, the United Kingdom and the United States backed and engineered a coup against the democratically elected Iranian Prime Minister Mohammed Mossadegh.

dramatic, heated conflicts towards valuing peace (Lynch, 2014a). Loyn (2007, p. 3), however, argues that the task of journalists is to find "what is going on, not carrying any other baggage. If there is conflict resolution, we report on it in context. We do not engage in it. Reporters need to preserve their position as observers, not players".

Lynch (2007) responds that PJ does not require journalists to involve themselves. What it asks them for is to include "causes and effects, based on their observer status" (Lynch, 2007). Moreover, while journalists in the West tend to think that their role is to "report the facts" only, this is really not the case (Lynch, 2007). This is highlighted especially in our "media-savvy world" where politicians, viewers, listeners and even ordinary people know exactly how to create facts for the media to cover (Lynch & McGoldrick, 2000). Journalists and political players are both involved in a "feedback loop" in which sources/elites depend on their previous experience as "observers and audience" to create certain "facts" that they predict will be reported in a particular way (Lynch & McGoldrick, 2005a). Thus, every time journalists report these facts or "frames", they influence the statements and actions of these sources in the future (Lynch & McGoldrick, 2005a).

In a nutshell, "what media report and what people do is related" (Lynch & Galtung, 2010). That is why journalists have to practise "self-reflection" or as mentioned earlier "reflexivity" (Lynch & McGoldrick, 2005a). They have to ask themselves, "What do we want, to stimulate more violence or more peace?" (Lynch & Galtung, 2010, p. 60). Therefore, it can be concluded that PJ is concerned about the "ethics of consequences rather than the ethics of intentions" and the "ethics of action rather than the ethics of conviction" (Lynch & Galtung, 2010). Again, to the founders of PJ, the main issue is selectivity, not objectivity. They say:

> To report or not report, a shot fired in anger or a word spoken with love is not a problem of factual objectivity but of criteria objectivity, of having explicit criteria that are also communicable and reproducible; a shot may be more consequential than a word. Any selectivity against peace smells of bias. We can and should demand explicitness: on what basis we select and discuss the criteria that would be a working version of objectivity. (Lynch & Galtung, 2010, p. 53)

3.8.2 Objectivity Regime

Lynch and McGoldrick (2005a) contend that the conventions of objectivity "lead us—or leave us—to overvalue violent, reactive responses to conflict, and undervalue non-violent developmental ones". Hackett (2006) names these conventions the "regime of objectivity". According to this regime, journalists should balance their coverage by interviewing "both sides" and reporting "credible facts" that they themselves observed or official sources confirmed (Hackett, 2011). Furthermore, reporters have to separate facts from opinions and prioritise characters and events over structures and process (Hackett, 2011). These conventions could produce "a bias in favour of official sources, a bias in favour of event over process and a bias in favour of dualism in reporting conflicts" (Lynch & McGoldrick, 2005a, p. 209). McGoldrick (2006, p. 4) concludes that these particular practices are in disagreement with the liberal theory of press freedom in which media should act as a "civic tool" that is supposed to shed light on problems and report "facts" without "fear or favour". Interestingly, according to a global survey conducted by Lynch and McGoldrick (2004), 60% of participants/journalists think that the media in their countries is not able to implement this crucial role due to journalistic conventions (cited in McGoldrick, 2006). For instance, the practice of balance or what Lynch (2014a) refers to as "on-the-one-hand-on-the-other-hand-in-the-end-only-time-will-tell" can result in simplifying complex issues in a conflict between two sides, therefore marginalising other perspectives and giving more time and space to polarised voices (Hackett, 2011, p. 39). It can also be strongly misleading and misrepresenting (Lynch, 2014a). As an illustration, a study conducted by Philo and Berry (2004) found that the majority of British television viewers believed that Palestinians are the ones who occupy the Occupied Territories, not the other way around (cited in Lynch, 2014a). Lynch and Galtung (2010) further argue that the practice of balance is problematic. They state that it can be possible to find the balance when covering a conflict between two legitimate sides or two equal illegitimate sides that are involved in conventional wars. Yet, how is it possible to create the balance where the conflict itself is imbalanced, as in the cases of conflicts between an occupier and occupied, colonial powers and colonies, brutal government and unarmed protesters and slave owners and slaves? This imbalance, according to the PJ approach, should be reflected in the media coverage (Lynch & Galtung, 2010). In addition, depending on authorities and elites as the main sources of obtaining "facts" could sideline millions of people who are suffering from poverty, labour exploitations and private sector corruption (Hackett, 2011). It can also encourage unauthorised groups which are usually neglected by journalists to adopt violence and "disruptive tactics in order to attract media attention" (Bagdikian, 2014). Giving prominence to political leaders makes it easy for them to undermine their rivals [as was the case of Saddam Hussain]. Most importantly, they can utilise their space to deflect and distract the audience from their violations and deadly implications of their policies (Hackett, 2011). Therefore, the ethos of objectivity can manipulate and misinform public opinion, undermine democratic public life (Hackett, 2011) and give credibility to officials' claims (Lynch, 2014b). That is why PJ has a completely different interpretation of "balance". According to Lynch and Galtung (2010), balanced and accurate reporting can be achieved through presenting all goals of all parties, presenting all phases [before, during and after] of the conflict equally, giving voice to elites as well as ordinary people and empathising with all parties. They, however, note that balanced empathy "does not imply balanced sympathy", as "those who tramples on others' basic needs, on their life and livelihood, their freedom, and identity have the right to be understood [empathy], but not to be sympathised with. Sympathy is granted for victims only" (Lynch & Galtung, 2010, p. 60). Although there is no framework that can replace the regime of objectivity, PJ is a "promising challenger" and an "internal reform movement" that can help revise the professional norms of journalism (Hackett, 2011). In the most recent research, however, PJ scholars tend to adopt more pragmatic, flexible and practical approaches towards objectivity. For example, in conflict-torn areas where journalists face deadly threats, they will have to compromise with the media and political structure to achieve their goal: peace (Lynch & Hussain, 2015). On the basis of "critical pragmatism", objectivity [ontology] can be considered as "the achievable part of reality which serves humanity" (Lynch & Hussain, 2015).

3.8.3 Objectivity and Propaganda

The practice of "objectivity" could promote and facilitate "propaganda". For instance, one of the systematic reasons that the main US news media failed to uncover the lies over the WMD was the conventional practice of [objectively] quoting "men and women with high titles" (Kamalipour & Snow, 2004). This absolute reliance on "officialdom" during the war in

Iraq has given a "stark lesson" to the American media institutions (Kamalipour & Snow, 2004). As George Orwell said in his "famous dictum":

> One ought to recognize that the present political chaos is connected with the decay of language, and that one can probably bring about some improvement by starting at the verbal end... Political language—and with variations this is true of all political parties from Conservatives to Anarchists—is designed to make lies sounds truthful and murder respectable, and to give an appearance of solidity to pure wind. (Kamalipour & Snow, 2004)

This study adopts Herman's and Chomsky's (2010) explanation of "propaganda" in which "the media serve, and propagandise on behalf of, the powerful societal interests that control and finance them". They further say:

> The representatives of these interests have important agendas and principles that they want to advance, and they are well positioned to shape and constrain media policy. This is normally not accomplished by crude intervention, but by the selection of right-thinking personnel and by the editors' and working journalists' internalisation of priorities and definitions of newsworthiness that conform to the institution's policy. (Herman & Chomsky, 2010, p. xi)

In a propaganda system, media outlets will implement several techniques that include "worthy and un-worthy victims", "legitimisation and de-legitimisation" and "dual standard coverage" between client and enemy states (Herman & Chomsky, 2010). These double standards are typical in Propaganda-Orientated coverage in which an ally to the media owners is constantly focused on, legitimised and framed as "worthy". In contrast, the enemy of that ally is delegitimised, considered "unworthy" and marginalised (Herman & Chomsky, 2010).

3.9   Peace Journalism and Advocacy Role

3.9.1   Good Journalism or Advocacy Journalism?

One of the most repetitive misconceptions of PJ is associating it with advocating peace. For instance, Loyn (2007, p. 2) says, "Galtung misunderstood our role and power; journalists are reporters, not peacemakers...

we are not there to make peace". In response, PJ scholars explain that PJ does not promote peace, but instead gives it a chance (Lynch & McGoldrick, 2005a; Lynch & Galtung, 2010). PJ simply "creates opportunities … to consider and value non-violent responses to conflict". "If such responses—once considered—are rejected, there is nothing else journalism can do about it while remaining journalism" (Lynch, 2014a, p. 46). Lynch and Galtung (2010, p. 60) further elaborate:

> Journalists should not be politicians, activists or social scientists. Others do that. We want journalists to do something very special, indispensable, and to do it well. We want journalists to be our eyes and ears to be where we cannot be in social space, and report to us what they saw and heard objectively, with balance inquisitively, and ethically, we do not want them to sit in hotel bar confusing gossip with other journalists with eyewitness' report. We want them to see with a wide angle, without blinkers.

Despite the fact that PJ's main scholars indicate in early stages that they reject PJ as a form of advocacy (Lynch & McGoldrick, 2005a; Kempf, 2003), Ross (2006) says, "peace journalists are divided" as some view the concept through activism and advocacy lenses (see Peleg, 2007; Lee, 2010; Benn, 2015; Aslam, 2016). Others look at it as "quality journalism" (Kempf, 2003) or "good journalism" (Lynch, 2014a) that aims to present marginalised accounts and create a better and deeper understanding of conflicts (Lynch & McGoldrick, 2005a; Lynch & Galtung, 2010). To explain this division further, Peleg (2007, p. 5) calls for narrowing the gap between journalism and peace-making by "modifying the latter [journalism] in order to better accommodate the former [peace-making]". Peleg (2006) suggests that PJ should act as a "third party" that facilitates communication, arbitrates and mediates between the "two rivalling sides" in conflicts.

Hanitzsch (2007) describes this approach as an "interventionist mode" of PJ that is closer to journalism of attachment and, hence, should be considered—according to journalism theory—as part of public relation practices (Hanitzsch, 2007). The "good journalism mode" of PJ (Hanitzsch, 2007), however, refuses to compare the concept with "journalism of attachment" (Kempf, 2003), which justifies siding with victims and promoting military interventions to save them. Kempf (2003) explains how the coverage of the war in Bosnia fabricated news under the pretext of "noble moral goals". He further states that:

Journalism of attachment "neglects conflict analysis, divides parties to good and evil and- its task is to put 'moral pressure' on the international community to take sides and use military means. It allows journalists to abandon their professional rules and standards of truthfulness in the name of a higher moral duty. (Kempf, 2003, p. 2)

Interestingly, both critics (Hanitzsch, 2007) and scholars of PJ (Kempf, 2008; Lynch, 2014a) believe that the term "Peace Journalism" causes difficulties to the concept itself and risks misrepresenting it among journalists and academics. Kempf (2008, p. 156) says, "Raise 'Peace Journalism' by that name in many newsrooms and people will assume you mean a form of advocacy, which would endanger the acceptance of the Peace Journalism project in the journalistic community" (cited in Lynch, 2014a, p. 46). This can explain why PJ initiatives in the Philippines and the United Kingdom avoided using the word "peace" in their projects. They named them instead "Conflict-Sensitive Reporting" and "Reporting the World", respectively (Lynch, 2014a). For the same reason, Nohrstedt and Ottosen (2015) suggest replacing PJ with a more "appropriate term", proposing to name it "Consequence-Ethical Reflexivity".

3.9.2   Advocacy Frameworks

Inspired by the different approaches of PJ researchers towards advocacy, Benn (2015) proposes the pyramid of "PJ spectrum" which aims at reconciling all conflicting views on the PJ debate into one framework. The first level of the pyramid includes the characteristics of good traditional journalism [passive PJ], whereas the second level contains the people, solution and advocacy orientations [active PJ]. Benn's (2015) pyramid, however, might be seen as problematic because it assumes that Jake Lynch and Robert Hackett are supporters of the advocacy form of PJ [second level] and PJ's critics (Loyn, 2007; Hanitzsch, 2007) are advocates of traditional journalism [first level]. One might consider this assumption baseless because Lynch and Galtung (2010) state very clearly that peace journalists are not peacekeepers or peace advocates, and PJ is not a departure from professional journalism (Lynch, 2014a).

In agreement with Benn's (2015) advocacy model, Aslam (2016) proposes the "inverted trident framework" of PJ. This model considers PJ as a "cohesive and synergised strategy" that should be developed by journalists, researchers and peace workers in order to de-escalate conflicts.

According to the framework, the tasks of intervention, prevention and peace-building are cooperatively conducted by journalists' creativity, researchers' skills and peace workers' initiatives (Aslam, 2016).

3.10 Challenges Facing Peace Journalism

3.10.1 News Values

While PJ is not unfamiliar with the journalism research that Hanitzsch (2007) describes as an "old wine in a new bottle", some of its orientations are "impractical" due to the routines of media production and "professional journalism". For instance, PJ challenges the conventional news values that guide journalists and affect the way they select and construct their news narratives (Hackett, 2011). In a study that aims at updating the results of Galtung and Ruge's (1965) article, Harcup and O'Neill (2001) found that the news values of the British media include: "power elite, celebrity, entertainment, surprise, bad news, good news [events], magnitude or scope, relevance [to the audience], follow-up [continuity], and the newspaper's own agenda" (cited in Hackett, 2011, p. 42).

These values along with journalists' tight deadlines, tendency to report immediate events and simplification without giving any context contribute to divide the world to "us" and "them", "rich" and "poor" and "good" and "evil" (Kempf, 2006). They also make escalation-orientated coverage more newsworthy than de-escalation-orientated coverage (Kempf, 2006). Although media routines can hinder displaying PJ on the ground, Hackett (2006) argues that these conventions can be in some circumstances in favour of the concept. For example, presenting "both sides" of the Vietnam War in the American media in the last few years of the conflict gave a platform for anti-war voices. Also, the "human interest" stories that focused on reconciliation are consistent with the ethos of PJ. In a similar vein, Loyn (2007) who is critical of PJ says that the claims that the media focuses only on reporting the visible damage without highlighting the context and peace initiatives are "incomprehensible". For example, the mainstream media focused on humanitarian suffering more than the violence occurring in Darfur in their coverage of the war (Loyn, 2007).

3.10.2 Media Structure

Other obstacles that can harden the practice of PJ are the institutional, national and international regimes that govern the media structure (Tehranian, 2002). It is widely argued that media content is more likely to serve government propaganda, advertisers and owners of media outlets especially in times of war, where the "the first casualty is the truth" (Tehranian, 2002). For instance, US broadcasters framed the Persian Gulf and Afghanistan wars in 1991 and 2001, respectively, as "just wars", presenting Saddam Hussain and Osama bin Laden as "aggressors and terrorists".

At the same time, they failed to mention how these "monsters had been manufactured by the United States" (Tehranian, 2002). These broadcasters also overlooked the fact that the United States [along with its Arab allies, Saudi Arabia and Kuwait] had excitedly supported Saddam Hussain in his war against Iran in the period from 1980 to 1988. Although Saddam invaded Kuwait in 1990, President Bush decided to keep him in power as an "insurance policy against Iran", condoning the ruthless violations of his regime against Shia dissenters (Tehranian, 2002).

Likewise, the coverage of the US media omitted the fact that the United States and its allies [Saudi Arabia and Pakistan] supported the most "fanatical Islamic elements" [Mujahedeen] in their fight against the Soviet occupation in Afghanistan (Tehranian, 2002). Such subjective coverage shows clearly how money, power and structure can "filter out the news fit to print" and shape "the message" (Herman & Chomsky, 2010, p. 2; Tehranian, 2002, p. 80).

Hackett (2006) examined the possibility of practising PJ principles within propaganda, the hierarchy of influence models and field theory. Not surprisingly, he found that the filters of the propaganda model [ownership of media, relying on advertising revenues, right-wing pressure campaigns or "flak", ideology of anti-communism, free market fundamentalism] present War Journalism characteristics such as double standards, framing "our" side as moral and righteous and "them" as evil and aggressive. Hackett (2006) argues that the model is functionalist and "reductionist", because it oversimplifies the news system by neglecting the role of journalists and audiences in constructing meanings. On the other hand, "field theory" founded by Bourdieu (1998) can be promising for practising PJ as it considers the media as an independent institutional sphere or a field that structurally functions and interacts with other fields. Furthermore, he

3 PEACE JOURNALISM MODEL: CHARACTERISTICS, MISCONCEPTIONS... 77

found that the hierarchy of influences model, theorised by Shoemaker and Reese (2013), is more exclusive and comprehensive than the propaganda model. Hackett (2006) argues that the levels of the model [the levels of individuals, media routines and organisation, extra-media and the ideological level] can work for and against PJ at the same time. For example, if personal values and social background of journalists [the first level] tend to value peace and liberalism, they might support anti-war and human rights campaigns (Hackett, 2006). Nonetheless, journalists are still citizens that cannot be immune from the nationalist bias (Hackett, 2006).

Kempf (2003) elaborates that journalists, like other people, are members of their communities who can be influenced by institutional as well as social-psychological pressures. Therefore, it can be very difficult if not impossible for journalists who are part of a group involved in violence or probably trapped in a conflicted area [where being balanced may put their lives in danger] to adopt PJ orientations (Hanitzsch, 2007). For example, during the clashes between religious groups in Indonesia's province, *Maluku*, in 1999, the coverage of the only daily newspaper, *Suara Maluku*, was supportive of Christian groups in order to protect its staff and office which was located in Christian territory (Hanitzsch, 2004).

Moreover, practising PJ can be possibly handicapped from within because of what is perceived as an "inherent contradiction between the logic of a peace process and the professional demands of journalists" (Wolfsfeld, 1997). Wolfsfeld (1997, p. 67) says:

> A peace process is complicated; journalists demand simplicity. A peace process takes time to unfold and develop; journalists demand immediate results. Most of a peace process is marked by dull, tedious negotiations; journalists require drama. A successful peace process leads to a reduction in tensions; journalists focus on conflict.

Due to the financial crisis, media organisations reduced resources and editorial staff meaning that the majority of journalists were not privileged to benefit from what is needed to put PJ into practice (Hanitzsch, 2007). Therefore, creating change from within, Hanitzsch (2007) argues, cannot be really accomplished on the ground, with the exception of some rare cases in which journalists are prominent and have the power to influence. What is more, several studies show that journalists can be effectively restrained by the political structure (Sahin & Ross, 2012; Ersoy, 2016). For instance, in a region like Northern Cyprus, journalist culture is contradictory with Western standards meaning journalists do not have any other option but to quote one side only, mainly from official sources and the state media agency. This means that the model obviously cannot be displayed (Sahin & Ross, 2012). As a result, Sahin and Ross (2012) suggest that PJ scholars should develop a comprehensive strategy that takes into consideration the political, historical, cultural and geographical factors that affect news production.

A study based on PJ orientations that examined Turkish newspapers' coverage of Syria's downing of a Turkish jet plane in 2012 and Turkey's downing of a Syrian jet plane in 2014 found that the Turkish press was dominated by a "win–lose framing" (Ersoy, 2016). A significant proportion of the coverage accused, blamed and suspected the "other side" (Ersoy, 2016). Ersoy (2016) attributes these results to the influence of ownership structure, political pressure, regulations, mainstream news values and market conditions.

In response to the domination of the political, economic and media structure, Tehranian (2002) suggests pluralising media ownership and control so as to be able to produce a pluralistic content that can reflect diverse views. Lynch (2007) suggests that "media activism" which is defined as "campaigning through the media and campaigning on the media" should be utilised to reveal the shortcomings of the existing structures and advocate for more pluralism. Tehranian (2002) explains that having ethical codes for PJ is significant, but not sufficient as ethics without laws and sanctions cannot be more than "pious wishes". He suggests founding a "World Media Development Bank" to fund disadvantaged communities and balance the flow of information.

In parallel with existing journalism, Hackett (2006) proposes creating an autonomous new field that is independent from corporate and state domination of the media that is supported by civil society. Shinar (2007) offers more practical techniques to implement PJ within conventional media structures. Shinar (2007, p. 7) suggests journalists should (1) utilise the current news values to promote positive attitudes towards peace and peace coverage, (2) increase the elements of newsworthiness in news stories that relate to peace, (3) set up journalistic policies that can restrain propaganda and external pressure and (4) encourage "media peace discourse" that is consistent with the news values.

Kempf (2003) states that journalists should be trained and equipped with communicative skills that can enable them to interact effectively with their institutions in order to overcome institutional constraints (Kempf,

2003). However, Keeble (2010) argues that it is very "utopian" to assume that journalism training can make crucial changes. Similarly, Hanitzsch (2007) says that it is an "illusion" that changing the attitude of journalists can result in getting different content and altering professional routines. Hence, Keeble (2010) suggests launching a radical political project and redefining journalism to include journalists as well as intellectuals, campaigners and citizens.

3.10.3 *Journalists*

Lynch (2007, 2014a) and Hackett (2006, 2007, 2011) do not underestimate the powerful impact of governments and commercial structures in shaping media content. They still find the space and scope however for journalistic agency and alternative practices, especially in countries that are going through crisis or transitional periods such as Indonesia, the Philippines and some sub-Saharan African states. For instance, a study done by Onyebadi and Oyedeji (2011) argues that unlike the role of the radio in escalating the 1994 genocide in Rwanda, the coverage of Kenyan newspapers during the post-2007 presidential election violence shows a tendency towards PJ. Because "some journalists" in "some conflicts" practise PJ more than others, Lynch (2014a) infers that there is an interaction between journalistic agency and restraining the media structure. He further states:

> It is still possible to exert agency and creativity; to expand scope and create resources to enjoy greater personal autonomy over the selection and execution of story ideas. It is, as I have argued, the enduring capacity for insurgent forms of representation that is the 'good thing' about journalism, even if they are occasional deviations from a norm. (Lynch, 2014a, p. 173)

In his article, Is Peace Journalism feasible? Lynch (2013) presents two inspirational anecdotes in which two journalists, one from the Philippines and the other from Lebanon, have notably changed the content of their journalistic work, after attending PJ workshops. They have succeeded in promoting and practising the model, using social media and online journalism (Lynch, 2013). A study carried out by Hussain and Rehman (2015) shows that the personal views of Baluchi journalists have made their coverage of Baluchistan's crisis "de-escalation-orientated", although they are not aware of the theory and practice of the PJM. Sixty-eight percent of their coverage displayed PJ frames, but the journalists themselves expressed their readiness—in interviews conducted by the researchers—to act as conflict-solvers (Hussain & Rehman, 2015). It should be noted that the consistency between the journalists' views and Pakistani officials helped increase the percentage of PJ (Hussain & Rehman, 2015). Interestingly, while the attitudes of journalists can enhance the practice of PJ, it can raise the tendency towards WJ at the same time. This has been manifested in Hussain's (2016) study which concludes that the trend of Pakistani journalists to prioritise national interests and support the government in its fight against Taliban has resulted in "escalation-orientated" coverage that neglects the sufferings and miseries of the ordinary tribesmen. Likewise, Siraj (2008) argues that the dependence of the US media on American and Indian reporters is the reason behind its WJ framing and representation of Pakistan as a foe and India as a friend.

3.11 Possibility of Practising Peace Journalism

Several studies have proved that PJ orientations can still be implemented even within existent media and political structures (see Lacasse & Forster, 2012; Ross, 2009; Hackett & Schroeder, 2009; Ozohu-Suleiman, 2014; Shinar, 2009; Lee & Maslog, 2005; Lee et al., 2006a, 2006b; Lee, 2010). For instance, Shinar's (2009) analysis of the Israeli and Canadian coverage of the 2006 Lebanon War found that while WJ dominated the coverage, PJ was not completely excluded, and a significant proportion of the coverage gave voice to ordinary people and used "less victimising language". A qualitative study that examined the *Seattle Times*' reporting of the same war found that non-elite sources and differing views were quoted during the peak of the conflict (Ross, 2009).

Another study over the same conflict shows that the coverage of four media outlets in different countries [Canada, the United States, Qatar and Israel] presented both PJ and WJ frames. This is not because the journalists of the examined news organisations intended to, but because of professional and media routines (Hackett & Schroeder, 2009). A comparative study that examined AJE, Press TV, BBC and CNN coverage of the Palestinian-Israeli conflict shows that all of them recorded high percentages of PJ frames [AJE = 61.7%, Press TV = 32.3%, BBC = 45% and CNN = 46.7%] (Ozohu-Suleiman, 2014). The researcher attributes the high proportion of PJ to the reporting on events/activities of peace initiatives that were proposed during the research period.

Comprehensive empirical research conducted by Lee and Maslog (2005) found that the coverage of Asian internal conflicts in four Asian newspapers [Sri Lankan, Indonesia, India and Pakistan] recorded a significant percentage (38%) of PJ indicators. However, another study demonstrates that eight Asian newspapers displayed a higher percentage of PJ orientations while covering the war in Iraq [international conflict], especially by newspapers located in Muslim Asian countries (Lee et al., 2006a, 2006b). Lee et al. (2006a, 2006b) note that the most displayed PJ characteristics are classified by Lynch (2008) as passive PJ, in which coverage avoids partisan and motive language and quotes different views and perspectives. These particular categories of PJ are doable due to their agreement with the objectivity and media routines (Lee et al., 2006a, 2006b).

A quantitative research conducted by Lee (2010) shows that the language, story type and the length and intensity of conflicts can impact on the proportion of PJ in coverage. Similarly, in an analysis of Taliban's representation, Siraj (2010) infers that the English-Pakistani media is dominated by the WJ approach more than the Urdu press. Lee (2010) found that the dependence on news wires increases the percentage of WJ. Fahmy and Neumann (2012a) studied to what extent the "visual coverage" of the most prominent Western news wire services—Associated Press, Reuters and AFP/Getty Images—applied the PJ and WJ frames during the war in Gaza in 2008. Their findings unveil that the news wires tend in general to use the WJ approach in their visual coverage (Fahmy & Neumann, 2012a). However, the study shows that AP focused more than AFP and Reuters on the international summits, anti-war demonstrations, victims and people (Fahmy & Neumann, 2012a). On the other hand, Lacasse and Forster (2012) argue that WJ orientations do not necessarily dominate the media. They found that 60% of local US newspapers' coverage of the drug war in Mexico presented the PJ ethos and 47% of the US regional press [*New York Times*, *The Washington Post* and *USA Today*] did so as well. Shaw, Lynch and Hackett (2011) conclude that the media outlets that display PJ frames can be divided into three types: (1) some of them deliberately apply PJ in particular places and times, such as the coverage of the Philippine media (Lynch, 2008), (2) some journalists practise PJ not because they are aware of its practice and theory, but because they tend to seek a common ground between conflicted parties and (3) some PJ tenets are reported accidently due to its consistency with the objectivity regime and media routines (Shaw et al., 2011).

3.12 AUDIENCE RESPONSES

Hanitzsch's (2007) contends that convincing viewers or readers of the content of PJ is not an easy task especially if the target audience is involved in the conflict itself. Hanitzsch's (2007) argues that conventional news values do not only govern media routines but also are in line with the expectations of the audience and "marketplace of public attention". However, Kempf and Thiel (2014) refute the argument that "violence sells", as a survey conducted by them found that the participants were "annoyed with violent news". In a disagreement with Hanitzsch's (2007) assumption, a measurement of the responses of 128 German readers show that "de-escalation-orientated" articles were accepted to a greater degree and resulted in "less polarised mental models of the events". Also 23% of the readers were interested in receiving more information. McGoldrick (2008) interviewed a group of professionals in the United Kingdom after asking them to watch two versions of a news story coded as War and Peace journalism. The findings show that the WJ news stories cause "more serious negative psychological feelings than the Peace Journalism ones" (McGoldrick, 2008). By the same token, an experiment conducted in Australia and the Philippines gathered audience responses to television news stories coded as WJ and PJ (Lynch & McGoldrick, 2013). The study concludes that "watching Peace Journalism left people less angry and fearful, and more hopeful and empathic" (Lynch & McGoldrick, 2013). Interestingly, a study carried out in four countries [Australia, the Philippines, South Africa and Mexico] showed that media content "encoded into the medium according to Shinar's (2007) five headings, are usually decoded, in like fashion, by most viewers of most stories" (Lynch & McGoldrick, 2016, p. 643). Lynch and McGoldrick (2016) prove that the main contention of the PJ movement [which argues that coverage that focuses on background, history, causes, creative ideas as well as solutions and reveals propaganda manipulations] can "enable audiences to consider and value non-violent responses to conflict" (Lynch & McGoldrick, 2016, p. 643). They also argue that giving voice to a marginalised "character" [people orientation] is very effective in challenging the dominant narratives and triggering attention, engagement and empathy. An analysis of the responses of German students that have read PJ- and WJ-Orientated news stories of the Israeli-Palestinian conflict found that escalatory and de-escalatory frames can directly affect the way the recipients understand the content (Kempf & Thiel, 2014). However, this effect remains "limited" if the audience has a prior position towards the conflict (Kempf & Thiel, 2014). At the same time, they state that the propaganda function can be "neutralised" if reports about victims and violence were "de-escalation-orientated". Kempf (2006) explains that there are factors that influence audiences' responses to PJ. They are as follows: "1) The level of conflict escalation, 2) the cognitive framework, 3) the audience's entanglement in the conflict, 4) societal beliefs, 5) journalists' assumptions about audience preferences, 6) the text genre, 7) the format of the media [and] 8) the audience itself" (Kempf, 2006, p. 2).

3.13 CONCLUSION

Nearly 20 years after its foundation, PJ has notably progressed on the conceptual, theoretical, operational and epistemological levels. Its four orientations [Peace, Truth, People and Solution] (Galtung, 1998) have been developed and expanded to frameworks, headings and thorough characteristics (Kempf, 2003; Shinar, 2007; Lynch, 2014a; Shaw, 2011; Jacobson, 2010; Benn, 2015; Aslam, 2016). Moreover, it has stimulated critics to design comprehensive models for the coverage of conflicts (see El-Nawawy & Powers, 2008; Gilboa, 2009; Hanitzsch et al., 2016). While some researchers understand PJ as a form of advocacy (Peleg, 2007; Lee, 2010; Benn, 2015; Aslam, 2016), its founders clarify that the concept does not require journalists to promote peace or play the role of peace-makers. It instead "creates opportunities to consider and value non-violent responses to conflict" (Lynch & McGoldrick, 2005a, p. 5). Therefore, PJ can be considered as a "shift" in the way of reporting and is not a complete "departure from professional journalism" (Lynch, 1998, 2014a). Due to its critical stance towards objectivity, the concept has not been widely welcomed among journalists (Loyn, 2007). Lynch and McGoldrick (2005a) argue that journalists cannot be mere observers that "report facts only". Whether they like it or not, they are involved in a "feedback loop" in which elites/sources depend on their previous experience with the media to create facts/statements/quotes that are more likely to be reported in a particular way. Some researchers view PJ as a normative concept (Hanitzsch, 2007), despite the fact that Lynch (2006) suggests "critical realism" as its theoretical foundation. Based on this approach, the world cannot be represented as it is [truth], but it can be assembled as-agreed [social truth] through (1) conducting a dialogue between the observer and the thing observed (Wright, 1996) and (2) encouraging journalists to practise "reflexivity" (Lynch & McGoldrick, 2005a; Lynch, 2007, 2014a, 2014b).

Reviewing official statements/interpretations/press releases can help journalists distinguish between facts and claims, determine what facts should be included and what facts are missing and most importantly can enable the audience to resist manipulation and de-code propaganda (Lynch, 2014b). Since very few studies have focused on the effect of the absence of certain facts in the representation of conflicts (see Lynch & McGoldrick, 2005b; Lynch, 2006; Ottosen, 2010; Nohrstedt & Ottosen, 2015), this study extracts evaluative criteria [particular facts] on the basis of Galtung's (1998) table and measures to what extent the inclusion and exclusion of the proposed facts impact on Al-Jazeera's overall framing of Bahrain's and Syria's conflicts. It also explores whether the absence or presence of these criteria have any role in promoting Qatar's foreign policy and propaganda.

Both opponents and proponents of PJ acknowledge the role of professional, economic and political structures in restricting the implementation of the model (Tehranian, 2002; Hackett, 2006; Hanitzsch, 2007; Shinar, 2007). Some even argue that since "the structure is the message", PJ cannot be practised without pluralising the ownership of the media (Tehranian, 2002) and initiating a radical change in the political system and media routines (Keeble, 2010). However, the aforementioned studies in this chapter can be used as evidence that PJ can still be displayed to some degree in spite of limitations and challenges. It should be noted though, empirical examinations and research show that the extent of including PJ indicators while reporting depends on journalists' views, intensity and proximity of conflicts, political involvement of states, types and sources as well as the languages of media outlets (Lacasse & Forster, 2012; Ross, 2009; Hackett & Schroeder, 2009; Ozohu-Suleiman, 2014; Shinar, 2009; Lee & Maslog, 2005; Lee et al. 2006a, 2006b; Lee, 2010; Shaw et al., 2011; Lynch, 2006, 2008, 2013; Fahmy & Neumann, 2012a, 2012b; Siraj, 2008, 2010; Hussain, 2016; Hussain & Rehman, 2015). The results of this study will further help identify the type of factors that hamper or enhance Al-Jazeera's practice of PJ. This study is the first of its kind that examines the coverage of Bahrain's uprising and Syria's second chemical weapon attack based on the PJM. It is one of very rare studies that explores the extent of implementing the model in two channels [AJA and AJE] that differ in their language, journalism culture, audiences and journalists. At the same time, however, they are sponsored by the same political leaders

3 PEACE JOURNALISM MODEL: CHARACTERISTICS, MISCONCEPTIONS... 85

and influenced by the same economic and political structure. It additionally analyses how the differing degrees of Qatar's political involvement in Syria and Bahrain and dissimilar intensity and proximity of both conflicts can increase or decrease the percentage of PJ frames.

REFERENCES

Abbott, H. P. (2008). *The Cambridge introduction to narrative.* Cambridge University Press.

Allan, S. (2011). Documenting war, visualising peace: Towards peace photography. In I. S. Shaw, J. Lynch, & R. A. Hackett (Eds.), *Expanding peace journalism: Comparative and critical approaches* (pp. 147–167). Sydney University Press.

Aslam, R. (2016). Building Peace through Journalism in the Social/Alternate Media. *Media and Communication, 4*(1), 63–79.

Bagdikian, B. H. (2014). *The media monopoly* (5th ed.). Beacon Press.

Benn, J. (2015). From passive to active: The spectrum of peace journalism. *Conflict & Communication, 14*(2), 1–9. Accessed September 3, 2016, from http://www.cco.regener-online.de/2015_2/pdf/benn2015.pdf

Bourdieu, P. (1998). *Practical Reasons.* Cambridge: Polity Press.

Calcutt, A., & Hammond, P. (2011). The truth about journalism. *Ethical Space, 8*(1/2), 8–13.

Cottle, S. (2006). *Mediatized conflict: Developments in media and conflict studies.* McGraw-Hill Education.

Danermark, B., Ekstrom, M., Jakobsen, L., & Karlsson, J. (2002). *Explaining society: Critical realism and the social sciences.* Routledge.

Dewey, J. (1938). *Logic: The theory of inquiry.* Henry Holt.

El-Nawawy, M., & Powers, S. (2008). *Mediating conflict: Al-Jazeera English and the possibility of a conciliatory media.* Figueroa Press.

Ersoy, M. (2016). War–peace journalism in the Turkish press: Countries come to the brink of war. *International Communication Gazette, 78*(3), 247–266.

Fahmy, S., & Neumann, R. (2012a). Shooting war or peace photographs? An examination of newswires' coverage of the conflict in Gaza (2008–2009). *American Behavioral Scientist, 56*(2), NP1–NP26.

Fahmy, S., & Neumann, R. (2012b). Analyzing the spell of war: A war/peace framing analysis of the 2009 visual coverage of the Sri Lankan civil war in Western newswires. *Mass Communication and Society, 15*(2), 169–200.

Fahmy, S., & Eakin, B. (2014). High drama on the high seas Peace versus war journalism framing of an Israeli/Palestinian-related incident. *International Communication Gazette, 76*(1), 86–105.

Fawcett, L. (2002). Why peace journalism isn't news. *Journalism Studies, 3*(2), 213–223.

86   Z. ABDUL-NABI

Galtung, J., & Ruge, M. H. (1965). The structure of foreign news. *Journal of Peace Research, 2*(1), 64–91.

Galtung, J. (1986). On the role of the media in worldwide security and peace. In T. Varis (Ed.), *Peace and communication* (pp. 249–266). Universidad para La Paz.ed.

Galtung, J. (1993). *Preface.* In C. Roach (Ed.). *Communication and culture in war and peace* (pp. xi–xiv). London: Sage

Galtung, J. (1998). High road, low road – Charting the course for peace journalism. *Track Two, 7*(4). Accessed September 14, 2015, from http://reference.sabinet.co.za/webx/access/electronic_journals/track2/track2_v7_n4_a4.htm

Galtung, J. (2000). The task of peace journalism. *Ethical perspectives-Katholieke Universiteit Leuven, 7*(2–3), 162–167.

Galtung, J. (2002). Peace Journalism – A challenge. In W. Kempf & H. Loustarinen (Eds.), *Journalism and the new world order* (Vol. 2, pp. 259–272). Nordicom.

Galtung, J., & Fischer, D. (2013). *Johan Galtung: Pioneer of peace research.* Springer.

Gilboa, E. (2009). Media and conflict resolution: A framework for analysis. *Marquette Law Review, 93*(9), 87–110.

Habermas, J., & Cooke, M. (2000). *On the pragmatics of communication.* MIT Press.

Hackett, R. A. (2006). Is peace journalism possible? Three frameworks for assessing structure and agency in news media. *Conflict & Communication, 5*(2), 1–13. Accessed July 14, 2016, from http://www.cco.regener-online.de/2006_2/pdf/hackett.pdf

Hackett, R. A. (2007). Journalism versus peace? Notes on a problematic relationship. *Global Media Journal: Mediterranean Edition, 2*(1), 47–53.

Hackett, R. A., & Schroeder, B. (2009). Does anybody practice Peace Journalism? A cross- national comparison of press coverage of the Afghanistan and Israeli–Hezbollah wars. *Peace and Policy, 13*(1), 26–47.

Hackett, R. A. (2011). New vistas for peace journalism: Alternative media and communication rights. In I. S. Shaw, J. Lynch, & R. A. Hackett (Eds.), *Expanding peace journalism: Comparative and critical approaches* (pp. 35–69). Sydney University Press.

Hall, S. (1980). Encoding/decoding. In S. Hall, D. Hobson, A. Lowe, & P. Willis (Eds.), *Culture, media, language: Working papers in cultural studies, 1972 – 1979* (pp. 128–138). Hutchinson.

Hammond, P. (2002). Moral combat: Advocacy journalists and the new humanitarianism. In D. Chandler (Ed.), *Rethinking human rights* (pp. 176–195). Palgrave Macmillan.

Hanitzsch, T. (2004). Journalists as peacekeeping force? Peace journalism and mass communication theory. *Journalism Studies, 5*(4), 483–495.

Hanitzsch, T. (2007). Situating peace journalism in journalism studies: A critical appraisal. *Conflict and Communication online, 6*(2), 1–9. Accessed July 20, 2016, from http://cco.regener-online.de/2007_2/pdf/hanitzsch.pdf

3 PEACE JOURNALISM MODEL: CHARACTERISTICS, MISCONCEPTIONS... 87

Hanitzsch, T., Tenenboim-Weinblatt, K., & Nagar, R. (2016). Beyond Peace Journalism reclassifying conflict narratives in the Israeli news media. *Journal of Peace Research, 53*(2), 151–165.

Harcup, T., & O'Neill, D. (2001). What is news? Galtung and Ruge revisited. *Journalism Studies, 2*(2), 261–280.

Herman, E. S., & Chomsky, N. (2010). *Manufacturing consent: The political economy of the mass media.* Random House eBooks.

Howard, R. (2002). *An operational framework for media and peacebuilding.* Institute for Media, Policy and Civil Society.

Howard, R. (2003). *Conflict Sensitive Journalism.* Institute for Media, Policy and Civil Society.

Hussain, S., & Rehman, H. (2015). Balochistan: Reaping the benefits of peace journalism. *Conflict & Communication, 14*(2), 1–13. Accessed August 28, 2016, from http://s3.amazonaws.com/academia.edu.documents/40404936/hussain-rehman2015.pdf?AWSAccessKeyId=AKIAJ56TQJRTWSMTNPEA&Expires=1472356624 &Signature=lBT9oduOmbKu3seKG37cuCAc8TY%3D&response-content-disposition=inline%3B%20filename%3DBalochistan_Reaping_benefits_of_Peace_Jo.pdf

Hussain, S. (2016). Media coverage of Taliban: Is Peace Journalism the solution? *Asia Pacific Media Educator, 26*(1), 31–46.

Jacobson, A. S. (2010). When peace journalism and feminist theory join forces: A Swedish case study. In R. Keeble, J. Tulloch, & F. Zollmann (Eds.), *Peace Journalism, War and Conflict Resolution* (pp. p105–p119). Peter Lang Publishing.

Kamalipour, Y. R., & Snow, N. (2004). *War, media, and propaganda: A global perspective.* Maryland: Rowman & Littlefield.

Keeble, R. (2010). Peace journalism as political practice: A new, radical look at the theory. In R. Keeble, J. Tulloch, & F. Zollman (Eds.), *Peace journalism, war and conflict resolution* (pp. 49–68). Peter Lang Publishing.

Kempf, W. (2003). Constructive conflict coverage–A social-psychological research and development program. *Conflict & Communication Online, 2*(2), 1–13. Accessed June 22, 2016, from http://cco.regener-online.de/2003_2/pdf_2003_2/kempf_engl.pdf

Kempf, W. (2006). *Acceptance and impact of de-escalation-oriented conflict coverage.* Diskussionsbeiträge der Projektgruppe Friedensforschung Konstanz, Nr. 60. Regener. Accessed June 25, 2016, from https://kops.unikonstanz.de/bitstream/handle/123456789/10452/60.pdf?sequence=1

Kempf, W. (2008). *The Peace Journalism Controversy.* Berlin: Regener

Kempf, W., & Thiel, S. (2014). Audience reactions to peace journalism: How supporters and critics of the Israeli policy process escalation and de-escalation oriented media frames. *Conflict & Communication Online, 13*(1), 1–28. Accessed September 4, 2016, from http://www.cco.regener-online.de/

88   Z. ABDUL-NABI

Lacasse, K., & Forster, L. (2012). The war next door: Peace journalism in US local and distant newspapers' coverage of Mexico. *Media, War & Conflict, 5*(3), 223–237.

Lee, S. T., & Maslog, C. C. (2005). War or peace journalism? Asian newspaper coverage of conflicts. *Journal of Communication, 55*(2), 311–329.

Lee, S. T., Maslog, C. C., & Kim, H. S. (2006a). Framing analysis of a conflict: How newspapers in five Asian countries covered the Iraq War. *Asian Journal of Communication, 16*(1), 19–39.

Lee, S. T., Maslog, C. C., & Kim, H. S. (2006b). Asian Conflicts and the Iraq War: A comparative framing analysis. *International Communication Gazette, 68*(5–6), 499–518.

Lee, S. T. (2010). Peace journalism: Principles and structural limitations in the news coverage of three conflicts. *Mass Communication and Society, 13*(4), 361–384.

Loyn, D. (2007). Good journalism or peace journalism? *Conflict & Communication Online, 6*(2), 1–10. Accessed June 1, 2013, from http://www.cco.regener-online.de/2007_2/pdf/loyn.pdf

Lynch, J. (1998). *The Peace Journalism option*. Conflict and Peace Forums.

Lynch, J., & McGoldrick, A. (2000). Peace journalism – How to do it? *Transcend Website* (Peace Journalism). Accessed March 30, 2013, from https://www.transcend.org/tri/downloads/McGoldrick_Lynch_Peace-Journalism.pdf

Lynch, J., & McGoldrick, A. (2004). Reporting conflict–an introduction to Peace Journalism. Agents of Peace. *Jakarta: Friedrich Ebert Stiftung*, 142–143.

Lynch, J., & McGoldrick, A. (2005a). *Peace journalism*. Hawthorn Press.

Lynch, J., & McGoldrick, A. (2005b). War and Peace Journalism in the holy land. *Social Alternatives, 24*(1), 11–15.

Lynch, J. (2006). What's so great about Peace Journalism. *Global Media Journal, Mediterranean Edition, 1*(1), 74–87.

Lynch, J. (2007). Peace journalism and its discontents. *Conflict and Communication Online, 6*(2), 1–13. Accessed June 3, 2013, from http://www.cco.regener-online.de/2007_2/pdf/lynch.pdf

Lynch, J. (2008). *Debates in Peace Journalism*. Sydney University Press.

Lynch, J., & Galtung, J. (2010). *Reporting conflict: New directions in peace journalism*. University of Queensland Press.

Lynch, J., & McGoldrick, A. (2013). Responses to peace journalism. *Journalism, 14*(8), 1041–1058.

Lynch, J. (2013). Is Peace Journalism feasible? Pointers for research and media development. *Ethical Space: The International Journal of Communication Ethics, 10*(2/3), 15–24.

Lynch, J. (2014a). *A global standard for reporting conflict*. Routledge.

Lynch, J. (2014b). Critical realism, peace journalism and democracy. *Ethical Space: The International Journal of Communication Ethics, 11*(1/2), 29–36.

Lynch, J., & Hussain, S. (2015, June 1). *Analysing Peace Journalism: A critical pragmatic perspective.* Paper presented at Peace and Conflict Studies Centre, University of Sydney, Sydney, Australia.

Lynch, J., & McGoldrick, A. (2016). Audience responses to Peace Journalism: Merging results from a four-country research study. *Journalism Studies, 17*(5), 628–646.

McGoldrick, A. (2008). Psychological effects of war journalism and peace journalism. *Peace and Policy, 13*, 86–98.

McGoldrick, A. (2006). War journalism and "objectivity." *Conflict and Communication Online, 5*(2), 1–7. Accessed June 14, 2016, from http://cco.regener-online.de/2006_2/pdf/mcgoldrick.pdf

Nohrstedt, S. A., & Ottosen, R. (2015). Peace journalism: A proposition for conceptual and methodological improvements. *Global Media and Communication, 11*(3), 219–235.

Onyebadi, U., & Oyedeji, T. (2011). Newspaper coverage of post political election violence in Africa: An assessment of the Kenyan example. *Media, War & Conflict, 4*(3), 215–230.

Ottosen, R. (2010). The war in Afghanistan and Peace Journalism in practice. *Media, War & Conflict, 3*(3), 261–278.

Ozohu-Suleiman, Y. (2014). War journalism on Israel/Palestine: Does contraflow really make a difference? *Media, War & Conflict, 7*(1), 85–103.

Peleg, S. (2006). Peace Journalism through the lense of conflict theory: Analysis and practice. *Conflict and Communication Online, 5*(2), 1–17. Accessed July 12, 2016, from http://cco.regener-online.de/2006_2/pdf/peleg.pdf

Peleg, S. (2007). In defense of Peace Journalism: A rejoinder. *Conflict & Communication Online, 6*(2), 1–9. Accessed April 2, 2013, from http://cco.regener-online.de/2007_2/pdf/peleg.pdf

Philo, G., & Berry, M. (2004). *Bad news from Israel.* Pluto Press.

Rimmon-Kenan, S. (2002). *Narrative fiction: Contemporary poetics.* Routledge.

Ross, S. D. (2006). (De) Constructing conflict: A focused review of war and Peace Journalism. *Conflict & Communication Online, 5*(2), 1–19. Accessed July 14, 2016, from http://www.cco.regener-online.de/2006_2/pdf/ross_2006.pdf

Ross, S. D. (2009). A Summer's pastime: Strategic construction of the 2006 war in Lebanon. In S. D. Ross & M. Tehranian (Eds.), *Peace journalism in times of war* (pp. 59–78). Transaction Publishers.

Şahin, S., & Ross, S. D. (2012). The uncertain application of Peace Journalism: The case of the Turkish Cypriot press. *Conflict & Communication Online, 11*(1), 1–12. Accessed August 29, 2016, from http://www.cco.regener-online.de/2012_1/pdf/sahin-ross.pdf

Shaw, I. S., Lynch, J., & Hackett, R. A. (Eds.). (2011). *Expanding peace journalism: Comparative and critical approaches.* Sydney University Press.

Shaw, I. S. (2011). Human rights journalism a critical conceptual framework of a complementary strand of Peace Journalism. In I. S. Shaw, J. Lynch, & R. A. Hackett (Eds.), *Expanding peace journalism: Comparative and critical approaches* (pp. 96–121). Sydney University Press.

Shinar, D. (2007). Peace Journalism: The state of the art. *Conflict & Communication Online, 6(1)*, 1–9. Accessed July 1, 2013, from http://cco.regener-online.de/2007_1/pdf/shinar_2007.pdf

Shinar, D. (2009). Can Peace Journalism make progress? The coverage of the 2006 Lebanon War in Canadian and Israeli media. *International Communication Gazette, 71(6)*, 451–471.

Shoemaker, P. J., & Reese, S. D. (2013). *Mediating the message in the 21st century: A media sociology perspective.* Routledge.

Siraj, S. A. (2008, May). *War or Peace Journalism in elite US newspapers: Exploring news framing in Pakistan-India conflict.* Paper presented at the annual meeting of the International Communication Association, Montreal, Quebec. Accessed June 14, 2016, from http://www.issi.org.pk/wp-content/uplo ads/2014/06/1303370133_44311323.pdf

Siraj, S. A. (2010). Framing War and Peace Journalism on the perspective of talibanisation in Pakistan. *Media Asia, 37(1)*, 13.

Siraj, S. A., & Hussain, S. (2012). War media galore in Pakistan: A perspective on Taliban conflict. *Global Media Journal: Pakistan Edition, 5(1)*. Accessed August 28, 2016, from http://scholar.google.com.au/scholar_url?url=http%3A%2F%2Fwww.academia.edu%2Fdownload%2F40715694%2FWar_Media_galore_in_Pakista_.doc&hl=en&sa=T&oi=ggp&ct=res&cd=0&ei=03jCV4H8OMO5jAHp-4moAw&scisig=AAGBfm1VLQnmFMeimgV-Yp_alSlKfoOM6Q&nossl=1&ws=1350x638

Spencer, G. (2004). The impact of television news on the Northern Ireland peace negotiations. *Media, Culture and Society, 26(5)*, 603–623.

Tehranian, M. (2002). Peace Journalism negotiating global media ethics. *The Harvard International Journal of Press/Politics, 7(2)*, 58–83.

Wolfsfeld, G. (1997). *Media and political conflict: News from the Middle East.* Cambridge University Press.

Wolfsfeld, G. (2004). *Media and the path to peace.* Cambridge University Press.

Wright, N. T. (1996). *The New Testament and the people of God.* Augsburg Fortress.

CHAPTER 4

Theoretical Framework and Research Questions

4.1 Introduction

The monograph analyses the AJA and AJE coverage of two conflicts, Bahrain's uprising and the Al-Ghouta CW attack in Syria.

The study examines the online coverage of the Bahraini uprising during the Saudi military intervention in 2011 and during the periods before and after the 2017 Gulf crisis, from 2014 to 2021. The study of coverage of the Syrian conflict includes the first three weeks of the Al-Ghouta CW attack from August 21 to September 14, 2013.

As indicated in Chap. 1, the Al-Jazeera coverage of the Bahrain and Syria cases was specifically selected to (1) measure whether or not Qatar's "double standards policies" in both countries were reflected in the AJA and AJE coverage and (2) determine to what extent having different degrees of drama, intensity, proximity and political agenda in both conflicts can influence the amount of PJ orientations included or excluded from coverage.

The study utilises the PJM (Galtung, 1986, 1998), framing theory (Entman, 1993) and quantitative content analysis methods to examine Al-Jazeera's coverage of both conflicts. All relevant news stories and features (unit analysis) that were published/posted on the websites of AJA and AJE during the research periods have been selected and analysed.

This chapter presents the theoretical framework of the study and explains what PJ frames are. It also clarifies on which basis the evaluative

---

© The Author(s), under exclusive license to Springer Nature Switzerland AG 2022
Z. Abdul-Nabi, *Al-Jazeera's "Double Standards" in the Arab Spring*, https://doi.org/10.1007/978-3-031-14279-6_4

91

92 Z. ABDUL-NABI

criteria of PJ frames are proposed and founded. This chapter will then state the study questions and methods.

4.2 Theoretical Framework

4.2.1 *Peace Journalism Frames*

This study mainly depends on the PJM that has been reviewed and discussed thoroughly in Chap. 3. When the main founder of PJ, Johan Galtung, was asked about the best way to define PJ, he said "it is to ask two questions: What is the conflict about, and what could be the solutions?" (Galtung and Fischer, 2013). As mentioned in the previous chapter, J. Lynch and McGoldrick (2005, p. 5), the developers of PJ, defined it as "when editors and reporters make choices—about what to report, and how to report it—that create opportunities for society at large to consider and to value non-violent responses to conflict". J. Lynch (2008) elaborates that PJ is "that which abounds in cues and clues to prompt and equip us to 'negotiate' our own readings, to open up multiple meanings, to inspect propaganda and other self-serving representations on the outside". Galtung and Fischer (2013, pp. 93–94) describe practically what tools journalists should obtain in order to practise PJ:

> Peace Journalism does essentially what journalists do anyhow, keeping in mind a maximum number of items from the left-hand column. The eye for the essential, the devotion both to facts and to hope, the need to be a good writer, to work quickly and hence to be a good administrator of own time; all of that remains the same. But new types of knowledge would be needed, such as identifying the conflict formation, the parties, their goals and the issues, and not fall into the trap of believing that the key actors are where the action (violence, war) is.

In his designed Peace/War Journalism table, Galtung (1986, 1998) classifies PJ and War Journalism (WJ) through four orientations: (1) Peace/War, (2) Truth/Propaganda, (3) People/Elites and (4) Solutions/Victory (see Table 4.1) (see Chap. 1).

The PJM is supported by framing theory on the theoretical level (Lee et al., 2006). Youngblood (2017) indicates that frames and word choices are the main elements of PJ.

4 THEORETICAL FRAMEWORK AND RESEARCH QUESTIONS 93

Table 4.1 Peace Journalism model of Johan Galtung (1986, 1998)

Peace and/or Conflict Journalism	*War and/or Violence Journalism*
I. Peace and/or Conflict-Orientated • Investigates the formation of conflict: X parties, Y aims, Z objects general win-win orientation. • Open space and time. Causes and solutions are looked for everywhere, also in history and culture. • Make conflicts transparent. • All parties are interviewed. Capacity for empathy, understanding. • Conflict/War seen as the problem. Focus on creative conflict solutions. • Humanisation of all sides (the more so the worse the weapons) • Preventive: prevention of violence/war. • Focus on the invisible effects of violence (trauma and reputation, structural and cultural damage).	**I. War and/or Violence-Orientated** • Describes the conflict arena: 2 parties, 1 aim (victory) war, general zero-sum orientation. • Restricted space and time. Reasons and solution sought on the battlefield: "who threw the first stone?" • Wars made obscure. • "We-them" journalism. Propaganda, vote for us. • They are seen as the problem. Focus on who gets the upper hand in the war. • Dehumanisation of the others, the more so, the worse the weapons. • Reactive: only violence is worth reporting. • Only considers the visible effects of violence (dead, wounded and material damage).
III. Truth-Orientated • Exposes untruths of all sides. • Discloses all cover-up attempts.	**II. Propaganda-Orientated** • Exposes the untruths of others. • Supports [our] cover-up attempts/lies.
IV. People-Orientated • Focuses on all suffering: suffering of women, old people, children, gives the voiceless a voice. • Names all wrongdoers. • Stresses peace tendencies in the population.	**III. Elite-Orientated** • Focuses on our suffering: the men who make up the military elite; it is their mouthpiece. • Names their wrongdoers. • Stresses that only the elite can make peace.
IV. Solution-Orientated • Peace = freedom from violence + creativity. • Points to freedom initiatives, also to prevent the expansion of war. • Structure and culture are important: a peaceful society. • Reports about the post-war phase: conflict solution, reconstruction, reconciliation.	**IV. Victory-Orientated** • Peace = victory + armistice. • Conceals peace initiatives as long as it is not clear who is winning. • Treaties and institutions are important: a controlled society. • After the war is over, turns to the next source of conflict; goes back when the old one breaks out again.

Entman (1993, p. 52) states that "to frame is to select some aspects of a perceived reality and make them more salient in a communicating text, in such a way as to promote a particular problem definition, causal interpretation, moral evaluation, and/or treatment recommendation for the item described". Entman (1991, 1993) argues that repeatedly mentioning, placing as well as reinforcing certain text or an image could make a particular interpretation more "salient" than others. Entman (1993, p. 52) further says that frames can be determined by the inclusion and exclusion of "certain keywords, stock phrases, stereotyped images, sources of information, and sentences that provide thematically reinforcing clusters of facts or judgments". In short, the mere presence of certain aspects of reality in media coverage is as significant as the absence of them, especially in political communication, as frames can be utilised to draw attention to particular factors or elements of an event while obscuring others (Entman, 1993).

Therefore, the use of Peace/Conflict, Truth, People and Solution frames will be determined based on (1) what PJ characteristics are included as well as excluded and (2) the frequency of the inclusions and exclusions of these orientations.

Media scholarship divides framing theory into three levels and approaches. More specifically, framing-orientated studies measure—either all or one of—frames created by (1) journalists or the media system, (2) recipients or society and (3) political, economic and cultural actors or organisations (Scheufele, 2004). This study focuses only on the first level of framing as it aims to analyse how Al-Jazeera has framed the conflicts in Bahrain and Syria.

The second level of framing (which is out of the scope of this study) has received more revisions and critiques by media scholars. Carragee and Roefs (2004) criticise framing research for neglecting "the relationship between media frames and broader issues of political and social power". Carragee and Roefs (2004) attribute this "neglect" to the "conceptual problems in the definition of frames, the inattention to frames sponsorship, the failure to examine framing contests within wider political and social contexts, and the reduction of framing to a form of media effects".

The relationship between framing and power, however, might not have been as widely ignored as Carragee and Roefs (2004) have argued. For instance, Scheufele (1999) already explained how political power, interests and pressures could affect framing. Scheufele (1999) mentioned five factors that influence the way journalists frame an issue. They include (1) social norms and values, (2) organisational pressures and constraints, (3) pressures of interest groups, (4) journalistic routines and (5) ideological or political orientations of journalists.

This study does not neglect the relationship between Al-Jazeera's coverage and its founder, Qatar. It actually measures the extent of agreement between Qatar's foreign policy and Al-Jazeera's framing in both examined conflicts. Chapter 2 of this study has already analysed the influence of Qatar's politics on Al-Jazeera's content. Furthermore, the following chapters utilise the propaganda model (Herman & Chomsky, 2010) and hierarchy of influences (Shoemaker & Reese, 2013) to explain how Qatar's interests have shaped Al-Jazeera's framing of Bahrain's uprising and Syria's CW attack. London (1993) says:

> The frames for a given story are seldom conscientiously chosen but represent instead the effort of the journalist or sponsor to convey a story in a direct and meaningful way. As such, news frames are frequently drawn from, and reflective of, shared cultural narratives and myths and resonate with the larger social themes to which journalists tend to be acutely sensitive.

4.2.2 Evaluative Criteria of Peace Journalism Frames

As framing relies on "selection" and "salience", the four frames of the PJM will be determined based on the selection or inclusion of certain texts/facts/ideas/phrases and the frequency of their mentions. As explained in Chap. 1, in this study these selected facts are called "evaluative criteria". The criteria of each frame were proposed based on two key elements: (1) the context of the analysed conflict and (2) the characteristics of the PJ orientations.

Therefore, measuring the extent of applying a particular frame in Al-Jazeera's coverage on Bahrain or Syria can be done through quantifying the frequency of including certain evaluative criteria or "facts".

For instance, a news story about the Al-Ghouta CW attack in Syria (analysis unit) will be framed as People-Orientated if it included the following three criteria: (1) voices of the survivors, (2) voices of ordinary people/civilians who are against a military intervention in Syria and (3) suffering and implications caused by the CW attack. The extent of mentioning as well as the repetition of these three criteria can determine the percentage to which the People-Orientated frame was implemented in Al-Jazeera's articles on Syria.

The Truth, Peace/Conflict and Solution-Orientated frames will be measured based on the presence/inclusion and absence/exclusion of certain evaluative criteria or "facts". This approach was operationalised previously by J. Lynch (2006) in his article "What is So Great About Peace Journalism". The article analysed the United Kingdom's press coverage of Iran's nuclear crisis. J. Lynch (2006, p. 76–77) measured the extent of implementing the first orientation of Galtung's model (Peace/Conflict frame) in UK newspapers by proposing five analytical criteria:

1. Does the article mention the Non-Proliferation Treaty (NPT)?
2. Does it report, as a fact—as distinct from something Iran 'claims' or 'insists' upon—that this gives Iran the right to develop civil nuclear power?
3. Does the article mention our nuclear weapons and/or failure to engage in disarmament negotiations, as a factor to be taken into consideration when assessing Iran's behaviour under the NPT?
4. Does the article mention any evidence that Iran is not, in fact, engaged in a process of developing nuclear weapons?
5. Does the article mention Iran's possible reasons for seeking a nuclear arsenal, if it were to do so, in terms of deterrence against threats from outside actors?

In J. Lynch's (2006) article, the number of "Yes's" determined the percentage of the presence of the Peace/Conflict-Orientated frame. The number of "No's", however, determined the percentage of the War-Orientated frame.

Hackett and Schroeder (2009) criticised this approach due to its "selectivity". However, since every conflict is different, then every conflict will have its own analytical factors that are derived from PJ distinctions and the context of certain conflicts. For example, the criteria which determine the presence of PJ in the Bahrain case will be different to the criteria of the Syrian one.

The proposed analytical criteria of the PJ frames for this study are stated and explained in detail in the research questions section.

4.3 Time Frame of Selected Online Articles

1. **Bahrain's uprising coverage will be analysed during two main periods**:

    (a) From March 14, 2011 (when Saudi-led troops were deployed), to June 1, 2011 (when King Hamad bin Isa bin Salman Al-Khalifa lifted martial law). This period was selected because the AJA and AJE coverage of Bahrain intensified and violence escalated.

    (b) Bahrain's uprising before and after the 2017 Gulf crisis. These periods include two diplomatic crises between Qatar and Bahrain. The first one was in March 2014, when Bahrain, Saudi Arabia and the United Arab Emirates (UAE) withdrew their ambassadors from Doha. The second was in June 2017 when these states (along with Egypt) imposed a blockade on Qatar. Qatar reconciled with its neighbours in the period between the 2014 and 2017 crises. This "in-between period" is classified in this research as a "non-conflict period". These three periods were selected because they can help measure the extent to which the deterioration of ties between Qatar and Bahrain (Qatar's policy) affected AJA's and AJE's media coverage (editorial policy). The specific details of the periods are as follows:

    - 2014 diplomatic crisis (first conflict): From March 5 to November 16, 2014
    - Non-conflict period: From November 17, 2014, to June 4, 2017
    - 2017 diplomatic crisis (second conflict): From June 5, 2017, to September 28, 2021

2. **Syrian conflict**: From August 21, 2013 (the first day of the Al-Ghouta attack), until September 14, 2013 (when the United States and Russia reached a deal to eliminate Syria's CW). This period was selected because Syria was (for the first time during the civil war) threatened by a possible military strike by US forces. The CW elimination deal, however, abruptly altered the events that followed.

98   Z. ABDUL-NABI

4.3.1   *Data Collection*

The terms "Bahrain" [in Arabic: البحرين], "Bahrain protests" [in Arabic: احتجاجات البحرين] and "Bahrain's uprising" [ثورة البحرين] were used as key words in the research engine of AJE's and AJA's website coverage of Bahrain.

In relation to Syria's data, the terms "Syria CW attack" [الهجوم/ الكيماوي في سوريا الكيميائي] and "Al-Ghouta attack" [هجوم الغوطة] were searched in the search engine on the AJA and AJE websites.

Reports under the sport and economy sections or articles that did not relate directly to Bahrain's uprising or Syria's second CW attack were not considered. Very short paragraphs that were written as introductions or descriptions for video news reports, interviews or programmes were also excluded from this study. All articles that were published before or after the time frame of the research periods were not used. All news stories and features related to Syria's second CW attack and Bahrain's uprising during the Saudi military intervention in 2011 were selected. Only news stories were selected from the coverage of Bahrain's conflict during the periods before and after the 2017 Gulf crisis (from 2014 to 2021). This was due to the lack of published features, especially in AJA, during these periods.

The following table demonstrates the time frame of each conflict as well as the period and the number of selected relevant articles (Table 4.2).

4.4   RQ1 AND 6: PEACE JOURNALISM FRAMING IN BAHRAIN'S AND SYRIA'S CONFLICTS

Unlike the order of the research questions in Chap. 1, the order of the questions in this chapter will be based on the methods used to analyse them. The questions of PJ framing of Bahrain (RQ1) and Syria (RQ6) will be gathered with each other, for instance.

4.4.1   *Peace Journalism Frames and Evaluative Criteria in Bahrain and Syria Coverage*

RQ (1): **To what extent did AJE and AJA display PJ frames in their coverage of Bahrain's uprising during (1) the Saudi military intervention (from March 14 to June 1, 2011) and (2) during the periods before and after the 2017 Gulf crisis (from March 5, 2014, to September 28, 2021)?**

4 THEORETICAL FRAMEWORK AND RESEARCH QUESTIONS

Table 4.2 Time frames and number of selected articles for each conflict during a specific research period

	Bahrain's uprising during the Saudi military intervention and periods before and after 2017 Gulf crisis				CW attacks on Syria
	Saudi military intervention	2014 diplomatic crisis/first conflict	Non-conflict period	2017 diplomatic crisis/second conflict	
Conflict period	March 14, 2011, to June 1, 2011	March 5, 2014, to November 16, 2014	November 17, 2014, to June 4, 2017	June 5, 2017, to September 28, 2021	August 21, 2013, to September 14, 2013
Research terms	Bahrain protests/ uprising/ revolution	Bahrain protests/ uprising/ revolution	Bahrain protests/ uprising/ revolution	Bahrain protests/ uprising/ revolution	Syria CW attack, Al-Ghouta attack
Type of genre/ analysis unit	News stories and features	News stories	News stories	News stories	News stories and features
Number of selected articles from AJA	80 news stories 6 features	19 news stories	61 news stories	161 news stories	71 news stories 22 features
Number of selected articles from AJE	38 news stories 3 features	9 news stories	26 news stories	30 news stories	82 news stories 5 features

RQ (6): To what extent did AJE and AJA display PJ frames in their coverage of the Al-Ghouta attack in Syria?

As explained earlier in this chapter, PJ and WJ frames will be measured based on the frequency of the presence and absence of certain evaluative criteria. As mentioned above, in this study, the components of the proposed analytical criteria are derived from (1) PJ orientations, Peace, Truth, People and Solution (see Table 4.1), and (2) the context/history/roots/ causes of both conflicts. The following section elaborates the reasons behind the significance of conflicts' context/background/history in shaping the criteria.

4.4.2 Significance of Context in Founding Evaluative Criteria of PJ Frames

As mentioned in Chap. 3, PJ coverage depends on the insights of conflict analysis and transformation field, while conventional coverage aims at answering six questions: what, who, where, when, why and how. A PJ approach, however, focuses on the questions of "conflict dynamics" which include contexts, background, history, and perspectives of all involved parties, their interests, goals and relationships (J. Lynch, 2007). For example, if a suicide bombing attack took place, a PJ news story/report would not focus specifically on the details of the death and destruction of the incident. It would instead "probe why the bombers did it, what was the process leading up to it, what were their grievances and motivations" (J. Lynch, 2008).

In order to put PJ into practice, media practitioners should be equipped with a solid knowledge of (1) political/economic and historical contexts of conflicts, (2) interests and goals of involved parties, (3) types of conflicts and (4) methods of resolution (Blasi, 2004). McGoldrick (2006) says that if media coverage does not shed light on contexts, causes, background and alternative or marginalised views, violence will appear as the only proper response. McGoldrick (2006, p. 4) elaborates:

> Without some exploration of underlying causes, violence can be left to appear, by default, as the only response that 'makes sense.' Wars remain opaque, in the sense that we are given no means to see through the violence to problems that lie beneath. It therefore makes no sense to hear from anyone wanting those problems to be addressed and set right, as a contribution to ending or avoiding violence.

If the mainstream media, for instance, explained the real reasons behind the American invasion of Iraq instead of focusing only on Weapons of Mass Destruction (WMDs), it might have put pressure on the Bush administration to stop the war (Bagdikian, 2014). J. Lynch (2010, p. 545) says that prohibiting such explanations can automatically make conflict representation "more receptive to the proposition that further violence will prove an appropriate and effective response".

Fahmy and Eakin (2014) state that shallow and narrow coverage that lacks explanation of the roots, causes and consequences of conflicts makes reaching reconciliation or convincing audiences of possible resolutions more difficult. On the other hand, including detailed explanations/

context/history/roots in coverage can "create opportunities for society at large to consider and value non-violent responses to conflict" (J. Lynch & McGoldrick, 2005, p. 5). Furthermore, linking the present (threats to launch a strike against Syria for using CWs, for instance) with the past (striking Iraq for allegedly having WMDs) could help audiences decode propaganda and "develop critical awareness of attempts to pass off claims as facts, or 'social truths' as merely 'interpersonal'" (J. Lynch, 2014, p. 33).

As indicated in Chap. 3, PJ is principally concerned about what facts are allowed "through the gate" and what facts are not (J. Lynch, 2007). J. Lynch and McGoldrick (2000) state that omitting "some facts" from media coverage affects the understanding of conflicts and leads to conveying a distorted image of social reality.

In order to effectively enable PJ-orientated analysis to observe excluded facts, Nohrstedt and Ottosen (2011) suggest utilising Pierre Bourdieu's notion of "Doxa" and a Discourse-Historical Approach (DHA) (developed by Ruth Wodak (2001)). Therefore, implementing Peace Journalism or "Consequence-Ethical Reflexivity" (as Nohrstedt and Ottosen (2011) calls it) requires studying the history and contexts of conflicts before covering them. That is why the proposed evaluative criteria of PJ frames rely heavily on the context/history/process of both conflicts in this study. The following section introduces the main contexts/aspects and causes of both conflicts before stating the evaluative criteria.

4.4.3 Context of Bahrain's Uprising

Al-Khalifa's Invasion of Bahrain
Bahrain has been ruled by the Al-Khalifa dynasty since 1783. They came from Najd, the heartland of Saudi Arabia where the alliance between Al-Saud and Wahhabism emerged in the seventeenth century (Matthiesen, 2013). The Al-Khalifa tribe which was based in Zubara, Qatar, invaded the island in the eighteenth century, toppled the Persian rulers at the time and has maintained power to this day. The Al-Khalifa dynasty was officially recognised as the rulers of Bahrain during the period of British colonisation in 1820 (Matthiesen, 2013). The strategy of the Al-Khalifa family and other Sunni monarchies in the Gulf states was to strengthen their ties with the British to secure their positions and guarantee that they would be protected from external neighbours and internal uprisings (Matthiesen, 2013). Since the Al-Khalifa dynasty invaded the country, they have

102   Z. ABDUL-NABI

supressed the indigenous people (the Shia majority) of the country (Louër, 2013). Al-Mdaires (2002) elaborates that the Shia community in Bahrain was in "a state of great humiliation, slavery, and subject to public massacres" in the 1920s. Louër (2013, p. 35) says:

> They [Al-Khalifa] took control of the arable land and the pearl fishing, subjecting the Shia peasants, indigenous to the country, to a form of servitude that created a rift between the state and the Shia population which continues [and] largely accounts for current conflicts.

The people of Bahrain revolted in the 1920s, 1930s, 1950s and 1990s, demanding political and economic reforms, greater freedom, democracy and the elimination of the systematic discrimination and poverty in the oil-rich Gulf state. Given this history, Shias in Bahrain (who make up the majority of the population of around 65 to 75%) consider themselves the "original inhabitants" of the country (Mabon, 2012).

Shias of Bahrain and Iran

Before the independence of Bahrain in 1971 from the British, Iran's Shah claimed that Bahrain was historically part of the Persian Empire. In order to solve the dispute, a United Nations (UN) mission conducted a referendum, giving the people of Bahrain the right to choose between independence under the Al-Khalifa regime or the Shah of Iran. The majority of Bahraini citizens voted for independence under the rule of the Al-Khalifa (Mabon, 2012) in spite of the long tense relations between the Shia and the Sunni tribal dynasty. The Al-Khalifa ruling family, however, still perceive Shias as a "potential Iranian fifth column" (Mabon, 2012). The lack of trust between Shias of Bahrain and Saudi Arabia and their rulers intensified after the success of the 1979 Iranian revolution. Al-Mdaires (2002) says that in February 1979, thousands of Shias in Bahrain marched in support of the Iranian revolution and its Shia leader, Ayatollah Khomeini, "condemning the American government and raising slogans to overthrow the pro-American conservative regimes in the region".

Two years after the Iranian revolution, the Al-Khalifa regime arrested members of an unlicensed opposition group, the Islamic Front for the Liberation of Bahrain (IFLB), and accused them of planning to topple the regime (Mabon, 2012). Shias in Saudi Arabia protested at the time and demanded more rights (Al-Rasheed, 2011). Clearly, the success of the revolution in Iran with its Shia majority population raised fears in the Gulf states of the exportation of the Iranian uprising to the Shia populations in

Bahrain and Saudi Arabia (Al-Mdaires, 2002). Since then, the Al-Khalifa dynasty "began to embrace a sectarian definition of concepts of loyalty and disloyalty, being tempted to see any Shia as a potential threat" (Louër, 2013, p. 247).

Bahrain's Uprising
Days after the downfall of Egypt's dictator Hosni Mubarak, the people of Bahrain took to the streets on February 14, 2011, demanding democracy, an elected government and resignation of the longest-serving Prime Minister in the world, Khalifa bin Salman Al-Khalifa[1] (the uncle of the current King, Hamad bin Isa Al-Khalifa). Zunes (2013) said that Bahrain's uprising was very popular, as more than 200,000 people (40% of the Bahraini population) protested in one day in 2011. Inspired by the Tahrir Square in Cairo, the demonstrators staged a sit-in protest in the Pearl Roundabout in Manama, the capital of Bahrain. The roundabout had been built in 1982 as a sign to welcome the third Gulf Cooperation Council (GCC) summit that took place that year (Matthiesen, 2013). The irony of history has turned this roundabout from an official symbol into a revolutionary one.

While protesters were calling it the "Pearl Roundabout" or even "Pearl Square", state media referred to it by its official (unknown) name: the GCC Roundabout or *Dowar Majlis Al Ta'awon* دوار مجلس التعاون (Khalaf, 2015). In March 2011, the regime ordered that the roundabout be demolished. Bahrain's Foreign Minister Sheikh Khaled bin Ahmed Al-Khalifa stated that it was done to "erase bad memories" (AJE, March 19, 2011). After tearing it down, the authorities—"in a symbolically sectarian move"— renamed it to the "Al-Farooq Junction[2]" (Matthiesen, 2013, p. 71). Khalaf (2015, p. 274) states:

> The Pearl Roundabout was literally removed from the state narrative by a government hoping to create a clean slate with which to rewrite post-uprising memories... the area was provocatively renamed the 'Al Farooq Junction'... the naming of the junction as 'Al-Farooq' is seen as a sectarian dig to the largely Shia population.

---

[1] Sheikh Khalifa was appointed as a Prime Minister by the previous Emir, Isa bin Salman Al-Khalifa [his brother] in 1971.

[2] "Al-Farooq" refers to Umar bin Al-Khattab, the second Caliph in the Islamic history, who "is viewed negatively in the Shia literature" (Khalaf, 2015, p. 274).

104   Z. ABDUL-NABI

The GCC pointed their fingers at Iran, blaming it for supporting the opposition. However, M. Lynch (2013b, p. 138) states that these allegations have been repeated to gain the support of the Sunni population to justify the intensive crackdown and intimidation of the "moderate Shias who had no love for Iran but hoped for more democracy and respect for human rights". Along with taking diplomatic actions, the GCC states—in an unprecedented move—deployed 1500 Saudi Arabian and 500 Emirati troops on March 14, 2011, in Manama to suppress the protest movement (Davidson, 2013). Qatar (which has created an important regional diplomatic role for itself during the last ten years) was not able to adopt an independent stance from the GCC policy over Bahrain (Friedman, 2012). Khatib (2013) concludes that Qatar took a decision not to go against the foreign and domestic policies of Saudi Arabia (Khatib, 2013).

Kamrava (2012) states that bringing in Saudi-led troops has not only propped up the Al-Khalifa regime, but it has also worsened the division between Shias and Sunnis in the region. Zunes (2013) says that Saudi Arabia deployed its troops to prevent Bahrain's uprising from spreading to its Shia population in its Eastern Province. The Al-Saud regime has exaggerated these religious differences within Saudi Arabia and Bahrain to hinder any attempt or possibility of the founding of a united opposition. It has at the same time sent a message to its Sunni majority that it would protect them from Shia conspirators and "foreign agents" (Al-Rasheed, 2011).

Using Sectarianism as a Counterrevolution Tool

After the deployment of Peninsula Shield Force (PSF) troops and the heavy crackdown on the sit-in protests at the Pearl Roundabout on March 14, 2011, King Hamad bin Isa Al-Khalifa declared martial law for three months. Following the declaration, several people were killed and hundreds injured. Activists, journalists, bloggers, lawyers, students, teachers, unionists, medical staff who treated injured protesters and anyone who participated in the Pearl Roundabout protests were targeted, dismissed from their work and arrested. The Bahrain Centre for Human Rights (BCHR) documented that activists were humiliated, insulted based on their sectarian affiliation, arrested and in some cases subjected to severe torture that led to death.

The Bahrain Independent Commission of Inquiry (BICI) (that was established by King Hamad bin Isa Al-Khalifa in June 2011 to investigate violations that occurred in February and March 2011) revealed that Shia political prisoners were called by the police *"Ibn/bint al muta'aa* ابن المتعة [son/daughter of a temporary marriage], *Rafidi/a* رافضي [deserters];

Safawi/a صفوي[relating to the Safavid Iranian dynasty], filth, animal, spy, and traitor" (2011, p. 289). Matthiesen (2013) says that the state media used anti-Shia rhetoric in their television programming to delegitimise the demands of the protesters.

Zunes (2013) concludes that the Bahraini regime has used sectarianism to obtain the support from the West and Sunni population. The Al-Khalifa regime and Bahraini officials represented to the public that the pro-democracy movement was an unfortunate "sectarian division" triggered by their enemy, Iran. King Hamad bin Isa Al-Khalifa (2011) wrote in *The Washington Times*, "The sectarian divide has created a schism in our society that is a major challenge. As monarch of all Bahrainis, it pains me to see many harmed by the actions of a few". Al-Rasheed (2011) argues that the sectarian discourse has proved to be successful in suppressing the Bahraini pro-democracy movement.

Sectarian Measures of the Regime: Demolishing Shia Mosques
Given the history of the alliance in 1744 between the founder of Wahhabism, Sheikh Mohammed bin Abdul-Wahhab, and Prince Mohammed bin Al-Saud (that led to establishment of Saudi Arabia Kingdom in the nineteenth century (Gelvin, 2012)), demolishing Shia shrines and religious institutions during Bahrain's uprising was not an unusual occurrence. Wahhabi doctrines (which the State of Saudi Arabia was and is still grounded on) consider Muslims that do not follow the teachings of Abdul-Wahhab—and of course non-Muslims—as *Kafir* كافر [infidels/heretics] who should be killed (Haroon, 2014).

Haroon (2014) and Vassiliev (2000) state that Wahhabis backed by the Al-Saud dynasty demolished shrines and mosques in Medina and Mecca in Saudi Arabia in the eighteenth and nineteenth centuries. In 1803, the alliance attacked Karbala, a Shia city in Iraq, demolishing the holy Shrine of Imam Hussain, the grandson of the Prophet Mohammed, and killing 4000 Shias in one day (Vassiliev, 2000). Murawiec (2005, p. 155) cited a detailed description of the incident:

> 12,000 Wahhabis suddenly attacked [the mosque of] Imam Husain; after seizing more spoils than they had ever seized after the greatest victories, they put everything to fire and the sword . . . Old people, women and children— everybody died at the barbarians' sword. Besides, it is said that whenever they saw a pregnant woman, they disembowelled her and left the foetus on the mother's bleeding corpse. Their cruelty could not be satisfied; they did not cease their murders and blood flowed like water. As a result of the bloody catastrophe, more than 4,000 people perished.

106   Z. ABDUL-NABI

Matthiesen (2013) says that anti-Shi'ism has been one of the essentials of Saudi Arabian domestic and foreign policy and also Wahhabi interpretations of Islam.

Double Standards of the West

Matthiesen (2013) says that the West did not adopt a sectarian discourse, but they have not admonished it. Zunes (2013) states that the former President of the United States (US) Barack Obama "seemed convinced" that the conflict was sectarian. Obama said on September 21, 2011, that he believes that "the patriotism that binds Bahrainis together must be more powerful than the 'sectarian forces' that would tear them apart. It will be hard, but it is possible" (White House, 2011). Obama failed to mention, however, that it is the Bahraini authorities and not the protesters that are discriminating against Shias and playing the sectarian card (Zunes, 2013).

As Bahrain is the home to the US Fifth Fleet, the United States "kept its head down during the repression", an attitude which undermined its credibility in the region (M. Lynch, 2013b, p. 140). While the United States supported a military intervention in Libya and imposed sanctions on the regime in Syria, the Obama administration refused to condemn the presence of Saudi-led troops in the streets of Manama (Zunes, 2013). US Senator (at the time) John Kerry said that PSF troops were "not looking for violence in the streets" as they would "like to encourage the King and others to engage in reforms and dialogue" (Mitchell, 2012). In spite of the systematic violations committed by the Bahraini security forces against unarmed peaceful protesters, the US administration tried to convince Congress to approve a US$53 million arms deal with the Al-Khalifa regime (Mitchell, 2012).

Matthiesen (2013) indicates that the GCC regimes are very crucial to the United States as they are not only hosting its military bases in the region, but are key buyers of Western military technology and arms. Most importantly, the GCC regimes control about two thirds of the world's proven oil reserves and one third of natural gas reserves. From 2007 to 2009, the Bahraini authorities spent US$386 million on US-made ammunitions and fighting vehicles (Zunes, 2013). Saudi Arabia spends over US$10 billion a year (10% of its annual oil revenues) on weapons and arms that are unfortunately used for oppressing their own population (Jones, 2011).

Relationship Between Qatar and Bahrain Before and After 2017 Gulf Crisis

As discussed thoroughly in Chap. 2, Qatar has always had uneasy relations with Bahrain whose internal and foreign policies are heavily dependent on Saudi Arabia (M. Lynch, 2017). Bahrain and Qatar were "at odds" even before the 2014 and 2017 GCC rifts (Congressional Research Service, 2021). They had a long-standing territorial disagreement over the Hawar Islands and other land since the eighteenth century, when Al-Khalifa and Al-Thani dynasties were controlling parts of the Arabian Peninsula (Congressional Research Service, 2021).

Unlike Saudi Arabia, the UAE and Bahrain, all of which were threatened by protests in their streets, Qatar's leadership sided with the uprisings during the Arab Spring due to its political and economic stability (Ulrichsen, 2019). Despite this, Qatar decided not to oppose its neighbours during the 2011 uprising in Bahrain and went further by being part of the PSF.

Regardless, the relations between Qatar and its neighbours have remained unsettled. Their rivalry could be seen clearly when Qatar supported the Muslim Brotherhood (MB) in Egypt, while Saudi Arabia and the UAE financially and politically backed the military coup led by General Abdel-Fatah al-Sisi in July 2013 (Ulrichsen, 2019). The dispute between Qatar and the GCC countries could also be observed in Syria, where Doha and Riyadh have been funding different opposition groups.

Qatar's constant support to the MB in the region has increased the disapproval of Qatar's foreign policy among the GCC countries. The conflict escalated in March 2014 when Saudi Arabia and the UAE declared the MB as a "terrorist organisation". The GCC members along with Bahrain withdrew their ambassadors from Doha in protest at supporting the MB and other "parties" that aim at threatening the security as well stability in the Gulf (Ulrichsen, 2019). They said in their joint statement that they tried to "convince Qatar" to implement an agreement they signed in November 2013 not to back "anyone threatening the security and stability of the GCC whether as groups or individuals—via direct security work or through political influence, and not to support hostile media" (BBC, March 7, 2014).

The 2014 nine-month diplomatic spat was resolved by an agreement in late-November 2014, after Qatar made several concessions. These included closure of Al-Jazeera Egypt Live, expelling exiled Egyptian MB leaders who sought refuge in Qatar and sending 1000 Qatari forces to join the

Saudi-led coalition in Yemen. Ulrichsen (2019, p. 33) argues that even though the concessions conducted by Qatar were "meaningful acts", they were not sufficient to satisfy "Qatar's detractors".

On June 5, 2017, the conflict reached its peak when Saudi Arabia, the UAE, Bahrain and Egypt severed diplomatic and economic relations with Qatar, imposing a blockade by air, land and sea on the country. The Saudi-led coalition attributed their escalatory move to Qatar's "support for terrorism" and violation of the 2014 agreement that ended the diplomatic crisis at the time.

On June 22, 2017, the blockading countries released a statement that included 13 demands that Qatar was required to agree to "within 10 days".

The main demands included closing the Al-Jazeera channel; closing the Turkish military base; reducing relations with Iran (especially military and intelligence coordination); severing ties with the MB, Hamas, the Islamic State of Iraq and the Levant (ISIL), Al-Qaeda, Hezbollah and Jabhat Fateh al Sham; stopping the funding for organisations designated as terrorists; not interfering in the four countries' affairs; and not granting citizenship to wanted nationals from the four countries.

Despite the fact that none of these demands were fulfilled, the Qatari Emir Sheikh Tamim bin Hamad Al Thani and the Saudi crown prince Mohammed bin Salman signed the Al-Ula declaration agreement on January 5, 2021, ending five years of blockade and one of the worst disputes in the GCC's recent history.

Interestingly, Qatar's ties have never gone back to normal with Bahrain (until the writing of this book), although the former sent at least two formal invitations to Doha—without response according to Bahrain's Foreign Ministry (Reuters, June 22 2021).

Al-Jazeera's channels, especially AJA, have kept airing documentary films that focus on human rights violations in Bahrain, causing more tension between the authorities in Manama and Doha. For instance, on September 28, 2021, Bahrain's Ministry of Interior said in response to a critical documentary film "the aggressive defaming campaigns against Bahrain through the Qatar-sponsored Al Jazeera channel are systematic and are staged at particular times" (Bahrain National Agency, September 28th, 2021).

4.4.4 Proposed Evaluative Criteria of PJ Frames in Bahrain's Coverage

A. Analytical Criteria of the Peace/Conflict-Orientated Frame

Since the PJ approach focuses on the roots of the conflict and not only on what is happening at the time of reporting, it is significant for coverage on Bahrain's uprising to include that the pro-democracy struggle in Bahrain began long before 2011. Bahrainis have been demanding greater freedoms and political reform since the 1920s. A year before the uprising, in 2010, the regime intensified its crackdown, as prominent activists and opposition leaders were arrested and subjected to torture. The first analytical criterion in measuring the extent of implementing the Peace/Conflict frame is:

1. **Does the article give a historical background about the protest movement in Bahrain?**

The pro-democracy movement has been labelled by the Al-Khalifa regime as a "sectarian conflict" backed by Iran. Therefore, mentioning that it has been inspired by the Arab Spring and not Iran can provide a more accurate context to the uprising. Bahraini slogans in the Pearl Roundabout which was the focal point of the protests were dominated by what Egyptians and Tunisians chanted during the Arab Spring: *Al-Sha`ab yurid isqat Al-Nidham* الشعب يريد إسقاط النظام [the people want the downfall of the regime]. Davidson (2013, pp. 205–206) says:

> On the back of the Egyptian revolution, the Bahraini protests saw an estimated 150,000 nationals streaming onto the streets of Manama following an initial 'day of rage,' on 14 February 2011. Organised by various youth groups, rather than established political societies, the size and strength of this movement took many by surprise.

Hence, the second analytical criterion is:

2. **Does the article mention that the protesters have been inspired by the downfall of the regimes in Egypt and Tunisia? Or by the Arab uprisings/Arab Spring?**

In order for readers and viewers to understand why the majority of the protesters were "Shia", it is significant to mention that they make up the majority of the population. Although Bahrain's regime has not published statistics showing the percentage of Shia and Sunni in the country, the academic literature has stated that Shias make up the majority of the population (around 65–75%) (Davidson, 2013; Matthiesen, 2013; M. Lynch, 2013b; Kamrava, 2013; Mabon, 2012). Consequently, the third analytical criterion is:

3. **Does the article mention that Shias make up the majority of the population?**

Peace/Conflict-Orientated coverage focuses on structural, cultural and direct violence. Hence, the coverage would mention that the Al-Khalifa regime has been institutionally discriminating against Shias (structural violence) in employment (in government institutions particularly in the Ministry of Interior and Defence), housing and education (scholarships) (Mitchell, 2012). Davidson (2013) says that increasing systematic discrimination against Shia populations in the GCC states in recent years has created resentment and weakened the legitimacy of the Sheikhs in the region. Therefore, the fourth analytical criterion of the Peace/Conflict frame is:

4. **Does the article mention that the Shias of Bahrain have been discriminated against?**

Peace/Conflict-Orientated coverage explains the context of the demands of protesters from their own perspective, not from official ones. A PJ journalist would mention that although the majority of the protesters were Shia, their calls for democracy, unity and peaceful demonstrations dominated the scene in the Pearl Roundabout. Thus, the fifth analytical criterion is:

5. **Does the article mention that the protesters called for unity between Shias and Sunnis from day one of the protests? Or does the article mention that there is no evidence that the protesters were supported by Iran? Or does the article mention that the protesters have "democratic demands"?**

Explaining the geopolitical significance of Bahrain to the United States and the fact that it is home to the US Navy's Fifth Fleet is essential to understand the reasons behind the uncritical stance of the West towards regime violations. Michael Rubin from the American Enterprise Institute said that the Fifth Fleet is "our most important strategic asset in the Persian Gulf" and that Bahrain is "pretty much the one country where we can't afford regime change" (Ambrosio, 2014). This is because "Bahrain is not Syria" in David Cameron's words. Hence, the sixth analytical criterion is:

6. **Does the article mention that Bahrain is the home of the US Fifth Fleet?**

In response to the rise of Shia/Iranian power in the region, the kingdoms, sheikhdoms and emirates which include Saudi Arabia, the UAE, Qatar, Kuwait, Oman and Bahrain founded the GCC in 1981 (Mitchell, 2012). While the Iraq-Iran war was escalating in 1984, the GCC established the PSF to protect and defend the GCC states from any external threats or attack. The PSF was not deployed during the Iraqi invasion of Kuwait in 1990. It was, however, deployed for the first time since its foundation against the domestic population in Bahrain to quell the uprising in 2011. Therefore, the seventh analytical criterion is:

7. **Does the article mention that 1500 Saudi and 500 Emirati troops were deployed in Manama?**

The house of Al-Saud will do whatever it takes to "ensure the survival" of the Al-Khalifa family and prevent Bahrain's Shias from gaining more democratic power (Mabon, 2012). Friedman (2012) states that the GCC "fears Iran's expanding conventional military capabilities because it would decisively alter the regional balance of power and make Iran a potential Persian Gulf hegemon". Saud Al-Faisal, Saudi Arabia's Foreign Minister, accused Tehran's policy of "violating their [GCC states'] sovereignty and independence" (Friedman, 2012). Therefore, Peace/Conflict-Orientated coverage would highlight the fact that Shias in Bahrain are marginalised and deprived from gaining political rights for the fear that they might be a potential ally to Iran, Saudi's primary rival in the region. Consequently, the eighth analytical criterion is:

112   Z. ABDUL-NABI

8. **Does the article mention the context of the rivalry between Saudi Arabia and Iran? Or does the article mention as a part of its context/analysis that the GCC or their allies fear the rise of a Shia power in the Gulf?**

The lack of trust in the Bahraini Shia population has prompted the regime to change the sectarian demography of the country by bringing in Sunnis from Jordan, Yemen, Syria and Pakistan. They have been employed in the Ministry of Interior as security forces and granted Bahraini citizenship (Davidson, 2013). These new citizens are more loyal to the regime and are more likely to support it (even violently) against pro-democracy protesters (Matthiesen, 2013). Mitchell (2012) says that by early 2011, 7000 of Bahrain's 25,000-member police force were Pakistanis. Since Peace/Conflict-Orientated coverage mentions causes and reasons behind conflicts, it would mention that eliminating sectarian naturalisation is one of the main demands of the opposition. A Peace-Orientated approach will alternatively mention that the Al-Khalifa royal family belongs to the Sunni sect which makes up the minority of the population. This can help to interpret the dynasty's constant need for legitimisation that they aim to gain from the new, naturalised citizens.

Therefore, the ninth analytical criterion is:

9. **Does the article mention the political naturalisation process? Or does the article mention that the regime recruits foreigners in their riot police/security forces? Or does the article mention that the royal family belongs to the Sunni sect?**

B. **Analytical Criteria of the Truth-Orientated Frame**

In its World Report, Human Rights Watch (HRW) (2012) documented the Bahraini security force violations that were committed at the beginning of the uprising. The report states:

> Bahraini authorities used lethal force to suppress peaceful anti-government and pro-democracy protests... Security forces' use of birdshot pellets, rubber bullets, and tear gas as well as live ammunition caused the most deaths and injuries of protesters and bystanders.... After troops from Saudi Arabia entered Bahrain and Bahraini military and security forces launched a systematic campaign of retribution, arresting thousands of demonstrators or indi-

4 THEORETICAL FRAMEWORK AND RESEARCH QUESTIONS **113**

viduals who supported the protests. Authorities fired hundreds of public sector employees suspected of supporting the protests, as did large private firms in which the state had a substantial stake (HRW, 2012).

Therefore, the first analytical criterion in measuring the extent of displaying the Truth-Orientated frame is:

1. **Does the article mention the human rights violations committed by the Bahraini security forces or by the regime in general?**

International human rights organisations that documented the violations in March and April 2011 stated that Saudi troop played a significant role in the crackdown. One report by the Physicians for Human Rights (PHR) (which visited Bahrain in April 2011 to document the abuses against doctors, medical staff and the injured protesters) stated that the military forces sieged the main hospital in Bahrain (Salmaniya Medical Complex) and prevented the injured protesters from being treated. It revealed that the forces (some of them from Saudi Arabia) tortured the injured protesters and arrested them. In his testimony, Ali, one of the injured protesters, narrated to the PHR (2011) what he witnessed:

> An Indian nurse told the armed men, 'Don't hurt them. They are our patients.' One of the Bahraini security forces yelled back, 'They are not your patients—they are criminals.' One of the armed men with a Saudi accent hurled insults at the bloodied patients on the floor and cursed, 'Grave worshippers! Sons of whores! Sons of Muta'a!' [derogatory references to Shi'a Muslims]. Another armed man in black shouted, 'We're going to hang you. We're going to kill you.'

The PHR (2011) continues, "Ali and the other patients lay on the floor for four hours until they were transferred to ward 62 on the sixth floor". Truth-Orientated coverage would expose the violations carried out by Saudi troops and name those responsible. Therefore, the second analytical criterion is:

2. **Does the article mention the role of the GCC troops in the crackdown or the violations they committed?**

The criterion above will be used only for the coverage of Bahrain uprising in 2011. It is not relevant in the periods from 2014 to 2021 as the Saudi troops were not present in the country during that time.

The mainstream opposition has used peaceful forms of dissent, but small factions have engaged in confrontations with security officials (Congressional Research Service, 2021).

As some protesters clashed with security forces due to the heavy crackdowns and non-coverage/non-attention from the mainstream media, the following criterion will replace criterion No. 2 in the three periods from 2014 to 2021:

(2)-(PV): Does the article mention that some protesters clashed with security forces and explain the reasons behind it?

BICI (2011) stated that the security forces demolished a number of Shia mosques in the country. The International Religious Freedom Report released by the U.S. Department of State (2011) annually, documented that the regime destroyed 53 Shia religious structures. In addition, Davidson (2013, p. 209) said that after participating in the uprising, "5,000 Shias were fired from their jobs" and US$10 million was "looted by security personnel from Shia communities". State media outlets have portrayed the pro-democracy movement as a sectarian conflict between Sunnis and Shias, accusing the Shia protesters of being "Iranian agents" and "traitors" (Jones, 2011). Such sectarian measures and the subsequent crackdown would be clearly highlighted in Truth-Orientated coverage. Therefore, the third analytical criterion is:

3. **Does the article mention any sectarian acts/abuses committed by the regime and/or its forces?**

C. **Analytical Criteria of the People-Orientated Frame**

When the security forces attacked sleeping protesters at 3 am at the Pearl Roundabout on February 17, 2011, the protesters started demanding the downfall of the regime, chanting "Down Down with Hamad [the King]" (Davidson, 2013). The authorised opposition had been calling for political reforms and constitutional monarchy, but the 14 February Coalition, an unauthorised youth group founded during the sit-in protests in the Pearl Square, was clearly calling for the downfall of the Al-Khalifa dynasty. These voices have not only been ignored by the media but have

4 THEORETICAL FRAMEWORK AND RESEARCH QUESTIONS   115

also been marginalised by licensed opposition groups. Madawi Al-Rasheed, a prominent Saudi professor at King's College London, told BBC Arabic in an interview that "there are voices that are demanding the downfall of the Al-Khalifa regime in Bahrain but no one in the world wants to listen". Since People-Orientated coverage would not marginalise such voices, then the first criterion of the People-Orientated frame is:

1. **Does the article mention that there are voices in Bahrain demanding the downfall of the regime?**

The criterion above will be examined only in the coverage of Bahrain's uprising in the period from March 2011 to June 2011. Given changes to the protest movement that occurred after continuous crackdowns, demands for the overthrow of the regime during the period from 2014 to 2021 are not as controversial as they once were at the beginning of the uprising. Indeed, most prominent activists and leaders of the opposition (that both support and do not support the "downfall of the regime") were arrested and subjected to torture. As such, the main demand of the protesters in the aftermath of these arrests, especially in the recent years, has been to release the prisoners and achieve a meaningful resolution that can help get the country out of deadlock. As this criterion is not very relevant in the later periods of the uprising, it was excluded from the People frame.

People-Orientated coverage is all about people and their voices, perspectives and views. According to M. Lynch (2016), 30% of the Bahraini population participated in one rally in one day (M. Lynch, 2016); therefore, it is necessary to hear what they want to say. So, the second analytical criterion is:

2. **Does the article give voice to civilians, ordinary people or victims?**

A People-Orientated approach would focus on the implications (such as psychological damage, trauma and fear) that were caused by the crackdown. For example, Médecins Sans Frontières (MSF) (2011) stated that many people in Bahrain were unable to access medical care at Salmaniya Hospital—the most well-equipped hospital in the country—when the Saudi troops were deployed. MSF (2011, p. 1) further says:

> Hospitals and health clinics are no longer places to go for the sick or injured, but are rather places to be feared. As the military cracks down on protesters

and medical personnel, Médecins Sans Frontières/Doctors without Borders (MSF) has witnessed patients with critical and life-threatening injuries refusing to go to the hospital due to high levels of fear.

BICI (2011), which depended on official records, revealed that 4400 Shia employees were sacked from their jobs (from both the governmental and private sectors) for participating in the uprising. A PJ approach would focus on the social implications and economic hardships of such a move on the daily lives of the people who lost their jobs. Therefore, the second analytical criterion is:

3. **Does the article mention the suffering that the crackdown caused?**

D. **Analytical Criteria of the Solution-Orientated Frame**

Solution-Orientated coverage would give space and time to the implications of the regime's sectarian measures on the people. It would ask questions such as: To what extent a sectarian crackdown will divide the country? How does such a crackdown reinforce the Sunni-Shia division in the region? How does demolishing Shia mosques impact on collective identity of Bahraini Shias? For example, the Office of the United Nations High Commissioner for Human Rights (2014) indicates how demolishing Shia institutions represents a destruction of their culture and identity. OHCHR (2014, p. 2) explains:

> Some of the mosques are hundreds of years old and represent Shia Muslims' past and influence on the island of Bahrain. Their destruction, and the restriction of their sites, represents a concerted attempt to destroy not only the physical manifestation of Shi'ism in Bahrain, but also its cultural impact on the island. Their destruction thus prevents Bahraini Shias from engaging in their cultural practices and beliefs.

Therefore, the first analytical criterion in measuring the extent of implementing the Solution-Orientated frame is:

1. **Does the article mention the implications of the regime's violations and sectarian crackdown/measures?**

Since Solution-Orientated coverage depends mainly on initiating and covering peace proposals, the second analytical criterion is:

2. Does the article give any possible solution/initiative from any source to break the deadlock and de-escalate the conflict?

Peace initiatives can be one of the following (or any other suggestions):

- Restrictions on supplying arms to the regime
- Exerting international pressure on the Al-Khalifa regime
- Withdrawal of Saudi troops from the country (in the 2011 research period)
- Releasing political prisoners to pave the way for a meaningful dialogue where the opposition and regime are equally represented
- Emphasising a political solution instead of a security solution

4.4.5   Context of the Al-Ghouta Attack

As Syria's analytical criteria are derived from PJ orientations and the context of the conflict, this chapter gives a brief history and background about the Al-Ghouta CW attack before introducing and explaining each analytical criterion.

Syria's 2011 Uprising
Bashar Al-Assad, the current embattled president of Syria, has been ruling the country since the death of his father, Hafez Al-Assad, in 2000. Hafez played a significant role in the 1963 coup d'état which brought the Ba'ath Party to power. After having been appointed as a Commander of the Syrian Air Force, Al-Assad participated in another coup that brought Salah Jadid to power in 1966. Four years later, Al-Assad (Defence Minister at the time) led another coup against Jadid and toppled him. Since then, the power has remained within the Al-Assad family.

Basil Al-Assad, Hafez's eldest son, was supposed to inherit the throne after his father. However, after his unexpected death in a car accident in 1994, the responsibility fell on Bashar's shoulders. Bashar was doing his postgraduate studies in ophthalmology in London when he was recalled home (Erlich, 2014). The young ophthalmologist was seen by the West as a reformer (McHugo, 2014). Even though Bashar Al-Assad implemented economic reforms in the beginning of his rule, he did not carry out meaningful and significant measures in relation to the political restrictions and authoritarian system (Erlich, 2014). The Al-Assad family which belongs to the Alawite minority (10–12% of the population) rules over the Sunni majority (around 60%) and other minorities (Christians = 10–12% and Druze = 6%) (Carpenter, 2013).

M. Lynch (2013b) described Syria before the 2011 uprising as the "kingdom of silence". The iron fist and the centralised system of government did not allow opponents of the regime to protest openly or to even create their own organisations. The only organised Syrian movement was the exiled MB. Freedom of press was restricted and, unlike Egypt and Tunisia (during their uprisings), there were very few online Syrian activists and bloggers (M. Lynch, 2013b). Given the high level of total suppression and fear of the intensive pressure by the intelligence and security forces, few analysts expected that an uprising would make its way to Damascus (M. Lynch, 2013b). The Hama Massacre in which thousands were killed in 1982 was still fresh in people's memories. The Hama Massacre occurred two years after the MB's failed assassination attempt of Hafez Al-Assad. In a swift retaliation, Hafez Al-Assad ordered the execution of 12,000 imprisoned Islamists in Tadmor Prison.

Bashar Al-Assad thought that his popular foreign policy and "resistance identity" (against Israel) would protect his regime from the Arab uprising wave that toppled the dictatorships in Egypt and Tunisia (M. Lynch, 2013b). Lesch (2011) who met and interviewed Al-Assad regularly from 2004 to 2009 says:

> I can almost guarantee that he [Al-Assad] was absolutely shocked when the uprisings in the Arab world started to seep into his own country by March 2011. I believe he truly thought he was safe and secure and popular in the country, and beyond condemnation.

Al-Assad believed that his limited reforms had already met the expectations of the Syrian population, telling *The Wall Street Journal* that "if you didn't see the need of reform before what happened in Egypt and Tunisia, it's too late to do any reform" (M. Lynch, 2013b, p. 178).

The protests in Syria began in March 2011, as a peaceful movement that called for democracy, greater freedoms and meaningful reforms. In return, however, the protesters were faced by live ammunition and excessive force. A young Damascene activist said, "It's just time to be free. We

4 THEORETICAL FRAMEWORK AND RESEARCH QUESTIONS   119

learnt from other [Arab] revolutions not to remain silent, and that if we don't take advantage of this opportunity we will remain cowards forever" (M. Lynch, 2013b, p. 180).

As a result of the violent killings, significant numbers of soldiers from the Arab Syrian Army defected, founding the Free Syrian Army (FSA) which would later be funded and armed by the West and Gulf states (Hughes, 2014). Al-Jazeera's former reporter in Beirut, Ali Hashem (2012), stated that the uprising in its early stages was not overly peaceful. He revealed that he saw and filmed Syrian opponents smuggling arms from Lebanon into Syria only one month after the uprising began.

If Al-Assad offered real and deeper reforms, he could have avoided the escalation of the conflict that his international and regional opponents have taken advantage of (M. Lynch, 2013b). M. Lynch (2013b, p. 180) says, "It's fair to say that Al-Assad did to himself what his external enemies had failed to bring about for a decade". Despite having been intensively supported by the international community, the Syrian opposition has not been able to unite their efforts against Al-Assad's regime. Their disagreements and divisions have escalated and turned into infighting since 2013.

Geopolitics of Syria's Conflict
While the United States finance and arm the moderate opposition in Syria, Saudi Arabia funds both the moderates and radicals (Erlich, 2014). Erlich (2014) states that some rebel groups deliberately let their beards grow to look like Islamists, so that they could receive funds from Saudi Arabia. Patrick Cockburn, a columnist in *The Independent* and Middle East correspondent for the *Financial Times* since 1979, reveals:

> The directors of Saudi policy in Syria—the Foreign Minister Prince Saud Al-Faisal, the head of the Saudi intelligence agency Prince Bandar bin Sultan and the Deputy Defence Minister Prince Salman bin Sultan—plan to spend billions raising a militant Sunni army some 40,000 to 50,000 strong. Already local warlords are uniting to share in Saudi largesse for which their enthusiasm is probably greater than their willingness to fight. (Cockburn, 2013)

Carpenter (2013) states that Saudi Arabia has been responsible for escalating the sectarian division in Iraq by funding and arming Sunni groups. It is not coincidental that the increase of the sectarian/suicidal attacks in Iraq was accompanied with the advancement of the Islamist radicals in Syria (Carpenter, 2013).

Khan Al-Assal Chemical Weapons Attack

The Syrian Observatory for Human Rights said that "16 government soldiers and 10 civilians were killed, and more than 86 were injured" in the Khan Al-Assal CW attack (Barnard, 2013). The CW attack that occurred on March 19, 2013, was condemned heavily by the Obama administration and considered as crossing the United States' "red line". Both the regime and the Syrian opposition groups traded accusations over the responsibility of the attack. At the time, the Al-Assad regime asked the UN Secretary-General Ban Ki-moon to establish an enquiry in order to investigate the incident. When UN inspectors finally entered Syria on August 19, 2013, Eastern Ghouta, which was held by the Syrian opposition, was hit by a CW attack only two days later, killing hundreds of people.

As mentioned previously, the UN Commission to investigate the use of CW in Syria was founded in March 2013 to find out if CW were used or not. They were not charged with determining who was responsible or who had used CW. The commission released its final report in December 2013, indicating that sarin gas was used against civilians in Al-Ghouta on August 21, 2013, and that the nerve agent was also used against regime soldiers in Jobar on August 24 and in Ashrafiah on August 25, 2013 (UNMIAUCWSAR, 2013b). While the Al-Ghouta's attack got the most coverage in the media, the Jobar and Ashrafiah incidents were barely mentioned. Robert Fisk, a veteran and well-known Middle East reporter, stated that:

> In Iraq, we went to war on the basis of lies originally uttered by fakers and conmen. Now it's war by YouTube. This doesn't mean that the terrible images of the gassed and dying Syrian civilians are false. It does mean that any evidence to the contrary is going to have to be suppressed. For example, no-one is going to be interested in persistent reports in Beirut that three Hezbollah members—fighting alongside government troops in Damascus— were apparently struck down by the same gas on the same day, supposedly in tunnels. They are now said to be undergoing treatment in a Beirut hospital. So if Syrian government forces used gas, how come Hezbollah men might have been stricken too? Blowback? (Fisk, 2013)

A few weeks before the Al-Ghouta attack, a US intelligence consultant learned that Erdoğan expressed his "need to do something that would precipitate a US military response" (Hersh, 2014). The former intelligence official said:

4 THEORETICAL FRAMEWORK AND RESEARCH QUESTIONS   121

After the advancement of the Syrian troops on the ground, Erdoğan felt he was left hanging on the vine. It was his money and the cut-off was seen as a betrayal, Erdoğan's hope was to instigate an event that would force the US to cross the red line. (Hersh, 2014)

The New York Times (Chivers, 2013) and HRW (Lyons, 2013) said that the Al-Ghouta rocket attack was launched from over nine kilometres away. However, a study published by missile experts has contradicted this analysis. Richard Lloyd, a former UN weapons inspector who currently works at Tesla Labs in Arlington Virginia, and Theodore A. Postol, professor of science, technology and national security policy at the Massachusetts Institute of Technology in Boston, inferred that the rockets would have a maximum range of two kilometres. In support of this analysis, the head of the UN CW inspection team, Ake Sellstrom, stated that the rockets could have been fired as close as two kilometres (Erlich, 2014). This could lead to the conclusion that the rockets were launched from an area that was very close to or under rebel control (Erlich, 2014).

Fisk (2013) says that the gas used in the Al-Ghouta attack was sold from the Soviet Union to Libya, Yemen and Egypt but not to Syria. He wrote in his investigative article:

> Since Al-Gaddafi's fall in 2011, vast quantities of his abandoned Soviet-made arms have fallen into the hands of rebel groups and Al-Qaeda-affiliated insurgents. Many were later found in Mali, some in Algeria and a vast amount in Sinai. The Syrians have long claimed that a substantial amount of Soviet-made weaponry has made its way from Libya into the hands of rebels in the country's civil war with the help of Qatar—which supported the Libyan rebels against Al-Gaddafi and now pays for arms shipments to Syrian insurgents. (Fisk, 2013)

Regional powers (which have been campaigning for a military action against Syria for years) found the Al-Ghouta attack as an opportunity to finally rid Syria of the Al-Assad regime (M. Lynch, 2016). The United States was enthusiastically gearing up for launching a "tightly limited military strike". The US Secretary of State, John Kerry, likened Al-Assad with Hitler and referred to the Al-Ghouta attack as a "genocide" (M. Lynch, 2016). The then Prime Minister of the United Kingdom David Cameron failed to gain approval from the House of Commons. President Barack Obama (who later decided to seek congressional approval) expected to

122   Z. ABDUL-NABI

face the same defeat (M. Lynch, 2016). In a dramatic turn of events, on September 9, 2013, a reporter asked John Kerry if there was anything Al-Assad could do to avoid the imminent military strike. Kerry responded, "Sure, he could turn over every single bit of his CW in the next week. But he isn't about to do it, and it can't be done". Russia grabbed the opportunity and declared its peace proposal which aimed at eliminating Syria's CWs. On September 10, 2013, Obama described "Russia's offer as a possible breakthrough and a potentially positive development" (The Guardian, 2013). On September 14, 2013, the negotiation between Russia and the United States resulted in reaching an agreement that "called for Syria's arsenal of CW to be removed or destroyed by the middle of 2014" (Gordon, 2013).

The Russian peace proposal saved face for the Obama administration but further frustrated and provoked the Syrian opposition, the Gulf states, Turkey and Israel (M. Lynch, 2016). Saudi Arabia perceived the US deal with Russia as a betrayal. Such was the extent of this perception of betrayal that Prince Bandar bin Sultan, former Saudi ambassador to the United States and director general of the Saudi Intelligence Agency from 2012 to 2014, "warned ominously of major changes in the US-Saudi relationship" (M. Lynch, 2016, p. 205).

4.4.6   Proposed Evaluative Criteria of PJ Frames in Syria's Coverage

A. Analytical Criteria of the Peace/Conflict-Orientated Frame

Since Peace/Conflict-Orientation focuses on the history, background, causes and roots of conflicts, it is critical to mention in media coverage that the conflict between the opposition and the Syrian regime goes back far before the Al-Ghouta CW attack in 2013 or even the uprising in 2011. The conflict between these parties began in 1982 when Hafez Al-Assad heavily repressed the MB, carrying out what is widely known as "Hama Massacre". At the time, thousands were killed, injured and displaced. Since then, Hafez Al-Assad and the Syrian regime did not make any meaningful efforts towards recognition and reconciliation with the opposition. Therefore, the first analytical criterion in measuring the extent of displaying the Peace/Conflict frame is:

4 THEORETICAL FRAMEWORK AND RESEARCH QUESTIONS   123

1. Does the article mention the Hama Massacre?

Implementing the Peace/Conflict frame requires revealing the context and background of the regime's capabilities of using and producing CWs. Before October 14, 2013, Syria was one of seven countries that did not join the 1993 Chemical Weapons Convention (CWC) (Pita & Domingo, 2014). When Al-Assad was asked about Syria's production of CW during an interview conducted in 2009, he said, "Chemical weapons, that's another thing. But you don't seriously expect me to present our weapons program to you here? We are in a state of war" (Pita & Domingo, 2014). The Independent International Commission of Inquiry on the Syrian Arab Republic (IICISAR) (2013) stated that "the [Syrian] regime possesses a number of chemical weapons". Stating this fact in media coverage will imply that the regime is possibly capable of using CWs when it is needed. Therefore, the second analytical criterion is:

2. Does the article mention that the Syrian regime possess CWs already?

A PJ journalist will not focus on the current attack in Al-Ghouta only (here and now). They will instead mention previous or similar attacks that occurred and who were possibly responsible for them. A PJ approach would not neglect the fact that five months before the Al-Ghouta incident, on March 19, 2013, Khan Al-Assal—a regime-held area—was struck by sarin gas, killing and injuring regime soldiers and civilians. The UN Mission to Investigate Allegations of the Use of Chemical Weapons in the Syrian Arab Republic (UNMIAUCWSAR) (2013b) corroborated these allegations. On May 6, 2013, Carla del Ponte, a former war crimes prosecutor and a member in the UNMIAUCWSAR, said, "According to the testimonies we have gathered, the rebels have used chemical weapons, making use of Sarin gas". She continued, "there was still not irrefutable proof, [but] very strong suspicions, concrete suspicions that Sarin gas has been used... by opponents, by rebels, [and] not by government authorities" (Erlich, 2014). Including such accounts and perspectives could widen the possibilities and options of potential CWs' users. Therefore, the third analytical criterion is:

3. Does the article mention that soldiers from the Syrian Arab Army (SAA) were injured in the first CW attack that struck Khan Al-

Assal on March 19th, 2013? Or does the article mention that the Khan Al-Assal area was under regime control during the attack? Or does the article mention that Carla del Ponte stated that the rebels are responsible for the Khan Al-Assal attack?

On March 20, 2013, one day after Khan Al-Assal attack, the Deputy Prime Minister of Syria requested the Secretary-General to form an independent investigation of the attack. The next day, March 21, 2013, the UN Secretary-General founded the UNMIAUCWSAR, which was later endorsed by the UN Security Council (UNSC) (UNMIAUCWSAR, 2013b, p. 6). The UN investigative team (which was invited into the country by the Syrian regime) arrived on August 18, 2013, three days before the Al-Ghouta attack (UNMIAUCWSAR, 2013b, p. 7). Therefore, a PJ journalist would mention as background that the inspectors had just arrived in Damascus to investigate the use of CW in March 2013. Critical coverage of events would raise questions such as: Is it a coincidence that the Al-Ghouta attack took place in conjunction with the arrival of the UN investigators? Who can politically benefit more from such attack? Therefore, the fourth analytical criterion is:

4. **Does the article mention that UN inspectors had been in the country three days prior to the Al-Ghouta attack?**

When the Al-Ghouta attack occurred, the Syrian army was gaining ground. The SAA backed by Hezbollah captured the strategic city, Qusayr (located close to the Lebanese border), in June 2013, from the Farouq Brigade and Jabhat Al-Nusra (Anderson, 2015). At the same time, parts of Aleppo and Eastern Syria were under the control of Islamist groups, while Western Syria, a majorly populated area, was under regime control (Anderson, 2015). Therefore, a PJ journalist would question the need of using CW while the SAA (at the time of the attack) were advancing on the ground using traditional ones. Thus, the fifth analytical criterion is:

5. **Does the article mention that the regime troops were advancing on the ground before and during the attack?**

The United States, the United Kingdom, Turkey, Saudi Arabia and Qatar have politically and financially supported opposition groups (M. Lynch, 2016). They publicly condemned Al-Assad's violations and cried out for a "limited strike" to "save the people of Syria". While these powers were beating the drums of war, PJ journalists would not have conveyed their statements and allegations at face value. They would have revealed the real causes and motivations behind the military intervention. Therefore, the sixth analytical criterion is:

6. **Does the article mention the geopolitical interests of Syria's allies and enemies in Damascus? Or Iran and Saudi rivalry? Or the rivalry between the West and Russia?**

A Peace/Conflict-Orientated coverage would practise "reflexivity" and provide deep analysis of hidden factors. It would link the present with the past and remind audiences of similar conflicts, such as when the United States intervened in Iraq depending on "intelligence sources" that were later proved to be false. Consequently, the seventh criterion is:

7. **Does the article mention that Iraq was invaded in 2003, which was justified due to their alleged possession of WMD?**

On March 16, 1988, 5000 were killed in Halabja (a Kurdish town) in one day when Saddam Hussein's regime used CWs (sarin gas) against civilians (Bretton-Gordon, 2016). The final death toll reached 12,000, mostly women and children (Bretton-Gordon, 2016). At the time, the United States did not describe their ally (Saddam) as "Hitler"—like they do to Al-Assad—and did not threaten to "punish" or "deter" the perpetrator and save the Kurdish people. A PJ approach would highlight these double standards and reveal the untold reasons behind the imminent US strike. Therefore, the eighth analytical criterion is:

8. **Does the article mention any previous incidents where CW were used but the West did not take any action and did not militarily intervene?**

A Peace/Conflict-Orientated coverage would mention the fact that striking Syria without the authorisation of the UNSC is illegal. It would also mention that striking Syria is inconsistent with Article 2(4) of the UN Charter which states, "All Members shall refrain in their international relations from the threat or use of force against the territorial integrity or political independence of any state, or in any other manner inconsistent with the purposes of the United Nations". Hence, the ninth analytical criterion is:

9. **Does the article mention that striking Syria without obtaining authorisation from the UNSC is unlawful and breaches International Human Rights Law?**

It is crucial to mention that Eastern Al-Ghouta was under rebel control when it was struck by CWs on August 21, 2013. This might possibly imply that it is not very logical to accuse opposition groups of using such weapons against itself, in an area where its people and supporters live. Therefore, the tenth analytical criterion is:

10. **Does the article mention that the Al-Ghouta area was under the control of the rebels when the attack occurred on August 21, 2013? Or does the article mention that rebels were killed in the attack?**

B. **Analytical Criteria of the Truth-Orientated Frame**

Truth-Orientated coverage would expose the wrongdoing of all sides. It would mention that two months before the Al-Ghouta attack, the IICISAR (2013, p. 21) released a report stating that both sides could use and might have access to CW. Therefore, the first analytical criterion of the Truth-Orientated frame is:

1. **Does the article mention that "both sides" could use CW according to a UN report released in June 2013, two months before the Al-Ghouta attack?**

As media coverage could be manipulated by propaganda and allegations of officials, elites and conflicted parties, it is necessary for a Truth-Orientated approach to equip readers with independent, informed and non-propaganda-based analysis about who possibly could have used CW in Syria. Given that both sides of the conflict claim that they have evidence that the other side is responsible for the CW attack, the second analytical criterion is:

4 THEORETICAL FRAMEWORK AND RESEARCH QUESTIONS   127

2. Does the article present a non-propagandistic analysis about the responsibility of the use of the CW? Or, does the article present an analysis by an independent and well-experienced military or CW expert about who possibly committed the attack?

Truth-Orientated coverage would name and expose all human rights abusers. It would mention that both sides committed war crimes and human rights violations. The IICISAR (2014, p. 1) summarises the violations of the Syrian regime as following:

> Government forces continued to perpetrate massacres and conduct widespread attacks on civilians, systematically committing murder, torture, rape and enforced disappearance amounting to crimes against humanity. Government forces have committed gross violations of human rights and the war crimes of murder, hostage-taking, torture, rape and sexual violence, recruiting and using children in hostilities and targeting civilians. Government forces disregarded the special protection accorded to hospitals, and medical and humanitarian personnel. Indiscriminate and disproportionate aerial bombardment and shelling led to mass civilian casualties and spread terror. Government forces used chlorine gas, an illegal weapon.

On the other hand, the report reveals the violations of opposition groups as well:

> Non-State armed groups named in the report, committed massacres and war crimes, including murder, execution without due process, torture, hostage-taking, violations of international humanitarian law tantamount to enforced disappearance, rape and sexual violence, recruiting and using children in hostilities and attacking protected objects. Medical and religious personnel and journalists were targeted. Armed groups besieged and indiscriminately shelled civilian neighbourhoods, in some instances spreading terror among civilians through the use of car bombings in civilian areas. Members of the Islamic State of Iraq and Al-Sham (ISIS) committed torture, murder, acts tantamount to enforced disappearance, and forcible displacement as part of an attack on the civilian population in Aleppo and Al-Raqqah governorates, amounting to crimes against humanity. (IICISAR, 2014, p. 1)

Therefore, the third analytical criterion is:

128   Z. ABDUL-NABI

3. **Does the article mention that both sides of the conflict committed human rights violations?**

C. Analytical Criteria of the People-Orientated Frame

Since civilians are the ones who paid the highest price, their voices should be prioritised and given space and time in a PJ approach. Hence, the first analytical criterion of the People-Orientated frame is:

1. **Does the article give voice to the victims/survivors of the attack?**

A People-Orientated coverage would shed light on the views, accounts and peace initiatives presented by civilians and human rights activists that are working on the ground. It would not give space to elite perspectives only. Therefore, the second analytical criterion is:

2. **Does the article give voice to Syrian activists/civilians (that are not necessarily members of known organisations) who were campaigning against military intervention?**

Focusing on suffering of ordinary people, children and women is essential in People-Orientated coverage. Therefore, the third analytical criterion is:

3. **Does the article focus on or show the suffering of Al-Ghouta's people after the attack?**

D. Analytical Criteria of the Solution-Orientated Frame

Solution-Orientated coverage would focus on the invisible consequences of (1) the CW attack and (2) potential military intervention such as trauma, psychological damage, difficulties and challenges of displacement and daily life. Therefore, the first and second analytical criteria in measuring the Solution-Orientated frame are:

1. **Does the article mention the implications/future effects of the use of CW on civilians?**
2. **Does the article mention the implications/future effects of military intervention on escalating the conflict and civil war?**

PJ should "pick up and explore peace initiatives wherever they come from" (J. Lynch & McGoldrick, 2000). Hence, the third analytical criterion is:

3. **Does the article mention any peace initiative that can prevent war or de-escalate the conflict?**

Peace initiatives in the Syrian conflict can be one of the following (or any other creative suggestions):

- Participating in the Geneva II conference.
- Peaceful transition of power.
- Truce/ceasefire.
- Restricting the transfer of military arms.
- Destroying the regime's CW.
- UN inspectors are still in Syria and the United States should wait for the results before it takes any action.

Measuring evaluative criteria and PJ frames in the Bahrain and Syria coverage:

The frames of the PJM (Peace/Conflict, People, Truth and Solution) and the frames of the War Journalism Model (WJM) (War, Elite, Propaganda and Victory) will be determined based on the absence (WJM) or presence (PJM) of the proposed facts/analytical criteria. If the article includes/mentions the proposed analytical criteria, it will be marked with Y = Yes. If the article excludes/does not mention the criterion, it will be marked with N = No. Each Y = 1 point for the PJ frame. The number of Ys will determine the percentage of PJ framings, and the number of Ns will determine the percentage of WJ framings.

4.5   RQ 2 and 7: Influence of "Here and Now" on Absence and Presence of PJ Frames

RQ (2): To what extent did the developments of the events [here and now] impact on including or excluding Peace Journalism frames in Al-Jazeera's coverage of Bahrain's uprising during the Saudi military intervention in 2011?

RQ (7): To what extent did the developments of the events [here and now] impact on including or excluding Peace Journalism frames in Al-Jazeera's coverage of Syria's second chemical weapons attack?

Measuring how events have influenced the percentage of the PJ frames during different periods in both conflicts is conducted in the following stages:

1. The most mentioned analytical criterion in each frame is selected to represent a frame. For instance, assuming that "violations committed by the Bahraini regime" is the most mentioned criterion among the analytical criteria of the Truth-Orientated frame, then this criterion will represent the [Truth] frame itself.
2. The frequency of mentioning the selected criterion will be measured in different phases [in the beginning of the research period, in the middle and at the end].
3. The frequencies of this criterion will be compared with each other while taking into consideration the developments of each phase.
4. If the frequency of the criterion increases or decreases in conjunction with certain developments [negotiations, peace initiatives or escalation/de-escalation of conflicts], then "here and now" have an influence on including and excluding PJ orientations in media coverage.
5. Selecting one criterion and measuring the difference in its frequency during different phases in the conflict is more practical than measuring the whole frame.

4.6   RQ 3 and 8: Dominant Sources in the Bahrain and Syria Coverage

RQ (3): What were the dominant [quoted] sources in AJA's and AJE's coverage of Bahrain's uprising during all research periods?

RQ (8): What were the dominant sources in AJA's and AJE's coverage of Syria's second CW attack?

Coding list of Bahrain's uprising quoted sources, during all research periods:

- Unauthorised opposition: opposition groups that are unlicensed by the regime
- Authorised opposition or licensed opposition groups

- Bahraini officials
- Al-Jazeera reporter
- Activists or human rights organisations
- Victims/civilians

Coding list of Syria's quoted sources:

- Moderate opposition groups that opposed air strikes in Syria
- Opposition and its allies
- Syrian regime and its allies
- The UN and human rights groups
- Survivors, victims, civilians
- Doctors [including Doctors Without Borders]
- CW experts
- Al-Jazeera reporter

4.7 RQ 4 AND 9: FRAMING OF SYRIAN AND BAHRAINI CONFLICTS

RQ 4: How did AJA and AJE frame the conflict and the protesters in Bahrain during all research periods?

RQ 9: How did AJA and AJE frame the Al-Ghouta attack and the Syrian conflict?

Framing of the Bahraini conflict:

- Uprising
- Revolution
- Conflict
- Crisis/unrest/turmoil
- Protests
- Peaceful protest/movement
- Pro-democracy or anti-government movement

Framing of Bahraini protesters:

- Protesters or opposition/demonstrators/opponents
- Pro-democracy or anti-government protesters/opposition or protesters that demanded reforms and/or greater freedoms

- Shia protesters or Shia opposition/Shia-led protests
- Peaceful protesters
- Revolutionaries

Framing of Al-Ghouta's attack

- Chemical weapons attack or gas attack
- Alleged chemical weapons attack or suspected attack
- Deadly or horrific attack
- Massacre
- Crime or criminal act
- Attack

Framing of Syrian conflict:

- Uprising
- Revolution
- Civil war
- Syrian/Syria crisis

4.8   RQ 5 AND 10: PRO- AND ANTI-QATAR FRAMING IN THE BAHRAIN AND SYRIA COVERAGE

RQ (5): To what extent the framing of the AJA and AJE coverage of Bahrain's conflict during all research periods conform to Qatar's foreign policy?

A. **Measuring pro- and anti-Qatar framing in the coverage of Bahrain's uprising during all analysed periods [from 2011 to 2021]**

Given that Qatar was part of the PSF deployed in the streets of Manama in March 2011 to crack down on protesters, the legitimisation of the presence of these troops in the coverage will be categorised as "pro-Qatar" framing and delegitimising them will be categorised as "anti-Qatar" framing. Therefore, utilising Entman's (1993) definition of framing [selection and salience] and quantitative content analysis method:

- Each article [news stories or features] will be framed as "pro-Qatar" if it states as a "fact" that:
  - The GCC troops were sent to restore order and security.
  - To protect the government facilities.
  - To face Iran's threat/agents.
  - Sending the troops is part of the GCC coordination and agreement.

- The article will be classified/framed as "anti-Qatar" if the following reasons were mentioned as facts:
  - The GCC troops were sent to quell the protesters or to put an end to the protests.
  - To participate in the crackdown.
  - To prevent Bahrain's uprising from spreading to the Saudi Arabia's Eastern province.
  - The presence of the troops could escalate the sectarianism in Bahrain and in the region.
  - It is an invasion.

- An article will be classified as neutral—neither pro- nor anti-Qatar framing—if it mentions both reasons equally.

B. **Measuring pro- and anti-Qatar framing in the coverage of Bahrain's during the periods before and after the 2017 Gulf crisis [only]**

1. A news story will be framed as "pro-Qatar" if it includes frequent lexical choices that delegitimise the Bahraini regime, such as:
   - Quelling or crushing protests
   - Torture of protesters
   - Sexual assaults/rape/abuse by the Bahraini regime security forces
   - The role of Sheikh Naser, the son of the King in the human rights violations

2. As Qatar stands formally against the "Abraham accord" or the normalisation deal signed between Bahrain and Israel on September 15, 2020, the study intends to measure the extent of agreement between Al-Jazeera's framing of the deal and Qatar's declared foreign policy. Some news stories related to the normalisation deal were published during

the 2017 Gulf crisis [second conflict period]. As they were irrelevant to Bahrain's uprising coverage, the news stories [64 from AJA and 36 from AJE] were excluded from the analysis. However, they were selected and analysed separately.

- The frequency of including the following frames will be examined:
  - Peace deal
  - Normalisation deal
  - Crime [or partners in crime]
  - Betrayal and/or stab in the back/shame
  - Abraham accord

- For further analysis, articles will be classified as "critical" and "uncritical" to the normalisation deal based on the following:
  - Critical framing: Reporting on the deal while including critical/challenging accounts to it
  - Uncritical framing: Reporting on the deal while not including critical/challenging accounts to it

RQ (10): How did AJA and AJE frame the responsibility of using chemical weapons in Syria and to what extent does this framing conform to Qatar's foreign policy?

Due to the nature of the Al-Ghouta incident, Al-Jazeera has rarely mentioned or named who was responsible for the chemical attack as a "fact". However, AJA and AJE mentioned and repeated the "claims" of both sides. Hence, using a quantitative content analysis method, the number of pro- and anti-Qatari claims will determine the framing of the whole coverage.

- Pro-Qatar claim [allegations or quotes]: the Al-Assad regime has used chemical weapons.
- Anti-Qatar claim [allegations or quotes]: the opposition has used chemical weapons.
- Neutral [as a fact]: Both sides could have used chemical weapons.

4.9 RQ11: Estimation of the Number of Syrian Victims

RQ (11): As the estimated number of the victims killed in the chemical attack varied widely from one source to another [from 100 to 1600], which estimation dominated the coverage of AJA and AJE during the first three weeks of the Al-Ghouta attack?

The United States estimated the number of the victims killed in the attack at 1429. The Doctors Without Borders, however, estimated that 355 were killed in the Eastern Al-Ghouta attack (Erlich, 2014). Similarly, MI6 said that 350 were killed, and the Syrian Observatory for Human Rights stated that the number of the deaths reached 502 (Erlich, 2014). The head of the UN chemical weapons inspection team, Ake Sellstrom, pointed out that the rebels overstated the number of victims. He said, "We saw the capability of those hospitals, and it is impossible that they could have turned over the amount of people that they claim they did" (Erlich, 2014).

This study uses quantitative content analysis to measure which estimation dominated the coverage of both channels.

- 100–500 victims
- 1300–1600 victims
- "Hundreds"

4.10 RQ12: Extent of Depending on News Wires in the Coverage of Bahrain and Syria

RQ (12): To what extent did Al-Jazeera (AJA and AJE) depend on news wires in its coverage of Bahrain's uprising during all research periods and Syria's second chemical weapon attack?

A. **Measuring the extent [frequency] of depending on news wires in the coverage of Bahrain's uprising during the Saudi military intervention in 2011 and Al-Ghouta CW attack in 2013:**
   - News wires only
   - Al-Jazeera and news wires
   - Al-Jazeera only

B. Measuring the extent [frequency] of depending on news wires in the coverage of Bahrain's uprising in the periods before and after the 2017 Gulf crisis:

As "social media", "human rights organisations" and "international journalism" sources were observed while analysing the articles of Bahrain's uprising in the periods before and after the 2017 Gulf crisis, these sources were added to the coding list of these periods accordingly.

- News wires
- Al-Jazeera
- Social media, websites
- International journalism
- Human rights origination

4.11 Conclusion

To conclude, this study depends on measuring the extent of displaying PJ frames [which are coined based on framing theory (Entman, 1993) and PJ orientations (Galtung, 1986, 1998)] in the AJA and AJE coverage of Bahrain's uprising and Syria's second CW attack. Each frame includes a number of evaluative criteria that are proposed on the basis of PJ characteristics and contexts/history of both conflicts. Along with framing and PJ theories, this study utilises quantitative content analysis methods to answer the research questions.

To sum up, this study aims to answer 12 research questions about (a) the extent of the presence and absence of PJ and WJ frames in the AJA and AJE coverage of both conflicts, (b) the influence of developments/here and now on including and excluding PJ frames, (c) representations of the Bahrain and Syrian conflicts, (d) measurement of the most quoted sources, (e) degree of conformity between Qatar's foreign policy and Al-Jazeera's framing, (f) dominant estimations of the number of victims killed in the Al-Ghouta attack and (g) the level of dependence on news wires by both channels in covering both conflicts.

References

Al-Khalifa, H. I. (2011, April 19). Stability is prerequisite for progress. *The Washington Times.* http://www.washingtontimes.com/news/2011/apr/19/stability-is-prerequisite-for-progress/

Al-Mdaires, F. (2002). Shicism and political protest in Bahrain. *Digest of Middle East Studies, 11*(1), 20–44.

Al-Rasheed, M. (2011). Sectarianism as counter-revolution: Saudi responses to the Arab Spring. *Studies in Ethnicity and Nationalism, 11*(3), 513–526.

Ambrosio, T. (2014). Democratic states and authoritarian firewalls: America as a black knight in the uprising in Bahrain. *Contemporary Politics, 20*(3), 331–346.

Anderson, T. (2015). *The dirty war on Syria.* Montreal: Global Research.

Bagdikian, B. H. (2014). *The media monopoly* (5th ed.). Beacon Press.

Bahrain Independent Commission of Inquiry. (2011). *Report of the Bahrain Independent Commission of Inquiry.* Bahrain Independent Commission of Inquiry.

Barnard, A. (2013, March 19). Syria and Activists Trade Charges on Chemical Weapons. *The New York Times.* https://www.nytimes.com/2013/03/20/world/middleeast/syria-developments.html?pagewanted=all

BBC. (2014, March 5). *Gulf ambassadors pulled from Qatar over 'interference.'* https://www.bbc.com/news/world-middle-east-26447914

Bläsi, B. (2004). Peace journalism and the news production process. *Conflict & Communication Online, 3*(1/2), 1–12. Accessed January 4, 2016, from http://www.cco.regener-online.de/2004/pdf_2004/blaesi.pdf

Bretton-Gordon, D. H. (2016). Remembering Halabja chemical attack. *Al-Jazeera English.* http://www.aljazeera.com/indepth/opinion/2016/03/remembering-halabja-chemical-attack-160316061221074.html

Carpenter, T. G. (2013). Tangled web: The Syrian civil war and its implications. *Mediterranean Quarterly, 24*(1), 1–11.

Chivers, C. J. (2013, September 17). U.N. data on gas attack point to Assad's top forces. *The New York Times.* Accessed September 22, 2014, from http://www.nytimes.com/2013/09/18/world/middleeast/un-data-on-gas-attack-points-to-assads-top-forces.html

Cockburn, P. (2013, December 8). Mass murder in the Middle East is funded by our friends the Saudis. *The Independent.* http://www.independent.co.uk/voices/comment/mass-murder-in-the-middle-east-is-funded-by-our-friends-the-saudis-8990736.html

Congressional Research Service. (2021). *Bahrain: Unrest, security, and U.S. policy updated April 20, 2021.* https://sgp.fas.org/crs/mideast/95-1013.pdf

Davidson, C. M. (2013). *After the Sheikhs: The coming collapse of the Gulf monarchies.* Hurst & Company.

Entman, R. M. (1991). Framing US coverage of international news: Contrasts in narratives of the KAL and Iran Air incidents. *Journal of communication, 41*(4), 6–27.

Entman, R. M. (1993). Framing: Toward clarification of a fractured paradigm. *Journal of Communication, 43*(4), 51–58.

Erlich, R. (2014). *Inside Syria: The backstory of their civil war and what the world can expect.* Prometheus Books.

Fahmy, S., & Eakin, B. (2014). High drama on the high seas Peace versus war journalism framing of an Israeli/Palestinian-related incident. *International Communication Gazette, 76*(1), 86–105.

Fisk, R. (2013, August 27). Does Obama know he's fighting on al-Qa'ida's side? *The Independent.* Accessed August 30, 2013, from http://www.independent.co.uk/voices/comment/does-obama-know-hes-fightingon-alqaidas-side-8786680.html

Friedman, B. (2012). Battle for Bahrain: What one uprising meant for the Gulf states and Iran. *World Affairs, 174*(6), 74–84.

Galtung, J. (1986). On the role of the media in worldwide security and peace. In T. Varis (Ed.), *Peace and communication* (pp. 249–266). Universidad para La Paz.ed.

Galtung, J. (1998). High road, low road – Charting the course for peace journalism. *Track Two, 7*(4). Accessed September 14, 2015, from http://reference.sabinet.co.za/webx/access/electronic_journals/track2/track2_v7_n4_a4.htm

Galtung, J., & Fischer, D. (2013). *Johan Galtung: Pioneer of peace research.* Springer.

Carragee, K. M., & Roefs, W. (2004). The neglect of power in recent framing research. *Journal of Communication, 54*(2), 214–233.

Gelvin, J. L. (2012). *The Arab uprisings: What everyone needs to know.* Oxford University Press.

Gordon, M. R. (2013, September 14). U.S. and Russia reach deal to destroy Syria's chemical arms. *The New York Times.* http://www.nytimes.com/2013/09/15/world/middleeast/syria-talks.html

Hackett, R. A., & Schroeder, B. (2009). Does anybody practice Peace Journalism? A cross-national comparison of press coverage of the Afghanistan and Israeli–Hezbollah wars. *Peace and Policy, 13*(1), 26–47.

Haroon, A. (2014). *History of Saudi Arabia & wahabism.* Xlibris Corporation.

Hashem, A. (2012, April 3). The Arab Spring has shaken Arab TV's credibility. *The Guardian.* Accessed March 12, 2016, from http://www.theguardian.com/commentisfree/2012/apr/03/arab-spring-arab-tv-credibility

Herman, E. S., & Chomsky, N. (2010). *Manufacturing consent: The political economy of the mass media.* Random House eBooks.

Hersh, S. (2014). The red line and the rat line. *The London Review of Books.* http://www.lrb.co.uk/v36/n08/seymour-m-hersh/the-red-line-and-the-rat-line

Hughes, G. A. (2014). Syria and the perils of proxy warfare. *Small Wars & Insurgencies, 25*(3), 522–538.

Human Rights Watch. (2012). *World report 2012: Bahrain: Events of 2011.* Accessed March 22, 2013, from https://www.hrw.org/world-report/2012/country-chapters/bahrain

Independent International Commission of Inquiry on the Syrian Arab Republic. (2013). *Report of independent international commission of inquiry on the Syrian Arab Republic.* Accessed September 14, 2014, from http://www.ohchr.org/Documents/HRBodies/HRCouncil/CoISyria/A-HRC-23-58_en.pdf

Independent International Commission of Inquiry on the Syrian Arab Republic. (2014). *Report of independent international commission of inquiry on the Syrian Arab Republic.* Accessed September 14, 2014, from http://www.ohchr.org/Documents/HRBodies/HRCouncil/CoISyria/A.HRC.27.60_Eng.pdf

Jones, T. C. (2011). Saudi Arabia versus the Arab spring. *Raritan, 31*(2), 43–59,164.

Kamrava, M. (2012). The Arab Spring and the Saudi-led counterrevolution. *Orbis, 56*(1), 96–104.

Kamrava, M. (2013). *Qatar: Small state, big politics.* Cornell University Press.

Khalaf, A. (2015). The many afterlives of Lulu: The story of Bahrain's Pearl Roundabout. In A. Shehabi & J. O. Marc (Eds.), *Bahrain's uprising: Resistance and repression in the Gulf* (pp. 135–150). Zed Books.

Khatib, L. (2013). Qatar's foreign policy: The limits of pragmatism. *International Affairs, 89*(2), 417–431.

Lee, S. T., Maslog, C. C., & Kim, H. S. (2006). Framing analysis of a conflict: How newspapers in five Asian countries covered the Iraq War. *Asian Journal of Communication, 16*(1), 19–39.

Lesch, W. D. (2011, May 4). *Shock in Syria – The messy and unlikely alternatives for Bashar.* http://yalebooksblog.co.uk/2011/05/04/author-article-by-david-lesch-shock-in-syria-the-messy-and-unlikely-alternatives-for-bashar/

London, S. (1993). *How the media frames political issues. Scott London.* http://www.scottlondon.com/reports/frames

Louër, L. (2013). Sectarianism and coup-proofing strategies in Bahrain. *Journal of Strategic Studies, 36*(2), 245–260.

Lynch, J., & McGoldrick, A. (2000). Peace journalism – How to do it? *Transcend Website* (Peace Journalism). Accessed March 30, 2013, from https://www.transcend.org/tri/downloads/McGoldrick_Lynch_Peace-Journalism.pdf

Lynch, J., & McGoldrick, A. (2005). *Peace journalism.* Hawthorn Press.

Lynch, J. (2006). What's so great about Peace Journalism. *Global Media Journal, Mediterranean Edition, 1*(1), 74–87.

Lynch, J. (2007). Peace journalism and its discontents. *Conflict and Communication Online, 6*(2), 1–13. Accessed June 3, 2013, from http://www.cco.regener-online.de/2007_2/pdf/lynch.pdf

140 Z. ABDUL-NABI

Lynch, J. (2008). *Debates in Peace Journalism.* Sydney University Press.
Lynch, J. (2010). Peace Journalism. In S. Allan (Ed.), *The Routledge Companion to News and Journalism,* (pp. 542–554). Oxon & New York: Routledge.
Lynch, J. (2014). *A Global Standard for Reporting Conflict.* Routledge.
Lynch, M. (2013b). *The Arab uprising: The unfinished revolutions of the new Middle East.* PublicAffairs.
Lynch, M. (2016). *The new Arab wars: Uprisings and anarchy in the Middle East.* New York : Public Affairs.
Lynch, M. (2017). Three big lessons of the Qatar crisis. In N. Anayiss (Ed.), *The Qatar Crisis* (pp. 14–17). Project on Middle East Political Science.
Lyons, J. (2013). *Dispatches: Mapping the sarin flight path.* Accessed September 22, 2014, from Human Rights Watch: https://www.hrw.org/news/2013/09/17/dispatches-mapping-sarin-flight-path
Mabon, S. (2012). The battle for Bahrain: Iranian-Saudi rivalry. *Middle East Policy, 19*(2), 84–97.
Matthiesen, T. (2013). *Sectarian gulf: Bahrain, Saudi Arabia, and the Arab Spring that wasn't.* Stanford University Press.
McGoldrick, A. (2006). War journalism and "objectivity." *Conflict and Communication Online, 5*(2), 1-7. Accessed June 14, 2016, from http://cco.regener-online.de/2006_2/pdf/mcgoldrick.pdf
McHugo, J. (2014). *Syria: from the great war to civil war.* Saqi.
Médecins Sans Frontières. (2011). *Health Services Paralyzed: Bahrain military crackdown on patients.* Accessed April 12, 2013, from http://www.doctor-swithoutborders.org/news-stories/special-report/health-services-paralyzed-bahrains-military-crackdown-patients
Mitchell, M. (2012). The aborted revolution: The demise of Bahrain's democracy movement. *Harvard International Review, 33*(4), 32–36. Accessed April 12, 2014, from http://ezproxy.library.usyd.edu.au/login?url=http://search.pro-quest.com/docview/151869 3969?accountid=14757
Murawiec, L. (2005). *Princes of darkness: The Saudi assault on the West.* New York: Rowman & Littlefield.
Nohrstedt, S. A., & Ottosen, R. (2011). Peace journalism–critical discourse case study: Media and the plan for Swedish and Norwegian defence cooperation. In I. S. Shaw, J. Lynch, & R. A. Hackett (Eds.), *Expanding peace journalism: Comparative and critical approaches* (pp. 217–238). Sydney University Press.
Office of the United Nations High Commissioner for Human Rights. (2014). *International destruction of cultural heritage as a violation of human rights in Bahrain and Saudi Arabia.* Accessed June 24, 2016, from http://www.ohchr.org/Documents/Issues/CulturalRights/DestructionHeritage/NGOS/ADHRB.pdf

4 THEORETICAL FRAMEWORK AND RESEARCH QUESTIONS 141

Physicians for Human Rights. (2011). *Do no harm: A call for Bahrain to end systematic attacks on doctors and patients.* https://s3.amazonaws.com/PHR_Reports/bahrain-do-no-harm-2011.pdf

Pita, R., & Domingo, J. (2014). The use of chemical weapons in the Syrian conflict. *Toxics, 2*(3), 391–402.

Reuters. (2021, June 22). Bahrain has invited Qatar twice for bilateral al-Ula talks – ministry. https://www.reuters.com/world/middle-east/bahrain-has-invited-qatar-twice-bilateral-al-ula-talks-ministry-2021-06-22/

Scheufele, D. A. (1999). Framing as a theory of media effects. *Journal of Communication, 49*(1), 103–122.

Scheufele, B. (2004). Framing-effects approach: A theoretical and methodological critique. *Communications, 29*(4), 401–428.

Shoemaker, P. J., & Reese, S. D. (2013). *Mediating the message in the 21st century: A media sociology perspective.* Routledge.

Ulrichsen, K. C. (2019). Perceptions and divisions in security and defense structures in Arab Gulf States. In S. Wright & A. Baabood (Eds.), *Divided gulf* (pp. 19–36). Palgrave Macmillan.

United Nations Mission to Investigate Allegations of the Use of Chemical Weapons in the Syrian Arab Republic. (2013b). *Final report.* Accessed June 3, 2014, from https://unoda-web.s3.amazonaws.com/wp-content/uploads/2013/12/report.pdf

U.S. Department of State. (2011). *International religious freedom report for 2011.* Accessed April 11, 2014, from http://www.state.gov/j/drl/rls/irf/2011religiousfreedom/index.htm#wrapper

Vassiliev, A. (2000). *The history of Saudi Arabia.* Saqi Books.

White House. (2011). *President Obama's address to the United Nations General Assembly.* Accessed May 2, 2012, from https://geneva.usmission.gov/2011/09/21/obama-remarks-unga/

Wodak, R. (2001). The discourse-historical approach. In R. Wodak & M. Meyer (Eds.), *Methods of critical discourse analysis* (pp. 87–122). Sage.

Youngblood, S. (2017). *Peace journalism principles and practices: Responsibly reporting conflicts, reconciliation, and solutions.* London and New York: Routledge.

Zunes, S. (2013). Bahrain's arrested revolution. *Arab Studies Quarterly, 35*(2), 149–164.

CHAPTER 5

Bahrain's Uprising: Pro-democracy Protests or Sectarian Movement?

5.1 Introduction

This chapter presents and discusses the empirical findings of analysing Al-Jazeera's coverage of the Bahraini uprising in 2011. All news stories and features that were published from the beginning of the Saudi military intervention on March 14, 2011, until the lifting of martial law on June 1, 2011, were selected and analysed. After excluding irrelevant articles, 80 news stories and 6 features were collected from AJA, and 38 news stories and 3 features were collected from AJE.

The empirical content analysis found that the coverage of Bahrain's uprising in AJA and AJE was dominated by War Journalism (WJ) framing. However, AJE-N&F presented PJ frames and characteristics more than AJA-N&F.

This chapter discusses how the inclusion as well as exclusion of PJ framing in AJA and AJE has affected the representation of Bahrain's protests, and protesters. It argues that the lack of implementation of PJ criteria in AJA aided the Al-Khalifa regime in promoting baseless allegations as factual statements. AJA, for example, reported as unquestioned "facts" that Bahraini protesters were supported by Iran and driven by "sectarian reasons". AJA similarly legitimised the presence of the Saudi troops deployed to allegedly "protect government facilities and maintain security and order". AJA also reported well-documented "facts" such as

© The Author(s), under exclusive license to Springer Nature 143
Switzerland AG 2022
Z. Abdul-Nabi, *Al-Jazeera's "Double Standards" in the Arab Spring*,
https://doi.org/10.1007/978-3-031-14279-6_5

discrimination against Shias, demolition of Shia mosques and violations committed against protesters as merely "claims".

The chapter argues that the turning of "claims" into "facts" and vice versa in AJA is attributed to the reporting of officials' statements "as factual", Qatar's influence on the channel's editorial policy, the selectivity of AJA's journalists and local restrictions on AJA's reporter in Bahrain.

The findings demonstrated major differences between the coverage of AJA and AJE. Although some parts of AJE's coverage associated Bahrain's uprising with Shi'ism and "sectarian clashes", significant percentages of its reporting uncovered violations, challenged dominant accounts and focused on the context of the pro-democracy struggle in the country. It is this coverage that enabled AJE to effectively counter the propaganda of the Qatari, Bahraini and Saudi Arabian regimes in the beginning of the Arab Spring.

5.2   Key Findings

Before analysing and dissecting the findings of the AJA's and AJE's coverage of Bahrain's uprising in depth, the following key points summarise the main quantitative results:

- More than 60% of the news stories and features of the Arabic and English channels were dominated by WJ framing.
- PJ framing was displayed in AJE-N&F (25.9% and 34.7%) more than AJA-N&F (13.25% and 9.3%).
- More than one third of AJE Features (AJE-F) applied PJ frames, whereas less than 10% of AJA Features (AJA-F) did so.
- Pro-Qatar and Gulf Cooperation Council (GCC) sources dominated AJA News (AJA-N, 44.8%), while human rights organisations dominated AJE News (AJE-N, 36.8%).
- Sources from elites were quoted more than 40% in the news of both channels, whereas the quotations of ordinary people scored less than 10%.
- More than 50% of the coverage of both channels framed the Bahraini conflict as merely "protests", while less than 10% referred to it as an "uprising".
- A significant percentage of AJA-N (26.2%) and AJE-N (30.6%) associated the protesters with Shi'ism.

- Pro-Qatar framing dominated AJA-N&F (47.7% and 100%), whereas anti-Qatar framing prevailed AJE-N&F (75% and 100%).

5.3 AJA Coverage of Bahrain's Protests (March–June 2011): A Quantitative Analysis

5.3.1 AJA: Sectarian Framing of Bahrain's Protests and Protesters

Unlike Al-Jazeera's framing of the Libyan and Egyptian protests as "revolutions" (El-Nawawy & El-Masry, 2015; Al-Nahed, 2015), this monograph determined that AJA-N&F barely framed Bahrain's pro-democracy demonstrations in 2011 as an "uprising" (1.8% and 0%) or "revolution" (0.9% and 0%) (as shown below in Table 5.1). The clear majority of AJA-N&F (67% and 77.3%) downplayed the movement as merely "protests" in spite of their popularity among Bahrainis (see Table 5.1). For example, 30% of the population participated in its rallies, and 80% went on a general strike organised by the Bahraini Labour Union in March 2011 (M. Lynch, 2016).

Similarly, more than 60% of the N&F of AJA referred to the Bahraini demonstrators as "protesters" (see Table 5.2). Table 5.2 illustrates that a significant percentage of AJA-N (26.2%) framed the opposition as "Shia protesters", whereas limited percentages portrayed them as "pro-democracy protesters" (4.8%).

Since "language is an available set of options" (Machin & Mayr, 2012), describing protesters as "Shia" while excluding their "pro-democracy" demands reflects the lexical choices of AJA's editors. Machin and Mayr

Table 5.1 Framing of Bahrain's conflict in AJA's coverage

Conflict framing	AJA News	AJA Features
Uprising	4 (1.8%)	0 (0%)
Revolution	2 (0.9%)	0 (0%)
Conflict	0 (0%)	0 (0%)
Crisis/Unrest/Turmoil	38 (17%)	2 (9.1%)
Protests	150 (67%)	17 (77.3%)
Peaceful protest/movement	3 (1.3%)	0 (0%)
Pro-Democracy or Anti-Government movement	27 (12.1%)	3 (13.6%)

146 Z. ABDUL-NABI

Table 5.2 Framing of the protesters in AJA's coverage of Bahrain's uprising

Protesters' framing	AJA News	AJA Features
Protesters/Opposition /Demonstrators/Opponents	171 (67.9%)	15 (88.2%)
Pro-Democracy or Anti-Government Protesters	12 (4.8%)	0 (0%)
Shia Protesters/ Shia Opposition /Shia-led Protests	66 (26.2%)	2 (11.8%)
Peaceful protesters	3 (1.2%)	0 (0%)
Revolutionaries	0 (0%)	0 (0%)

(2012) argue that media choices aim at suppressing certain meanings and focusing on others. These choices are never "neutral", as journalists select them based on "the way they wish to signpost what kind of person they are representing, or how they wish to represent them as social actors engaged in action". Such selections can implicitly help legitimise and delegitimise social actors, participants or actions. Machin and Mayr (2012) contend that using functional terms (such as pro-democracy protesters) can make participants appear more "legitimate" than using generic terms (such as Shias). Given the context of the Saudi-Iranian rivalry and Sunni-Shia division in the Arab world (especially after the war in Iraq), referring to protesters as merely Shia without highlighting their peaceful methods and pro-democracy demands can give an impression that they and their movement are sectarian, and hence illegitimate.

5.3.2 Implications of Excluding the Peace/Conflict-Orientated Frames in AJA

More Emphasis on "Sectarian Framing"
The quantitative findings show that the criteria of the Peace/Conflict frame are hardly displayed in the AJA-N (7.4%) (see Table 5.3). As explained in Chaps. 1 and 4, these criteria are designed on two elements: the PJ characteristics and the historic context of the Bahraini conflict. Chapter 4 states that the criteria of the Peace/Conflict-Orientated frame

5 BAHRAIN'S UPRISING: PRO-DEMOCRACY PROTESTS OR SECTARIAN... 147

Table 5.3 Percentage of including/mentioning the Peace/Conflict-Orientated criteria in AJA's coverage of Bahrain's uprising

Peace/Conflict-Orientated Frame										
Peace/Conflict Orientated Criteria	(HB) Historical Background	(AS) Arab Spring	(SM) Shia Majority	(SD) Shia discrimination	(SSU) Shia-Sunni unity	(US5) US 5TH fleet	(PSF) Peninsula Shield Force	(SIR) Saudi-Iranian Rivalry	(PN) Political Naturalisation	(Total) Peace/Conflict Frame
AJA (80) News stories	0%	2.5%	5%	2.5%	3.75%	2.5%	47.5%	2.5%	0%	(7.4%)
AJA (6) Features	16.7%	16.7%	0%	16.7%	16.7%	33.3%	50%	33.3%	0%	(20.4%)

include nine facts[1] that were derived from the background, roots and contextual history of the long pro-democracy struggle in Bahrain.

The nine facts (or criteria) of the Peace-Orientated frame were explained thoroughly in Chap. 4, but as a quick reminder, they include highlighting facts related to the contextual history of Bahrain's protest movement, the structural discrimination against the Shias' majority population, peaceful struggle and the geopolitical context (Iranian-Saudi rivalry) of the Bahraini conflict.

The following section argues that a lack of applying these criteria has strengthened the "sectarian framing" of the AJA coverage and therefore

---

[1] Analytical criteria of Peace/Conflict-Orientated frame (the selection of these criteria was explained thoroughly in Chap. 4).

1. (HB): Does the article give a historical background about the protest movement in Bahrain?
2. (AS): Does the article mention that the protesters have been inspired by the Arab uprisings/Arab Spring?
3. (SM): Does the article mention that Shias make up the majority of the population?
4. (SD): Does the article mention that the Shias of Bahrain have been discriminated against?
5. (SSU): Does the article mention that the protesters called for unity between Shias and Sunnis from day one of the protests? Or does the article mention that there is no evidence that the protesters are supported by Iran?
6. (US5): Does the article mention that Bahrain is the home of the US Fifth Fleet?
7. (PSF): Does the article mention that 1500 Saudi and 500 Emirati troops have been deployed in Manama?
8. (SIR): Does the article mention the context of the rivalry between Saudi Arabia and Iran?
9. (PN): Does the article mention the political naturalisation process?

148   Z. ABDUL-NABI

helped promote the Bahraini regime narrative that the conflict is based on "sectarian" motivations, not democratic demands.

As shown previously in Table 5.2 that a significant percentage of AJA coverage referred to the protesters as "Shia" yet the channel's N&F focused minimally on the fact that these "Shia protesters" were peacefully calling for unity between Shias and Sunnis (3.75% and 16.7%) (see Table 5.3). Such examples include carrying flowers in one hand and the country's flag in the other chanting: "No Shias, no Sunnis, we are all brothers".

Since "frames are defined by what they omit as well as include" (Entman, 1993, p. 57), associating protesters with their sect (Shi'ism) repeatedly in AJA-N&F while almost excluding the fact that Shias make up the majority of the population (5% and 0%) and the fact that they are discriminated against (2.5% and 16.7%) has resulted in framing Bahrain's protests as "sectarian" (Table 5.3).

In other words, the inclusions of some facts (sect of the protesters) and exclusions of others (discrimination and marginalisation of Shias) have effectively reproduced a key framing of the Al-Khalifa regime discourse and propaganda. J. Lynch and McGoldrick (2005, p. 109) state:

> Propaganda works in the same way as advertising, using the same techniques—association and repetition. Advertisers associate their product, service or brand with certain images, ideas or values—then the message is repeated often enough for the rest of us to make the association for ourselves.

The following texts from AJA's coverage[2] clearly demonstrate the channel's use of sectarian framing:

> The protests put the Shia majority in confrontation with the Sunni ruling family who accused Iran of fomenting these protests. (AJA, May 11, 2011i)

> The King of Bahrain, Hamad bin Isa Al-Khalifa has said, "a foreign plot against the Kingdom has been foiled," referring to the protests which have taken on a sectarian dimension. Sheikh Hamad bin Isa thanked PSF troops for restoring order in the country. (AJA, March 22, 2011d)

---

[2] All cited AJA's Arabic texts from news stories and features in this chapter were translated by the author.

The sectarian factor is the most prominent factor of instability in Bahrain, as the opposition is founded on a sectarian basis, not a political one. Shias complain that they are marginalised and excluded by the Sunni ruling family. The government, however, constantly asserts that it does not discriminate between its citizens, as it has already employed a large number of Shias in its public sectors. (AJA, March 16, 2011a)

As clearly shown in the quotes above, the editors of AJA portrayed the Bahrain protest movement as having a "sectarian dimension" and that it is "founded based on a sectarian basis". This representation can significantly give credibility to the "sectarian narrative", adopted by the Bahraini regime.

The Al-Khalifa regime has tried to convince the Arabic public opinion that the protests were not part of the Arab Spring uprisings, but instead a societal Shia-Sunni conflict fuelled by Iran. For example, the Bahraini Foreign Minister Khalid bin Ahmad said on March 30, 2011, "We want to confirm to the world that we do not have a government-opposition problem, there is a clear sectarian issue in Bahrain, and there is a division in society" (BNA, 2011). The Crown Prince, Salman bin Hamad Al-Khalifa, stated on April 4, 2011, "There will be no lenience given to those who are trying to divide the country" (BNA, 2011).

The Al-Khalifa regime's use of sectarianism has always been the most trusted strategy to confront any political threats to their power (Jones, 2015). The same "survival tactic" has succeeded in portraying calls for democratisation in the 1990s as a "radical Shia agenda" (Fuller & Francke, 2001).

The regime has used the sectarian card to delegitimise the protest movement and deflect attention from its pro-democracy demands (Matthiesen, 2013; Wehrey, 2013). Moore-Gilbert (2016) argues that the Al-Khalifa regime has displayed the "classic divide-and-rule" policy to prevent a powerful and unified cross-sectarian opposition in Bahrain. Other scholars argue that associating the protesters with being Shia, and hence sympathetic somehow to Iran, has aided the regime's representation of itself as the "protector of Sunni populations" (Gengler, 2015, p. 9) while at the same time toning down the criticisms by the West against its repression of the protest movement (Ulrichsen, 2012).

The hostility between the GCC and Iran and its allies (Syria and Iraq) in the region has reinforced this "sectarian narrative" (Gengler, 2015, p. 9). Instead of uncovering the context and goals behind the regime's propaganda, AJA coverage has only strengthened it. Protesters have

150   Z. ABDUL-NABI

refused to be labelled as Shias and being associated with Iran. A representative of February 14 Youth Coalition (unpermitted opposition group founded in 2011 by mostly young activists) said:

> This is a big lie through which the Al-Khalifa regime seeks to mislead international public opinion at media and international forums as well as centres of decision making in order to distort the image of the legitimate revolution. This is in addition to the regime's media blackout on its sectarian and racist practices against all Bahraini citizens... How can it be called 'sectarian,' when the goal of the revolution is for all citizens, regardless of sect, whether Sunni or Shia, to become equal in their rights and duties. (Jones, 2015)

Analysis or quotes by the February 14 Youth Coalition never appeared in AJA's coverage during the research period. Table 5.6 will show that none of AJA-F quoted the unlicensed youth group and only 3.8% of its news reported this group. The absence or limited proportions of such accounts have led to further support of the "sectarian narrative" which—according to M. Lynch (2016)—has eventually succeeded in reshaping Arab public opinion about Bahrain's uprising.

Representation of Regime Crackdown as "Sectarian Clashes"
Shortly after the deployment of Saudi-led troops in the country, AJA referred to the regime's crackdown as "sectarian clashes". AJA stated in March and April 2011:

> Bahrain witnessed last February [2011] its worst sectarian clashes between the Shia majority and government security forces. (AJA, April 6, 2011g)

> Schools and universities have been shut down in order to prevent any sectarian clashes that have started to occur on a daily basis. (AJA, March 19, 2011c)

The examples above illustrate the regime's claims (sectarian clashes in streets and schools) as facts without mentioning the other side of the story. Amnesty International and Human Rights Watch (HRW) refuted these claims reporting that school and university students who participated in the protests and went on strike have been targeted, arrested and tortured by security forces. HRW (2011) documented on March 13, 2011, that masked, armed and plain-clothed men, accompanied by police officers, raided the University of Bahrain (UOB); attacked the student protesters with swords, knives and sticks and prevented ambulances from entering the campus. Dr. Michael Vaughn Diboll, a former professor at UOB, witnessed and documented what kind of "clashes" that took place in the university. The management of the university fired Diboll in June 2011, for revealing what happened and speaking up on social media. Diboll said in his testimony to the Bahrain Centre for Human Rights (2011):

> On the morning of March 13th 2011, Bahraini students protested peacefully on campus against the Bahraini regime. Soon after, the University of Bahrain was attacked by government-sponsored thugs and politically naturalised citizens. Students began posting videos of the unidentified thugs on YouTube, some of who were obviously non-students and each of them carrying a deadly weapon, vandalizing the university and putting lives of student demonstrators at risk. As students panicked the campus went from peaceful protests to chaos, leading to many injuries.

Hana Hussain, a former teacher at the Al-Ahad Al-Zaher Female Secondary School, witnessed how her students were arrested by security forces from the school for participating in the uprising in 2011. She says:

> Security forces raided the school and arrested teachers and students who participated in the protests. I saw some students being arrested while they were in the middle of doing their final exams. Other students were arrested from the school's public bus. The forces beat them in front of everyone. They abused the girls physically and sexually, swore at them, called them names, insulted their Shia belief... I was not able to save my own students, I felt so helpless. (H. Hussain, personal communication, May 16, 2016)

This side of the narrative was never mentioned on AJA. In another news story, AJA stated:

> A local newspaper has mentioned that two workers, one of them being Indian and the other one Bengali, were killed following sectarian clashes. (AJA, March 23, 2011e)

AJA continued to report what the regime claimed but did not mention what the activists said about the workers. According to opponents, the security forces killed the foreigners while firing indiscriminately at close range at protesters in Sitra, a Shia village.

The term "sectarian clashes" is consistently repeated during the coverage. According to AJA reports, the "sectarian clashes" caused the death of foreign workers and prevented students from attending school. One might infer that the protesters were possibly violent. Otherwise, how were the Indian and Bengali workers "killed" during the "sectarian clashes?" Who killed them? Why was the killer not mentioned? Machin and Mayr (2012) argue that the use of passive tense aims to "conceal responsibility". If the editors want to reveal who is behind an action, they will use active sentences.

The term "sectarian clashes" could also imply that both sides are equal. It could even mean that Shia protesters were colliding with Sunni people, as most of the news stories did not clarify that the "clashes" were between armed security forces and unarmed protesters. This "imbalance" between the two sides is not highlighted in the coverage. J. Lynch and Galtung (2010) suggest that if a conflict is between an occupier and occupied, slave owners and slaves, colonial subjects and colonial authorities and a brutal government and its own people, such structural imbalance should be reflected in media coverage. Galtung (2000, p. 163) says that in a "conflict between Soviet dissidents and Stalinists, I know on which side I stand…, I am willing to humanise all sides but I am not willing to legitimise all goals".

Representation of Bahraini Protesters as "Iranian Proxies"
In line with Al-Khalifa's depiction of protestors as "Iranian proxies", AJA-N&F (2.5% and 16.7%) have rarely contextualised Bahrain's pro-democracy movement as part of the Arab Spring uprisings (see Table 5.3). AJA-N&F also barely mentions the fact that there is no evidence that the protesters are supported by Iran (3.75% and 16.7%) (Table 5.3). This study observes that AJA's tendency to promote the Al-Khalifa regime's propaganda and narrative about Iran's threat was expressed more clearly in the features than in the news. For example, AJA-F stated in March 2011:

> Although some Shias deny having any relationship with Iran, journalistic reports have shed lights on the Iranian influence in the country. The relationship between Iranian and Bahraini Shias has reached a degree of cooperation that some Iranians have demanded that Bahrain be considered an Iranian province. The tension between the countries [Iran and Bahrain] peaked in 1996 when Bahrain's [government] disclosed a secret organisation named 'Hezbollah of Bahrain.' The authorities said that the organisa-

tion [whose members were trained in Tehran], aimed at overthrowing the Bahraini government. (AJA, March 16, 2011b)

Using the verb "deny" when quoting Shias and "declare" when referring to Bahrain's regime can show exactly how certain choices of quoting verbs can make editors' "ideology" explicit (Machin & Mayr, 2012). According to Caldas-Coulthard (1994), the verb "declare" is one of the "meta-propositional verbs" which can "mark the author's interpretation of a speaker". Moreover, Volynets (2013) classifies "declare" as an "introduction verb" that "introduce[s] factual information produced by respectable sources", whereas "deny" is a "disagreement verb" which implies "a critical response to another source or position the author is advancing". In other words, AJA represents the Shia population's refusal to acknowledge the allegation that they have an influential relationship with Iran as a "claim". Yet, it portrays the regime's "disclosure" of a secret cell that is "trained by Iran" as a "fact".

The Bahrain Independent Commission of Inquiry (BICI), which was appointed by the King to investigate human rights violations that occurred in February and March 2011, concluded that there was no evidence of Iranian intervention. When BICI (2011, p. 387) asked the Bahraini authorities to provide more information about Iran's involvement in its internal affairs, they declined to share their intelligence findings "due to security and confidentiality considerations". A highly classified United States (US) cable released by WikiLeaks revealed that Bahrain's accusations around the threat that Iran posed and its support to protesters were baseless (Black, 2011). In that cable, the US embassy in Bahrain wrote, "To date, we have seen no convincing evidence of Iranian weapons or government money here since at least the mid-1990s. If the GOB (Government of Bahrain) had convincing evidence of more recent Iranian subversion, it would quickly share it with us" (Black, 2011).

Neglecting the Peaceful Struggle in Bahrain
AJA-N&F hardly mentions the peaceful aspect of Bahrain's uprising (1.2% and 0%) (as shown earlier in Table 5.3) despite the fact that the Arabic word "*Silmiyya* /سلمية [peaceful]" dominated the scene, banners, slogans and chants of protestors in 2011. Bahrainis emulated the Egyptian protesting style as they—after long discussions between members of the popular online forum, BahrainOnline.com—selected the Pearl Roundabout as a location for their sit-in protest (M. Lynch, 2016). The protestors set up

154   Z. ABDUL-NABI

tents at the Pearl Roundabout in the capital Manama, or what they would later call "Pearl Square", named after "Tahrir Square" during the Egyptian protests (M. Lynch, 2016). Ali Salman, the head of *Al-Wefaq*, the largest Shia opposition group, said, "Bahrainis shared the Egyptian and Tunisian demands for peaceful change" (M. Lynch, 2016). Bhatia and Shehabi (2015, p. 94) argue that the Bahrain uprising is the "most steadfast and longest standing peaceful movement" in the Arab world. Even though there was a sophisticated crackdown by the Bahraini authorities, banning all sorts of gatherings and targeting, arresting and torturing activists, Bahrainis continued to protest on a daily basis (Bhatia & Shehabi, 2015).

Although opponents in Bahrain are divided between demanding the "downfall of the regime" and "political reform", both sides are adherent to peaceful methods of demonstration and non-violent activism (Bhatia & Shehabi, 2015, p. 122). Ibrahim Sharif, a Sunni opponent and the head of a secular opposition group *Waad* (who was arrested and tortured on March 17, 2011, for his political activities), said:

> Inspired by the other Arab uprisings, our youth proved its connection to the wider Arab nation and its determination to use peaceful protest to force the regime into comprehensive reform. Instead of throwing them in jails and detention centres, the government should have engaged in dialogue with these young Bahrainis, who continued to use peaceful means despite the use of arms against them. (2015, p. 46)

This degree of commitment to peaceful methods especially in the early stages of the uprising has been ignored by AJA. J. Lynch and Galtung (2010) state that the media tend to neglect covering non-violent struggles. They simply "don't see them even if they are unfolding right before their eyes" (J. Lynch & Galtung, 2010, p. 59). For example, the "heroic" peaceful demonstrations in Leipzig, in the former German Democratic Republic in 1989, were largely underreported (J. Lynch & Galtung, 2010). Focusing on non-violent struggles reinforces protesters' devotion to peaceful means of protest (J. Lynch and Galtung, 2010), whereas ignoring these movements encourages its members to "turn to terror in order to make a difference in the media agenda" (Nohrstedt & Ottosen, 2008, p. 13). Galtung (2000) argues that inattention is the main reason behind violence. He elaborates:

5 BAHRAIN'S UPRISING: PRO-DEMOCRACY PROTESTS OR SECTARIAN... 155

So let me formulate it as a thesis: in a conflict you stand for something, you yearn for it but you have a feeling that there is something—whatever it may be—that makes it impossible for others to listen to it; you have a voice but they don't have an ear and whatever you say is twisted into unrecognition, and if you experience that over a period of let us say fifty years you may become tired and you may get the feeling that it doesn't matter the slightest, and you may just as well get violent because that seems to be the only language they understand. (Galtung, 2000, p. 162)

5.3.3 AJA: Implications of Excluding the Truth- and Solution-Orientated Frames

Concealing the Sectarian Narrative of the Regime
Categorising protesters as "Shia" and framing their protests as a "sectarian movement" that is influenced by Iran meant that AJA did not focus on the sectarianism narrative employed by the regime. AJA-N&F never mentioned that the regime has been granting Bahraini citizenships on a predominately sectarian basis to change the demographic majority of the country (Table 5.3). Reports state that the regime naturalised 8000–10,000 Sunnis from Pakistan, Jordan, Syria and Yemen during the 1990s (Jones, 2015). The percentage of this sectarian naturalisation increased from 6% in 1935 to 50% in 2015 (Jones, 2015). Shias are currently excluded from employment in the Ministry of Interior and the Ministry of Defence. Most of the new naturalised citizens, however, have been employed as "security forces" and officers at these Ministries (Jones, 2015). Salah Al-Bandar, a former adviser to the Minister of Cabinet Affairs, disclosed a secret plan that aims to "manipulate the country's sectarian balance and ensure Sunni domination over the country's majority Shias" (Jones, 2015, p. 106).

AJA-N&F barely mention the criteria of the Truth-Orientated frame. The criteria of this frame include three facts[3] that highlight the sectarian

---

[3] Analytical criteria of the Truth-Orientated frame

1. (SFV): Does the article mention the human rights violations committed by the Bahraini security forces or by the regime in general?
2. (PSFV): Does the article mention the role of the GCC troops in the crackdown or the violations they committed?
3. (DSM): Does the article mention that Shia religious structures and mosques were demolished during the pro-democracy movement in 2011? Or does the article mention any sectarian acts/abuses committed by the regime and/or its forces?

156   Z. ABDUL-NABI

measures and human rights violations committed by the Bahraini regime against the protesters. None of the AJA-F and only 3.57% of its news stories focus on the regime's sectarian abuses (see Table 5.4). These include such acts as demolishing Shia mosques, forced resignations of Shia protesters from their jobs after participating in a general strike and demonising and accusing protesters of being traitors and agents of Iran and Hezbollah.

When AJA covered Obama's speech about the Arab Spring on May 19, 2011, it reported everything he said about Bahrain's protests except his criticisms on the destruction of Shia mosques. The following part of Obama's speech was omitted from AJA's coverage on May 20, 2011:

> And for this season of change to succeed, Coptic Christians must have the right to worship freely in Cairo, just as Shia must never have their mosques destroyed in Bahrain. (White House, 2011)

AJA-N&F never covered the demolitions of Shia places of worships as a "fact" during the research period. It was mentioned as an "accusation" once during the whole coverage. AJA stated in April 2011:

> The participants of a rally that took place after Friday's prayers have accused Saudi troops of demolishing mosques/Hussaineyas,[4] and violations against Shia institutions. They chanted slogans against Peninsula Shield Forces (PSF) troops and demanded their departure. (AJA, April 23, 2011h)

Table 5.4 Percentage of including/mentioning the Truth-Orientated criteria in AJA's coverage of Bahrain's uprising

Truth-Orientated Frame				
Truth-Orientated Criteria	(SFV) Security Forces Violations	(PSFV) PSF Violations	(DSM) Demolishing Shia Mosques	(Total) Truth-Orientated Frame
AJA (80) News stories	70%	7.5%	3.75%	(27.1%)
AJA (6) Features	50%	0%	0%	(16.7%)

---

[4] Shia places of worship.

The regime justified destroying Shia mosques because they did not conform to "building regulations" (although most of them were built many years before). In an interview with *The Washington Times* newspaper, Professor M. Cherif Bassiouni (who was appointed by the King Sheikh Hamad bin Isa Al-Khalifa to lead the investigation of BICI) considers the regime's justification as "stupid" (Birnbaum, 2011). Jones (2015) argues that the regime demolished Shia mosques deliberately to inflame sectarian tensions. BICI (2011) describes the demolitions as "collective punishment" against Shias.

When asked about the reasons behind not reporting the demolitions, Bahrain's AJA online reporter said that he covered it but "not everything gets published". Mahfood[5] further reveals:

> I wrote about it but AJA did not publish my story. The demolitions were shocking to AJA's management. No one expected that the government would go that far. They didn't publish it because the topic was very sensitive. Let's face it, Al-Jazeera is a Qatari channel that is based in a GCC country [ally with Bahrain], so there are limitations on what we can write. I cannot write everything; I have to censor myself at times so I can guarantee that I will not be suspended. I hate it when editors change my own story, so I do omit what they do not like, just to protect it from being damaged. (personal communication, January 26, 2016)

This is completely in line with Shoemaker and Reese's (2013) argument that reporters recognise their boundaries and limitations by the way editors change their stories. They add that journalists prefer self-censorship based on "unwritten policies" rather than having it changed by editors.

Concealing the Implications of Sectarianism

The criteria of the Solution-Orientated frame were hardly mentioned in AJA-N (13.1%) and never mentioned in the features (0%) (see Table 5.5).

---

[5] Some interviews in this chapter were conducted/published by the author and reproduced (from the article: Al-Jazeera's relationship with Qatar before and after Arab Spring: Effective public diplomacy or blatant propaganda?) with permission from the *Arab Media & Society* journal.

158   Z. ABDUL-NABI

These criteria include two facts[6] that focus on potential solution/peace initiatives and the after-effects of sectarian violations. Table 5.5 illustrates that the implications of these sectarian acts were rarely reported by AJA-N&F (3.75% and 0%) although they virtually affected "every corner of public life" (Wehrey, 2013, p. 216). Moore-Gilbert (2016) argues that the Al-Khalifa regime's divide-and-rule policy affected Bahraini society to such an extent that the opposition may not be able to find a cross-sectarian opposition movement again that is similar to the ones that emerged in the 1950s, 1970s and 1990s.

Reporting the Regime's Violation and Torture as "Claims"
As shown previously in Table 5.4, only 7.5% of the news and none of the features in AJA focused on the violations carried out by the Saudi-led troops. High percentages of AJA-N&F (70% and 50%), however, mentioned the abuses committed by the Bahraini regime during the first three months of the uprising (Table 5.4). This study observes that editors generally used passive tense and ambiguous language when referring to the regime's wrongdoings. Many violations that have been documented by HRW and Amnesty International were reported as "claims" and "accusations". To cite examples, AJA stated in March and May 2011:

Table 5.5 Percentage of including/mentioning the Solution-Orientated criteria in AJA's coverage of Bahrain's uprising

Solution-Orientated frame			
Solution-Orientated Criteria	(ISA) Implications of Sectarian Acts	(PS) Possible Solution	(Total) Solution-Orientated frame
AJA (80) News stories	3.75%	22.5%	(13.1%)
AJA (6) Features	0%	0%	(0%)

[6] Analytical criteria of the Solution-Orientated frame:

1. (ISA): Does the article mention the implications of deploying Saudi troops? Or does the article mention the implications of demolishing Shia mosques or the political naturalisation process?
2. (PS): Does the article give any possible solution/initiative from any source to break the deadlock and de-escalate the conflict?

5 BAHRAIN'S UPRISING: PRO-DEMOCRACY PROTESTS OR SECTARIAN... 159

The opposition has accused the local authorities of killing three people while dispersing protesters today, in the capital city. (AJA, March 16, 2011a)

A report, released by Reuters states that a human rights group, based in the US, says that a prominent activist was apparently tortured in detention. (AJA, May 12, 2011j)

Two journalists, Karim Fakhrawi, founder of the opposition newspaper Al-Awasat, and Zakariya Al-Asheri, writer at the same newspaper, died in prison under mysterious circumstances. (AJA, May 22, 2011k)

From the examples above, it can be clearly established that "torture" against participants in Bahrain's uprising was represented as a contested allegation. In regard to the third example, Al-Asheri, 40, and Karim, 49, did not die under "mysterious circumstances" as the article claimed. Amnesty (2016) documented that they were arrested in April 2011 and tortured to death by security forces. At the time, thousands of aggravated protesters took to the street and participated in their funeral, despite the heavy crackdown. Activists took photos of the victims' bodies while they were washed and prepared for burial in the cemetery.[7] The images blatantly show fresh marks and signs of torture. The images were circulated and shared widely on social media. A PJ approach would include these accounts in media coverage and would not use vague terms (like "mysterious circumstances") that could cover up violations and exonerate the wrongdoers.

5.3.4 AJA: Implications of Including Official Sources and Excluding the Marginalised

Reporting "Claims" as "Facts": Protesters' Occupation
of Salmaniya Hospital
The People-Orientated criteria, which focuses on the voice of the voiceless and their demands, include three facts.[8] These were significantly sidelined

---

[7] Washing dead bodies in the cemetery is part of Islamic funeral and burial procedures.
[8] Analytical criteria of People-Orientated frame:

1. (DRD): Does the article mention that there are voices in Bahrain demanding the downfall of the regime?
2. (VV): Does the article give voice to civilians, ordinary people or victims?
3. (SC): Does the article mention the suffering that the crackdown caused?

in the AJA-N&F. More specifically, the People-Orientated frame was never applied in the AJA-F and recorded only 5.4% in the news of the channel (see Table 5.6).

The marginalisation of the People-Orientated frame and domination of Bahraini official sources in AJA-N (44%)—as shown in Table 5.7—have helped promote the narrative of the regime. This study further observes that AJA represented the "claims" stated by these officials as "facts" without reviewing their statements or quoting alternative accounts.

Although AJA published a news story on March 25, 2011, under the title "Tens of protesters injured in Bahrain", it did not include the views of the protesters. The article was full of allegations by officials on how "protesters occupied the main hospital in Bahrain [*Salmaniya* Hospital]" and "beat up hospitalised patients". The editor wrote/copied officials' statements that were released by the Bahrain National Agency (BNA) without adding any background or other accounts that could challenge the regime's propaganda and narrative. The article stated:

> Minister of Social Development, Dr. Fatima Mohamed Baluchi adds that 'protesters occupied the Salmaniya Medical Complex (SMC), beat up hospitalised patients, attacked ambulances and used them to transfer weapons'. (AJA, March 25, 2011f)

The side of this story that was omitted was that the Saudi troops and Bahraini soldiers were the ones who seized and occupied *Salmaniya*

Table 5.6 Percentage of including/mentioning the People-Orientated criteria in AJA's coverage of Bahrain's uprising

People-Orientated frame			
People-Orientated Criteria	(DRD) Downfall of the Regime Demand	(VV) Voice of Voiceless	(SC) Suffering caused by the Crackdown	(Total) People-Orientated frame
AJA (80) News stories	5%	5%	6.25%	(5.4%)
AJA (6) Features	0%	0%	0%	(0%)

Hospital, arresting and preventing the injured protesters from getting treatment (HRW, 2011). HRW (2011) said that Bahraini security forces beat up medics and attacked ambulances transporting injured people in order to prevent them from reaching hospitals. Physicians for Human Rights (PHR) (which came to Bahrain in April 2011) documented how medical staff were attacked and arrested when leaving the operating rooms. It also described in detail how injured protesters were "dragged from their beds" and tortured by forces and soldiers that spoke "with a Saudi accent" (PHR, 2011). On March 30, HRW (2011) released a statement appealing to "stop targeting patients injured in protests". The statement said:

> Security and military forces have sought out and threatened, beaten and detained patients injured by teargas, rubber bullets, birdshot pellets, and live ammunition. These patients also have been removed from hospitals or forcibly transferred to other medical facilities, often against medical advice. (HRW, 2011)

Reporting "Claims" as Facts: Iranian-Backed Terror Cells

AJA's coverage consistently conveys regime allegations of Iran's "military training" to Shias and "Iranian/Hezbollah-backed terror cells", without counterbalancing their coverage with alternative accounts. For example, AJA stated:

> Minister of Public Information and the Minister of Shura Council Affairs Isa bin Abdul-Rahman Al-Hamadi said that the authorities have discovered that terrorists received their orders from Tehran and depend morally, technically and logistically on Iranian support. (AJA, October 20, 2015)

> Bahrain's Foreign Minister Khalid bin Ahmed Al-Khalifa said that his country would not tolerate the threats of Hezbollah. The "terrorists" [Hezbollah] have organised training for some of the "provocateur's" [Bahraini opposition leaders] and we know that they have participated in them. (AJA, March 23, 2011e)

> Bahrain Ministry of Foreign Affairs has warned its citizens not to travel to Lebanon and advised those who are in Lebanon to leave the country immediately. Bahrain News Agency said, due to the terrorists' [Hezbollah] threats and their intervention [in Bahrain], the Ministry advises its citizens not to travel to the Republic of Lebanon. (AJA, March 23, 2011e)

As shown in the quotes above, the Bahraini regime's claims about "discovering terrorism cells" backed by Iran and Hezbollah were simply taken from news wires and reported as facts. A PJ approach would mention the context and background of such allegations. It also should explain how the regime has accused pro-democracy activists of committing acts of "terrorism" and "hooliganism" since 1965 (Khalaf, 2015, p. 147). It would also indicate how the same pretexts (the alleged involvement of Bahraini protesters in "terrorism cells") were used by the regime in the 1980s and 1990s to justify quelling the protest movements in the country (Fuller & Francke, 2001). Nash (2016) argues that journalism is like history, as both are more than just facts and textual narrative. They are instead "the moment of contemporary significance where the present and the past are created as meaningful in relation to each other" (Nash, 2016, p. 225).

After the deployment of GCC troops and the escalation of the crackdown in March 2011, the authorities arrested 13 prominent opposition leaders and subjected them to severe torture (Bhatia & Shehabi, 2015). These opposition figures have been sentenced to life in prison for "founding a terror cell" and "plotting to overthrow the regime" (Bhatia & Shehabi, 2015). Many activists who were already in exile during 2011 uprising were charged of taking part in "terror activities" and tried in absentia (Horne, 2015, p. 188). Dr. Saeed Shehabi, a prominent activist and head of Bahrain Freedom Movement which is based in London, is continually accused of being a founder of these cells. Shehabi stated:

> Terrorism did not exist in Bahrain and it does not exist. It is only in the minds of the royal family. Terrorism is when you speak your mind and oppose the regime... I have been implicated in every single terror cell since 2001, with people I have never met, and never heard of. I am always the mastermind of the plot, named at the top of some fictional organisational structure, of course aligned with Hezbollah and supported by Iran, and always with all the headlines 'MoI [Ministry of Interior] has uncovered a cell'. (Holman, 2015, p. 200)

Such quotes never appeared on AJA during the research period. The Arabic channel never included activists' views despite the fact that they are approachable and active on social media. Only 3.8% of the news broadcast delivered the views of activists who belonged to unlicensed opposition groups (Table 5.7). Recognising and quoting marginalised opponents or implementing what Howard (2002) called "mediatised recognition"

5 BAHRAIN'S UPRISING: PRO-DEMOCRACY PROTESTS OR SECTARIAN... 163

could facilitate reconciliation and integration between conflicting groups. However, Herman and Chomsky (2010, p. 29) explain that such voices are usually avoided by the media because they are not in line with the "ideology or interests of the gatekeepers and other powerful parties that influence the filtering process".

Regime Manipulation
AJA's coverage of the regime's claims over the "protesters' occupation of *Salmaniya* Hospital" and "Iranian-backed cells" demonstrates how statements by regime officials can effectively manipulate the news, impose their own agenda and divert media attention to their desired direction (Herman & Chomsky, 2010). It demonstrates how officials deliberately flood media outlets with "facts" that "help chase unwanted stories off the front page or out of the media altogether" (Herman & Chomsky, 2010, p.21). This study observes that AJA considered Bahraini officials' accounts as "factual" (Fishman, 1988) without reviewing their statements or practising what PJ calls "reflexivity" (J. Lynch, 2014a). This kind of coverage has turned AJA's editors into channels for official propaganda. Hoijer et al. (2002, p. 4) argue that:

> The media are subject to massive propaganda from the parties involved, and are often without their own knowledge representing the necessary link between the propaganda machinery and the audience. If they are not aware

Table 5.7 Quoted sources in AJA's coverage of Bahrain's uprising

Quoted sources	AJA (80) News stories	AJA (6) Features
Unauthorised Opposition	7 (3.8%)	0 (0%)
Authorised Opposition	33 (18%)	2 (66.7%)
Bahraini Officials	82 (44.8%)	0 (0%)
AJ Reporter	1 (0.5%)	0 (0%)
Activists or Human Rights Organisations (HRO)	51 (27.9%)	1 (33.3%)
Victims/Civilians	9 (5%)	0 (0%)

of this potential role themselves, the danger of playing a role as a catalyst for propaganda will be even greater. (cited in J. Lynch, 2007, p. 3)

Officials are always privileged in coverage because media workers take bureaucratic sources seriously and consider them as "competent knowers" that provide "hard facts" (Fishman, 1988). Moreover, what makes media reporting more vulnerable to their propaganda is that "objective journalists" deliver statements by officials as they are, without including context or fact-checking, to avoid being perceived as "biased" (Shoemaker & Reese, 2013). Fishman (1988) explains that journalists are not "detectives" or "social workers" as they rely only on the interview method to gather their "facts". That is why including PJ characteristics[9] is increasingly crucial to prevent media coverage from being dominated and manipulated by what J. Lynch (2014b) calls "officials' garbage".

5.3.5 AJA: Pro-Qatar and GCC Framing

In addition to promoting Al-Khalifa's sectarian propaganda and sidelining voices that demanded the downfall of the regime (as shown previously in Table 5.6), the majority of AJA-N&F (47.6% and 100%) legitimised the Saudi military intervention of the country (see Table 5.8). The coverage did not highlight their role in cracking down on protesters and carrying out sectarian-oriented violations (PHR, 2011). All the GCC countries endorsed sending the Saudi-led soldiers into Bahrain, including Qatar who did not want to challenge Saudi Arabia[10] (which considers Bahrain as part of its sovereignty) (Friedman, 2012).

The data above confirms that Qatar's reluctance to oppose Saudi Arabia in 2011 was reflected in Al-Jazeera's legitimisation of the presence of the Saudi-led troops in Bahrain during the uprising.

An anchor for AJA, Lina Zahr Al-Deen, resigned from the channel in 2009 and said in her book "*Al-Jazeera is not the End of the Journey*" (2010) that the AJA editors are not allowed to publish any news story about Saudi

---

[9] As explained thoroughly in the introduction chapter, PJ characteristics include (1) explaining contexts/background/history/reasons of conflicts, (2) quoting people and marginalised accounts, (3) uncovering propaganda and (4) highlighting implications of conflicts and possible solutions.

[10] The relationship between Qatar and Saudi Arabia, the United Arab Emirates (UAE) and Bahrain was not as strained in 2011 as they are since 2017 when these Gulf States cut diplomatic ties with Doha.

5 BAHRAIN'S UPRISING: PRO-DEMOCRACY PROTESTS OR SECTARIAN... 165

Table 5.8 Pro- and anti-Qatar framing in AJA's coverage of Bahrain's uprising

Pro/Anti Qatar Framing in the:	Pro-Qatar Framing	Anti-Qatar Framing	Neutral
AJA News 21 news stories out of 80 mentioned the reasons behind the GCC troop deployment.	10 articles 47.6%	6 articles 28.6%	5 articles 23.8%
AJA Features 1 feature out of 6 mentioned the reason behind the GCC troop deployment	1 article 100 %	0%	0%

Arabia without consulting with the (former) managing director, Wadhah Khanfar. She reveals that the management classifies Saudi matters and news as "sensitive". In consistency with Zahr Al-Deen, Samuel-Azran's (2013) empirical content analysis covering eight years of AJA's reporting found that the channel toned down its coverage of Saudi affairs after Qatar and Riyadh signed an agreement in 2007. Zahr Al-Deen criticises AJA's coverage of Bahrain's uprising and describes the channel as "Qatar's mouthpiece" (Haddad, 2011).

AJA's coverage of Bahrain and Syria has led to a series of resignations among well-known anchors and reporters such as Ghassan bin Jeddo, former head of Al-Jazeera's Beirut bureau; Ali Hashem, AJA's reporter in Lebanon; and Aktham Suliman, AJA's reporter in Germany, all of whom resigned in 2011. Bin Jeddo says in an interview with Russia Today (RT):

> I do believe that Al-Jazeera and other channels were not balanced in dealing with the events. For instance, with respect to the events in Syria and Bahrain, we started to invite guests from America who only criticised the regime in Syria and supported the regime in Bahrain, and persons who justified NATO intervention [in Libya]. This was unacceptable. (RT, 2012)

Hashem (2012) wrote in *The Guardian* newspaper after his resignation, "It was clear that Gulf-financed stations were more interested in regional security than Bahrainis' dreams of democracy and freedom, and their revolt against tyranny". However, the former managing director of the Al-Jazeera network, Wadah Khanfar, disagrees entirely with this analysis. He said in an interview (conducted by the author) that other "bigger" revolutions were taking place during Bahrain's uprising, and hence there were other "priorities". The former director elaborates:

Bahrain is a case which has been complicated for both Arabic and English channels. Why? When the Bahrain uprising was taking place, during the same period, we have the revolutions taking place or big revolutions taking place in Egypt, in Libya, in Yemen and so on. So, with the weight of the story of Bahrain, if you have one hour to define your priorities during this one hour, you would give Bahrain much less coverage of course. Then give, for example [the rest of the coverage] to Egypt. Egypt was the major story, or Libya, or Yemen. And besides that, we do not really have access. And I remember that our chief correspondent was kicked out from Bahrain. (W. Khanfar, personal communication, March 16, 2017)

The reasons behind the criticisms of the Bahrain coverage are not predominately about quantity, frequency and the prominence of Bahrain's news compared to other uprisings in the region. They are instead about the framing and representation of the protest movement and protesters compared to others. AJA's reporter in Bahrain, Mahfood (personal communication, January 26, 2016) reveals that he was restricted by the channel's editorial policy. He understood the "unwritten rules" of not criticising the Saudi military intervention and its violations. Consequently, he had to write in his news stories and features that Saudi troops were sent to Bahrain to "protect public facilities, maintain security, and restore order". He was personally convinced, however, that they were deployed to "quell protesters" (H. Mahfood, personal communication, January 26, 2016). He reveals:

> Editorial policy sometimes determines what terms I use and how I refer to certain events. I know that if I don't use certain phrases, they [editors] would use them so I would rather use them myself, so they do not change my own story. There is an editorial policy; we have to be realistic. Qatar did not want to damage its relations with the GCC countries... AJA is very careful when dealing with the news that relates to the Gulf states. Qatar is part of GCC, and it does not want to take a unilateral foreign policy in regard to Bahrain. (H. Mahfood, personal communication, January 26, 2016)

The findings of this study together with Mahfood's revelation reflect the great extent of Qatar's involvement in AJA's editorial policy and illustrate that the interests of media owners have an "unmistakable impact on media content" (Shoemaker & Reese, 2013, p. 163). The above demonstrates the importance of what Herman and Chomsky (2010) argue: that emphasis, inclusions, exclusions, framings of issues and tones are all selected based on the needs of governments and powers.

5.3.6 Can PJ Still Be Implemented in AJA?

Through analysing AJA-N&F, this study observes that some articles have a different tone and percentages of PJ criteria than others. Unlike the overall sectarian framing of AJA, Mahfood's articles tended to avoid associating protesters with their Shi'ism. His articles also include more details, context, background and a variety of sources including ordinary people. In an article published on May 31, 2011, Mahfood linked the 2011 pro-democracy movement to the 1990s uprising. He attributed the reasons behind the previous and current protests to unemployment, a lack of freedom and political reforms.

Another reporter, Awadh Rajoob, stated in a feature published on March 16, 2011 (just two days after the crackdown of the Saudi-led troops), that "the sectarian factor" and "the sectarian-orientated opposition" have been the main reasons behind the "instability" in the country in the 1990s and 2011. Although both journalists work at the same channel and are restrained by the same editorial policy, their representation of the "reasons" behind the "protests" or "instability" in the country during the 1990s and 2011 were entirely different. Mahfood's reporting can be seen as a "scattered opposition" which stands against the dominant framing, but it is still not strong enough to challenge it (Entman, 2003). Some might argue, however, that this "little dissent" might have been strategically allowed by AJA to gain credibility and "influence public opinion in the desired direction" (Herman & Chomsky, 2010, p. XII). Mahfood's distinct style of reporting was consistent during the whole research period which proves that "some journalists" in "some conflicts" practise PJ more than others (J. Lynch, 2014a).

Several studies concluded that the background and political association of journalists can influence—positively as well as negatively—their tendency to apply PJ orientations in their coverage (Siraj, 2008; Onyebadi & Oyedeji, 2011; Hussain & Rehman, 2015; Hussain, 2016). Hackett (2006) argues that while journalists have a limited space to create some change, the institutional framework of media will not enable them to fully implement PJ orientations. Some media scholars suggest that journalists can have greater influence on media coverage (Chang & Lee, 1992), whereas others consider "individuals" as one of four other factors that determine media content: (1) media routines, (2) media organisations, (3) social institutions and (4) social system/ideology (Shoemaker & Reese, 2013).

In their proposed model "Hierarchy of Influences", Shoemaker and Reese (2013) conclude that the social system layer or what they call "the base of the cake" can significantly affect media organisations, values of individuals, media routines and social institutions. Therefore, "decisions are not only made at the whim of the individuals" (Shoemaker & Reese, 2013). Tehranian (2002, p. 18) argues that journalists tend to be "moral", but they are confined by two major restrictions: government and commercial structures of ownership and control. These limitations are manifested in Mahfood's reporting, as he unveils that he omitted the main reasons behind the deployment of Saudi troops (supressing protesters) and sectarian acts (demolishing Shia mosques) committed by the Al-Khalifa regime (personal communication, January 26, 2016).

5.4 AJE Coverage of Bahrain's Protests: Quantitative Analysis

5.4.1 AJE: Implications of Applying the Peace-, Solution- and Truth-Orientated Frames

Less Sectarian Framing of Bahrain's Conflict and Protesters
Similar to AJA, very limited percentages of the N&F of AJE referred to Bahrain's pro-democracy movement as an "uprising" (3.8% and 10%) or revolution (1.1% and 0%) (see Table 5.9). Additionally, more than 50% of the coverage framed the movement as merely "protests" (Table 5.9) and portrayed the pro-democracy opponents as "protesters" (Table 5.10). At the same time, more than a third of the AJE's news referred to them as "Shia protesters" (Table 5.10).

Although one third of the AJE coverage described the protesters as "Shias" (as shown above in Table 5.10), the channel's application of the Peace-Orientated criteria, which explains the history of marginalisation of the Shia majority by the Al-Khalifa regime, has notably made the coverage less sectarian than AJA. Displaying these criteria has lessened the sectarian framing, as AJE has been able to provide a solid context of "why" Shias dominated the protests. For instance, 55.3% of the news and 66.7% of the features mentioned that Shias made up the majority of the population (see

5 BAHRAIN'S UPRISING: PRO-DEMOCRACY PROTESTS OR SECTARIAN... 169

Table 5.9 Framing of Bahrain's conflict in AJE's coverage

Conflict framing	AJE-news	AJE-features
Uprising	7 (3.8%)	2 (10%)
Revolution	2 (1.1%)	0 (0%)
Conflict	0 (0%)	0 (0%)
Crisis/unrest/turmoil	20 (11%)	1 (5%)
Protests	100 (54.9%)	14 (70%)
Peaceful protest/movement	5 (2.7%)	2 (10%)
Pro-democracy or anti-government movement	48 (26.4%)	1(5%)

Table 5.10 Framing of the protesters in AJE's coverage of Bahrain's uprising

Protesters' framing	AJE news	AJE features
Protesters/opposition/demonstrators/opponents	127 (58.8%)	17 (94.4%)
Pro-democracy or anti-government protesters	18 (8.3%)	1 (5.6%)
Shia protesters/Shia opposition/Shia-led protests	66 (30.6%)	0 (0%)
Peaceful protesters	5 (2.3%)	0 (0%)
Revolutionaries	0 (0%)	0 (0%)

Table 5.11). Furthermore, 23.7% of the news and 66.7% of the features stated that Shias have been discriminated against by the regime (see Table 5.11).

While terms like "sectarian clashes" still appeared in AJE, a significant amount of coverage explained the context, reasons of the conflict and structural violence (discrimination) against Shias. AJE stated in April and May 2011:

> In Bahrain, where a Sunni minority monopolises political power, the government has cast the popular revolt in a sectarian light, arguing that the Shia-led opposition movement is being supported by Iran and Hezbollah. (AJE, April 24, 2011d)
>
> Shias make up about 70 per cent of the population in the Kingdom ruled by a 200-year-old Sunni dynasty, but are largely excluded from top government and security posts. (AJE, May 17, 2011i)

Unlike AJA, AJE mentions that there were Sunnis protesting along with Shias at the beginning of the uprising. Highlighting this fact in the

Table 5.11   Percentage of including/mentioning the Peace/Conflict-Orientated criteria in AJE's coverage of Bahrain's uprising

Peace/Conflict-Orientated frame

Peace/ Conflict-Orientated criteria	*(HB) Historical background*	*(AS) Arab Spring*	*(SM) Shia majority*	*(SD) Shia discrimination*	*(SSU) Shia-Sunni unity*	*(US5) US 5TH fleet*	*(PSF) Peninsula Shield Force*	*(SIR) Saudi-Iranian rivalry*	*(PN) Political naturalisation*	*(Total) Peace/ Conflict frame*
AJE (38) News stories	5.3%	26.3%	55.3%	23.7%	0%	39.5%	73.7%	21.1%	0%	(27.2%)
AJE (3) Features	0%	100%	66.7%	66.7%	0%	66.7%	100%	0%	0%	(44.4%)

coverage effectively refutes the Al-Khalifa's sectarian narrative and propaganda. AJE stated in May 2011:

> He [AJE's reporter] said Al-Jazeera found it very difficult to find Sunni voices since the crackdown began in mid-March. 'A lot of the sympathisers who were pushing for reform from the Sunni side have gone into hiding, seemingly very intimidated by the crackdown,' our correspondent added. 'It is important to recognise that before the crackdown on the roundabout there were sizable demonstrations by the Sunni population'. (AJE, May 14, 2011g)

On May 15, 2011, AJE referred to the head of *Waad* Party (the largest liberal association in the country), Ibrahim Sharif, as "Sunni". This could imply that the protest movement was not dominated by Shias and that some Sunnis were part of the pro-democracy uprising. In contrast, AJA (which usually associates opposition groups with being "Shia") never introduced Sharif as "Sunni" although he was mentioned 11 times in AJA during the research period.

A significant percentage of AJE features (33.3%) covered the sectarian measures implemented by the Al-Khalifa regime against the protesters during the uprising (see Table 5.12). Unlike AJA, AJE reported the demolition of Shia mosques as a "fact", attributing the responsibility to the regime directly. As shown below in Table 5.12, AJE did not shy away from naming the wrongdoers. The Truth-Orientated frame recorded high percentages in the N&F of the channel (39.5% and 44.4%).

For example, AJE stated in March and April 2011:

> The Bahraini government has destroyed a number of mosques in continuation of its aggressive crackdown on pro-democracy protesters, a special Al-Jazeera investigation has revealed. (AJE, March 14, 2011g)
>   Meanwhile, the authorities have demolished many Shia places of prayer and old mosques, saying they were built without authorisation. (AJE, April 27, 2011e)

Along with focusing on the Al-Khalifa's sectarian directives, a relatively high percentage of AJE features (33.3%) went that extra mile and covered the implications of such acts (see Table 5.13). Table 5.13 shows that more than 15% of the N&F of AJE applied the criteria of the Solution-Orientated frame which focuses on proposed solutions as well as the implications of the regime's sectarian policies.

172   Z. ABDUL-NABI

Table 5.12 Percentage of including/mentioning the Truth-Orientated criteria in AJE's coverage of Bahrain's uprising

Truth-Orientated frame in the:

Truth-Orientated criteria	*(SFV) Security forces violations*	*(PSFV) PSF violations*	*(DSM) Demolishing Shia mosques*	*(Total) Truth-Orientated frame*
AJE (38) News stories	92.1%	15.8%	10.5%	(39.5%)
AJE (3) Features	100%	0%	33.3%	(44.4%)

Table 5.13 Percentage of including/mentioning the Solution-Orientated criteria in AJE's coverage of Bahrain's uprising

Solution-Orientated frame in the:

Solution-Orientated criteria	*(ISA) Implications of sectarian acts*	*(PS) Possible solution*	*(Total) Solution-Orientated frame*
AJE (38) News stories	2.6%	28.9%	(15.8%)
AJE (3) Features	33.3%	0%	(16.7%)

5.4.2   AJE: Implications of Applying the People-Orientated Frame

Giving Voice to the Voiceless

It is clear from this analysis that AJA marginalised unlicensed opposition groups and quoted elite sources and pro-Bahraini regime sources more frequently than other sources. On the contrary, AJE-N&F were notably dominated by quotations by activists and human rights organisations (36.8% and 60%) as shown below (Table 5.14).

The criteria of the People-Orientated frame which focuses on quoting ordinary people and victims was displayed in AJE-N&F (21.1% and 33%) (see Table 5.15) far more than AJA-N&F (5.4% and 0%) (as shown previously in Table 5.6).

5 BAHRAIN'S UPRISING: PRO-DEMOCRACY PROTESTS OR SECTARIAN... 173

The results above are in line with previous studies which found that AJE gives a voice to the voiceless and marginalised (Al-Najjar, 2009; El-Nawawy & Powers, 2008; Firdous, 2009; Figenschou, 2011). Incompatible with AJA-N, AJE-N tended to include more details about people's suffering and the implications of human rights violations during the research period. AJE did not avoid naming the "wrongdoers" by using passive sentences or nominalisation.

This study found that AJE did not take the statements and claims of the Bahraini regime at face value. It investigated, included marginalised accounts and challenged the Al-Khalifa regime and Bahrain state media propaganda. It published a feature on April 6, 2011, under the title "Bahrain's Hospital of Ghosts". In this feature, AJE refuted the regime's claims about occupation by protestors of *Salmaniya* Hospital. AJE-F

Table 5.14 Quoted sources in AJE's coverage of Bahrain's uprising

Quoted sources	*AJE* *(38) News stories*	*AJE* *(3) Features*
Unauthorised opposition	0 (0%)	0 (0%)
Authorised opposition	19 (17.9%)	1 (10%)
Bahraini officials	31 (29.2%)	2 (20%)
AJ reporter	4 (3.8%)	0 (0%)
Activists or human rights organisations (HRO)	39 (36.8%)	6 (60%)
Victims/civilians	13 (12.3%)	1 (10%)

Table 5.15 Percentage of including/mentioning People-Orientated criteria in AJE's coverage of Bahrain's uprising

People-Orientated frame in the:

People-Orientated criteria	*(DRD)* *Downfall of the regime demand*	*(VV)* *Voice of voiceless*	*(SC)* *Suffering caused by the crackdown*	*(Total)* *People-Orientated frame*
AJE (38) News stories	23.7%	28.9%	10.5%	(21.1%)
AJE (3) Features	0%	33.3%	66.7%	(33.3%)

174   Z. ABDUL-NABI

Table 5.16   Pro- and anti-Qatar framing in AJE's coverage of Bahrain's uprising

Pro/anti-Qatar framing in the:	Pro-Qatar framing	Anti-Qatar framing	Neutral
AJE News	2 articles	15 articles	3
20 news stories out of 38 mentioned the reasons behind the GCC troop deployment	10%	75%	articles 15%
AJE Features	0%	1 article	0%
1 feature out of 3 mentioned the reason behind the GCC troop deployment		100%	

covered in detail how injured protesters (by live ammunitions, bird shots and tear gas) were afraid to seek treatment. The article stated:

> The victim's family tried everything possible to avoid sending him to hospital. His sister had recently completed nursing training and attempted to treat him from home. 'I tried to stop the bleeding and the pain for three days,' she said. 'We were afraid to take him to Salmaniya [Hospital]. We also took him to almost all of the private and international hospitals in Bahrain. They brought him into emergency and took x-rays but said he needed ICU treatment. As a last choice, we took him to Salmaniya. It looked almost empty in emergency ... and there were more military officers around than patients. They were all walking around with their guns inside and outside the hospital. We saw him being taken after to ward 63 on the sixth floor. They told us to leave then and that we were not allowed to visit him. We have not heard any more information on him after that'. (AJE, April 6, 2011b)

AJE did not use the "sectarian clashes" narrative when reporting on the crackdown on school and university students. AJE stated on May 11, 2011, that the security forces raided 15 female schools, arresting and torturing teenage girls. AJE secretly interviewed and filmed a 16-year-old female student, revealing how she was assaulted and tortured. AJE quoted the schoolgirl:

> 'He [police officer] hit me on the head, I started bleeding. I fell down; he told them [guards] to keep me in the rest-room,' she said during the secretly filmed interview. 'He hit and banged me against the wall to scream. Since we did not cry out or scream, we were beaten more and more, stronger and stronger. Beating was severe, but being afraid of what comes next, we were senseless to the pain' [She said]. (AJE, May 11, 2011f)

It can be observed that AJE quoted women whose voices were systematically marginalised and neglected in the mainstream media (Jacobson, 2010) far more than AJA. For instance, AJE stated in May 2011:

> A woman who only identified herself as Yasmine said she feared for herself and her family. 'I am hiding my identity because I might be targeted. My children and family might be targeted, and my husband inside may suffer even more,' she told Al-Jazeera. Yasmine said her husband was arrested almost two months ago when ten masked men in civilian clothes climbed over the family's garden walls and forced their way into their home. (AJE, May 15, 2011h)

Such detailed interviews with ordinary people never appeared in AJA regularly during the research period. The executive producer of AJE news, Kelly Jarrett, says that she considers giving voice to the voiceless a priority. She stated, "Our mandate is always to focus on the underdog as it were... That's always been our modus operandi" (K. Jarrett, personal communication, April 14, 2016).

5.4.3   AJE: Anti-Qatar Framing

The majority of AJE-N&F (75% and 100%) delegitimised the presence of the Saudi-led troops stating that "they were invited into the country to help quell pro-democracy protesters" (see Table 5.16). For example, AJE stated in April 2011:

> Bahrain has sharply tightened internet and media controls under the emergency rule imposed last month after the anti-government protests. It also called in Gulf Co-operation Council troops to quell the pro-democracy protests. (AJE, April 3, 2011a)
>
> Saudi Arabia led a joint Gulf force that deployed there last month, enabling Bahraini authorities to quell protests calling for democratic reforms. (AJE, April 7, 2011c)

5.4.4   AJE's Shouting in the Dark: An Ideal Example of Peace Journalism

In August 2011, AJE aired a documentary film about Bahrain's uprising called "Shouting in the Dark". The shocking documentary which revealed human rights violations and sectarian acts that were committed by the

176   Z. ABDUL-NABI

Bahraini forces and Saudi-led troops caused tensions between Bahrain and Qatar authorities. Even though the 50-minute critical documentary won at least six international awards, AJA has never broadcast this documentary on its channel.

The documentary was not aired during the selected research period, so this study separately analysed it based on PJ evaluative criteria (Chap. 4). The author also analysed how the film framed Bahrain's conflict and on which sources it depended. The findings show that the film was extensively dominated by PJ framing (84.7%). Peace-, Truth-, People- and Solution-Orientated frames scored notably high percentages (88.9%, 100%, 100% and 50%, respectively) (see Table 5.17).

The film framed the protests as a "revolution" (42.9%) and pro-democracy movement (28.6%) (see Table 5.18). It significantly quoted ordinary people (37.5%) and doctors who were targeted for treating injured protesters (20%). A relatively high percentage of quotes were given by regime officials and Bahraini state media segments (32.5%); however, their views were challenged by the presenter and countering accounts (see Table 5.19).

May Ying Welsh, the director and writer of the documentary, filmed and conducted interviews with doctors and activists while she was undercover. She managed to send the footage to Doha before leaving the country. She was searched and interrogated for hours in Bahrain's airport. Welsh said in the first lines of the documentary script:

> Bahrain: An island kingdom in the Arabian Gulf where the Shia Muslim majority are ruled by a family from the Sunni minority. Where people fighting for democratic rights broke the barriers of fear, only to find themselves alone and crushed. This is their story, and Al-Jazeera is their witness—the only TV journalists who remained to follow their journey of hope to the carnage that followed. This is the Arab revolution that was abandoned by

Table 5.17 Percentages of PJ frames in Shouting in the Dark documentary film aired by AJE

AJE	Peace frame	Truth frame	People frame	Solution frame	Overall PJ frames
Shouting in the dark film	88.9%	100%	100%	50%	84.7%

5 BAHRAIN'S UPRISING: PRO-DEMOCRACY PROTESTS OR SECTARIAN... 177

Table 5.18 Framing of Bahrain's conflict in Shouting in the Dark documentary

Framing of the conflict	Shouting in the Dark-AJE
Uprising	0 (0%)
Revolution	6 (42.9%)
Conflict	0 (0%)
Crisis	0 (0%)
Protests	1 (7.1%)
Pro-democracy movement	4 (28.6%)
Peaceful protest	3 (21.4%)
Shia protest	0 (0%)

Table 5.19 Percentages of quoted sources in Shouting in the Dark documentary

Dominant sources	Shouting in the Dark-AJE
Unauthorised opposition	1 (2.5%)
Authorised opposition	1 (2.5%)
Bahraini officials	13 (32.5%)
Ordinary people	15 (37.5%)
Doctors treating the injured	8 (20%)
Activists or lawyers	2 (5%)

the Arabs, forsaken by the West and forgotten by the world. (Shouting in the Dark, August 4, 2011)

The last lines of the award-wining documentary were:

Each night the people of Bahrain go to their rooftops and call out... To God and each other... The world's cameras have left... And their revolution remains as it began: A people shouting in the dark. (Shouting in the Dark, August 4, 2011)

Between the first and last lines, Welsh explains the context, history and background of the conflict. She demonstrates the peaceful aspect of Bahrain's pro-democracy struggle while revealing the GCC troops' violations, uncovering the regime's sectarian propaganda and challenging allegations by officials over the "sectarian clashes" in schools and universities. Welsh also unveiled the ordeal that physicians and injured protesters went through in March and April 2011, when the military surrounded *Salmaniya* Hospital.

The Bahraini regime has repeatedly asked the Qatari authorities to prevent the broadcast of the documentary. Two of the scheduled broadcasts were never aired on AJE (Safdar, 2012). Mahfood said:

> Shouting in the Dark caused problems between Bahrain and Qatar. The Qatari authorities wanted to stop it, but AJE had taken a decision to broadcast it. If AJA produced it, it would have never been aired. AJA tends not to anger the Bahraini authorities to guarantee that they can stay in the country and continue reporting. (personal communication, January 26, 2016)

Although AJE's coverage seems less influenced by Qatar's foreign policy than AJA, it is still confined by ownership structure. A prominent Bahraini human rights activist was supposed to be interviewed by AJE to comment on the documentary, yet the channel cancelled the interview with the activist at the last minute. They instead presented the views of the director and a member of the Bahraini regime (Davidson, 2013). Moreover, the commenting option on Bahraini videos on AJE's website was disabled, while commenting on other videos was allowed (Kamrava, 2013). Professor Mehran Kamrava, director of the Centre for International and Regional Studies at Georgetown University in Qatar, discloses that he has never been interviewed by AJE after strongly criticising the Bahraini Prime Minister, Sheikh Khalifa bin Salman Al-Khalifa, on air. He says:

> At the beginning of the Bahraini uprising, exactly in March 2011, I said during an interview with AJE, 'Bahrainis want to see the Prime Minister gone. He is so corrupted, imagine that, he bought the Bahrain Financial Harbour by 1 BD [less than USD$3] only.' After that interview, I have never been invited by AJE. (M. Kamrava, personal communication, April 5, 2016)

Jarrett, however, states that the coverage of AJE is not restricted by the Qatari regime:

> I have never ever in 10 years of working here had anybody from [Qatar] at the government level tell me what to do or not to do. (personal communication, April 14, 2016)

5.5 Differences Between AJA and AJE

Overall, the percentages of PJ framing in AJA-N&F (13.3% and 9.3%) and AJE-N&F (25.9% and 34.7%) varied significantly (see Table 5.20). The differences between both channels are more clearly demonstrated in the Peace- and People-Orientated frames. The frames scored 27.2% and 21.1% in AJE-N, respectively. However, they recorded only 7.4% and 5.4% in AJA-N (Table 5.20).

These results are inconsistent with other studies that found no major differences between AJA and AJE coverage (Fakhri, 2011; Al-Nahed, 2015; Fahmy & Al-Emad, 2011). The findings of this study disagree with Kraidy (2008, p. 24) who argues that although the channels are "different" in many aspects, their coverage of the Middle East is generally analogous with some dissimilarities in the tone and use of terms and language.[11]

The five filters/levels of the hierarchy of influences model (Shoemaker & Rees, 2013) can effectively explain why the coverage of AJA and AJE were different in representing Bahrain's conflict. Both channels are

Table 5.20 Percentage of Peace Journalism frames in AJA's and AJE's coverage of Bahrain's uprising

Overall Peace Journalism Framing: News					
PJ Frames	Peace-Orientated Frame	Truth-Orientated Frame	People-Orientated Frame	Solution-Orientated Frame	Overall Peace Journalism Framing
AJA (80) News stories	7.4%	27.1%	5.4%	13.1%	(13.25 %)
AJE (38) News stories	27.2%	39.5%	21.1%	15.8%	(25.9%)
Features					
AJA (6) Features	20.4%	16.7%	0%	0%	(9.3%)
AJE (3) Features	44.4%	44.4%	33.3%	16.7%	(34.7%)

[11] While the results of the Bahrain coverage do not agree with Kraidy's (2008) analysis, his argument is in line with the results of the Syria coverage (Chap. 7) which found no salient difference between both channels in displaying PJ frames.

180   Z. ABDUL-NABI

governed by the same organisational level (Qatar's ownership); however, they differ at the individual level (Arab and non-Arab journalists), extra-media level (advertisers, market, news sources, interest groups and competitors), routines level (Arab journalistic culture and English objective reporting standards) and ideology level (journalist and audience ideologies) (Rees & Shoemaker, 2013). Kraidy (2008) argues that unlike AJA, AJE has to compete and meet the standards of prominent Western media outlets such as the BBC and CNN. Fahmy and Al-Emad (2011) found that the majority of AJA's website readers are from the Arab world (98%) while the majority of AJE's viewers are from the United States and other Western countries (81.4%).

When asked about the factors behind having more restrictions and limitations on the Arabic channel, AJA's reporter said that the GCC countries (especially Saudi Arabia) are concerned about AJA's viewers and the Arabic audience, not about non-Arabs. Mahfood said:

> Saudi Arabia and Qatar do not care about the foreign [AJE] audience. The audience of AJA is different. Saudi Arabia is concerned about the Arab and Saudi people, not others. The Saudi authorities fear that their audience will get influenced by the uprising in Bahrain and that is why AJA was more restricted than AJE. (personal communication, January 26, 2016)

Furthermore, Mahfood argues that the reasons behind AJA's inclination towards the Al-Khalifa's sectarian narrative and legitimisation of deploying Saudi-led troops can be attributed to (1) Qatar's decision not to oppose and anger Saudi Arabia, (2) Al-Jazeera's cautiousness when covering any issue related to Saudi Arabia[12] (even before the Arab Spring), (3) the channel's concerns of being suspended and prevented from reporting from Bahrain and (4) domination of the Muslim Brotherhood (MB) and "sectarian journalists" inside the channel (personal communication, January 26, 2016). Mahfood uncovers that when he was reporting in the period before 2011, many of his stories about Bahrain's pro-democracy struggle were not published because the chief of the newsroom at the time was "a bit sectarian". He said:

> What is published and not, depends on the head of the newsroom. For instance, the head of the newsroom before 2011 was from the former mem-

---

[12] The sectarian nature of AJA's journalists is discussed in more detail in Chap. 7.

ber of the Iraq Baath Party. At the time, he didn't accept publishing any critical story about the Bahraini government. While I was reporting in 2011, the chief editor was Palestinian [Ahmed Al-Sheikh]. He doesn't belong to the Muslim Brotherhood, but he tends to adopt their views, so he was not very keen to publish Bahrain's stories as well. (H. Mahfood, personal communication, January 26, 2016)

5.6   Conclusion

The findings of AJA's coverage of Bahrain during the beginning of the 2011 uprising demonstrate very clearly the significance of implementing PJ orientations. This monograph indicates how the absence and low percentages of Peace-, People-, Solution- and Truth-Orientated frames have promoted the Al-Khalifa's sectarian narrative, representing Bahrain's protests as a special case that does not relate to the Arab Spring uprisings. Instead, there has been an omission of the history of Bahrain's prodemocracy struggle and neglecting protesters' peaceful means and their calls for unity between Shias and Sunnis. It demonstrates how the lack of "reflexivity" has resulted in giving credibility to bureaucratic accounts, downgrading human rights violations to merely "allegations", legitimising the crackdown of the GCC troops, sidelining people that demand the downfall of the regime and excluding implications of suppression and sectarianism.

On the other hand, AJE's critical representation of the Saudi military intervention and the moderate presence of PJ criteria in its coverage have made it stronger than AJA in challenging the sectarian narrative and propaganda of the Al-Khalifa regime and the GCC. AJE's adherence to what Hackett (2011) calls its "objectivity regime" allowed its news to be biased in favour of "elites" and "events", over the "voice of voiceless" and "process". Other genres such as features and documentary films gave significant space to ordinary people and presented the humanitarian side of the conflict. "Shouting in the Dark" is a model that reflects how "reflexivity" and PJ orientations are implemented in reality. This documentary—along with significant proportions of AJE's features—illustrates that PJ is "feasible" (J. Lynch, 2013) and can still be applied in the mainstream media that is confined by standards of "objective reporting".

In parallel with other studies (Kempf, 2006; Lee et al., 2006; Lee, 2010), the results of analysing the AJE coverage of Bahrain's uprising demonstrate that features and documentary films are more likely to implement PJ frames than actual hard news. This study agrees (in the case of Bahrain's coverage only) with previous studies (Firdous, 2009; El-Nawawy & Powers, 2008; Al-Najjar, 2009; Figenschou, 2010) that AJE tends to quote civilians, provide context and focus on reconciliation. This study disagrees with previous literature which found that English media scored higher percentages of WJ framing than other (mainly Asian) language-based media (J. Lynch, 2008; Lee, 2010; Siraj & Hussain, 2012; Rahman & Eijaz, 2014). While AJE and AJA differ significantly in Bahrain, their coverage of Syria was unexpectedly not very different. The next chapter will discuss the findings of AJA and AJE coverage of the Al-Ghouta attack and how the presence and absence of PJ criteria have affected the overall representation of the conflict.

References

Al-Nahed, S. (2015). Covering Libya: A framing analysis of Al Jazeera and BBC coverage of the 2011 Libyan uprising and NATO intervention. *Middle East Critique, 24*(3), 251–267.

Al-Najjar, A. (2009). How Arab is Al-Jazeera English? Comparative study of Al-Jazeera Arabic and Al-Jazeera English news channel. *Global Media Journal, 8*(14), 1–35.

Amnesty International. (2016). *7 stories of shocking injustice: Bahrain after the Arab Spring.* Accessed September 21, 2016, from https://www.amnesty.org/en/latest/campaigns/2016/02/7-stories-shocking-injustice-bahrain-after-arab-spring/

Bahrain Centre for Human Rights. (2011). *BCHR: Former university professor's testimony of March 13 University of Bahrain incident.* Accessed December 2, 2013, from http://bahrainrights.hopto.org/en/node/4862

Bahrain Independent Commission of Inquiry. (2011). *Report of the Bahrain Independent Commission of Inquiry.* Bahrain Independent Commission of Inquiry.

Bahrain News Agency. (2011, March 29). نحن مشغولون الآن بتثبيت الأمن والاستقرار :ةوالبحرين وزير الخارجي قوية. http://bna.bh/portal/news/451171?date=2011-04-7 . وتتحمل مسؤولية شعبها

Bhatia, L., & Shehabi, A. (2015). Shifting contours of activism and possibilities for justice in Bahrain. In A. Shehabi & M. O. Jones (Eds.), *Bahrain's uprising: Resistance and repression in the Gulf* (pp. 93–133). Zed Books.

Birnbaum, B. (2011, November 23). No Iranian role found in Bahrain unrest. *The Washington Times.* Accessed April 11, 2016, from http://www.washingtontimes.com/news/2011/nov/23/no-iranian-role-found-in-bahrain-unrest/

Black, I. (2011, February 15). WikiLeaks cables show no evidence of Iran's hand in Bahrain unrest. *The Guardian*. https://www.theguardian.com/world/2011/feb/15/wikileaks-no-evidence-iran-bahrain

Caldas-Coulthard, C. (1994). On reporting: The representation of speech in factual and factional narratives. In M. Coulthard (Ed.), *Advances in written text analysis* (pp. 295–308). Routledge.

Chang, T. K., & Lee, J. W. (1992). Factors affecting gatekeepers' selection of foreign news: A national survey of newspaper editors. *Journalism & Mass Communication Quarterly, 69*(3), 554–561.

Davidson, C. M. (2013). *After the Sheikhs: The coming collapse of the Gulf monarchies*. London: Hurst & Company Limited.

El-Nawawy, M., & Powers, S. (2008). *Mediating conflict: Al-Jazeera English and the possibility of a conciliatory media*. Figueroa Press.

El-Nawawy, M., & El-Masry, M. H. (2015). Revolution or crisis? Framing the 2011 Tahrir Square protests in two pan-Arab satellite news networks. *Journal of Applied Journalism & Media Studies, 4*(2), 239–258.

Entman, R. M. (1993). Framing: Toward clarification of a fractured paradigm. *Journal of Communication, 43*(4), 51–58.

Entman, R. M. (2003). Cascading activation: Contesting the White House's frame after 9/11. *Political Communication, 20*(4), 415–432.

Fahmy, S., & Al Emad, M. (2011). Al-Jazeera vs Al-Jazeera: A comparison of the network's English and Arabic online coverage of the US/Al Qaeda conflict. *The International Communication Gazette, 73*(3), 216–232.

Fakhri, F. (2011). *Content analysis of how Al-Jazeera English and Arabic channels framed the war on Gaza* (Master's thesis). Retrieved from ProQuest Dissertations and Theses. (Accession Order No. 1496764).

Figenschou, T. U. (2010). A voice for the voiceless? A quantitative content analysis of Al Jazeera English's flagship news. *Global Media and Communication, 6*(1), 85–107.

Figenschou, T. U. (2011). The south is talking back: With a white face and a British accent – editorial dilemmas in Al Jazeera English. *Journalism, 13*(3), 354–370.

Firdous, T. (2009). *Al Jazeera English presenting a non-western viewpoint and contesting western media dominance during the Gaza crisis* (Master's thesis). Retrieved from ProQuest Dissertations and Theses. (Accession Order No. 1507250).

Fishman, M. (1988). *Manufacturing the news*. University of Texas Press.

Friedman, B. (2012). Battle for Bahrain: What one uprising meant for the Gulf states and Iran. *World Affairs, 174*(6), 74–84.

Fuller, G. E., & Francke, R. R. (2001). *The Arab Shi'a: The forgotten Muslims*. Macmillan.

184   Z. ABDUL-NABI

Galtung, J. (2000). The task of peace journalism. *Ethical perspectives-Katholieke Universiteit Leuven, 7*(2–3), 162–167.

Gengler, J. (2015). *Group conflict and political mobilization in Bahrain and the Arab Gulf: Rethinking the Rentier State.* Indiana University Press.

Hackett, R. A. (2006). Is peace journalism possible? Three frameworks for assessing structure and agency in news media. *Conflict & Communication, 5*(2), 1–13. Accessed July 14, 2016, from http://www.cco.regener-online.de/2006_2/pdf/hackett.pdf

Hackett, R. A. (2011). New vistas for peace journalism: Alternative media and communication rights. In I. S. Shaw, J. Lynch, & R. A. Hackett (Eds.), *Expanding peace journalism: Comparative and critical approaches* (pp. 35–69). Sydney University Press.

Haddad, L. (2011, May 13). Lina Zahr Al-Deen: Hadhe quSati ma'a Al-Jazeera [This is my story with Al-Jazeera]. *Al-Akhbar.* http://www.al-akhbar.com/node/14125

Hashem, A. (2012, April 3). The Arab Spring has shaken Arab TV's credibility. *The Guardian.* Accessed March 12, 2016, from http://www.theguardian.com/commentisfree/2012/apr/03/arab-spring-arab-tv-credibility

Herman, E. S., & Chomsky, N. (2010). *Manufacturing consent: The political economy of the mass media.* Random House eBooks.

Hoijer, B., Nohrstedt, S. A., & Ottosen, R. (2002). *Kosovokonflikten, medierna och medlidandet.* SPF.

Holman, Z. (2015). On the side of decency and democracy: The history of British–Bahraini relations and transnational contestation. In A. Shehabi & M. O. Jones (Eds.), *Bahrain's uprising: Resistance and repression in the Gulf* (pp. 175–206). Zed Books.

Horne, J. (2015). Tn Tn Ttn and torture in Bahrain: Puncturing the spectacle of the Arab Spring. In A. Shehabi & M. O. Jones (Eds.), *Bahrain's uprising: Resistance and repression in the Gulf* (pp. 151–174). Zed Books.

Howard, R. (2002). *An operational framework for media and peacebuilding.* Institute for Media, Policy and Civil Society.

Human Rights Watch. (2011). *Bahrain injured people denied medical care.* Accessed February 21, 2016, from https://www.hrw.org/news/2011/03/17/bahrain-injured-people-denied-medical-care

Hussain, S., & Rehman, H. (2015). Balochistan: Reaping the benefits of peace journalism. *Conflict & Communication, 14*(2), 1–13. Accessed August 28, 2016, from http://s3.amazonaws.com/academia.edu.documents/40404936/hussain-rehman2015.pdf?AWSAccessKeyId=AKIAJ56TQJRTWSMTNPEA&Expires=1472356624&Signature=lBT9oduOmbKu3seKG37cuCAc8TY%3D&response-content-disposition=inline%3B%20filename%3DBalochistan_Reaping_benefits_of_Peace_Jo.pdf

Hussain, S. (2016). Media coverage of Taliban: Is Peace Journalism the solution? *Asia Pacific Media Educator, 26*(1), 31–46.

Jacobson, A. S. (2010). When peace journalism and feminist theory join forces: A Swedish case study. In R. Keeble, J. Tulloch, & F. Zollmann (Eds.), *Peace Journalism, War and Conflict Resolution* (pp. 105–119). Peter Lang Publishing.

Jones, M. O. (2015). Rotten apples or rotten orchards Police deviance, brutality, and unaccountability in Bahrain. In A. Shehabi & M. O. Jones (Eds.), *Bahrain's uprising: Resistance and repression in the Gulf* (pp. 207–238). Zed Books.

Kamrava, M. (2013). *Qatar: Small state, big politics.* Cornell University Press.

Kempf, W. (2006). *Acceptance and impact of de-escalation-oriented conflict coverage. Diskussionsbeiträge der Projektgruppe Friedensforschung Konstanz,* Nr. 60. Berline: Regener. Accessed June 25, 2016, from https://kops.unikonstanz.de/bitstream/handle/123456789/10452/60.pdf?sequence=1

Khalaf, A. (2015). The many afterlives of Lulu: The story of Bahrain's Pearl Roundabout. In A. Shehabi & M. O. Jones (Eds.), *Bahrain's uprising: Resistance and repression in the Gulf* (pp. 135–150). Zed Books.

Kraidy, M. M. (2008). *Al-Jazeera and Al-Jazeera English: A Comparative institutional analysis.* Woodrow Wilson International Center for Scholars, pp. 23–30. Accessed July 30, 2012, from http://repository.upenn.edu/cgi/viewcontent.cgi?article=1282&context=asc_papers

Lee, S. T., Maslog, C. C., & Kim, H. S. (2006). Asian Conflicts and the Iraq War: A comparative framing analysis. *International Communication Gazette, 68*(5-6), 499–518.

Lee, S. T. (2010). Peace journalism: Principles and structural limitations in the news coverage of three conflicts. *Mass Communication and Society, 13*(4), 361–384.

Lynch, J., & McGoldrick, A. (2005). *Peace journalism.* Hawthorn Press.

Lynch, J. (2007). Peace journalism and its discontents. *Conflict and Communication Online, 6*(2), 1–13. Accessed June 3, 2013, from http://www.cco.regener-online.de/2007_2/pdf/lynch.pdf

Lynch, J. (2008). *Debates in Peace Journalism.* Sydney University Press.

Lynch, J., & Galtung, J. (2010). *Reporting conflict: New directions in peace journalism.* University of Queensland Press.

Lynch, J. (2013). Is Peace Journalism feasible? Pointers for research and media development. *Ethical Space: The International Journal of Communication Ethics, 10*(2/3), 15–24.

Lynch, J. (2014a). *A global standard for reporting conflict.* Routledge.

Lynch, J. (2014b). Critical realism, peace journalism and democracy. *Ethical Space: The International Journal of Communication Ethics, 11*(1/2), 29–36.

Lynch, M. (2016). *The new Arab wars: Uprisings and anarchy in the Middle East.* Public Affairs.

Machin, D., & Mayr, A. (2012). *How to do critical discourse analysis: A multimodal introduction*. SAGE Publications.

Matthiesen, T. (2013). *Sectarian gulf: Bahrain, Saudi Arabia, and the Arab Spring that wasn't*. Stanford University Press.

Moore-Gilbert, K. (2016). From protected state to protection racket: Contextualising divide and rule in Bahrain. *Journal of Arabian Studies, 6*(2), 163–181.

Nash, C. (2016). *What is journalism? The art and politics of a rupture*. Palgrave Macmillan.

Nohrstedt, S. A., & Ottosen, R. (2008). War Journalism in the threat society: Peace Journalism as a strategy for challenging the mediated culture of fear? *Conflict & Communication Online, 7*(2), 1–17. Accessed August 29, 2016, from http://www.cco.regener-online.de/2008_2/pdf/nohrstedt_ottosen.pdf

Onyebadi, U., & Oyedeji, T. (2011). Newspaper coverage of post political election violence in Africa: An assessment of the Kenyan example. *Media, War & Conflict, 4*(3), 215–230.

Physicians for Human Rights. (2011). *Do no harm: A call for Bahrain to end systematic attacks on doctors and patients*. https://s3.amazonaws.com/PHR_Reports/bahrain-do-no-harm-2011.pdf

Rahman, B. H., & Eijaz, A. (2014). Pakistani media as an agent of conflict or conflict resolution: A case of Lal Masjid in Urdu and English Dailies. *Pakistan Vision, 15*(2), 238–263.

Russia Today. (2012, March 12). *Al Jazeera exodus: Channel losing staff over bias*. https://www.rt.com/news/al-jazeera-loses-staff-335/

Safdar, A. (2012). Filming undercover in Bahrain. *Doha Centre for Media Freedom*. Accessed March 29, 2016, from http://www.dc4mf.org/en/content/filming-undercover-bahrain

Samuel-Azran, T. (2013). Al-Jazeera, Qatar, and new tactics in state-sponsored media diplomacy. *American Behavioral Scientist, 57*(9), 1293–1311.

Sharif, I. (2015). A trial of thoughts and ideas. In A. Shehabi & M. O. Jones (Eds.), *Bahrain's uprising: Resistance and repression in the Gulf* (pp. 43–60). Zed Books.

Shoemaker, P. J., & Reese, S. D. (2013). *Mediating the message in the 21st century: A media sociology perspective*. Routledge.

Shouting in the Dark. (2011, August 4). *Bahrain: Shouting in the dark*. https://www.youtube.com/watch?v=xaTKDMYOBOU

Siraj, S. A. (2008, May). *War or Peace Journalism in elite US newspapers: Exploring news framing in Pakistan-India conflict*. Paper presented at the annual meeting of the International Communication Association, Montreal, Quebec. Accessed June 14, 2016, from http://www.issi.org.pk/wp-content/uploads/2014/06/1303370133_44311323.pdf

5 BAHRAIN'S UPRISING: PRO-DEMOCRACY PROTESTS OR SECTARIAN... 187

Siraj, S. A., & Hussain, S. (2012). War media galore in Pakistan: A perspective on Taliban conflict. *Global Media Journal: Pakistan Edition, 5*(1). Accessed August 28, 2016, from http://scholar.google.com.au/scholar_url?url=http%3A%2F%2Fwww. academia.edu%2Fdownload%2F40715694%2FWar_Media_galore_in_Pakista_.doc&hl=en&sa=T&oi=ggp&ct=res&cd=0&ei=03jCV4H8OMO5j AHp-4moAw&scisig=AAGBfm1VLQnmFMeimgV-Yp_alSlKfoOM6Q&noss l=1&ws=1350x638

Tehranian, M. (2002). Peace Journalism negotiating global media ethics. *The Harvard International Journal of Press/Politics, 7*(2), 58–83.

Ulrichsen, K. C. (2012). The temperature is rising: Sectarianism and reform in the Gulf. *Muftah.* Accessed May 2, 2013, from http://muftah.org/the-temperature-is-rising-sectarianism-political-reform-in-the-gulf/

Volynets, Y. (2013). Structural and semantic features of quotation in English media discourse. *Academic Journal of Interdisciplinary Studies, 2*(8), 554–559.

Wehrey, F. M. (2013). *Sectarian politics in the Gulf: from the Iraq war to the Arab uprisings.* Columbia University Press.

White House. (2011). *Remarks by the president on the Middle East and North Africa.* Accessed April 11, 2016, from https://www.whitehouse.gov/the-press-office/2011/05/19/remarks-president-middle-east-and-north-africa

Zahr Al-Deen, L. (2010). الجزيرة ليست نهاية المشوار. Baisan.

References of Al-Jazeera Arabic and English Articles:

Al-Jazeera Arabic. (2011a, March 16). جدل متجدد عن علاقات البحرين بإيران . http://www.aljazeera.net/home/print/f6451603-4dff-4ca1-9c10-122741d17432/533 1ee72-e8f4-48e1-8b80-10beff04cf9e

Al-Jazeera Arabic. (2011b, March 16). قتلى وجرحى بمواجهات البحرين. http://www.aljazeera.net/home/print/f6451603-4dff-4ca1-9c10122741d17432/1396b 4ef-8ac3-40f8-8003-bc21e8522776

Al-Jazeera Arabic. (2011c. March, 19). البحرين تقلص ساعات حظر التجول. http://www.aljazeera.net/news/arabic/2011/3/19/%d8%a7%d9%84%d8%a8%d8%ad%d8%b1%d 9%8a%d9%86-%d8%aa%d9%82%d9%84%d8%b5-%d8%b3%d8%a7%d8%b9%d8%a7%d8%aa-%d8%ad%d8%b8%d8%b1-%d8%a7% d9%84%d8%aa%d8%ac%d9%88%d9%84

Al-Jazeera Arabic. (2011d, March 22). اغلوا يحذر من الطائفية في البحرين. http://www.aljazeera.net/news/international/2011/3/22/%d8%a3%d9%88%d8%ba%d9%8 4%d9%88-%d9%8a%d8%ad%d8%b0%d8%b1-%d9%85%d9%86-%d8%a7%d9%84 %d8%b7%d8%a7%d8%a6%d9%81%d9%8a%d8%a9-%d8%a8%d8%a7%d9%84%d8 %a8%d8%ad%d8%b1%d9%8a%d9%86

Al-Jazeera Arabic. (2011e, March 23). الجامعة تؤيد درع الجزيرة بالبحرين. http://www.aljazeera.net/news/arabic/2011/3/22/%D8%A7%D9%84%D8%AC%D8%A7%D9%85 %D8%B9%D8%A9-%D8%AA%D8%A4%D9%8A%D8%AF-

%D8%AF%D8%B1%D8%B9-%D8%A7%D9%84%D8%AC%D8%B2%D9%8A%D8%B1%D8%A9-%D8%A8%D8%A7%D9%84%D8%A8%D8%AD%D8%B1%D9%8A%D9%86

Al-Jazeera Arabic. (2011f, March 25). البحرين تشتكي حزب الله للبنان. https://www.aljazeera.net/news/arabic/2011/3/25/%D8%A7%D9%84%D8%A8%D8%AD%D8%B1%D9%8A%D9%86-%D8%AA%D8%B4%D8%AA%D9%83%D9%8A-%D8%AD%D8%B2%D8%A8-%D8%A7%D9%84%D9%87-%D9%84%D9%84%D8%A8%D9%86%D8%A7%D9%86

Al-Jazeera Arabic. (2011g, April 6). مصر تؤيد التحرك الخليجي بالبحرين. http://www.aljazeera.net/news/arabic/2011/4/6/%d9%85%d8%b5%d8%b1-%d8%aa%d8%a4%d9%8a%d8%af-%d8%a7%d9%84%d8%aa%d8%ad%d8%b1%d9%83-%d8%a7%d9%84%d8%ae%d9%84%d9%8a%d8%ac%d9%8a-%d8%a8%d8%a7%d9%84%d8%a8%d8%ad%d8%b1%d9%8a%d9%86

Al-Jazeera Arabic. (2011h. April 23). الأمن يفرق مسيرات في البحرين. https://www.aljazeera.net/news/arabic/2011/4/23/%D8%A7%D9%84%D8%A3%D9%85%D9%86-%D9%8A%D9%81%D8%B1%D9%82-%D9%85%D8%B3%D9%8A%D8%B1%D8%A7%D8%AA-%D9%81%D9%8A-%D8%A7%D9%84%D8%A8%D8%AD%D8%B1%D9%8A%D9%86

Al-Jazeera Arabic. (2011i, May 11). البحرين تطرد مراسل رويترز. http://www.aljazeera.net/amp/news/arabic/2011/5/11/%D8%A7%D9%84%D8%A8%D8%AD%D8%B1%D9%8A%D9%86-%D8%AA%D8%B7%D8%B1%D8%AF-%D9%85%D8%B1%D8%A7%D8%B3%D9%84-%D8%B1%D9%88%D9%8A%

Al-Jazeera Arabic. (2011j, May 12). انتخابات تكميلية وفصل عمال بالبحرين. http://www.aljazeera.net/news/arabic/2011/5/11/%d8%a7%d9%86%d8%aa%d8%ae%d8%a7%d8%a8%d8%a7%d8%aa-%d8%aa%d9%83%d9%85%d9%8a%d9%84%d9%8a%d8%a9-%d9%88%d9%81%d8%b5%d9%84-%d8%b9%d9%85%d8%a7%d9%84-%d8%a8%d8%a7%d9%84%d8%a8%d8%ad%d8%b1%d9%8a%d9%86

Al-Jazeera Arabic. (2011k, May 22). انتقادات لمعاملة الصحفيين بالبحرين. http://www.aljazeera.net/home/print/c54c246c-3a58-42e6-8ebc-076c30f509ce/256f8061-709a-4a17-a4f4-bfb3e4818037

Al-Jazeera Arabic. (2015, October 20). اكتشفنا خاليا ارهابية تدعمها إيران :البحرين. http://www.aljazeera.net/home/print/f6451603-4dff-4ca1-9c10-122741d17432/b2d74e80-8cb9-4046-8532-2a6488f243a5

Al-Jazeera English. (2011a, April 3). *Bahrain bans main opposition newspaper.* http://www.aljazeera.com/news/middleeast/2011/04/2011438401186997.html

Al-Jazeera English. (2011b, April 6). *Bahrain's hospital of ghosts.* http://www.aljazeera.com/indepth/features/2011/04/20114512347348853.html

Al-Jazeera English. (2011c, April 7). *US and Saudi Arabia discuss Iran "meddling."* http://www.aljazeera.com/news/middleeast/2011/04/20114623362545 5108.html

5 BAHRAIN'S UPRISING: PRO-DEMOCRACY PROTESTS OR SECTARIAN... 189

Al-Jazeera English. (2011d, April 24). *Bahrain prince to skip UK royal wedding.* http://www.aljazeera.com/news/middleeast/2011/04/2011424165555715419.htm

Al-Jazeera English. (2011e, April 27). *Bahrain denies mass sackings over protests.* http://www.aljazeera.com/news/middleeast/2011/04/2011427134843707918.html

Al-Jazeera English. (2011f, May 11). *Schoolgirls "beaten" in Bahrain raids.* http://www.aljazeera.com/news/middleeast/2011/05/20115118146679800.html

Al-Jazeera English. (2011g, May 14). *Bahrain targets Shia religious sites.* http://www.aljazeera.com/video/middleeast/2011/05/201151311 2016389348.html

Al-Jazeera English. (2011h, May 15). *"Hundreds held" in Bahrain crackdown.* http://www.aljazeera.com/news/middleeast/2011/05/201151511050523260.html

Al-Jazeera English. (2011i, May 17). *Bahrain accepts resignation of opposition MPs.* http://www.aljazeera.com/amp/news/middleeast/2011/05/2011517134644881491.html

CHAPTER 6

Syria's CWs Coverage (2013): Peace Deal or Military Action to "Punish" the Perpetrator?

6.1 INTRODUCTION

This chapter demonstrates and dissects the findings of Al-Jazeera's coverage of Syria's second chemical weapons (CW) attack in 2013. All news stories and features published at the outset of the Al-Ghouta attack from August 21 until September 14, 2013, were selected for analysis. Following the exclusion of irrelevant articles, the study empirically examined 71 news stories and 22 features from Al-Jazeera Arabic (AJA) and 82 news stories and 5 features from Al-Jazeera English (AJE).

The quantitative content analysis found that the coverage of the second CW attack from both the channels was dominated by War Journalism framing. This chapter elucidates how a lack of displaying PJ orientations/frames in AJA and AJE has misrepresented the Syrian conflict and conveyed a distorted image of the reality of the situation. It explains how the low proportions of PJ criteria in the coverage have led to the omission of significant facts. Such omissions include the fact that the regime's soldiers were among those killed in the first CW attack in 2013 and that Al-Qaeda-affiliated groups in Syria had access to sarin. Other exclusions are the geopolitical interests of the regime's allies and antagonists, voices of civilians caught in the conflict, implications of military intervention and alternative accounts from independent experts and moderate opposition groups.

© The Author(s), under exclusive license to Springer Nature Switzerland AG 2022
Z. Abdul-Nabi, *Al-Jazeera's "Double Standards" in the Arab Spring*, https://doi.org/10.1007/978-3-031-14279-6_6

According to the results, both channels repeatedly covered the Al-Assad regime's "war crimes" but, to a great extent, excluded the human rights violations committed by the Syrian opposition. This study argues that these exclusions have contributed to promoting the opposition/Qatar's propaganda and make the coverage vulnerable to the manipulation of elites and bureaucratic accounts.

Similar to Bahrain's coverage (Chap. 5), not implementing "reflexivity" while covering the conflict has resulted in the reportage of claims as facts and vice versa. It has also caused the production of inaccurate, fabricated and imbalanced coverage. This can be observed through the legitimisation of the allegations by the Syrian opposition and American "intelligence sources" in relation to the location of the launching point of the rockets that struck Al-Ghouta on August 21, 2013, and the number of victims killed in the said attack.

Although both channels were similarly dominated by War Journalism (WJ) and pro-Qatar framings, AJE was notably more People-Orientated and used more "objective" language than AJA.

6.2   Key Findings

Before a detailed examination of the findings of the AJA and AJE's coverage of the second CW attack in Syria, it is important to note the following key points that summarise the main empirical results.

- War Journalism framing dominated AJA news and features (AJA-N&F) (92% and 90.4%) and AJE-N&F (91.6% and 77.3%).
- The Solution-Orientated frame was the most observed frame in the news (23%) from both channels, while the Truth-Orientated frame was the least presented one (less than 2%).
- More than 50% of the quotations in the news and features of both channels were dominated by elites, whereas the voice of the voiceless and human rights activists recorded lower percentages.
- The Syrian opposition sources were given more space in the news from AJA and AJE (nearly more than 45%) than the Al-Assad regime sources in both channels (25%).
- More than 80% of the news and features of both AJA and AJE were dominated by pro-Qatar framing.

- AJA used more emotive language than AJE—while the terms "crime", "massacre" and "deadly attack" appeared in AJA, they were hardly mentioned in AJE.
- More than a third of AJA news and features framed the Al-Ghouta attack as "the CW attack", while more than 35% of the AJE coverage portrayed it as "the alleged attack".
- Over 60% of AJA-N&F framed the Syrian conflict as a "crisis", while more than 56% of AJE-N&F framed it as a "civil war".
- Significant percentages of AJA-N&F (20% and 32%) framed the Syrian conflict as a "revolution", while such a term was never mentioned in AJE-N&F.
- More than half of AJA news estimated that 1300–1600 people were killed in the Al-Ghouta attack, whereas 42% of the AJE news' estimation did not exceed "hundreds".

6.3 Implications of Not Displaying Peace Journalism Framing in AJA and AJE

Table 6.1 shows that the Peace Journalism-Orientated frames, Peace, Truth, People and Solutions, were hardly implemented in the news and features of AJA and AJE. The overall PJ framing was applied less than 9% in the news from both channels (Table 6.1). The following table indicates that the Truth-Orientated frame was never applied in the AJA-N&F (0% and 0%) and hardly implemented in the AJE-N&F (1.2% and 6.7%). The

Table 6.1 Percentage of Peace Journalism frames in AJA's and AJE's coverage of Syria's chemical attack

Overall Peace Journalism framing					
News					
PJ frames	Peace frame	Truth frame	People frame	Solution frame	Overall Peace Journalism framing
AJA (71) News stories	7.2%	0%	1.9%	23%	**(8%)**
AJE (82) News stories	7.6%	1.2%	1.2%	23.6%	**(8.4%)**
Features					
AJA (22) Features	6.8%	0%	4.5%	27.3%	**(9.65%)**
AJE (5) Features	4%	6.7%	33.3%	46.7%	**(22.7%)**

People-Orientated frame was marginalised in the majority of AJA and AJE coverage with the exception of AJE features, wherein the frame was observed about 33.3% in the total coverage. However, the Solution-Orientated frame was displayed generally higher than other frames, scoring more than 20% in the news and features of both channels (Table 6.1).

The following section in this chapter argues that the lack of applying the Peace/Conflict-, Truth-, People- and Solution-Orientated frames has led to the omission of significant "facts"/criteria that could, if adequately mentioned, generate better understandings and relatively more accurate representations of the conflict.

6.4   Omission of Significant Facts

6.4.1   Geopolitics of the Syrian Conflict

As shown in Table 6.2, the AJA-N&F (7.2% and 6.8%) and AJE-N&F (7.6% and 4%) minimally implemented the criteria of the Peace/Conflict-Orientated frame.[1] These criteria include ten facts that explain the context,

---

[1] Analytical criteria of the Peace/Conflict-Orientated frame:

1. (**HM**): Does the article mention the Hama massacre?
2. (**CW**): Does the article mention that Syria has one of the world's largest stockpiles of chemical weapons?
3. (**KA**): Does the article mention that soldiers from the Syrian Arab Army (SAA) were injured in the first chemical attack that struck Khan Al-Assal on March 19, 2013?
4. (**UN**): Does the article mention that UN inspectors had been in the country three days prior to the Al-Ghouta attack?
5. **CQ**): Does the article mention that the regime troops were advancing on the ground before and during the attack?
6. (**GI**): Does the article mention the geopolitical interests of Syria's allies and enemies?
7. (**WMD**): Does the article mention that Iraq was struck in 2003 under the justification of possessing WMD?
8. (**PCW**): Does the article mention any previous incidents where CWs were used but the West did not take any action and did not militarily intervene?
9. (**BIL**): Does the article mention that striking Syria without obtaining authorisation from the UN Security Council is unlawful and breaches International Human Rights law?
10. (**RH**): Does the article mention that the Al-Ghouta area was under the control of the rebels when the attack occurred?

6 SYRIA'S CWS COVERAGE (2013): PEACE DEAL OR MILITARY ACTION... 195

Table 6.2 Percentage of including/mentioning the Peace/Conflict-Orientated criteria in AJA's and AJE's coverage of Syria's chemical attack

Peace-Orientated frame in the: News											
Peace/Conflict-Orientated criteria	(HM) Hama Massacre	(CW) Possession of the Chemical Weapons	(KA) Khan Al-Assal	(UN) UN Inspectors	(CQ) Capturing Qusayr	(GI) Geopolitical Interests	(WMD) Weapons of Mass Destruction	(PCW) Previous use of CW	(BIL) Breaching International Law	(RH) Rebel-held area	(Total) Peace/conflict frame
AJA (71) News stories	0%	29.6%	2.8%	9.9%	1.4%	0%	4.2%	0%	11.3%	12.7%	(7.2%)
AJE (82) News stories	0%	25.6%	1.2%	15.9%	3.7%	0%	1.2%	0%	14.6%	13.4%	(7.6%)
Features											
AJA (22) features	0%	50%	0%	0%	0%	0%	13.6%	4.5%	0%	0%	(6.8%)
AJE (5) features	0%	20%	0%	0%	0%	0%	0%	0%	0%	20%	(4%)

historical background, geopolitics and reasons underpinning the Syrian conflict and previous chemical weapons attacks.

Table 6.2 shows that the news and features from both channels focused solely on the allegations of the Syrian regime and opposition and never offer any background information concerning the geopolitical interests of all involved parties. The Al-Jazeera network has simplified the conflict by introducing the use of CW as the only reason for the launch of military action against the Syrian regime. For instance, both AJA-N&F (4.2% and 13.6) and AJE-N&F (1.2% and 0%) failed to focus on the possibility that the United States may employ Al-Assad's possession/use of CWs as a pretext to strike Syria, in the same way WMDs were used to invade Iraq in 2003 (Table 6.2).

The mainstream media represented WMDs as the major factor underpinning the invasion of Iraq while obscuring several other causes such as securing oil, granting an American military presence in the Middle East, decreasing the popularity of George W. Bush, turning attention away from internal financial and economic problems and possibly even the psychological fear of enduring another 9/11 (de Fransius, 2014).

If the mainstream media implemented PJ orientations before the invasion of Iraq, all possible causes [mentioned above] would have been highlighted (de Fransius, 2014). Critical accounts would have been focused on such as the views of the Kurdish minority in Iraq, UN weapons inspectors, French and German heads of states and protestors who opposed the war (de Fransius, 2014).

It would be crucial for a peace journalist covering Al-Ghouta's attack to ask what a CW attack means to Syria's allies and antagonists. Who would benefit most from this attack? Why did the United States not intervene militarily in the 1980s when Saddam Hussain used CW against civilians in Halabja? Was the Obama administration concerned about the use of CW and human rights violations in Syria or removing Iran's and Russia's only ally in the Middle East? What are the motives, background and history of US interventions in the region? Why would Al-Assad use CWs two days after the arrival of the UN inspectors [who finally visited the country after months of delay]? Why would Al-Assad cross Obama's "red line" while he was advancing and gaining ground using conventional weapons? "Is Al-Assad stupid? He may be evil, but he is not stupid" (Erlich, 2014). What did the Syrian people think of the talks about striking their country? Was there any opinion among the opposition that opposed the war? These questions were barely asked during the research period.

Chomsky (2011) says it is normal for the media not to ask "the necessary questions". He says that although Saddam Hussein had been supported by the United States, Soviet Union, Europe, Gulf states and Arabs in the 1980s, he was not able to defeat Iran. Yet all of a sudden, he had Weapon of Mass Destruction (WMD) and was ready to invade the world. "Did you find anybody who pointed that out? No. You found virtually nobody who pointed it out. That's typical" (Chomsky, 2011, p. 63). Nash (2016, p. 229) calls the process of failing to include and ask the relevant and significant questions "production of salience". Nash (2016) argues that this silence is generally [albeit not all the time] produced by the journalistic structure and imposed by systematic and organisational decisions, in which journalists cannot play an effective role. Journalists normally justify the absence of explanation and exploration of the "why" to the lack of time and space (McGoldrick, 2006). However, focusing only on a conflict arena without presenting the causes of a conflict can make media coverage inaccurate and vulnerable to dominant accounts and propaganda (J. Lynch, 2007).

6.4.2 Omission of the Context of Previous CW Attacks

Khan Al-Assal CW Attack
While covering the Al-Ghouta attack in August 2013, the news and features of AJA and AJE scarcely mentioned any contextual information

regarding the Khan Al-Assal CW attack which occurred five months prior, on March 19, 2013. As shown in Table 6.2, less than 3% of the news and features from AJA and AJE offered background information about the attack in Khan Al-Assal. According to the Syrian Observatory for Human Rights (SOHR), 16 soldiers from the regime's Syrian Arab Army (SAA) were killed in the Khan Al-Assal attack. Despite the Khan Al-Assal being a regime-held area, the United States and its allies were quick to blame Al-Assad and remind him of the consequences of crossing Obama's "red line".

The opposition and the regime traded accusations over the responsibility of using CW. Bassam Barakat, a pro-regime medical doctor and consultant, said that the Syrian regime sent blood samples to Russia for investigation (Erlich, 2014). The results concluded that rebels had used sarin.[2] According to the analysis, this particular sarin came originally from Muammar Al-Gaddafi's CW stockpiles which had been bought from the Soviet Union (Erlich, 2014). A highly classified US document revealed that the Obama and Erdoğan administrations had signed an agreement in 2012 to transfer weapons from Libya to the Syrian rebels through what the CIA calls "rat line"[3] (Hersh, 2014).

On March 20, 2013, one day after the attack, the Syrian regime asked the UN Secretary-General to form an independent mission to investigate the use of CW in Eastern Al-Ghouta (Anderson, 2015). On March 21, 2013, one day after Syria's request, the United States, the United Kingdom and France lodged a petition to the UN to investigate other CW attacks that allegedly occurred in 2012 and 2013. In total, the UN received 13 requests from the Syrian opposition allies. Nine of them were dismissed for failing to provide "sufficient and credible information" (UNMIAUCWSAR, 2013b). In its detailed report, the United Nations Mission to Investigate Allegations of the Use of Chemical Weapons in the Syrian Arab Republic (UNMIAUCWSAR, 2013b) corroborated the allegations that sarin was used against SAA's soldiers and civilians on March 19, 2013.

---

[2] The National Institute for Occupational Safety and Health (2015) defines sarin as an odourless and tasteless nerve agent that can cause death in minutes, as it is "one of the most toxic of the known chemical warfare agents".

[3] Rat line is "a back-channel highway into Syria" that was "used to funnel weapons and ammunition from Libya via southern Turkey and across the Syrian border to the opposition" (Hersh, 2014).

198 Z. ABDUL-NABI

Both AJA and AJE channels avoided mentioning the fact that the dead in Khan Al-Assal attack were SAA's soldiers.[4] For example, AJA stated:

> Damascus has accused the Free Syrian Army (FSA) and revolutionary brigades of firing a rocket, primed with CW in Khan Al-Assal, Aleppo, resulted in killing 26 civilians last Tuesday. (AJA, March 22, 2013a)[5]

Only one article out of eight published from March 19 to 25 on the AJA website referred to the victims as "soldiers". Six articles out of eight (75%) referred to them as "people" or "civilians". None of the eight articles mentioned the fact that Khan Al-Assal CW attack occurred in a regime-held area. Likewise, on the AJE website, only one article out of seven articles published from March 20 to June 5 referred to the victims as "soldiers". Selecting and repeating the word "civilians" while omitting the term "SAA soldiers" reflect what Machin and Mayr (2012) called "ideological interpretations" of the Al-Jazeera editors. According to Hofstetter and Buss (1978), selectivity or "bias" includes omission, abstraction and generalisation. This is why, "selectivity", not "objectivity", is what matters most to the PJ approach (J. Lynch & Galtung, 2010, p. 53).

Carla del Ponte, a former Chief prosecutor for two International Criminal Tribunals,[6] stated in May 2013 that rebels used CW in the Khan Al-Assal attack. She said in an interview with a Swiss TV channel that CWs were used by "the opposition, the rebels, [but] not by the government authorities" (BBC, 2013). After her media statements, the UNCW Mission asked her and other members to stop commenting on the issue (Erlich, 2014). Ponte's claims never appeared on AJA and AJE during the research period.

---

[4] The AJA and AJE coverage of Khan Al-Assal attack was not part of the research period. However, as it is part of the context of the second CW attack, I have analysed how both channels represented the victims that were killed in the attack. The results show that the majority of the coverage of both channels framed the victims as "civilians" although 16 out of 26 killed in the attack were SAA soldiers.

[5] All cited AJA's Arabic texts from news stories, features and interviews in this study are my own translation.

[6] Carla del Ponte was Chief prosecutor on the International Criminal Tribunal for the former Yugoslavia (ICTY) and the International Criminal Tribunal for Rwanda (ICTR).

The regime and Russia pointed the fingers to Jabhat Al-Nusra [Al-Qaeda-affiliated group[7]], as there were reports that the group had seized a chemical factory in Aleppo in December 2012 (Anderson, 2015). Other reports, on the other hand, state that the dead soldiers were found at a checkpoint close to a research and scientific lab, known for examining and working with CWs (Erlich, 2014). Erlich (2014), however, infers that it is more likely that Al-Nusra carried out the attack as the plan was to hit two birds with one stone: killing SAA's soldiers and discrediting the Syrian regime in front of the international community at the same time. Al-Jazeera [like Al-Assad's opponents] blamed the regime and excluded any other possibilities. For instance, in a live interview in May 2013, AJA's host, Nasser Abdul-Samad, asked his American guest, Richard Weitz, director of the Center for Political-Military Analysis at Hudson Institute:

> Why did the US not take a decisive move against the Al-Assad regime despite the fact that he crossed what the US administration considered a 'red line'? (AJA, May 20, 2013b)

In another example, in August 2013, an article in AJE stated:

> In June, the US said it had conclusive evidence that Bashar Al-Assad's regime used such arms against opposition forces. (AJE, August 22, 2013a)

The second quote mentioned that the United States had evidence that the regime had used CWs, but, at the same time, it did not say anything about Russia's evidence or Carla Del Ponte's statements.

Ashrafiyah and Jobar CW Attacks
The UNMIAUCWSAR (2013b) report that was released on December 12, 2013, corroborated that CWs were used five times during 2012 and 2013. Surprisingly, the victims of three of these five incidents were from SAA soldiers [Khan Al-Assal as mentioned earlier, Jobar on August 24, 2013, Ashrafiyah on August 25, 2013]. AJA and AJE never mentioned

---

[7] Al-Nusra Front, *Jabhat Al-Nusra* in Arabic, is an armed extremist group that had been formed on February 23, 2012. It pledged its allegiance to Al-Qaeda's leader, Ayman Al-Zawahiri. Soon after its foundation, the United States and United Nations Security Council classified it as a "terrorist group". It had united with Al-Qaeda in Iraq [or what is known as ISI] and broke away in April 2013. On July 28, 2016, Al-Nusra declared its independence from Al-Qaeda. Al-Zawahiri has endorsed and blessed the move.

the Ashrafiyah attack in their coverage. Both channels, however, mention the Jobar attack two times during the research period. If the SAA struck itself "accidently" [blowback] in Khan Al-Assal as the opposition said, could the other two incidents [Ashrafiyah's and Jobar attacks] occur "accidently" as well? Anderson (2015, p. 205) says, "Logically, those attacks came from groups which were fighting soldiers, not from government forces".

This study observes that the network framed the opposition's responsibility of the Jobar attack as a "claim" that "cannot be verified" (AJE, August 25, 2013b), whereas it [especially the Arabic channel] represented Al-Assad's responsibility of Al-Ghouta's attack as a "fact" in a number of articles (AJA, September 1, 2013f). For instance, AJA stated in September 2013:

> The meeting of Arab foreign ministers at the Arab League meeting in Cairo has started today—Sunday evening—to discuss the Syrian crisis and a number of issues, amid condemnation of the Al-Assad regime's use of chemical weapons and divergent views over the possible Western strike against Syria. (AJA, September 1, 2013f)

> Paris is working intensively on forming an international coalition that is supportive of punishing the Syrian regime for using CW. French intelligence has already revealed the details of the use of CW by Damascus in Al-Ghouta two weeks ago. (AJA, September 3, 2013f)

> The Russian proposal of eliminating Syria's CW has been met with a cautious international welcome as they fear that the initiative aims to gain time and spare the Syrian regime a military strike after its [the regime] use of CW against civilians last month. (AJA, September 10, 2013h)

In short, this study found that more than 20% of the news and features of AJA and AJE mentioned the fact that the Al-Assad regime obsessed one of the largest CW arsenals in the world (as shown in Table 6.2). However, it was also noted that the coverage failed to highlight the fact that SAA's soldiers were injured and killed in at least three CW attacks that took place in Khan Al-Assal, Jobar and Ashrafiyah.

6.4.3 Omission of Al-Qaeda-Affiliated Groups as Potential Suspects

The criteria of the Truth-Orientated frame[8] include facts that focus on the capability of the regime and the opposition to commit human rights violations and use CWs. The findings show that AJA-N&F never applied the Truth-Orientated frame. AJE-N&F was not any better than AJA, as it applied the frame in a limited manner (1.2% and 6.7%) (Table 6.3).

Thus, not mentioning the criteria of the Truth-Orientated frame has supported the exoneration of some opposition groups, namely, the Al-Qaeda-affiliated ones, from any involvement in the Al-Ghouta CW attack.

Table 6.3 Percentage of including/mentioning the Truth-Orientated criteria in AJA's and AJE's coverage of Syria's chemical attack

Truth-Orientated frame in the:				
News				
Truth-Orientated criteria	**(BSCW)** Both sides could use CW	**(EA)** Expert Analysis	**(HRV)** Human Rights Violations by both sides	**(Total)** Truth frame
AJA (**71**) news stories	0%	0%	0%	**(0%)**
AJE (**82**) news stories	0%	1.2%	2.4%	**(1.2%)**
Features				
AJA (**22**) Features	0%	0%	0%	**(0%)**
AJE (**5**) Features	0%	20%	0%	**(6.7%)**

[8] **Analytical criteria of the Truth-Orientated frame:**

1. **(BSCW):** Does the article mention that "both sides" could use chemical weapons according to a UN report released in June 2013?
2. **(EA):** Does the article present an analysis by an independent and well-experienced military or chemical weapons expert about who possibly committed the attack?
3. **(HRV):** Does the article mention that both sides of the conflict committed human rights violations?

Al-Nusra Front, Al-Qaeda-affiliated group, was mentioned four times in AJA during the study period, and none of the four articles associated it with the CW attack. The jihadi group was never mentioned in AJE during the research period.

In his investigative article "Whose Sarin", Hersh (2013) said that the CIA alarmed the US administration that Al-Nusra and Al-Qaeda in Iraq (AQI) had possession of sarin. In May 2013, the authorities of Iraq arrested five members of AQI [known as Islamic State in Iraq (ISI) as well] for manufacturing sarin and mustard gas (Hersh, 2013). ISI and Al-Nusra were already coordinating with each other during this period (Erlich, 2014). More specifically, a highly classified document, issued by US intelligence, stated that Ziyaad Tariq Ahmed [an Iraqi CW expert who was serving in the Iraqi military during Saddam's time] had been operating actively with Al-Nusra in the Al-Ghouta area (Hersh, 2013). The document which referred to him as the "Al-Nusra guy" detailed his activities in manufacturing mustard gas in Iraq (Hersh, 2013). Two months before the Al-Ghouta attack, a consultant to the US Defence Intelligence Agency (DIA) sent an analytical report to David Shedd, the deputy director of DIA, expressing his concerns over Al-Nusra's efforts in producing CW (Hersh, 2014). The DIA consultant states:

> [Al-Nusra's program] is the most advanced Sarin plot since Al-Qaeda's pre-9/11 effort. Previous IC [Intelligence Community] focus had been almost entirely on Syrian CW stockpiles; now we see ANF [Al-Nusra Front] attempting to make its own CW. Al-Nusra Front's relative freedom of operation within Syria leads us to assess the group's CW aspirations will be difficult to disrupt in the future. Turkey and Saudi-based chemical facilitators were attempting to obtain Sarin precursors in bulk, tens of kilograms, likely for the anticipated large scale production effort in Syria. (Hersh, 2014)

As mentioned in Chap. 4, a US intelligence source reveals that the Turkish National Intelligence Agency [known as MIT] and Gendarmerie [Turkish militarised law-enforcement organisation] trained Al-Nusra on how to develop CW (Hersh, 2014). In May 2013, ten members of Al-Nusra were detained in Turkey for possessing two kilograms of sarin. A US Defence Intelligence Agency source said that Haytham Qassab, a high-profile member of Al-Nusra, was one of the arrested suspects (Hersh, 2014). Peace Association and Lawyers for Justice in Turkey (PALJ) (2013), however, has stated that Qassab was not a member of Al-Qaeda

[Al-Nusra] as he confessed while being interrogated that he is a member of the Saudi-funded opposition group, *Liwa Al-Islam*.

After conducting personal interviews with doctors, Al-Ghouta's residents, rebel fighters and their families, Gavlak and Ababneh (2013) conclude that the Saudi-funded group *Liwa Al-Islam* might be responsible for the Al-Ghouta attack. In their report that was published on August 29, 2013, Aby Abdel-Moneim, father of an anti-Assad rebel, said his son along with 12 other rebels died on the same day of the attack while they were in a tunnel, used to store Saudi-supplied weapons. The father added that the stored weapons had "tube-like structures" and some of them were similar to "huge gas bottles" (Gavlak & Ababneh, 2013). A female fighter revealed that the rebels did not know that "these arms were CW". She continues:

> They [Saudi intelligence] didn't tell us what these arms were or how to use them. We did not know they were chemical weapons. We never imagined they were chemical weapons. When Saudi Prince Bandar [bin Sultan] gives such weapons to people, he must give them to those who know how to handle and use them. (Gavlak & Ababneh, 2013)

PALJ (2013) in Turkey said that on September 15, 2013, a *Peshmerga*[9] fighter found videos of the Al-Ghouta attack saved in a smartphone of a dead anti-Assad rebel. One of these videos shows gas masked rebels, declaring the launch of a mission called "Cold Wind Operation" on the same day of the Al-Ghouta attack (PALJ, 2013). According to PALJ (2013), the flag of *Liwa Al-Islam* was seen in the videos.

The International Support Team for Mussalaha in Syria (ISTEAMS) and Mother Agnes Mariam of the Cross analysed the YouTube footage that was uploaded by rebels on August 21, 2013. Their report which was released on September 11, 2013, concludes that the videos that showed dead children were "staged" and "fabricated". They said that these children [along with 150 women] were abducted by Al-Nusra on August 4, 2013, when the group attacked 11 Alawite villages in Latakia (ISTEAMS, 2013). This incident was already documented by the Independent International Commission of Inquiry on the Syrian Arab Republic

---

[9] Military forces of the Regional Government of Kurdistan (KRG) in the autonomous region of Iraqi Kurdistan.

[IICISAR] (2014) report, stating that *Ahrar Al-Sham* and Al-Nusra abducted 200 civilians from villages in Eastern Latakia in 2013.

At the same time, however, a British weapons expert, Eliot Higgins, refutes the claim that Al-Nusra used CWs (Erlich, 2014). He argues that producing 50 gallons of sarin needs a specific type of precursor. Higgins asks, "Where is their factory? Where is their waste stream?" (Erlich, 2014). After analysing photos of the rockets used in the attack, Theodore Postol, a professor of technology and national security at the Massachusetts Institute of Technology (MIT), concluded that the rockets used in the attack gave an indication that the production process was not very complex. It is "something you could produce in a modestly capable machine shop" (Hersh, 2013). Hersh (2013) infers that all this contradictory information might have been the reason behind Obama's decision to take the issue to the Congress and accept Russia's proposal later.

None of these allegations, views and reports were mentioned in the AJA and AJE news and features during the research period. If such context and accounts were highlighted, then threatening to launch a war against the regime might not have sounded reasonable. McGoldrick (2006) argues that if media coverage does not provide explanations and alternative accounts, violence will appear as a proper response, and avoiding it will not make any sense. A PJ approach would give space to all sides and include other possible CW users [such as Al-Nusra, Al-Qaeda in Iraq or ISI and *Liwa Al-Islam*]. J. Lynch and McGoldrick (2000) say that excluding some aspects or facts from media coverage conveys a distorted image of reality. They state:

> Mainstream media conveys a distorted picture by routinely missing out certain factors which an understanding of peace studies, conflict analysis and transformation sees as essential. It is this pattern of omission which is dangerous unless counterbalanced with peace journalism. (J. Lynch & McGoldrick, 2000, p. 48)

The findings of this book are in line with previous studies that show how the absence of certain facts has aided in misrepresenting conflicts and conveying inaccurate narratives that do not reflect the reality [or social reality] (see Fahmy & Eakin, 2014; J. Lynch & McGoldrick, 2005b; J. Lynch, 2006; Ottosen, 2010).

6 SYRIA'S CWS COVERAGE (2013): PEACE DEAL OR MILITARY ACTION... 205

Al-Jazeera's Legitimisation and Exoneration of Al-Nusra Front

As noted previously, Al-Jazeera did not only exclude the possibility that Al-Nusra Front could carry out a CW attack, but it has represented them as a "moderate" and "tolerant" group that does not resemble or is related to Al-Qaeda and ISIS. Ahmad Zaidan (2015), a Syrian reporter and AJA's Islamabad bureau chief, published an article on AJE website on June 2, 2015, in which he portrayed Al-Nusra and its leader Abu Mohammad Al-Jolani as distinct from Al-Qaeda. He wrote about his interview with Al-Jolani:

> The first thing that struck me was his [Al-Jolani's] traditional Syrian dress. He did not wear Al-Qaeda's trademark turban. Al-Jolani defied Al-Qaeda's legacy of going after minorities, telling the Alawite community—the backbone of dictator Bashar Al-Assad's support—they would be welcome in a Syria after Al-Assad. (Zaidan, 2015)

Zaidan (2015) adds that Al-Qaeda's leader, Ayman Al-Zawahiri, is to Al-Nusra "like the British monarch" as it "has symbolic resonance without much in the way of practical authority". Ahmad Mansour, one of AJA's prominent presenters since the 1990s, was the first journalist to interview Al-Jolani on May 27, 2015. In that interview Mansour criticised putting "Al-Nusra and ISIS in one basket" because—according to him—they are totally different on many levels. Before introducing Al-Jolani, Mansour said in the opening of his show:

> Unlike others [rebel groups] Al-Nusra is classified by the United States as a terrorist group. While the Syrian regime attack Al-Nusra's men and headquarters, the US-led coalition jet planes hit the same targets. Al-Nusra and its leaders are struck by the American missiles because the US put Al-Nusra and ISIS in one basket despite the intense disagreements between them intellectually, ideologically, and even militarily. (Bila Hudud, May 27, 2015a)

Like AJA, it was leaked that the executive producer of AJE news instructed AJE's news staff not to associate Al-Nusra with Al-Qaeda (Salih, 2015). Kelly Jarrett sent the following memo to the staff in September 2015:

> Please don't introduce Al-Nusra Front as 'Al-Qaeda-affiliated.' We have a hard enough time trying to explain the state of play without including labels that mislead. Al-Nusra Front is part of Syria's rebel coalition which is made up of multiple armed rebel groups including many based on religious

ideology with various funding streams; our viewers need to understand that these armed groups form the main opposition to the government led by President Assad. And these rebel groups are opposed to, and actively fighting ISIL. (Salih, 2015)

In an interview conducted for this book, Kelly Jarrett[10] has confirmed sending this memo to 4000 employees in AJE, but she insisted that this request does not have any political motivation. She states:

In that email, I was talking to producers who need to get the audience's attention in 20 seconds. So they don't want to be bogged down with explaining who is aligned to whom because it would take too long and it's too complicated. If people want to leak emails that is absolutely fine but you need to understand the context. I teach producers how to present information. Correspondents write reports, they write packages, they do live shots in which they have 2, 3, 4 minutes to give all of the background, all of the context. My producers have 20 seconds to direct the viewers' attention and tell you what the top line or the top story is backed by. You see? So that is the difference. (K. Jarrett, personal communication, April 14, 2016)

Representing the Qatari-funded group as more moderate than Al-Qaeda and ISIS is not only in contradiction with the human rights reports that documented Al-Nusra's violations (Amnesty International, 2015; HRW, 2015), but it is also inconsistent with the statements of the group itself. For instance, the group has proudly expressed its support and "full endorsement" to the deadly attacks in Paris that took place on November 13, 2015. Al-Nusra said, "We are happy if a deviant sect successfully executes an operation against the *Kufaar* كفار [infidels]" (MacDonald, 2015). Moreover, Abu Mariya Al-Qahtani, a prominent cleric and former Shariah official in Al-Nusra, backed ISIS' suicide bombings in Southern Beirut where 43 Shia civilians were killed on November 12, 2015. Al-Qahtani said:

Their [ISIS] fight against the Rawafid روافض [Shias] who wage war against the Muslims is something we are happy about. And their fight against Hizbu Shaytaan حزب الشيطان [Party of Satan; referring to Hezbollah] is something

---

[10] Some interviews in this chapter were conducted/published by the author and reproduced (from the article: Al-Jazeera's relationship with Qatar before and after Arab Spring: Effective public diplomacy or blatant propaganda?) with permission from the *Arab Media & Society* journal.

good. But they will remain Khawarij خوارج [renegades] to us. (SITE Intelligence Group, 2015)

HRW (2015) states that Al-Nusra claimed responsibility for explosions targeting "*Shabiha*[11] شبيحة [pro-Assad militias/thugs] and *Rawafid* [Shias]" in Sayida Zainab area in March and November 2013. On December 11 and 12, 2013, Al-Nusra and *Jaysh Al-Islam* raided civilians' houses in Rif Dimashq Governorate and shot dead 15 civilians based on their sectarian affiliation (IICISAR, 2014). On August 13, 2014, IICISAR (2014) reported that Al-Nusra claimed responsibility for car bombings in Al-Abassiya, a lower-class Alawite neighbourhood in Homs, killing 45 people, most of them were under 18 years old. On June 2, 2014, Al-Nusra claimed responsibility of detonating a car in Al-Hiraqe, an Alawite village in Homs, killing at least 15 civilians, including women and children (IICISAR, 2014). The IICISAR (2014, p. 41) report states:

> The war crime of attacking civilians was committed by Jabhat Al-Nusra and other unidentified armed groups in their car bomb attacks on Government-controlled neighborhoods of Homs city between 6 March and 19 June 2014. The attacks did not target any military objectives, nor was there any military equipment or personnel near the sites of the attacks.

Excluding Al-Nusra as a potential suspect that might have used CW in the Al-Ghouta attack, representing it as a "moderate group" and omitting its war crimes against civilians, cannot be fully interpreted without taking into consideration Qatar's foreign policy and its financial support to Al-Nusra. In an interview with CNN in September 2014, the Emir of Qatar, Sheikh Tamim bin Hamad Al-Thani, has denied that his country funds any Islamist groups in Syria and Iraq (Dorsey, 2015). However, Qatar's successful mediations [that led to the release of several hostages abducted by Al-Nusra in the recent years] have cast doubts on the extent of coordination between Doha and the Al-Qaeda-affiliated group (Dorsey, 2015). Reports reveal that Qatar has paid from US$5 to $150 million to release Al-Nusra's captives (Lister, 2016b).

Its mediation efforts have resulted in releasing nine Shia Iranian pilgrims in October 2013, 13 Greek Orthodox nuns in 2014 and 16

---

[11] Arabic word means literally "ghosts", referring to Alawite armed militias fighting with Al-Assad's regime.

Lebanese armed forces personnel in December 2015 (Roberts, 2015; Lister, 2016b). Al-Nusra has been known for being the best armed and funded group as it receives "generous supplies from sympathisers in Qatar and the Gulf states" (Sengupta, 2013). The Qatari Foreign Minister Khalid Al-Attiyah praised and described *Ahrar al-Sham* [which Al-Nusra is part of] as "purely Syrian" (Blair & Spencer, 2014). In addition, the authorities in Qatar have not taken any action against the Qatari academic and businessman Abdul Rahman Al-Nuaimi, who is well-known by the US Treasury as a "global terrorist" (Blair & Spencer, 2014). The US Treasury (2013) revealed that Al-Nuaimi transferred US$600,000 to Al-Qaeda's-affiliated groups in Syria. Another Qatari citizen known by the US Treasury as a "key link between Al-Qaeda's leadership in Pakistan and Gulf financiers" was arrested and released shortly after promising he would not "conduct terrorist activity in Qatar" (Burweila, 2014). Roberts (2015) argues that Qatar supports Al-Nusra due to its effectiveness and popularity compared to other opposition groups in Syria.

Qatar and Turkey's funding and coordination with Al-Qaeda-affiliated groups have angered the United States and the West (M. Lynch, 2016). Kamrava (2013, p. 80) says that Qatar is "the worst in the region when it comes to cooperation with the United States in counterterrorism efforts". The President of the United States Joe Biden said, when he was Vice President in October 2014:

> Our allies in the region were our largest problem... [They] were so determined to take down [Syrian President Bashar] Al-Assad and have a proxy Sunni-Shia war, they poured hundreds of millions of dollars and thousands of tons of weapons into anyone who would fight against Al-Assad. Except that the people who were being supplied were [Jabhat] Al-Nusra and Al-Qaeda, and the extremist elements of jihadis coming from other parts of the world. (M. Lynch, 2016, p. 25)

AJA's representation of Al-Nusra as a "tolerant" group that is not related to extremists or jihadists and AJE's request from its journalists not to associate Al-Nusra with Al-Qaeda echo Qatar's attempts to convince Al-Nusra of splitting from Al-Qaeda. According to Karouny (2015), Qatari intelligence officials met the leader of Al-Nusra, to persuade him to "abandon Al-Qaeda and to discuss what support they [Qatar] could provide". Khatib (2015) says that Qatar was trying to separate Al-Nusra from

Al-Qaeda in order to use it as a "winning card" in any international resolution of the Syrian conflict. Roberts (2015) states that the split will officially enable Qatar to "commence—with Western blessing—the supply of one of the most effective fighting forces in Syria".

On July 28, 2016, Al-Nusra has confirmed all these speculations by declaring its separation from Al-Qaeda. The group has changed its name to *Jabhat Fateh Al-Sham* فتح الشام جبهة [the Front for the Conquest of the Levant]. Six hours before this announcement, Ayman Al-Zawahiri, the main leader of Al-Qaeda, endorsed and blessed Al-Nusra's split. He said, "The bonds of Islamic brotherhood are stronger than any obsolete links between organisations... These organisational links must be sacrificed without hesitation if they threaten your unity" (Lister, 2016a). Lister (2016a) argues that this move makes the group more dangerous because it can be considered now as a "legitimate armed group" that is openly eligible of receiving funds from Qatar and Turkey.

6.4.4   *Omission of Alternative Accounts*

Elites' quotations [from both the Syrian regime and the opposition] dominated AJA-N&F (84.3% and 77.4%) and AJE-N&F (70% and 53.3%) (Table 6.4). Yet, members of the moderate opposition [who are against the regime and, at the same time, refuse a military strike against Syria] were barely quoted in either of the channels [AJA-N&F (0% and 1.6%) and AJE-N&F (0% and 0%)] (Table 6.4).

J. Lynch (2008) argues that quoting officials is more than a practice of media routines.

It is instead a "choice and preference". The absence of moderate opposition or activists' sights can give the impression that there are no challenges to the dominant accounts (J. Lynch, 2007). John Paul Lederach (1997), a prominent peace researcher, says that peace supporters can be found even in the most complicated conflicts, but they are usually ignored by the media. He says:

> I have not experienced any situation of conflict, no matter how protracted or severe, from Central America to the Philippines to the Horn of Africa, where there have not been people who had a vision for peace, emerging often from their own experience of pain. Far too often, however, these same people are overlooked and disempowered either because they do not repre-

210 Z. ABDUL-NABI

Table 6.4 Dominant sources in AJA's and AJE's coverage of Syria's chemical attack

Source	News		Features	
	AJA	AJE	AJA	AJE
Moderate opposition groups	0 (0%)	0 (0%)	1 (1.6%)	0 (0%)
Opposition and its allies	185 (59.1%)	218 (44.9%)	26 (41.9%)	12 (40%)
Syrian regime and its allies	79 (25.2%)	122 (25.1%)	22 (35.5%)	4 (13.3%)
The UN and Human Rights groups.	41 (13.1%)	53 (10.9%)	4 (6.5%)	1 (3.3%)
Survivors, victims, civilians	0 (0%)	2 (0.4%)	6 (9.7%)	9 (30%)
Doctors	2 (0.6%)	12 (2.5%)	0 (0%)	0 (0%)
CW expert/military expert	1 (0.3%)	5 (1%)	2 (3.2%)	4 (13.3%)
Al-Jazeera reporter	5 (1.6%)	74 (15.2%)	1 (1.6%)	0 (0%)

sent 'official' power, whether on the side of government or the various militias, or because they are written off as biased and too personally affected by the conflict. (Lederach, 1997, p. 94 cited in J. Lynch & McGoldrick, 2005a, p. 18)

Even though the majority of quoted elites are from the opposition and its allies in AJA-N&F (59.1% and 41.9%) and AJE-N&F (44.9% and 40%) (Table 6.4), extremist opposition groups that refused a foreign military intervention were also marginalised. For instance, the Syrian Islamic Front [close to the Salafist *Ahrar Al-Sham*] was not mentioned during the research period although it heavily criticised a US potential strike. *The Washington Post* stated on September 6, 2013:

[the Syrian Islamic Front] issued a statement on its Facebook page cautioning its followers against supporting U.S. intervention, saying it would only serve American interests and not the cause of those seeking to topple President Bashar Al-Assad. (Sly, 2013)

Except for AJE-F (30%), the coverage of the network marginalised the accounts of ordinary people and civilians (Table 6.4), though not giving a voice to the voiceless is not unusual in the mainstream media, even if they are the main actors in a story. For instance, a study that examined *The Guardian*, *Haaretz* and *The New York Times* coverage of the Turkish flotilla *Mavi Marmara* [that wanted to break the blockade against Gaza in 2010] shows that the passengers of the ship were significantly sidelined as sources and actors (Fahmy & Eakin, 2014). McGoldrick (2006) argues that the favouring of official sources is the most widespread practice in conventional media across the world. Fishman (1988, p. 144–145) says journalists consider bureaucratic sources as "authorised knowers". He states:

> Reporters operate with the attitude that officials ought to know what it is their job to know... In particular, a news worker will recognise an official's claim to knowledge not merely as a claim, but as a credible, competent piece of knowledge. This amounts to a moral division of labour: officials have and give the facts; reporters merely get them. (Fishman, 1988, p. 144–145)

Quoted sources can significantly affect media content especially if these sources obscure information or "lie" (Shoemaker & Reese, 2013). Elite sources have a control over the flow of information because they are normally the ones that organise events, monopolise journalists' time and have the power to answer or ignore the questions they want (Shoemaker & Reese, 2013). Journalists prefer to conduct interviews with them not only because they believe they have something important to say (Fishman, 1988) but also they are available and take less time, effort and expense (Shoemaker & Reese, 2013). Entman (2003, p. 420) explains in his "cascading activation model of political influence" that ideas come from powerful sources that have influence and strength and the ability to spread more than ideas that have come from lower levels. This is because "moving downward in a cascade is relatively easy, but spreading ideas higher, from lower levels to upper, requires extra energy—a pumping mechanism" (Entman, 2003, p. 420, cited in Shoemaker & Reese, p. 110).

6.5 FAVOURING OPPOSITION SOURCES OVER THE REGIME

As mentioned previously and stated in Table 6.4, the results of this study show that both channels favoured the opposition sources over the Syrian regime.

When asked about the reasons behind giving more space and time to the opposition, the executive producer of AJE news said that it is "extremely challenging" to be "fully balanced in Syria" due to safety considerations and difficulties in accessing the country. Kelly Jarrett (personal communication, April 14, 2016) says:

> It's extremely challenging in Syria, in Yemen, in Libya at the moment to give a fully balanced picture show by show, hour by hour, day by day, because it is moving so quickly and access is extremely difficult, and that's for all media outlets. Ours in particular because we had several safety breaches and our journalists have been killed and are threatened more than any other organisation. So that is a very, very real handicap for us.

However, a journalist working in the newsroom of AJE said that most journalists in the channel are "anti-Assad" because they normally "stand with people against governments". The editor who preferred to be anonymous says:

> Al-Jazeera couldn't get inside Syria; their coverage is so reliant on YouTube posts from protestors. The Syrian government stopped talking to Al-Jazeera very early in the conflict. I think most people feel anti-Assad at Al-Jazeera because they are just consuming online material from activists, so as journalists we naturally side with the people against the government. (AJE Journalist, personal communication, December 15, 2015)

Not having access to certain sources or difficulties in gathering information about the "other side" are not a "credible" justification according to Herman and Chomsky (2010). They argue that political factors are the only reasons that can explain the differences in quality when reporting on worthy and unworthy victims. If journalists want to obtain information about violations committed against "the other side", they can always refer to and quote human rights organisations (Herman & Chomsky, 2010). In today's world, the views and accounts of most sides of conflicts are available on social media.

Al-Jazeera's correspondent in Lebanon, Ali Hashem, resigned in 2011 when the channel refused to broadcast his exclusive footage in which members of the Syrian opposition were smuggling arms from the Lebanese border into Syria, two months after the protests [May 2011]. He believes that AJA wanted to conceal the fact that the opposition was armed from the early stages of the uprising. Hashem (2012) wrote in *The Guardian*:

> It was clear to me, though, that these instructions [rejecting to broadcast the footage] were not coming from Al-Jazeera itself: that the decision was a political one taken by people outside the TV centre—the same people who asked the channel to cover up the situation in Bahrain. I felt that my dream of working for a main news channel in the region was becoming a nightmare. The principles I had learned during 10 years of journalism were being disrespected by a government that—whatever the editorial guidelines might say—believed it owned a bunch of journalists who should do whatever they were asked.

In a leaked correspondence between Hashem and his colleague, anchorwoman, Rula Ibrahim, expressed her frustrations over the censorship in the channel (Kanaan, 2012). She told Hashem in that email:

> They [Al-Jazeera] wiped the floor with me because I embarrassed Zuheir Salem [spokesperson for Syria's Muslim Brothers/opposition] on air. As a result, I was prevented from doing any Syrian interviews and threatened with [a] transfer to the night shift on the pretext that I was making the channel imbalanced. (Kanaan, 2012)

The Syrian anchor reveals in her emails that Ahmed Ibrahim, who is responsible for the coverage of Syria, is the brother of one of the Syrian opposition leaders, Anas Al-Abdeh. According to *Al-Akhbar* newspaper, Al-Jazeera's editor stopped using his surname to "avoid drawing attention to the connection" (Kanaan, 2012).

214   Z. ABDUL-NABI

6.5.1   Double Standard Coverage of the Syrian Regime and Opposition

According to SOHR's[12] [opposition group] data, the number of the deaths among the Syrian regime forces and their allies is higher than the number of opposition and Al-Qaeda-affiliated groups (M. Lynch, 2016). In December 2013, SOHR stated that 50,000 regime's soldiers and 30,000 rebels were killed in the fighting (M. Lynch, 2016). SOHR also has said that 70,000 anti-Assad fighters and 82,000 pro-Assad soldiers had been killed in the civil war by June 2015 (M. Lynch, 2016).

The Independent International Commission of Inquiry on the Syrian Arab Republic (IICISAR) (2013) report has stated that both sides committed war crimes including executions without due process, murder, torture, hostage-taking and indiscriminately shelling civilians' neighbourhoods. Al-Jazeera however has only focused on the "massacres" committed by the regime and condoned the explosions carried out by opposition groups. For example, on September 5, 2013, AJA published a news report under the title "_Massacres_ by the Syrian regime since the beginning of the _revolution_". The article stated:

> Since the start of the revolution in mid-March in 2011, Syria has witnessed massacres and bloody operations that were carried out by the Syrian army, which have killed thousands of children, women and men. These massacres include attacks in the Eastern Ghouta, Homs and Houla in Altrimssh, Hama and others. Hundreds were killed and wounded in blasts that hit several cities in Syria. Some of these attacks have targeted the military and security headquarters of Syrian forces. (AJA, September 5, 2013g)

Just by looking at which lexical choices were used to describe the attacks [massacres] and Syrian conflict [revolution], readers can infer which side AJA inclines to. However, what cannot be observed clearly is that AJA listed 21 "massacres" against the "revolutionaries" [rebels], yet nine of these 21 massacres were either attacks against the Syrian army or explosions in Alawite areas. In this article, AJA mentioned the perpetrators [Al-Assad regime] very clearly if the listed attack was against rebels. However, when the attack was committed by rebels against pro-Assad areas or regime's soldiers, AJA did not mention who were the

---

[12] SOHR is headed by Rami Abdul-Rahman, human rights activist and anti-Assad opponent.

6 SYRIA'S CWS COVERAGE (2013): PEACE DEAL OR MILITARY ACTION...   215

perpetrators. It used instead passive sentences such as "hundreds were killed in blasts". In some cases, it uses "nominalisation"[13] [such as killing hundreds in blasts] to "obscure those responsible for the killing" and create intentional ambiguity (Machin & Mayr, 2012, p. 138). The following paragraphs show how AJA avoided attributing the responsibility of the attacks to rebels:

> On November 28th, 2012, two <u>car explosions killed 54</u> and injured 120 in Jaramana suburb of Christian and Druze majority in Damascus. (AJA, September 5, 2013g)

> On May 10th 2012, <u>55 people were killed, and 372</u> injured in two simultaneous bomb blasts in the Kazaz neighbourhood, south of Damascus in front of the Syrian security headquarters. (AJA, September 5, 2013g)

> On June 23rd 2013, <u>eight soldiers associated with Al-Assad forces were killed</u> in a car bomb attack near a police station in Jobar neighbourhood. (AJA, September 5, 2013g)

On the other hand, if the attacks were committed by the regime, AJA would clearly mention who is responsible, as shown in the following examples:

> On June 22, 2013, the Syrian opposition said that <u>the Syrian army killed</u> 191 people in a massacre in Aleppo. (AJA, September 5, 2013g)

> At the beginning of May 2013, the Syrian Observatory for Human Rights said 145 civilians were shot dead in a massacre <u>carried out by Al-Assad troops in</u> Banbas. (AJA, September 5, 2013g)

> In May 2013, the Syrian Revolution General Commission said that <u>Al-Assad forces executed 50 prisoners</u> jailed in central Aleppo prison. (AJA, September 5, 2013g)

> In April 2013, 483 people were killed, including women and children, in a massacre <u>committed by Syrian Republican Guard forces</u> in coordination with the Shabiha [thugs], which lasted for four days, according to the Local Coordination Committees of Syria. (AJA, September 5, 2013g)

---

[13] When verb is transformed into a noun, for example, kill is transformed to killing (Machin & Mayr, 2012).

216   Z. ABDUL-NABI

While suicide car bombs "are not less deadly" than the Al-Assad regime's barrel bombs, the media and social media circulated the abuses of the regime but not the opposition (M. Lynch, 2016). Entman (1993) argues that excluding certain facts, explanations and evaluations is as critical as including them in influencing the audience. In addition, selecting a frame calls attention to a particular aspect of reality and directs it away from another (Entman, 1993). Had Al-Jazeera conveyed accounts and perspectives from an Alawite or Christian area where suicide bombings and car explosions indiscriminately targeted pro-Assad civilians [as documented by HRW (2015)], its coverage would have been more balanced and less polarised.

Tehranian (2004) argues that when American journalists started to report from the front lines during the war in Vietnam, by sending "bloody images" that contradicted Pentagon statements and fabrications, American public opinion turned against the war. Tehranian (2004) says that uncovering the Pentagon's propaganda eventually led the Nixon administration to conduct a peace agreement with North Vietnam. Tehranian (2004) contends that the effective role of media during Vietnam's war had forced the Pentagon to adopt a new media policy in First and Second Gulf Wars. During the First Gulf War in 1991, journalists were not allowed to report from the front line and were instead kept in hotels in Riyadh. In the Second Gulf War in 2003, the Pentagon "moved a step further" by embedding journalists with US troops. This did not affect their role as "free agents" but created a sense of empathy and solidarity with the troops (Tehranian, 2004).

6.5.2   *Double Standards Between Al-Nusra's Captive and Leader*

The following section provides a specific example of the "double standards" between the representations of the regime and the opposition. It details how AJA interviewed and framed Al-Nusra's leader and one of Al-Nusra's captives.

During his interview with Al-Nusra's leader on May 27, 2015, Ahmad Mansour referred to Al-Nusra as a "resistance" that has achieved "victories". Mansour, who is known for asking provocative and interrogating questions, said while introducing Al-Nusra's Emir:

6 SYRIA'S CWS COVERAGE (2013): PEACE DEAL OR MILITARY ACTION...

I greet you and welcome you in a new episode of Bila Hudud بلا حدود [Without Borders] from a <u>liberated area</u> [under Al-Nusra's control] in northern Syria, as the <u>military victories</u> made by Jaysh Al-Fateh جيش الفتح [The Army of Conquest] has cast its shadow inside and outside Syria's arena. Al-Nusra Front is one of Jaysh Al-Fateh's army pillars. (Bila Hudud, May 27, 2015a)

Unlike his usual interviewing style, Mansour did not repeat, insist and challenge his guest. Instead, he seemed to agree with him. For instance, he said—in an agreement with Al-Jolani—that the Al-Qaeda-affiliated group was "actually protecting the minorities". The following part of the one-hour interview was about Al-Nusra's treatment to minorities:

Mansour: When I was walking around in the last days in the 'liberated areas' [under Al-Nusra's control], I found ten Druze [Islamic sect] villages and some Christian villages as well. I was really surprised that you [Al-Nusra] were actually protecting the people of these villages, this has really surprised me.

Al-Jolani: In respect to the Druze, they are welcome. We had sent preachers to them to explain to them their mistakes. Then, they showed that they retreated from their ideological mistakes, and we...

Mansour [interrupting]: You haven't attacked their villages, you haven't destroyed their homes?

Al-Jolani: No, No, not at all.

Mansour: You haven't taken their properties, you haven't sabotaged their temples? You haven't done anything yet?

Al-Jolani: No not at all, no not at all, in regard to temples, if there is anything that does not belong to Sharia law, we deal with it according to the Sharia law. For instance, they [Shias and Alawites] visit graves [Shrines]. We consider this as polytheism, so we make them avoid this. We have sent preachers to them in order to correct their ideologies and to teach them what they have missed [misunderstood] from this religion. We even haven't harmed Alawites although they committed massacres [against us]. Our religion is a religion of mercy; we are not killers and criminals; we fight who fights us; we stand against injustice. If Alawites abandon their arms and renounce Al-Assad's wrongdoings; if they renounce the tyranny [Al-Assad's regime], they will not only be safe, but they will be our brothers, and we will protect them like the way we protect ourselves.

Mansour: So you are sending this clear message to the Alawites?

Al-Jolani: Of course, if each village [Alawite village] took a decision to abandon Bashar Al-Assad.

Mansour: Each village alone?

Al-Jolani: Yes, if they renounce Al-Assad and what he did to Sunnis and prevent their men from fighting alongside Al-Assad, and they abandon what makes them different from the Islamic way [infidels], and they return back to Islam again and leave their beliefs, then they will be our brothers, and we will defend them. We will no longer consider them as stray people, and we will forget our wounds.

Mansour: So Abu Mohammed, excuse me here, is it possible that we consider this as an official declaration to each Alawite village including its men, women, and people who are under your fire now?

Al-Jolani: Of course, this is what we do already.... (Bila Hudud, May 27, 2015a)

Although Mansour asked Al-Jolani about Al-Nusra's violations, he did not confront the Emir with the mounting evidence and reports that documented Al-Nusra's war crimes against minorities in Syria. He gave Al-Jolani a significant amount of time and space to represent the Al-Qaeda group as a "merciful" and "forgiving" entity who fights against "tyranny" and "injustice", without challenging his allegations. Mansour did not ask Al-Jolani about how the group was able to convince the "Druze" to "retreat from their beliefs". He did not ask about Al-Nusra's suicidal explosions in Alawite and Christian areas where there were no military targets. If Al-Nusra is a "tolerant" group, why would it send preachers to "convince" minorities to change their religions? What if these minorities did not want to change their beliefs? Why is everyone that disagrees with Al-Nusra's ideology considered as "astray" and "non-Muslim?" Mansour—unlike his inquisitorial interviewing style—did not ask any of these questions. On the other hand, the same presenter used a stronger tone and questions with pro-regime guests even if they were prisoners. For instance, on July 8, 2015 [nearly two months after the interview with

Al-Nusra's leader], Mansour interviewed a pro-regime prisoner who was abducted by Al-Nusra. Ali Abboud, a colonel in the Syrian regime's air force, was taken hostage when the group shot down his plane. At the outset of his interview with Abboud, Mansour described Al-Nusra fighters as "revolutionaries", noting that "the interview is being conducted from a "liberated area" in Northern Syria. Mansour said that he "tried his best to convince Al-Nusra" to interview Abboud. Minutes later he said, "I do not like to do an interview with a person that is not free, but the colonel pilot insisted to" (*Bila Hudud*, July 8, 2015b). During the interview, Abboud seemed to be in an unstable condition. He was speaking with a low voice and giving very short answers. Mansour's strong and provocative questions made him look vulnerable and frightened. One might ask, if Abboud "insisted on doing the interview", as Mansour claimed, why would he respond with silence and brief answers most of time? Why would he call his enemies "revolutionaries" and "*mujahedeen*" [jihadists] while he supposedly considers them "terrorists" or "armed thugs"? In contrast with his interview with Al-Jolani, Mansour repeated his questions, insisted, confronted, interrogated, interrupted and intimidated Abboud. Below are some parts of the interview.

(Part 1)

Mansour: So, if they [the Syrian regime] told you to attack your house or an Alawite area, would you attack/hit it?

Abboud: No, I mean, if there was…

Mansour [Interrupting]: No, No, No, if it was an Alawite area and there are Alawite people in it, your family are in it [would you still hit it]?

Abboud: If my family were there, I wouldn't hit it

Mansour: Isn't this a military rebellion?

Abboud: No one hits his own family!

Mansour: So other Syrians are not your family?

Abboud: All of them are our family.

Mansour: So, you were already attacking your family?

Abboud: All of them are our family.

Mansour: So?

Abboud: You are right. **Mansour:** What does this mean? **Abboud:** It means….

Mansour: Tell me? **Abboud:** You are right. (Part 2)

Mansour: So your [air] bombings caused great destruction?

Abboud [remained silent]: …

Mansour [repeats]: So, your [air] bombings caused great destruction?

Abboud [after seconds of silence]: Yes (Part 3)

Mansour: Who are the leaders/officials that you have a relationship with?

Abboud: I have a relationship with the Airport Operation Officer only.

Mansour: So, you don't have any contacts with other Alawite leaders and officers in the Syrian Army at all?

Abboud: No, I don't have any, I don't because…

Mansour: There are no [Alawite] officers [serving in the Syrian Army] in your village?

Abboud: No

Mansour: There are no officers in your family?

Abboud: Only my brother…….

Mansour [interrupting]: So, there is no one serving in the army from your family?

Abboud: No, me and my brother only. **Mansour:** You and your brother only? **Abboud:** Only.

6 SYRIA'S CWS COVERAGE (2013): PEACE DEAL OR MILITARY ACTION... 221

Mansour: I didn't mean by your family your mother, father and siblings only **Abboud:** Oh, you mean the village? Yes, there are, but we don't see each other...

Mansour: Who are the main leaders/officers in your village?

Abboud: There aren't any

Mansour: What is your relationship with Suhail Al-Hassan [Major General in the Syrian Army and commander of its Tiger Forces]?

Abboud: I don't know him **Mansour:** Does he know you? **Abboud:** No.

Mansour: He does know you.

Abboud: I don't know him.

Mansour: He knows you and he cares about you.

Abboud: Maybe he knows me as he is a pilot as well

Mansour: No, he knows you personally, you are apparently relatives

Abboud: I don't know, I am from Jablah and he is from Dreikish

Mansour: See! You know him now, and you know which village he is from...

Abboud: Not personally, I know him from what people say

Mansour: What is his role in the Syrian army?

Abboud: He is a leader of a group

Mansour: Does he lead the air operation in the North?

Abboud: Yes, he moves from one area to another

Mansour: You as a pilot, do you have a relationship with him?

Abboud: He has contacts with his own pilots only **Mansour:** Which airports do they operate/depart from? **Abboud:** They go wherever he goes

Mansour: Which airports?

Abboud: Hama airport, Taifor airport.... (Bila Hudud, July 8, 2015b)

These two interviews with the anti-Assad [Al-Jolani] and pro-Assad [Abboud] guests reflect an implementation of what Herman and Chomsky (2010) call "double standard" coverage. Mansour challenged, intimidated, interrogated and confronted the prisoner [Abboud] far more than the free leader [Al-Jolani]. These interviews do not only raise questions about Al-Jazeera's editorial policy and its Propaganda-Orientated coverage, but they also send alarms about the degree of AJA's adherence to human rights and media ethics. Abboud's interview can be considered as a violation of the 1949 Geneva Convention, which states that the prisoners of war "must at all times be protected, particularly against acts of violence or intimidation, and against insults and public curiosity" (Saxon, 2013). Saxon (2013), a former legal adviser to the United Nations International Commission of Inquiry for Syria, has criticised a similar interview in which AJA's reporter intimidated a pilot that had been captured by the Free Syrian Army. Saxon (2013) says:

> There is a distinct difference, however, between a still photograph or video material that identifies prisoners and/or depicts the reality of harsh detention conditions, and an interview that extracts information from a prisoner which 1) may be false and 2) may place that prisoner and others in danger. The former can save prisoners' lives. The latter may constitute abuse.

6.6   Pro-Qatar Framing in AJA and AJE

Given that both AJA and AJE favoured the opposition sources, exonerated Al-Qaeda-affiliated groups from committing any CW attack and legitimised the Al-Nusra Front, it is not surprising that the news and features of AJA (90.6% and 90.9%) and AJE (82% and 100%) were overwhelmingly dominated by pro-Qatar framing (Table 6.5). In other words, more than 80% of the articles from both channels involved claims that attributed the responsibility of using CWs in Al-Ghouta to the Al-Assad regime.

Interestingly, the personal, political and economic relations between Al-Assad and Sheikh Hamad were more than stable before the Arab Spring uprisings. There were frequent visits to each other's countries, and their wives were "close friends" (Ulrichsen, 2014). For instance, Qatar

6 SYRIA'S CWS COVERAGE (2013): PEACE DEAL OR MILITARY ACTION... 223

Table 6.5 Pro- and anti-Qatar framing in AJA's and AJE's coverage of Syria's chemical attack

Pro/Anti Qatar framing	News		Features	
	AJA	AJE	AJA	AJE
Pro-Qatar framing	144 claims 90.6%	150 claims 82%	20 claims 90.9%	5 claims 100%
Anti-Qatar Framing	15 claims 9.4%	33 claims 18%	2 claims 9.1%	0%
Neutral	0%	0%	0%	0%

coordinated very closely with Syria in Southern Lebanon after Israel's war in 2006. More interestingly, after Gaza's war in 2009, Syria and Hezbollah attended Doha's regional summit which was boycotted by Saudi Arabia and Egypt (Ulrichsen, 2014). Aktham Suliman, Al-Jazeera's former reporter in Germany who resigned in protest at Al-Jazeera's coverage of Syria and Bahrain, said in an interview with Deutsche Welle (DW) [Germany's international broadcaster] that the channel did not cover the uprising in the beginning because Qatar was trying to convince Al-Assad to initiate reforms (Allmeling, 2012). However, when the negotiations between them failed, Al-Jazeera started reporting (Allmeling, 2012). Aktham Suliman says:

> Al-Jazeera barely reported about the rebellion in the first few weeks. Some of my colleagues and I protested, pointing out that there was stuff happening in Syria, and we needed to report on it, regardless of our personal opinions. Back then, however, the ruler of Qatar was trying to change the Syrian president's mind and encourage him to take certain steps toward political reform. When Al-Assad did not respond, Al-Jazeera then said: Now get to work on Syria! It is not a good feeling when you have the impression that you are no longer a journalist. (Allmeling, 2012)

The *Al-Khabar* newspaper unveils that AJA's staff were instructed to use the term "martyrs" while referring to the victims of the Syrian opposition, but not regime loyalists (Kanaan, 2012). This is entirely in line with Propaganda-Orientated coverage in which the victims of an ally "will be subject to more intense and indignant coverage than those victimized by the United States or its clients" (Herman & Chomsky, 2010, p. xix).

6.7   Reporting Claims as Facts

6.7.1   *Launching Point and Range of Rockets Fired at Al-Ghouta Claims*

Similar to the AJA coverage of Bahrain's uprising, its coverage of Syria presented claims by officials as mere "facts" without them being challenged or counterbalanced.

For example, on August 30, 2013, AJA reported that the then US Secretary of State, John Kerry, said that the CW rockets that struck Al-Ghouta were launched from a regime-controlled area. AJA covered this statement as a "fact" without challenging it or counterbalancing it by other accounts. AJA stated:

> John Kerry said, 'We know where the rockets were launched from and at what time. We know where they landed and when. We know rockets came only from regime-controlled areas and went only to opposition-controlled or contested neighborhoods'. (AJA, August 30, 2013e)

However, unlike AJA, AJE represented Kerry's statement as an allegation that lacks "evidence":

> 'We know that the regime has used those weapons multiple times this year... and we know that the regime was specifically determined to rid the Damascus suburbs of the opposition,' Kerry said. In a separate conference call on Friday, a senior Obama administration official, speaking on condition of anonymity, dodged questions about whether Al-Assad himself directly ordered the attack, <u>suggesting that the US government does not have evidence that he did.</u> (AJE, August 29, 2013c)

> Obama did not present any direct evidence to back up his assertion that the Syrian government bears responsibility for the alleged attack, and the government has <u>strongly denied</u> accusations that it was involved. (AJE, August 29, 2013c)

Both channels were covering the same story; however, AJA represented the US administration's statement about the responsibility of the Al-Assad regime as a fact, while AJE challenged it and represented it as a claim that lacks evidence. This clearly shows how editors have the choice of which quote they want to include or exclude in order to balance coverage.

6 SYRIA'S CWS COVERAGE (2013): PEACE DEAL OR MILITARY ACTION... 225

On November 12, 2013, AJA aired a documentary film about the Al-Ghouta CW attack, under the title "Al-Ghouta: The Plotted Attack". The 30-minute documentary concluded that the rockets [which contained CW] were fired by the Republican Guard 104th Brigade in Mount Qasioun, a regime-held area. The AJA report described its findings as "new" and "unprecedented evidence". It said that "Al-Jazeera's investigative team" analysed the graphics and maps of the UNMIAUCWSAR (2013a) report [which confirmed the use of CW in Al-Ghouta without determining who was responsible in September 2013]. The team determined the trajectory of the two rockets. The documentary showed figures and maps supposedly designed by "Al-Jazeera's investigative team". It presented a figure showing that the first rocket that struck Moadamiya had a range of 9.5 kilometres and was fired from the Republican Guard 104th Brigade [Regime's checkpoint]. It presented another figure showing that the second rocket that struck Zamalka had a range of 9.6 kilometres and was launched from the same point [regime-held area]. The AJA documentary stated:

There is no such thing as a perfect crime... Al-Jazeera found two rockets in two separate houses. The images, measurements and information were sent to 'Al-Jazeera's investigative team' for analysis. The findings of 'Al-Jazeera's investigative team' have depended on a method that is similar to the method adopted by the UN report [that was released in September 2013] and Human Rights Watch. (AJA, November 12, 2013j)

The documentary said, "Al-Jazeera adopted 'a similar method' to the UN and HRW". First, the UN did not use any "method" to determine who was responsible for the attack. Second, the HRW analysed the findings of the UNMIAUCWSAR (2013a) report and was the one who had measured the trajectory of the rockets. AJA did not give any details about its analytical "method" or any information about its "investigative team". It did not show or quote anyone from the team during the 30-minute documentary. It displayed instead archival interviews with UN experts [who already confirmed the use of CW but did not determine who was responsible]. The presenter did not mention if the members of this team were journalists, scientists or military experts. Machin and Mayr (2012, p. 48) say that if information and details about processes or events are replaced by abstractions and generalisations, then "this is a sign that there is ideological work being done". Blatantly, AJA described its findings [which were broadcasted on November 12th, 2013] as "unprecedented evidence", whereas in fact these particular findings had been already inferred and published by *The New York Times* (Chivers, 2013) and Human Rights Watch (Lyons, 2013) on September 17, 2013. The estimations of the rockets' ranges [9.5 and 9.6 kilometres], their directions and firing base that AJA showed as its own findings were actually identical to the findings and figures posted by the HRW website nearly two months before AJA's documentary. The only differences between AJA and HRW pictures are the language and graphic design. The content is exactly the same.

More importantly, the documentary presented AJA's findings as "scientific evidence" not as a "scientific analysis" of the UN report. Machin and Mayr (2012, p. 42) argue that using figures and scientific sounding terms can convey authority and "connote 'science' and 'specialist knowledge' where in fact there might be none".

Nearly one month after this documentary, on December 13, 2013, Dr. Ake Sellstrom, head of the United Nations Mission to Investigate Allegations of the Use of Chemical Weapons in the Syrian Arab Republic, refuted the "scientific analysis" of HRW, NYT and AJA. In a media conference conducted by the UN mission after the release of its final findings of the use of CW in Syria, Sellstrom estimated the range of the missiles at about two kilometres. He stated, "Two kilometres could be a fair guess" (Lloyd & Postol, 2014). In other words, the rockets were not fired from Qasioun Mount [regime-held area]. When asked about his own analysis of who might have carried out the attack, Sellstrom said, "I don't have information that would stand in court". In an interview with *The Wall Street Journal*, he said "both sides in the conflict had the 'opportunity' and the 'capability' to carry out chemical weapons attacks" (Lauria, 2013). Richard Lloyd, former UN weapons inspector, and Theodore A. Postol, professor of science, technology and national security policy at MIT (2014), stated that Sellstrom's measurement of the range of the rockets is "in exact agreement" with their findings. In their report, they criticised Kerry's claims about the range of the rockets stating that "this mistaken intelligence could have led to an unjustified US military action based on false intelligence".

Both AJA and AJE covered the UN mission conference but did not mention Sellstrom's analysis over the range of the rockets. AJA stated:

6 SYRIA'S CWS COVERAGE (2013): PEACE DEAL OR MILITARY ACTION... 227

While the report [UN report that released on December 13, 2013] has not determined who used CW, it still implies that the regime is responsible for the attack that killed hundreds of Syrian civilians. (AJA, December 13, 2013k)

The first report of the UN inspectors has already pointed the finger to the regime's involvement in the attack. Yet, Syria and Russia blame the opposition. (AJA, December 13, 2013k)

None of the UN mission reports attributed the responsibility to any side. The UN reports that were released in September and December 2013 stated very clearly that their role is to find out whether CWs were used or not, without determining who carried out the attack (UNMIAUCWSAR, 2013a, 2013b). Therefore, AJA's quote above is not only misleading and blatantly Propaganda-Orientated but is inconsistent with basic journalism standards of accuracy and credibility. Tehranian (2002, p. 15) says that "without credibility, media does not lose its audiences only but legitimacy, power, and eventually money".

6.7.2 Intelligence Claims

AJA reported as a "fact" that the US administration has been informed by "intelligence sources" that the Al-Assad regime used CW in Al-Ghouta. AJA stated in August and September 2013:

Depending on many intelligence sources, a CIA report publicized by the White House on Friday, states that the Syrian regime has used nerve agent in Al-Ghouta's attack. (AJA, August 30, 2013e)

According to the American president, US information confirms that Al-Assad is responsible for the CW attack [in Al-Ghouta]. The information also confirms that the regime distributed gas masks to its soldiers before the deadly gas attack. (AJA, September 11, 2013i)

Hersh (2014) has already refuted the claim that the Obama administration had "intelligence information" three days before the attack. He says an intelligence consultant revealed that the "Morning Report[14]" did not

[14] High classified document produced daily by military intelligence community to the Secretary of Defence and the chairman of the Joint Chiefs of Staff (Hersh, 2014).

mention anything about Syria and the Al-Ghouta attack on August 21 and 22, 2013. Furthermore, the US sensor system, implanted secretly in Syria's CW stores to provide warning about CW activities, did not detect any movement before August 21 (Hersh, 2014). In December 2012, this sensor had picked up signals of sarin production by the Syrian military (Hersh, 2014). At the time, Obama alerted Syria that the use of sarin is "totally unacceptable". Thus, Hersh (2014) asks, if the Obama administration had information already on the preparations of the attack, why did it not warn Syria again?

Hersh (2014) says that intelligent officers are concerned about the US "deliberate manipulation of intelligence". A senior consultant wrote to his colleague, "The administration's assurances of Al-Assad's responsibility is a ruse. The attack was not the result of the current regime". If Hersh's (2013, 2014) analysis and sources are accurate, then this is another confirmation of Sir Richard Dearlove's, the head of Britain's Secret Intelligence Service (MI6), statement that "the intelligence and the facts were being fixed around the policy" (J. Lynch, 2014b, p. 29). While campaigning for the war against Iraq, the US and UK claims about the WMDs depended mainly on "intelligence sources". George W. Bush declared that Iraq possessed 30,000 munitions that could deliver chemical agents, 500 tons of CW, 38,000 litres of Botulism toxin and 25,000 litres of Anthrax (Bagdikian, 2014, p. 76). These sources claimed that Saddam's regime was plotting with Al-Qaeda to destroy the United States and planning to import uranium to manufacture nuclear bombs (Bagdikian, 2014). Likewise, the British government released a dossier signed by then Prime Minister Tony Blair under the title "Iraq's Weapons of Mass Destruction". The document claimed that Iraq had rockets that could reach 500 kilometres and hence could threaten the British Military Base in Cyprus. It also claimed that Iraq's CWs could be launched within 45 minutes of an order (J. Lynch, 2014b). During this period, UK media outlets acted as a channel for the British intelligence and security services to "camouflage dubious claims under a vicarious veneer of facticity" (J. Lynch, 2014b, p. 33). Even though there were a few exceptions to this, like Andrew Gilligan, who was fired from BBC for refuting the 45-minute claim (J. Lynch, 2014b), the majority of the mainstream media accepted the "official briefings at face value" (Bagdikian, 2014, p. 84). They relied significantly on government sources and sidelined critical accounts such as statements by Senator Robert C. Byrd and Seymour Hersh's investigative articles (Bagdikian, 2014, p. 84). If the media reviewed the "known facts" and examined previous facts [context] about the First Gulf War and gave space to criticisms and unpopular analysis, this kind of coverage "might have given pause to the hand of Bush, the younger, in ordering the reduction of Iraq to rubble" (Bagdikian, 2014, p. 85).

Herman and Chomsky (2010) argue that if media content was represented in a convincing way and supported by "authority figures" without displaying criticisms or alternative interpretations, propaganda themes become "established truths". That is why, PJ considers facts as an "ongoing, reviewable social consensus" (J. Lynch, 2014a, p. 159) that must be evaluated and interrupted critically by including different accounts in coverage. As explained in Chap. 3, "reflexivity" or reviewable interpretation is significantly needed to enable journalists to distinguish between claims and facts. Nash (2016, p. 228) argues that "authentic journalism" requires "rigorous reflexivity". Nash (2016, p. 228) says, "Journalism like history, involves a constant process of contested evaluation of factual evidence and production of meaning". In other words, to counter propaganda, media coverage should provide "readers and audiences with cues and clues to prompt and equip them to develop critical awareness of attempts to pass off claims as facts, or social truths as merely interpersonal" (J. Lynch, 2014a, p. 33).

6.7.3 Number of Victims Claim

The majority of news from AJE (42.1%) estimated that "hundreds" were killed in the Al-Ghouta attack (Table 6.6). The AJE features were even

Table 6.6 Estimation of the number of the victims in AJA and AJE news and features

Estimation of the number of victims	News		Features	
	AJA	AJE	AJA	AJE
100 to 500 victims	6 (11.5%)	24 (25.3%)	1 (14.3%)	3 (75%)
1300 to 1600 victims	27 (52%)	31 (32.6%)	4 (57.1%)	1 (25%)
"Hundreds" of victims	19 (36.5%)	40 (42.1%)	2 (28.6%)	0%

more specific as 75% of them stated that 355 people were killed on that day—the same estimation released by the *Médecins Sans Frontières'* (MSF) [Doctors Without Borders]. In contrast, more than 40% of AJA news and features depended on the US and opposition sources, which estimated that 1300–1600 people were killed in the attack (Table 6.6).

Before any independent investigation, AJA stated in its first article after the attack—as facts [not quotes or claims, allegations or even opinions]—that a "new chemical massacre" had occurred killing "1300 to 1600 Syrians". AJA said:

> Amid the international condemnation of the massacre, many states have demanded the UN inspectors' team, which has been present already in Damascus to investigate the use of chemical weapons earlier [in March 2013], to go immediately to the countryside near Damascus and investigate the new chemical massacre that killed 1300 to 1600 and injured hundreds. (AJA, August 21, 2013c)

> The international controversy of the chemical weapons attack that killed more than 1000 Syrians in Al-Ghouta last Wednesday has been escalating. (AJA, August 23, 2013d)

> The attack killed 1400 people, according to human rights organisations. [Then one Syrian interviewee said while walking in Al-Ghouta] In this area only, there were more than 500 martyrs. (AJA, November 12, 2013j)

In the last example, AJA have not determined which human rights organisations put the number at 1400. This particular number is close to the US and the Free Syrian Army estimations but definitely not human rights organisations. As mentioned earlier, MSF (2013) [which had personal on the ground] estimated that 355 people were killed in the attack. SOHR [pro-opposition human rights group] estimated that 502 were killed (BBC News, 2013). HRW (2013) [which said that Al-Assad is the "likely culprit" of the attack] estimated the death toll to 837. J. Lynch (2008) says, "To report is to choose". Therefore, selecting certain estimations over others reflects AJA's choice and preference. Furthermore, representing the US and opposition claims [death toll= 1400] as a legitimate fact that is endorsed by "human rights organisations" camouflages reality, promotes US and opposition propaganda and violates professional media ethics of accuracy, veracity and fairness.

6.8 AJA AND AJE: DIFFERENCES AND SIMILARITIES

6.8.1 Significant Application of Solution Frame in AJA and AJE

The criteria of the Solution-Orientated frame[15] were the most implemented in the news stories and features from both channels. As shown in Table 6.7, the frame scored 23.6% and 46.7% in AJE-N&F, while 23% and 27.3% were observed in AJA-N&F.

This study argues that the significant application of the Solution-Orientated frame has recorded relatively high percentages in AJA and AJE as the Russian Peace proposal was suggested and reported during the research period (August 21 to September 14, 2013). Chapter 7 explains in more detail how certain events and developments have affected the frequency of applying the PJ frames in the Al-Jazeera coverage. It discusses thoroughly how the tendency to cover "here and now" among

Table 6.7 Percentage of including/mentioning the Solution-Orientated criteria in AJA's and AJE's coverage of Syria's CW attack

Solution-orientated frame in the: News				
Solution-Orientated criteria	**(ECW)** Effect of Chemical Weapons	**(EMI)** Effects of Military Intervention	**(PI)** Peace Initiative	**(Total)** Solution-Orientated frame
AJA (71) News stories	2.8%	21.1%	45.1%	**(23%)**
AJE (82) News stories	0%	32.9%	37.8%	**(23.6%)**
Features				
AJA (22) Features	0%	36.4%	45.5%	**(27.3%)**
AJE (5) Features	20%	60%	60%	**(46.7%)**

[15] **Analytical criteria of the Solution-Orientated frame:**

1. **(ECW):** Does the article mention the implications/future effects of the use of CW on civilians?
2. **(EMI):** Does the article mention the implications/future effects of military intervention on escalating the conflict and civil war?
3. **(PI):** Does the article mention any peace initiative that can prevent war or de-escalate the conflict?

232   Z. ABDUL-NABI

conventional journalists can lead to an increase, and at times decrease, in the possibility of putting Peace Journalism into practice.

6.8.2   AJE Is More People-Orientated than AJA

Less than 2% of the AJA and AJE news stories corresponded with the criteria of the People-Orientated frame.[16] However, the frame was displayed among the AJE features (33.3%) far more than those of the AJA (4.5%) (Table 6.8).

Among 22 features and 71 news stories, AJA published only one feature that quoted Syrian civilians on August 31, 2013. The interviews of this particular feature were not conducted by AJA itself. They were instead summarised and taken from a Turkish news agency. The selected quotes were about how Syrians of Aleppo view the expected war. It represented their opinions as part of a political debate between those who agree and

Table 6.8   Percentage of including/mentioning the People-Orientated criteria in AJA's and AJE's coverage of Syria's chemical attack

People-Orientated frame in the:

News

People-Orientated criteria	(VV2) Voice to the Voiceless	(SA) Syrian Activists	(SCW) Suffering caused by the CW	(Total) People-Orientated frame
AJA (71) News stories	0%	2.8%	2.8%	(1.9%)
AJE (82) News stories	1.2%	0%	2.4%	(1.2%)

Features

AJA (22) Features	9.1%	0%	4.5%	(4.5%)
AJE (5) Features	60%	0%	40%	(33.3%)

[16] **Analytical criteria of the People-Orientated frame:**

1. **(VV2):** Does the article give voice to the victims/survivors of the attack?
2. **(SA):** Does the article give voice to Syrian activists/civilians who were campaigning against military intervention?
3. **(SCW):** Does the article focus on or show the suffering of Al-Ghouta's people after the attack?

disagree. It did not mention humanitarian suffering, possible implications or what this war could mean personally to the people of Syria.

AJE on the other hand represented people's views and the humanitarian implications of a potential war. For instance, a feature in AJE stated:

> But on the question of Western intervention, Damascenes reached by Al-Jazeera over the weekend remained wary, even those who blame the conflict squarely on the Assad regime.
>
> [A] travel agent says all he wants is peace, and soon. But he says he doesn't know how that can happen. 'Civilians are confused,' he says, leaders 'talk too much.'
>
> M. [first initial of another citizen] a long-time disparager of the regime says not to ask her these questions, they are irrelevant.
>
> The pharmacist is unequivocal. She believes it's a well-worn script being prepared for Syria. 'We are witnessing a new Afghanistan and a new Iraq,' she says.
>
> But in Damascus, others like M, are focusing less on debating who carried out the attack—the regime? renegade elements within the regime? terrorists?—and more on adapting to the new reality directly confronting them this week. (AJE, August 29, 2013c)

Unlike AJA's features, this study observes that AJE's features follow the structure and style of feature writing where analysis, background, context, explanation [Peace/Conflict-Orientated Criterion], implications of the expected war [Solution-Orientated Criterion] and voice of voiceless [People-Orientated Criterion] are presented. The tendency of AJE-F to give a voice to the voiceless is in line with previous studies that examined the coverage of the channel (see Al-Najjar, 2009; El-Nawawy & Powers, 2008; Firdous, 2009; Figenschou, 2011). Despite the fact that most conventions of the "objectivity regime" sideline the marginalised and give more attention to "both sides" of any conflict (Hackett, 2011), it—at the same time—encourages the use of more balanced and less polarised terms as clearly shown in the AJE-N&F articles. While Lee et al. (2006) do not necessarily see quoting civilians or using balanced language as an inclination towards PJ, this study suggests that PJ can intersect with [traditional] professional journalism. For instance, AJE-F's adherence to conventional

234   Z. ABDUL-NABI

reporting and feature writing standards has resulted in having less polarised and more People-Orientated coverage. In other words, this study proves that PJ is not a full departure from current journalism practice (J. Lynch, 2014a).

6.8.3   AJA Uses More Emotive Language than AJE

In addition to their dissimilarities in the application of the People-Orientated frame, this study also found that both channels differ significantly in the use of language. AJE-N&F tended to use objective terms when referring to the Syrian conflict, the Al-Ghouta attack and the Syrian regime, whereas AJA-N&F tended to use polarised, emotive, demonising and inciting language. For instance, 19.1% and 5.6% of AJA-N&F referred to the Al-Ghouta attack as a "massacre", while the same term was barely mentioned in AJE-N&F (1.1% and 0%) (Table 6.9). Also, portraying the attack as a "crime" or "criminal act" appeared more in AJA-N (11.6%) than AJE-N (3.6%) (Table 6.9).

Although more than 40% of both channels favoured the opposition quotes as demonstrated previously in Table 6.4, AJA's selectivity and bias towards Syrian rebels were more blatant than that of AJE. For instance, significant proportions of AJA-N&F (20% and 32%) framed the Syrian conflict as a "revolution", while such a term has not been observed at all in the AJE coverage (Table 6.10).

Using the term "revolution" can be justified if the coverage was at the beginning of Syria's pro-democracy uprising in March 2011, when most

Table 6.9   Framing of Al-Ghouta's attack in AJA's and AJA's coverage

Framing of Al-Ghouta's attack	News		Features	
	AJA	AJE	AJA	AJE
CW attack or gas attack	68 (39.3%)	79 (21.9%)	7 (38.9%)	0 (0%)
Alleged CW attack or suspected attack	14 (8.1%)	128 (35.5%)	2 (11.1%)	10 (66.7%)
Deadly attack	4 (2.3%)	17 (4.7%)	0 (0%)	1 (6.7%)
Massacre	33 (19.1%)	4 (1.1%)	1 (5.6%)	0 (0%)
Crime or criminal act	20 (11.6%)	13 (3.6%)	0 (0%)	0 (0%)
Attack	34 (19.7%)	120 (33.2%)	8 (44.4%)	4 (26.7%)

6 SYRIA'S CWS COVERAGE (2013): PEACE DEAL OR MILITARY ACTION... 235

Table 6.10 Framing of the Syrian conflict in AJA and AJE

Framing of the Syrian conflict	News		Features	
	AJA	AJE	AJA	AJE
Uprising	0 (0%)	4 (14.3%)	0 (0%)	0 (0%)
Revolution	7 (20%)	0 (0%)	8 (32%)	0 (0%)
Civil war	2 (5.7%)	17 (60.7%)	3 (12%)	5 (62.5%)
Syrian/Syria crisis	26 (74.3%)	7 (25%)	14 (56%)	3 (37.5%)

victims lost their lives to Al-Assad forces (M. Lynch, 2016). However, using this term during 2013 when the opposition was fully armed, funded by external powers [mainly by the United States, Saudi Arabia, Qatar and Turkey] and involved in killing civilians and minorities [Alawites and Christians] (IICISAR, 2013, 2014; HRW, 2015) is totally misleading.

The results of this chapter are inconsistent with previous studies that found minor differences between the two channels (see Fakhri, 2011; Al-Nahed, 2015; Fahmy & Al-Emad, 2011). It is in line, however, with Kraidy's (2008) argument that although both channels are sponsored by the same source, they are still "dissimilar" especially in their "tone".

This study found that the leaning of using what Kraidy (2008) called "harsh language" is more obvious in the AJA features than the news. For instance, AJA-F stated:

There are several cues here and there that can bring good news for the Al-Assad regime regarding the American strike. One of them is, if this strike does not break Al-Assad, it would strengthen him. Observers confirm that such a strike would increase his [Al-Assad] brutality because it conveys a clear message to him that you can kill, bomb, destroy but you cannot use chemical weapons.

Such military action will give credibility to the regime accusation that there is a cosmopolitan conspiracy designed by the US, Israel and western colonial powers against the axis of resistance. Such claims will find listeners [supporters], and their numbers would definitely increase if the strike were carried out.

Safwat Al-Zayat, a military expert, says that the American strike should be painful and poignant, otherwise the US would lose its prestige and pride.

Many indications confirm that the <u>expected strike will not be more than an ear pulling.</u> (AJA, August 30, 2013e)

The feature did not mention how Syrian people viewed the possible foreign military intervention or what implications the potential strike could cause. As features are longer and depend on analysis more than news stories, this study found it easier to measure editors' selectivity in the features than the news. In this particular feature, for example, the stance of the editor against Al-Assad's "brutality" was very obvious. The editor relied only on the analysis of one "military expert" who used inciting language and called blatantly for a "painful strike" against the regime. Herman and Chomsky (2010) argue that the media creates "experts" who echo the views of the dominant accounts. For example, Arkady Shevchenko, Soviet defector, was portrayed by *The New York Times* as an "expert" in Soviet intelligence and arms matters despite his poor credentials (Herman & Chomsky, 2010). Steel (1990) says that producers and editors select experts knowing already what they would say before conducting the interview. None of the quoted "experts" in AJA-N&F during the research period presented non-propagandistic analysis [Truth-Orientated Criterion]. Shoemaker and Reese (2013) say that "experts" have a significant influence on the meaning of the news as they give the impression that they would say something important and provide informed and impartial analysis. In general, this study observes that AJA features used inciting language and scarcely included people's views, implications of war [People-Orientated Criterion], context, background, variety of voices [Peace/Conflict-Orientated Criterion] and non-propaganda-orientated analysis [Truth-Orientated Criterion].

In September 2016, Faisal Al-Qasim, a famous Syrian presenter in AJA [who is known for using inciting and sectarian language against the Syrian regime supporters], called in his show, the Opposite Direction, for "ethnic cleansing" of Alawites and Shias who are living in the "heart of a Sunni land". He asked his pro-rebel guest, general coordinator of the Syrian opposition factions, Abdul-Munim Zain Al-Din:

> **Al-Qasim:** "Let me ask you something. You are always whining about the [destruction] in Sunni areas... That's the problem. Why do you limit all your battles with the regime in the Sunni areas? Where are you from Damascus [pro-regime area]? Or where are you from the Alawites in the coast [pro-regime area]? Or where are you from all the areas that support

the regime? That's the problem. You have yourselves destroyed your own [Sunni] areas. You want to liberate Syria? Go to the coast! That's what the Syrians are saying. Go to Damascus. Go to the areas that support Bashar Al-Assad and curse their fathers [Arabic expression], as they say! Where are you from all this?

Anti-Assad guest: These areas are not protected by Iran and Russia only but even the US has had to intervene and protect them with their airplanes, because it [the US] knows that this criminal regime cannot hold out. So, it had to sign an agreement with Russia… even Russia hasn't been able to protect it…

Al-Qasim: But brother, why are you blaming the regime? Let me ask you, [for instance] Nubl and Al-Zahraa are Shia colonies in the heart of a Sunni land, together with Kafraya and Fua. They [Shias] are still there, in the middle of your areas… Why don't you expel them like they did to you and curse the ones who gave birth to them?

Anti-Assad guest: Children of Madaya and Zabadani are the only reason we are leaving those criminals alone.

Al-Qasim: Sir, there is no emotions in wars. He [Al-Assad] drove you out from your areas, and you are [busy] fighting in Aleppo and Daraya?! Go to the coast sir.

Anti-Assad guest: God willing, we will go to the coast and other [regime's] areas. We won't leave them alone. The time will come, the coast is ours, Damascus is ours [belong to us]. We won't leave a single area, we will liberate them all, God willing". (The Opposite Direction, September 13, 2016)[17]

These sectarian calls from AJA's host for fighting, expelling and at best displacing Shia and Alawite civilians based on their sect and political stance manifest Galtung's (1998) description of media as "violent in and of itself". How would such inflammatory and escalatory-orientated statements affect the conflict? What consequences could it cause? To what extent would it polarise the parties? How would an armed Sunni rebel listening to such sectarian incitements treat Shia and Alawite civilians? How would Shia and Alawite civilians perceive rebels while knowing that

---

[17] Translation of all AJA's texts/quotes are my own translation except this part as it is quoted from MEMRI TV (September 21, 2016).

their murdering was being legitimised on air? Would such inflammation bring parties to the negotiation table or worsen the sectarianism and civil war further? These are the kind of questions that PJ is concerned about while covering such conflicts.

Yanagizawa-Drott (2014) found that *Radio Télévision Libre des Mille Collines* (RTLMC) [which was inciting Tutsis to kill Hutus during Rwanda's genocide in 1994] was responsible for 10% of the participation in the killing and 30% of armed groups' violence. Yanagizawa-Drott (2014) concludes that RTLMC's propaganda alone resulted in 51,000 deaths. Al-Qasim's legitimisation and justification for killing Shias and Alawites do not seem very different from the popular RTLMC's song, "I Hate Hutus". This poem had been aired for the first time on April 6, 1994, and was repeated constantly during the genocide. Kellow and Steeves (1998, p. 119) cite the provocative poem:

– Me, I hate Hutus. Me, I hate Hutus. Me, I hate Hutus who become Tutsis.

– What are you saying, Mutawa?

– Let me say it. I'm getting things off my chest. I'm going to tell you why I do hate them. Me, I hate the Hutus. I hate their "Hutuness," which makes them want to be our equals.

Lina Zahr Al-Deen, a Lebanese presenter, who resigned from AJA in 2009, says that the channel has become a tool of war. She said to *Al-Safir* newspaper:

Every media outlet has a political agenda, but there is a difference between conveying messages, and incitement and mobilisation, Al-Jazeera has become a pawn of war... Arabic blood is being shed and Al-Jazeera is playing that role. (Kubaisy, 2011)

AJA's coverage was an ideal implementation of WJ which polarises, escalates and calls for hatred, violence and revenge (Galtung & Fischer, 2013).

6.9 Conclusion

Al-Jazeera's coverage of Syria's second CW attack has narrowed down the potential suspects to one perpetrator [Al-Assad] due to the following factors: (1) excluding any background about the Khan Al-Assal attack, (2) ruling out the possibility that Al-Nusra or *Liwa Al-Islam* might have been responsible for the Al-Ghouta attack and at the same time (3) obscuring the fact that these groups have already had an access to CWs.

This study argues that Al-Jazeera's coverage has aided in legitimising a military strike in the country by demonising the regime and exonerating the opposition from killings and violations. It has given more space to the opposition and their views and reported intelligence allegations as facts without practising "reflexivity".

This study concludes that there were no major differences between AJA and AJE in implementing the PJ criteria. However, AJE's commitment to objective reporting standards and conventional feature writing style has made it more People-Orientated and less emotive than AJA.

The study observes that the AJA reporting of Syria's second CW attack lacks basic journalism ethics, credibility and accuracy. What is more, AJA's coverage demonstrated what Herman and Chomsky call "outright lies". AJA, for instance, stated that the UNMIAUCWSAR (2013a) report attributed the responsibility of using CW to the Al-Assad regime, whereas all the UN reports that were released in 2013 confirmed that the CW were used but did not determine who was responsible for the attacks. Moreover, AJA said that "human rights organisations" estimated that "1400 were killed in Al-Ghouta" even though all well-known human rights organisations put the number of victims at 355, 502 and 837 (see MSF, 2013; BBC News, 2013; HRW, 2013). Furthermore, AJA claimed that its "investigative team" found "new evidence" that can determine the range of fired rockets and their launching point, whereas all these findings were published two months previously by HRW and NYT.

The next chapter (Chap. 7) discusses the main reasons and factors behind recording different percentages of PJ in Bahrain's and Syria's coverage. It also summarises the major factors that can help decrease and increase the proportions of PJ frames.

References

Allmeling, A. (2012, December 24). Suliman: Al Jazeera plays the piper, but Qatar calls the tune. *DW*. Accessed March 12, 2016, from http://www.dw.com/en/suliman-al-jazeera-plays-the-piper-but-qatar-calls-the-tune/a-16477490

Al-Nahed, S. (2015). Covering Libya: A framing analysis of Al Jazeera and BBC coverage of the 2011 Libyan uprising and NATO intervention. *Middle East Critique, 24*(3), 251–267.

Al-Najjar, A. (2009). How Arab is Al-Jazeera English? Comparative study of Al-Jazeera Arabic and Al-Jazeera English news channel. *Global Media Journal, 8*(14), 1–35.

Amnesty International. (2015). *Amnesty International Report 2014/15 – Syria.* Accessed March 20, 2016, from http://www.refworld.org/docid/54f07d919.html

Anderson, T. (2015). *The dirty war on Syria.* Global Research.

Bagdikian, B. H. (2014). *The media monopoly* (5th ed.). Beacon Press.

BBC News. (2013). *Syria chemical attack: What we know.* http://www.bbc.com/news/world-middle-east-23927399

Bila Hudud. (2015a, May 27). لقاء أبو محمد الجولاني أمير جبهة النصرة . https://www.youtube.com/watch?v=-hwQT43vFZA

Bila Hudud. (2015b, July 8). بال العقيد -حدود السوري الأسير: بادلونا إذا كانت لنا قيمة . https://www.youtube.com/watch?v=mbI2JSeWLoo

Blair, D., & Spencer, R. (2014, September 20). How Qatar is funding the rise of Islamist extremists. *The Telegraph*. Accessed March 14, 2016, from http://www.telegraph.co.uk/news/worldnews/middleeast/qatar/11110931/How-Qatar-is-funding-the-rise-of-Islamist-extremists.html

Burweila, A. (2014). How to lose a war: When your allies aid your enemies. *RIEAS*. Accessed November 24, 2015, from http://rieas.gr/images/islamic/ayarieas.pdf

Chivers, C. J. (2013, September 17). U.N. data on gas attack point to Assad's top forces. *The New York Times*. Accessed September 22, 2014, from http://www.nytimes.com/2013/09/18/world/middleeast/un-data-on-gas-attack-points-to-assads-top-forces.html

Chomsky, N. (2011). *Media control: The spectacular achievements of propaganda.* Seven Stories Press.

De Fransius, M. P. (2014). Peace journalism case study: US media coverage of the Iraq War. *Journalism, 15*(1), 72–88.

Dorsey, J. M. (2015). How Qatar is its own worst enemy. *The International Journal of the History of Sport, 32*(3), 422–439.

El-Nawawy, M., & Powers, S. (2008). *Mediating conflict: Al-Jazeera English and the possibility of a conciliatory media.* Figueroa Press.

6 SYRIA'S CWS COVERAGE (2013): PEACE DEAL OR MILITARY ACTION... 241

Entman, R. M. (1993). Framing: Toward clarification of a fractured paradigm. *Journal of Communication, 43*(4), 51–58.

Entman, R. M. (2003). Cascading activation: Contesting the White House's frame after 9/11. *Political Communication, 20*(4), 415–432.

Erlich, R. (2014). *Inside Syria: The backstory of their civil war and what the world can expect.* Prometheus Books.

Fahmy, S., & Al Emad, M. (2011). Al-Jazeera vs Al-Jazeera: A comparison of the network's English and Arabic online coverage of the US/Al Qaeda conflict. *The International Communication Gazette, 73*(3), 216–232.

Fahmy, S., & Eakin, B. (2014). High drama on the high seas Peace versus war journalism framing of an Israeli/Palestinian-related incident. *International Communication Gazette, 76*(1), 86–105.

Fakhri, F. (2011). *Content analysis of how Al-Jazeera English and Arabic channels framed the war on Gaza* (Master's thesis). Retrieved from ProQuest Dissertations and Theses (Accession Order No. 1496764).

Figenschou, T. U. (2011). The south is talking back: With a white face and a British accent – editorial dilemmas in Al Jazeera English. *Journalism, 13*(3), 354–370.

Firdous, T. (2009). *Al Jazeera English presenting a non-western viewpoint and contesting western media dominance during the Gaza crisis* (Master's thesis). Retrieved from ProQuest Dissertations and Theses (Accession Order No. 1507250).

Fishman, M. (1988). *Manufacturing the news.* University of Texas Press.

Galtung, J. (1998). High road, low road – Charting the course for peace journalism. *Track Two 7*(4). Accessed September 14, 2015, from http://reference. sabinet.co.za/webx/access/electronic_journals/track2/track2_v7_n4_a4.htm

Galtung, J., & Fischer, D. (2013). *Johan Galtung: Pioneer of peace research.* Springer.

Gavlak, D. & Ababneh, Y. (2013). Syrians in Ghouta claim Saudi-supplied rebels behind chemical attack. *Mint Press News.* Accessed July 1, 2016, from https://www.mintpressnews.com/author/dale-gavlak-and-yahya-ababneh/

Hackett, R. A. (2011). New vistas for peace journalism: Alternative media and communication rights. In I. S. Shaw, J. Lynch & R. A. Hackett, (Eds.), *Expanding peace journalism: Comparative and critical approaches* (pp.35–69). Sydney: Sydney University Press.

Hashem, A. (2012, April 3). The Arab Spring has shaken Arab TV's credibility. *The Guardian.* Accessed March 12, 2016, from http://www.theguardian. com/commentisfree/2012/apr/03/arab-spring-arab-tv-credibility

Herman, E. S., & Chomsky, N. (2010). *Manufacturing consent: The political economy of the mass media.* Random House eBooks.

Hersh, S. M. (2013). Whose sarin? *London Review of Books, 35*(24), 9–12.

242   Z. ABDUL-NABI

Hersh, S. (2014). The red line and the rat line. *The London Review of Books.* Accessed October 15, 2014, from http://www.lrb.co.uk/v36/n08/seymour-m-hersh/the-red-line-and-the-rat-line

Hofstetter, C. R., & Buss, T. F. (1978). Bias in television news coverage of political events: A methodological analysis. *Journal of Broadcasting & Electronic Media, 22*(4), 517–530.

Human Rights Watch. (2013). *Attacks on Ghouta: Analysis of alleged use of chemical weapons in Syria.* https://www.hrw.org/report/2013/09/10/attacks-ghouta/analysis-alleged-use-chemical-weapons-syria (accessed 25 September 2014).

Human Rights Watch. (2015). *"He didn't have to die:" Indiscriminate attacks by opposition groups in Syria.* Accessed March 21, 2016, from https://www.hrw.org/report/2015/03/22/he-didnt-have-die/indiscriminate-attacks-opposition-groups-syria

Independent International Commission of Inquiry on the Syrian Arab Republic. (2013). *Report of independent international commission of inquiry on the Syrian Arab Republic.* Accessed September 14, 2014, from http://www.ohchr.org/Documents/HRBodies/HRCouncil/CoISyria/A-HRC-23-58_en.pdf

Independent International Commission of Inquiry on the Syrian Arab Republic. (2014). *Report of independent international commission of inquiry on the Syrian Arab Republic.* Accessed September 14, 2014, from http://www.ohchr.org/Documents/HRBodies/HRCouncil/CoISyria/A.HRC.27.60_Eng.pdf

Kamrava, M. (2013). *Qatar: Small state, big politics.* Cornell University Press.

Kanaan, W. (2012, February 24). Syria's electronic warriors hit Al Jazeera. *Al-Akhbar English.* Accessed March 12, 2016, from http://english.al-akhbar.com/node/4525

Karouny, M. (2015). Insight – Syria's Nusra Front may leave Qaeda to form new entity. *Reuters.* Accessed March 14, 2016, from http://uk.reuters.com/article/uk-mideast-crisis-nusra-insight-idUKKBN0M00G620150304

Kellow, C. L., & Steeves, H. L. (1998). The role of radio in the Rwandan genocide. *Journal of Communication, 48*(3), 107–128.

Khatib, L. (2015). The Nusra Front's game changing rise in Syria. *Carnegie Middle East Center.* Accessed March 14, 2016, from http://carnegie-mec.org/2015/03/24/nusra-front-s-game-changing-rise-in-syria

Kraidy, M. M. (2008). *Al-Jazeera and Al-Jazeera English: A Comparative institutional analysis* (pp. 23–30). Woodrow Wilson International Center for Scholars. Accessed July 30, 2012, from http://repository.upenn.edu/cgi/viewcontent.cgi?article=1282&context=asc_papers

Kubaisy, F. (2011, July 12). عتوق اليوم كتابها عن «الجزيرة» لفضح كواليس الإدارة لينا زهر الدين وتخوض أدب تعوالأطفال كالتلفزيون قريا ...*Assafir Newspaper.* Accessed August 2, 2016, from https://assafir.com/Article/243998/Archive

6 SYRIA'S CWS COVERAGE (2013): PEACE DEAL OR MILITARY ACTION... 243

Lauria, J. (2013, December 16). Russia blames rebels for Syria gas attack. *The Wall Street Journal*. Accessed January 22, 2016, from https://www.wsj.com/articles/russia-blames-rebels-for-syria-gas-attack-1387245714?tesla=y

Lee, S. T., Maslog, C. C., & Kim, H. S. (2006). Asian Conflicts and the Iraq War: A comparative framing analysis. *International Communication Gazette, 68*(5–6), 499–518.

Lederach, J. P. (1997). *Building peace. Sustainable reconciliation in divided societies*. United States Institute of Peace Press.

Lister, C. (2016a). The Nusra Front is dead and stronger than ever before. *Foreign Policy*. Accessed January 2, 2017, from http://foreignpolicy.com/2016/07/28/the-nusra-front-is-dead-and-stronger-than-ever-before/

Lister, C. (2016b). Profiling Jabhat Al-Nusra. *Brookings Institution*. Accessed January 2, 2017, from https://www.brookings.edu/wp-content/uploads/2016/07/iwr_20160728_profiling_nusra.pdf

Lloyd, R. & Postol, T. A. (2014). *Possible implications of faulty US technical intelligence in the Damascus nerve agent attack of August 21, 2013*. Accessed September 22, 2014, from https://www.voltairenet.org/IMG/pdf/possible-implications-of-bad-intelligence.pdf

Lynch, J., & McGoldrick, A. (2000) Peace journalism – How to do it? *Transcend Website* (Peace Journalism). Accessed March 30, 2013, from https://www.transcend.org/tri/downloads/McGoldrick_Lynch_Peace-Journalism.pdf

Lynch, J., & McGoldrick, A. (2005a). *Peace journalism*. Hawthorn Press.

Lynch, J., & McGoldrick, A. (2005b). War and Peace Journalism in the holy land. *Social Alternatives, 24*(1), 11–15.

Lynch, J. (2006). What's so great about Peace Journalism. *Global Media Journal, Mediterranean Edition, 1*(1), 74–87.

Lynch, J. (2007). Peace journalism and its discontents. *Conflict and Communication Online, 6*(2), 1–13. Accessed June 3, 2013, from http://www.cco.regener-online.de/2007_2/pdf/lynch.pdf

Lynch, J. (2008). *Debates in Peace Journalism*. Sydney University Press.

Lynch, J., & Galtung, J. (2010). *Reporting conflict: New directions in peace journalism*. University of Queensland Press.

Lynch, J. (2014a). *A global standard for reporting conflict*. Routledge.

Lynch, J. (2014b). Critical realism, peace journalism and democracy. *Ethical Space: The International Journal of Communication Ethics, 11*(1/2), 29–36.

Lynch, M. (2016). *The new Arab wars: Uprisings and anarchy in the Middle East*. Public Affairs.

Lyons, J. (2013). *Dispatches: Mapping the sarin flight path*. Accessed September 22, 2014, from Human Rights Watch: https://www.hrw.org/news/2013/09/17/dispatches-mapping-sarin-flight-path

MacDonald, A. (2015). Syria's Nusra Front backs Paris attacks, despite opposition to Islamic State. *Middle East Eye*. Accessed March 21, 2016, from http://

244 Z. ABDUL-NABI

www.middleeasteye.net/news/al-nusra-front-back-attacks-paris-despite-opposition-islamic-state-976490550#sthash.1hhnCmXW.dpuf

Machin, D., & Mayr, A. (2012). *How to do critical discourse analysis: A multimodal introduction.* SAGE Publications.

McGoldrick, A. (2006). War journalism and "objectivity." *Conflict and Communication Online, 5*(2), 1–7. Accessed June 14, 2016, from http://cco.regener-online.de/2006_2/pdf/mcgoldrick.pdf

Médecins Sans Frontières. (2013). *Syria: Thousands suffering neurotoxic symptoms treated in hospitals supported by MSF.* Accessed September 22, 2014, from http://www.doctorswithoutborders.org/news-stories/press-release/syria-thousands-suffering-neurotoxic-symptoms-treated-hospitals-supported

MEMRI TV. (2016, September 21). *Al-Jazeeia l'V host Faisal Al-Qassem incites to ethnic cleansing of Shiites in Sunni iegions in Syiia.* https://www.youtube.com/watch?v=qIVYwhPFGuc

Nash, C. (2016). *What is journalism? The art and politics of a rupture.* Palgrave Macmillan.

Ottosen, R. (2010). The war in Afghanistan and Peace Journalism in practice. *Media, War & Conflict, 3*(3), 261–278.

Peace Association and Lawyers for Justice in Turkey. (2013). *War crimes committed against the people of Syria.* Accessed September 12, 2016, from http://www.wpc in.org/sites/default/files/documents/war-crimes-committed-againts-the-people-of-syria.pdf

Roberts, D. (2015). Is Qatar bringing the Nusra Front in from the cold? *BBC News.* Accessed September 16, 2016, from http://www.bbc.com/news/world-middle-east-31764114

Salih, R. M. (2015). Al Jazeera English instructs staff not to call Syria's Jabhat al Nusra "Al Qaeda". *5Pillars.* Accessed March 14, 2016, from http://5pillarsuk.com/2015/09/22/al-jazeera-english-instructs-staff-not-to-call-syrias-jabhat-al-nusra-al-qaeda/

Saxon, D. (2013). Humanitarian law, ethics and journalism in Syria. *Guest Blog.* Accessed March 14, 2016, from https://cpj.org/blog/2013/01/humanitarian-law-ethics-and-journalism-in-syria.php

Sengupta, K. (2013, July 26). Homemade grenades and catapults: Introducing the DIY weapons of the Free Syrian Army. *The Independent.* Accessed March 20, 2016, from http://www.independent.co.uk/news/world/middle-east/homemade-grenades-and-catapults-introducing-the-diy-weapons-of-the-free-syrian-army-8732634.html

Shoemaker, P. J., & Reese, S. D. (2013). *Mediating the message in the 21st century: A media sociology perspective.* Routledge.

SITE Intelligence Group. (2015). *NF commander condones IS attacks in Beirut, remains critical of IS.* Accessed March 21, 2016, from https://news.siteintel-

6 SYRIA'S CWS COVERAGE (2013): PEACE DEAL OR MILITARY ACTION... 245

group.com/Jihadist-News/nf-commander-condones-is-attacks-in-beirut-remains-critical-of-is.html

Sly, L. (2013, September 6). Syrian Islamists protest U.S. strikes; Americans exit embassy in Beirut. *The Washington Post*. Accessed August 22, 2016, from https://www.washingtonpost.com/world/middle_east/us-orders-partial-evacuation-of-embassy-in-beirut-as-tensions-rise-over-syria-strike/2013/09/06/6af006a8-16f5-11e3-804b-d3a1a3a18f2c_story.html?utm_term=.85598372a67d

Steele, J. (1990). Sound bite seeks expert. *Washington Journalism Review*, *12*(7), 28–29.

Tehranian, M. (2002). Peace Journalism negotiating global media ethics. *The Harvard International Journal of Press/Politics*, *7*(2), 58–83.

Tehranian, M. (2004). War, media, and propaganda: An epilogue. In Y. R. Kamalipour & N. Snow (Eds.), *War, media, and propaganda: A global perspective* (pp. 237–246). Rowman & Littlefield.

The International Support Team for Mussalaha in Syria. (2013). *The chemical attacks on East Ghouta to justify military right to protect intervention in Syria*. Accessed September 2, 2014, from http://www.globalresearch.ca/STUDY_THE_VIDEOS_THAT_SPEAKS_ABOUT_CHEMICALS_BETA_VERSION.pdf

The National Institute for Occupational Safety and Health. (2015). *Sarin (GB): Nerve agent*. https://www.cdc.gov/niosh/ershdb/emergencyresponse-card_29750001.html

The Opposite Direction. (2016, September 13). التجاه -المعأكس تطهير طائفي في سوريا أم أمني؟. https://www.youtube.com/watch?v=R2sgQDLLxMs

Ulrichsen, K. C. (2014). *Qatar and the Arab Spring*. Oxford University Press.

United Nations Mission to Investigate Allegations of the Use of Chemical Weapons in the Syrian Arab Republic. (2013a). *Report on the alleged use of chemical weapons in the Ghouta area of Damascus on 21 August 2011*. Accessed June 3, 2014, from http://www.globalsecurity.org/wmd/library/report/2013/un-syria-cw-report-130916.pdf

United Nations Mission to Investigate Allegations of the Use of Chemical Weapons in the Syrian Arab Republic. (2013b). *Final report*. Accessed June 3, 2014, from https://unoda-web.s3.amazonaws.com/wp-content/uploads/2013/12/report.pdf

U.S. Department of the Treasury. (2013). *Treasury designates Al-Qa'ida supporters in Qatar and Yemen*. Accessed June 11, 2016, from https://www.treasury.gov/press-center/press-releases/Pages/jl2249.aspx

Yanagizawa-Drott, D. (2014). Propaganda and conflict: Evidence from the Rwandan genocide. *The Quarterly Journal of Economics*, *129*(4), 1947–1994.

246   Z. ABDUL-NABI

Zaidan, A. (2015). Nusra Front's quest for a united Syria. *Al-Jazeera English.* Accessed March 14, 2016, from http://www.aljazeera.com/indepth/opinion/2015/06/nusra-front-quest-united-syria- 150602050740867.html

References of Al-Jazeera Arabic Articles:

Al-Jazeera Arabic. (2013a, March 22). واشنطن: في سوريا الكيماوي استخدام على دليل ال. http://www.aljazeera.net/news/arabic/2013/3/22/%D9%88%D8%A7%D8%B4%D9%86%D8%B7%D9%86-%D9%84%D8%A7-%D8%AF%D9%84%D9%8A%D9%84-%D8%B9%D9%89-%D8%A7%D8%B3%D8%AA%D8%AE%D8%AF%D8%A7%D9%85-%D8%A7%D9%84%D9%83%D9%8A%D9%85%D9%8A%D8%A7%D9%88%D9%8A-%D8%A8%D8%B3%D9%88%D8%B1%D9%8A%D8%A7

Al-Jazeera Arabic. (2013b, May 20). السوريين للثوار الميدانية المكاسب: الكيماوي النظام استخدام. http://www.aljazeera.net/home/print/0353c88a-286d-4266-82c66094179ea26d/b93d251c-c18c-4e32-8287-3974056175e9

Al-Jazeera Arabic. (2013c, August 21). سوريا في فوري لتحقيق ودعوة الأمن لمجلس اجتماع. http://www.aljazeera.net/home/print/f6451603-4dff-4ca1-9c10-122741d17432/364bfd93-e996-4a9a-a16e-1501c523585f

Al-Jazeera Arabic. (2013d, August 23). سوريا كيماوي بشأن دولي وجدال حراك. http://www.aljazeera.net/news/arabic/2013/8/23/%D8%AD%D8%B1%D8%A7%D9%83-%D9%88%D8%AC%D8%AF%D9%84-%D8%AF%D9%88%D9%84%D9%8A-%D8%A8%D8%B4%D8%A3%D9%86-%D9%83%D9%8A%D9%85%D9%8A%D8%A7%D9%88%D9%8A-%D8%B3%D9%88%D8%B1%D9%8A%D8%A7

Al-Jazeera Arabic. (2013e, August 30). سوريا ضد العسكري التحرك ببرران وكيري أوباما. http://www.aljazeera.net/home/print/f6451603-4dff-4ca1-9c10-122741d17432/c41ff8e6-34a2-461a-9899-d1728c5835bb

Al-Jazeera Arabic. (2013f, September 1). السورية الأزمة يبحثون العرب الخارجية وزراء. http://www.aljazeera.net/news/arabic/2013/9/1/%d9%88%d8%b2%d8%b1%d8%a7%d8%a1-%d8%a7%d9%84%d8%ae%d8%a7%d8%b1%d8%ac%d9%8a%d8%a9-%d8%a7%d9%84%d8%b9%d8%b1%d8%a8-%d9%8a%d8%a8%d8%ad%d8%ab%d9%88%d9%86-%d8%a7%d9%84%d8%a3%d8%b2%d9%85%d8%a9-%d8%a7%d9%84%d8%b3%d9%88%d8%b1%d9%8a%d8%a9

Al-Jazeera Arabic. (2013g, September 5). الثورة منذ السوري النظام مجازر. http://www.aljazeera.net/home/print/f6451603-4dff-4ca1-9c10-122741d17432/4b86b91b-eb1b-40a0-bb26-d89965903440

Al-Jazeera Arabic. (2013h, September 10). السوري الكيماوي نزع بمبادرة حذر دولي ترحيب. http://www.aljazeera.net/news/arabic/2013/9/10/%D8%AA%D8%B1%D8%AD%D9%8A%D8%A8-%D8%AF%D9%88%D9%84%D9%8A-%D8%AD%D8%B0%D8%B1-%D8%A8%D9%85%D8%A8%D8%A7%D8%AF%D8%B1%D8%A9-%D9%86%D8%B2%D8%B9-%D8%A7%D9%84%D9%83%D9%8A%D9%85%D9

6 SYRIA'S CWS COVERAGE (2013): PEACE DEAL OR MILITARY ACTION... 247

%8A%D8%A7%D8%A6%D9%8A-%D8%A7%D9%84%D8%B3%D9%88%D8%B1%D9%8A
Al-Jazeera Arabic. (2013i, September 11). أوباما يمنح الدبلوماسية فسحة ويبقى على خيار الضربة. http://www.aljazeera.net/home/print/f6451603-4dff-4ca1-9c10-122741d17432/f82331bf-bbce-4e16-a8fb-1ef703cfea57
Al-Jazeera Arabic. (2013j, November 12). الغوطة... الهجوم المدبر. https://www.aljazeera.net/programs/aljazeeraspecialprograms/2014/8/23/%D8%A7%D9%84%D-8%BA%D9%88%D8%B7%D8%A9-%D8%A7%D9%84%D9%87%D8%AC%D9%88%D9%85-%D8%A7%D9%84%D9%85%D8%AF%D9%91%D8%A8%D8%B1
Al-Jazeera Arabic. (2013k, December 13). التقرير الأممي يؤكد استخدام الكيمياوي بسوريا. http://www.aljazeera.net/news/arabic/2013/12/13/%D8%A7%D9%84%D8%AA%D9%8 2%D8%B1%D9%8A%D8%B1-%D8%A7%D9%84%D8%A3%D9%85%D9%85%D9%8A-%D9%8A%D8%A4%D9%83%D8%AF-%D8%A7%D8%B3%D8%AA%D8%AE%D8%AF%D8%A7%D9%85-%D8%A7%D9%84%D9%83%D9%8A%D9%85%D9%8A%D8%A7%D8%A6%D9%8A-%D8%A8%D8%B3%D9%88%D8%B1%D9%8A%D8%A7

REFERENCES OF AL-JAZEERA ENGLISH ARTICLES:

Al-Jazeera English. (2013a, August 22). *UN seeks clarity on Syria gas attack claim.* http://www.aljazeera.com/news/middleeast/2013/08/2013821215836835335.html

Al-Jazeera English. (2013b, August 25). Syria symptoms 'point to neurotoxic agent. https://www.aljazeera.com/news/2013/8/25/syria-symptoms-point-to-neurotoxic-agent

Al-Jazeera English. (2013c, August 29). *Obama advocates limited strikes in Syria.* http://www.aljazeera.com/news/middleeast/2013/08/20138295234621459.html

CHAPTER 7

Al-Jazeera's (2011–2013) "Double Standards" Coverage of the Bahraini and Syrian Conflicts

7.1 Introduction

Chapters 5 and 6 thoroughly analyse the AJA and AJE coverage of Bahrain's uprising during the Saudi military intervention in 2011 and Syria's second CW attack in 2013. They comprehensively dissect the empirical findings and explore the implications and consequences of including and excluding PJ frames from the coverage of both conflicts.

As the quantitative results of the AJA and AJE coverage of both conflicts demonstrate some commonalities and discrepancies, this chapter aims to examine the reasons behind such similarities and differences. More specifically, it explores why the WJ frames were applied in the AJA and AJE coverage of the Syrian conflict more than in the coverage of Bahrain's. The lack of displaying the PJ frames in Syria's coverage was analysed within the context of the intensity of both conflicts and the degree of Qatar's direct involvement with the Syrian and Bahraini actors.

More importantly, this chapter measures to what extent Qatar's support to the Syrian opposition and to the Bahraini regime in 2011, or what this book calls "double standards policy", has manifested in the AJA and AJE coverage of the Bahraini and Syrian conflicts.

Although it is thoroughly discussed in Chaps. 2, 5 and 6, this chapter further explores the reasons behind the similarities and differences between the AJA and AJE coverage of both conflicts.

© The Author(s), under exclusive license to Springer Nature Switzerland AG 2022
Z. Abdul-Nabi, *Al-Jazeera's "Double Standards" in the Arab Spring*,
https://doi.org/10.1007/978-3-031-14279-6_7

249

This chapter also examines to what extent including PJ frames is affected by the developments on the ground "here and now" in both conflicts. It further measures whether dependence on news wires can affect applying PJ frames in the AJA and AJE coverage of both conflicts.

Before digging deeper in the channels' coverage of both conflicts, the following section summarises the comparative findings of both conflicts.

7.2 Comparison Between the Findings of Bahrain's Uprising in 2011 and Syria's Second CW Attack in 2013

- The percentages of applying PJ framing in the AJA and AJE coverage of Bahrain's uprising during the Saudi military intervention in 2011 are higher than the percentages of displaying PJ frames in the AJA and AJE coverage of the Al-Ghouta CW attack in Syria.
- While the percentage of implementing PJ frames was generally close in the AJA and AJE coverage of both conflicts, the study found that AJE was more People-Orientated and used less emotive, sectarian and demonising language than AJA in both conflicts.
- A significant percentage of AJA coverage framed the Syrian conflict during Al-Ghouta CW attack in 2013 as a "revolution", while the same term was hardly mentioned when referring to Bahrain's uprising in 2011.
- The news of Bahrain and Syria in both channels quoted Qatar's allies (Syrian opposition groups and officials of the Bahraini regime) more than its antagonists.
- Both channels in both conflicts were dominated by pro-Qatar framing, except the AJE coverage of Bahrain.
- One third of the AJE features (AJE-F) of both conflicts displayed the People-Orientated frame.
- The frequency of including PJ frames in AJA and AJE is affected by certain developments during both conflicts.
- The frequency of the Peace/Conflict-Orientated frame increased in the beginning of the deployment of Saudi-led troops in Manama and the mentioning of the Solution-Orientated frame reached its highest point when the United Nations (UN), the United States (US), Iran and Kuwait called for a political solution.

- The frequency of the Peace- and Solution-Orientated frames increased significantly in both channels during the second week of September 2013 when Russia announced its peace proposal.
- There has not been a direct relationship between the degree of dependence on news wires and the applying of WJ or PJ frames in the coverage of both conflicts.

7.3   Politics of Media Ownership

AJA-N&F (13.25% and 9.3%) and AJE-N&F (25.9% and 34.7%) of Bahrain scored higher percentages of PJ than AJA-N&F (8% and 9.65%) and AJE-N&F (8.4% and 22.7%) of Syria (see Tables 5.20 and 6.1). This is possibly because Al-Jazeera's sponsor, Qatar, is more politically involved in the Syrian civil war than the Bahraini conflict. As explained in Chaps. 2 and 4, Qatar acted as a champion of human rights and democracy in the beginning of the Arab Spring, but it endorsed and participated in the Peninsula Shield Force (PSF) troops that were deployed to quell pro-democracy protesters in Bahrain in 2011 (Ulrichsen, 2014). Unlike its relative independence from the Gulf Cooperation Council (GCC), the Qatari regime took a decision not to oppose Saudi Arabia and the Gulf states' consensus over supporting their Gulf ally (Al-Khalifa dynasty) at the time (Khatib, 2013; Friedman, 2012).

In an interview conducted to enrich the quantitative findings of this study, Professor Mehran Kamrava, author of the book *Qatar: Small State, Big Politics*, said, "Qatar was not extremely against Bahrain's uprising, it was quiet, it didn't actively oppose the movement but it did not effectively support it at the same time" (personal communication, April 5, 2016).

Qatar, however, was directly involved in Syria through arming rebels (including Al-Qaeda-affiliated groups), criticising the Al-Assad regime in public and mediating effectively to release hostages captured by Al-Nusra (Ulrishsen, 2014; Khatib, 2013, M. Lynch, 2016; Kamrava, 2013; Roberts, 2015; Lister, 2016; Sengupta, 2013; Blair & Spencer, 2014; Burweila, 2014; Dorsey, 2015).

Blasi (2004) argues that if a state is politically involved in a conflict, then its own media is more likely to produce WJ-Orientated coverage. Blasi (2004, p. 10) further indicates:

We can assume that the realisation of Peace Journalism should be easier in conflicts where neither one's own country nor its closest allies are involved.

In this case, the chances look better for balanced, all-sided, truth-orientated, win-win orientated coverage. In contrast, if one's own country is involved, and possibly also if close allies are involved, then Peace Journalism will be more difficult.

Lee et al. (2006) argue that Western wires were dominated by WJ framing during the war in Iraq because the West participated directly in the conflict. In their analysis of the coverage from eight Asian newspapers, Lee et al. (2006) found that the reporting by Asian media of local conflicts recorded generally higher percentages of WJ (54%) than international conflicts (specifically the war in Iraq) (44.1%). Lee et al. (2006) attribute the reason of Asian media displaying more PJ criteria in coverage on Iraq with the objection of the Asian governments to the war.

Fahmy and Eakin (2014) conclude that *Ha'aretz* (an Israeli newspaper) displayed significantly higher percentages of dichotomising language than *The Guardian* and *The New York Times* when covering the Israeli raid on the Turkish ship *Mavi Marmara*. This was due to Israel's direct involvement in the incident and exposure to intense international condemnation. Similarly, Shinar (2009) found that the Israeli media used higher percentages of WJ framing, zero-sum discourse and military sources than the Canadian media during 2006 Lebanon War. On the other hand, the Canadian media was classified as People-Orientated because many Canadians (from Lebanese background) were trapped in Lebanon during the war (Shinar, 2009).

Conversely, in his examination of the international and Philippine media coverage during June 2006 (when the United States ordered the authorities in the Philippines to "eradicate a group of armed rebels" as part of the US-led War on Terrorism), J. Lynch (2008) found that the *Philippine Daily Inquirer* (PDI) newspaper scored higher percentages of active and passive PJ than the international media. J. Lynch (2008, p. 143) infers that "the country's ambivalent relationship with the United States" can be behind the high proportions of PJ indicators. Lee et al. (2006) found that unlike the coverage by Asian newspapers, Sri Lankan newspapers used significant percentages of PJ while covering the conflict between the Sri Lankan government and Liberation Tigers of Tamil Eelam (LTTE) during 2001–2002. The researchers associate the high proportion of PJ to the political environment at the time, as both sides accepted to negotiate taking part in a ceasefire agreement in December 2000. Therefore, this study is in an agreement with the PJ literature that the interests of a state can increase (like in the case of the Philippines and Sri Lanka) and decrease (such as Israeli media and Asian coverage of internal conflicts) the percentage of PJ practice.

The other reason behind Al-Jazeera displaying more WJ criteria in Syria's coverage than Bahrain's can be attributed to the different degree of intensity and drama in both conflicts. Wolfsfeld (1997) concludes that media coverage differs from one conflict to another based on political contexts, political power of involved players, journalists' ability to access the conflict arena and developments on the ground (cited in Cottle, 2006). Lee (2010) argues that intense conflicts tend to use higher percentages of WJ than others. Galtung and Ruge (1965, p. 66) say, "the event that takes place over a longer time-span will go un-recorded unless it reaches some kind of dramatic climax, the building of a dam goes unnoticed but not its inauguration".

7.4 Double Standards of Qatar's Foreign Policy in Bahrain and Syria

Qatar's contradictory policy in Bahrain and Syria is exhibited in Al-Jazeera (excluding AJE coverage of Bahrain). For instance, 20% and 32% of AJA-N&F framed the Syrian conflict as a "revolution" during August and September 2013 (Table 6.10) where (unlike the peaceful protests in Bahrain) the opposition and regime were intensively fighting in a civil war. On the other hand, the term "revolution" scored less than 1% in the AJA-N&F of Bahrain (Table 5.1). Al-Jazeera has thus legitimised the Syrian armed opposition (including Al-Qaeda-affiliated groups that murder civilians based on their sect affiliations) (Chap. 6), whereas it (especially AJA) associated the Bahraini peaceful protesters with Shi'ism, describing them as having a "sectarian agenda" (Chap. 5).

Although AJA-N&F unreservedly blamed Al-Assad for committing war crimes and CW attacks, the channel hesitated in directly and indirectly naming the Al-Saud and Al-Khalifa regimes' violations in Bahrain. In line with Qatar's foreign policy (at the time), Bahraini regime officials were given space in the news of AJA (44.8%) and AJE (29.2%) more than pro-democracy opponents in both channels (18% and 17.9%, respectively) (Tables 5.7 and 5.14). In Syria, however, the opposition dominated the news of AJA (59.1%) and AJE (44.9%), whereas the regime was given approximately 25% of the overall quotations in both channels (Table 6.4).

254   Z. ABDUL-NABI

In short, both channels gave more space to Qatar's allies, the Al-Khalifa regime in Bahrain and opposition groups in Syria. In addition, the clear majority of AJA-N&F (90.6% and 90.9%) legitimised a military action against Syria to "punish" Al-Assad for "using CW against his own people" (Table 6.5). On the contrary, significant proportions of AJA-N&F (47.6% and 100%) justified the Saudi military intervention to guarantee the survival of the Al-Khalifa regime (Table 5.8). With the exception of AJE's coverage of Bahrain, the Al-Jazeera network[1] omitted sectarian-orientated violations carried out by the Bahraini authorities (demolishing Shia mosques) and Syrian opposition (suicide attacks in Alawite areas). Moreover, the network took allegations made by Syrian rebels and Bahraini officials at face value, contributing the promotion of their claims and propaganda.

Even though some scholars criticised Al-Jazeera's imbalanced coverage of Bahrain and Syria (Barakat, 2011; M. Lynch, 2013, 2015, 2016; Kraidy, 2014; Ayaad, 2014; Khatib, 2013; Ulrichsen, 2014; Kamrava, 2013), this is the first quantitative study that demonstrates the dual standards in both coverages.

AJA's reporter in Sydney, Salih Al-Saqqaf, stated in a research interview (conducted for this study) that the channel did not allow him to cover the pro-Bahraini uprising rallies in Sydney that were organised in solidarity with the Bahraini people. AJA however asked Al-Saqqaf to cover every anti-Assad march in Australia even if they were a small group of demonstrators. The former AJA reporter says:

> When Saudi troops were deployed in Bahrain in March 2011, the Lebanese and Iraqi community in Sydney organised a rally in Hyde Park where nearly 2000 people attended. I saw journalists from Australian outlets in the rally. I asked AJA whether I can cover it or not, as I should take their permission before I do any news report. I explained to them how big it was and that other media outlets were definitely going to report on it. They [AJA] said, 'Do not cover it.' I asked, 'Why?' They replied, 'Please understand our situation.' Three months later, on the 18th of June, nearly no more than 25 anti-Assad people, I swear no more than 25, protested in front of the Australian Parliament in Canberra [the capital city], demanding the 'downfall of Syria's dictator.' The channel had given me a permission to cover it and aired it on the same day. (S. Al-Saqqaf, personal communication, February 26, 2017)

[1] Both AJA and AJE are referred to as the "Al-Jazeera network".

Al-Saqqaf also revealed that the channel did not accept reporting pro-Assad rallies in Sydney although there were "significant numbers" of participants. Al-Saqqaf (who is well-known in the Arab community in Sydney for his work for Australian SBS Radio) said that he was "bombarded by questions from people about the reasons behind covering some rallies and neglecting others" (personal communication, February 26, 2017). Al-Saqqaf revealed that the camera operator was so "embarrassed" about the coverage and the outrage from the community that he resigned from AJA.

Therefore, Al-Jazeera can no longer act as Qatar's public diplomacy tool because—as mentioned in Chap. 2—"good public diplomacy has to go beyond propaganda" (Nye, 2008).

However, the former managing director of the Al-Jazeera network, Wadah Khanfar, totally disagrees with this analysis. He said in an interview (done for this study) that other "bigger" revolutions were taking place during Bahrain's uprising, and hence there were other "priorities". The former director elaborates:

Bahrain is a case which has been complicated for both Arabic and English channels. Why? When the Bahrain uprising was taking place, during the same period, we have the revolutions taking place or big revolutions taking place in Egypt, in Libya, in Yemen, and so on. So, with the weight of the story of Bahrain, if you have one hour to define your priorities during this one hour, you would give Bahrain much less coverage of course. Then give, for example [the rest of the coverage] to Egypt. Egypt was the major story, or Libya, or Yemen. And besides that, we do not really have access. And I remember that our chief correspondent was kicked out from Bahrain. (W. Khanfar, personal communication, March 16, 2017)

When challenged further about Qatar's intervention and pressure not to cover Bahrain, Wadah responded:

Sometimes Qataris were annoyed of our coverage; there is no doubt about it. I can't tell you that Al-Jazeera is fully independent like BBC or CNN. We are an Arabic channel based in Qatar. But we have been always aware of our bias. We are aware that we should never become the voice of the foreign affairs of Qatar, or Sunni majority in the Middle East, or a voice of this part against another. We are aware of that. Given the fact that we are in Qatar, we may by one way or another be influenced by certain narratives... So to answer your question, we try not to be the voice of Qatar and I think we have succeeded to a large extent, but I can't say that it is a 100% independent organisation. It's funded by Qatar and we try to find the balance regardless of this fact. (W. Khanfar, personal communication, March 16, 2017)

7.5 AJA and AJE: Journalism Culture, Journalists and Target Audience

This study concludes that the AJA and AJE coverage of both conflicts were to a varying extent different. In Bahrain, AJE practised "reflexivity" and scored higher percentages of PJ frames than AJA. AJE was significantly able to counter the propaganda of the Bahraini regime and reveal the role of GCC troops in participating in the crackdown on protesters. AJA, on the other hand, reinforced the sectarian framing of the conflict and legitimised the Saudi military intervention.

In Syria, both channels promoted the opposition and its allies' narrative, revealing violations of one side and pointing the finger at one perpetrator only. They were dominated by WJ frames and selectivity in favour of rebel sources, claims and propaganda. AJA, however, used noticeably polarising terms and tone while referring to the Al-Assad regime and its supporters.

The findings of the analysis of coverage by both channels in the two conflicts contradict previous studies that there were no major dissimilarities between AJA and AJE (Fakhri, 2011; Al-Nahed, 2015; Fahmy & Al-Emad, 2011). In both conflicts, AJE used less emotive language than AJA and recorded a significant percentage of the People-Orientated frame, especially in its features. The findings agree with the previous literature that AJE has a tendency to give voice to the voiceless (Firdous, 2009; El-Nawawy & Powers, 2008; Al-Najjar, 2009; Figenschou, 2010). On the other hand, AJA in both conflicts marginalised accounts of ordinary people and used sectarian language while referring to "Shia protesters" in Bahrain and "Alawite supporters" of the Syrian regime.

While there might be several reasons behind the differences between AJA and AJE (some of these were discussed already in Chaps. 5 and 6), the most obvious dissimilarities between them are the nationalities and ideologies of their journalists and directors. AJA's programme director, Aref Hijjawi, says that AJA is closer to Arabic hearts than AJE, as its reporters are "impassioned about Arab and Islamic issues" (Kamrava, 2013, p. 78). It is widely reported that Islamists, certainly the Muslim Brotherhood (MB) movement, dominate Al-Jazeera's channel (Fandy,

2007). Interviews with Al-Jazeera's editorial staff, conducted by Ferjani (2010) between 2005 and 2007, revealed that there was dissatisfaction among the editors and anchors of AJA with "pro-Islamist bias" (cited in Ayaad, 2014). For instance, the former Washington bureau chief of AJA, Hafez Al-Mirazi, resigned from the channel in 2007 in protest over the "Islamists drift" in the channel (Ayaad, 2014). Al-Mirazi says, "From the first day of the Wadah Khanfar era, there was a dramatic change, especially because of him selecting assistants who are hard-line Islamists" (Ayaad, 2014).

The Lebanese *Al-Safir* newspaper reported that five female anchors resigned from AJA for having been harassed and criticised over their clothing and modesty by the deputy editor, Ayman Jaballa, who is known for being close to the MB movement (Kubaisy, 2010). After the military coup that overthrew the first elected Egyptian President, Mohammed Morsi, in July 2013, 22 staff members from Al-Jazeera *Mubashir Misr* (Al-Jazeera Egypt) and four Egyptian editors from Al-Jazeera's headquarters in Doha resigned in protest against what they called a "biased editorial policy" in favour of the MB (Sharaf, 2013). Karem Mahmoud, a former Egyptian anchor at the channel, says to the Gulf News newspaper that Al-Jazeera used to "instruct each staff member to favour the Muslim Brotherhood". He further adds that "there are instructions to us to telecast certain news…, the management in Doha provokes sedition among the Egyptian people" (Sharaf, 2013).

The ideological inclination of AJA's prominent anchors to the MB can be clearly seen on their social media accounts. For instance, on March 15, 2015, Jamal Rayyan (who has been working with AJA since its foundation in 1996) posted a picture of the overthrown President Mohammad Morsi on his Twitter account. Above that picture Rayyan tweeted, "This great [giant] man was challenged by the whole state, corrupted institutions, thugs, army, media and the security as well as judicial authorities".

Kraidy (2014) says that there are several well-known anchors in AJA that are affiliated with the MB. For instance, Ahmad Zaidan (responsible for the Syria desk) was exiled by the Baath Syrian regime after accusations of being involved in the MB-led armed uprising against Hafez Al-Assad in 1982 (Kraidy, 2014). Interestingly, Zaidan was the only invited journalist to the wedding of bin Laden's son, Muhammad, in 2001 (Miles, 2010). Zaidan's sympathy with Al-Nusra (see Chap. 6) and other radical Islamic movements is not new or unusual. On November 12, 2015, Zaidan described the ISIS suicide bombers who attacked Southern Beirut, killing

43 Shia civilians, as "martyrs". He tweeted on the same day of the attack, "Targeting [attacking] Dahiya [Southern Beirut] by 'four martyrs,' one of them was killed and the others managed to escape, reflects that this attack is more professional than the previous attacks". He deleted this tweet after being widely criticised and shared on social media.

Taysir Alluni, another prominent Syrian reporter at AJA, was accused of supporting Al-Qaeda when he was reporting from Afghanistan during the war in 2001 (Miles, 2010). The former chief of Al-Jazeera's bureau in Kabul was the only reporter that interviewed Osama bin Laden (Miles, 2010). Alluni fled Syria in 1980 when the Syrian army was targeting students that belonged to the MB movement (Miles, 2010). He was arrested in Spain in 2001 and accused of "performing acts of support, finance, supervision and coordination" with Al-Qaeda. It was reported that the court had evidence of Alluni's telephone conversations with "known Al-Qaeda operatives" since the 1990s (Miles, 2010).

Rula Ibrahim, a Syrian Alawite anchor in AJA, said that some journalists in the channel are sectarian to the extent that they "have refused to greet me [her] ever since the outbreak of events in Syria because they hold a grudge against my [her] sect" (Kanaan, 2012). Ibrahim further states that AJA interviews activists who use sectarian language that "Syrians understand very well" (Kanaan, 2012). The domination of journalists with certain ideologies cannot be a coincidence, as media institutions tend to employ journalists that are more likely to produce content that conforms to the agenda of governments or media owners (Herman & Chomsky, 2010).

In addition to the domination of the MB and Sunni Islam in AJA, Al-Najjar (2011) found that Arab journalists, in general, are not committed to the ethos of objectivity and balanced reporting when their countries are involved. This is because "patriotism is viewed as a virtue among many Arab audiences, journalists, and government officials" (Al-Najjar, 2011, p. 747). As all journalists are themselves citizens of certain countries or belong to certain national cultures, they are not immune to nationalist bias, especially when covering international conflicts (Hackett, 2006). Arab media, in general, is more restricted than Western media outlets. A survey conducted by Pintak and Ginges (2009) found that 50% of Arab journalists stated that they are not fully independent, as their regimes manipulate their media organisations. In addition, a significant percentage of Arab journalists (40%) evaluate Arab media as "poor" in relation to its professionalism and journalistic standards (Pintak & Ginges, 2009, p. 161 cited in Al-Najjar, 2011, p. 750).

When asked about the reasons behind having completely different coverage by both channels, the former managing director of AJA and AJE, Wadah Khanfar, said in an interview conducted for this study that both channels have the "same editorial policy" but they have "different priorities". He says:

> We have one editorial policy and the same budget as well. We have one code of ethics. We have one professional set of rules. But we have different priorities [when it comes to] running the news. So, you have, for example, in AJA more reporters in the Arab World, whereas AJE has more reporters in Africa, Latin America, the US, and Europe for instance. Our audiences are the ones that define our priorities. So it's not actually about policies, but I'll go with [having different] priorities. (W. Khanfar, personal communication, March 16, 2017)

Therefore, based on the discussion of this chapter and previous ones (Chaps. 2, 5 and 6), this book concludes that the differences between AJA and AJE in their coverage of Bahrain and Syria can be attributed to the following reasons: (1) different nationalities and ideologies of journalists, (2) different target audiences, (3) different competitors, (4) different degrees of commitment to "objective reporting" and professional journalism and (5) different degrees of pressure and intervention from the Qatari owners.

7.6 Developments of Events: Here and Now

The quantitative findings of this study show that the frequency of including PJ frames in the AJA and AJE coverage of the Bahraini and Syrian conflicts increased and decreased based on certain events and developments.

For example, Tables 7.1 and 7.2 show that the frequency of including the Peace/Conflict-Orientated frame in the AJA and AJE coverage of Bahrain' surprising reached its peak (90% in both channels) at the beginning of the deployment of GCC troops, during the period from March 14 to March 31, 2011. It then decreased in both channels gradually at the end of the research period (Tables 7.1 and 7.2). Similarly, the frequency of applying the Solution-Orientated frame hits its highest point (50% in AJA and AJE equally) at the beginning of the crackdown in March, in which

260   Z. ABDUL-NABI

Table 7.1 Frequencies (F) of the PJ frames displayed in AJA during the three months that followed the deployment of GCC troops in Manama

Bahrain's uprising: AJA: (80) news stories

Date and number of articles	Developments	Peace	Solution	People	Truth
14/3 to 31/3/2011 20 articles	+ Deployment of the PSF. + US called on Bahrain to "take steps now" towards a political resolution. + Iran demanded UN exert pressure on Saudi. + Kuwait's Emir had offered to mediate between Bahrain's regime and opposition groups.	18 (90%)	10 (50%)	2 (10%)	17 (85%)
1/4 to 30/4/2011 22 articles	+ Excessive human rights violations and violent crackdown against the protesters.	9 (40.9%)	2 (9.1%)	0 (0%)	11 (50%)
1/5 to 1/6/2011 38 articles	+ The violent crackdown intensified. + HR groups and UN condemned the crackdown and called for an investigation. + US and United Kingdom (UK) expressed their concerns over the violations. + Bahrain's regime lifted martial law.	12 (31.6%)	6 (15.7%)	4 (10.5%)	29 (76.3%)

the United States, Iran and Kuwait called on the Bahraini regime to take steps towards a political solution. The frequency of this frame decreased gradually in April in AJA (9.1%) (Table 7.1) and AJE (30%) (Table 7.2). However, it went up again in AJA (15.7%) at the end of May 2011 (Table 7.1). This increase came in conjunction with Obama's speech that criticised the regime's human rights violations. As the violent crackdown was heavy during the first three months of the uprising, the frequency of applying the Truth-Orientated frame remained mostly high and stable (around 90%) in AJE during the research period (Table 7.2). However, the frequency of the same frame in AJA fluctuated, reaching its peak (85%)

7 AL-JAZEERA'S (2011–2013) "DOUBLE STANDARDS" COVERAGE... 261

Table 7.2 Frequencies (F) of the PJ frame displayed in AJE during the three months that followed the deployment of GCC troops in Manama

Bahrain's uprising: AJE: (38) news stories

Date and number of articles	Developments	Peace	Solution	People	Truth
14/3 to 31/3/2011 10 articles	+ Deployment of the PSF. + US called on Bahrain to "take steps now" towards a political resolution. + Iran demanded UN exert pressure on Saudi. + Kuwait's Emir had offered to mediate between Bahrain's regime and opposition groups.	9 (90%)	5 (50%)	3 (30%)	9 (90%)
9/4 to 11/5/2011 20 articles	+ Excessive human rights violations and violent crackdown against the protesters. + The violent crackdown intensified. + HR groups and UN condemned the crackdown and called for investigation.	15 (75%)	6 (30%)	5 (25%)	18 (90%)
17/5 to 1/6/2011 8 articles	+ US and UK expressed their concerns over the violations. + Bahrain's regime lifted martial law.	4 (50%)	0%	3 (37.5%)	8 (100%)

at the beginning of the crackdown, dropping in April (50%) and then increasing again in May (76.3%) (as shown in Table 7.1). The People-Orientated frame in AJE and AJA did not seem to be affected by any developments or time period (Tables 7.1 and 7.2).

Likewise, in Syria, the results show that the frequencies of including PJ frames in both channels were affected by certain developments. In AJA, the frequency of displaying the Peace/Conflict-Orientated frame recorded 10%, went down to 5% and then raised significantly to 58.1% during the second week of September (Table 7.3). Similarly, in AJA, the Solution-Orientated frame scored 40% at the beginning of the attack, dropped to 25% in the middle and went up sharply to 61.3% in the period from September 8 to 13 (Table 7.3).

262   Z. ABDUL-NABI

Table 7.3 Frequencies (F) of the PJ criteria mentioned in AJA during the first three weeks of Syria's CW attack

Syria's chemical attack: AJA: (71) news stories

Date + number of articles	Developments	F of CW: Peace	F of PI: Solution	F of SCW and MO: People	F of HRV: Truth
From 21/8 to 3/9/2013 20 articles	+ Al-Ghouta's attack took place on 21/8/2013. + Obama considered limited military action against Syria.	2 (10%)	8 (40%)	Both criteria scored equally: 2 (10%)	0%
From 3/9 to 7/9/2013 20 articles	+ Obama said he will seek approval from the Congress before striking Syria. + Putin demanded convincing evidence that Al-Assad's regime used CW. + G20 leaders were divided over Syria.	1 (5%)	5 (25%)	0%	0%
From 8/9 to 14/9/2013 31 articles	+ A UN report revealed that both sides of the conflict committed human rights violations. + Russia introduced CW peace proposal. + Syria accepted the Russian proposal. + US discussed the Russian proposal. + Syria's CW talks started in Geneva.	18 (58.1%)	19 (61.3%)	0%	0%

In AJE, both the Peace and Solution-Orientated frames scored 5% equally at the outset of the attack (Table 7.4). The frequencies of both frames increased gradually during the research period and hit their highest percentages (54.5% and 81.8%, respectively) in the second week of September (Table 7.4). This sharp and notable increase of the Peace- and Solution-Orientated frames in the period from September 7 to 13, 2013, in both channels was paralleled by the introduction of the Russian

7 AL-JAZEERA'S (2011–2013) "DOUBLE STANDARDS" COVERAGE... 263

Table 7.4 Frequencies (F) of the PJ criteria mentioned in AJE during the first three weeks of Syria's CW attack

Syria's chemical attack: AJE: (82) news stories

Date and number of articles	Developments	F of CW: Peace	F of PI: Solution	F of SCW: People	F of HRV: Truth
From 21/8 to 26/8/2013 20 articles	+ Al-Ghouta's attack took place on 21/8/2013.	1 (5%)	1(5%)	2 (10%)	0%
From 26/8 to 31/8/2013 20 articles	+ Obama considered limited military action against Syria.	4 (20%)	6 (30%)	0%	0%
From 31/8 to 6/9/2013 20 articles	+ Obama said he will seek approval from the Congress before striking Syria. + Putin demanded convincing evidence that Al-Assad's regime used CW. + G20 leaders were divided over Syria.	4 (20%)	6 (30%)	0%	0 %
From 7/9 to 14/9/2013 22 articles	+ A UN report revealed that both sides of the conflict committed human rights violations. + Russia introduced CW peace proposal. + Syria accepted the Russian proposal. + US discussed the Russian proposal. + Syria's CW talks started in Geneva	12 (54.5%)	18 (81.8%)	0%	2 (9.1%)

proposal that aimed at preventing imminent US military action against Syria. Furthermore, the Truth-Orientated frame in AJE was presented only at the end of the research period when the UN released a report revealing that both sides had committed human rights violations (Table 7.4).

Therefore, this study concludes that the focus on the Solution-Orientated frame in Bahrain and Syria does not necessarily reflect a tendency towards practising PJ. It instead implies their (AJA and AJE) commitment to cover the developments (here and now) on the ground. While covering the Russian peace initiative, both channels depended significantly on statements and information provided by officials. The coverage did not cover the proposal in depth and did not ask any of the following significant questions that a peace journalist should highlight:

> To what extent is the plan based on what only elites can do, what only people can do, or on what both can do? Does the plan foresee an ongoing conflict resolution or is the idea a single-shot agreement? Is peace/conflict transformation education for people, for elites or for both, built into the plan?
>
> ... To what extent does the plan contain elements of reconciliation? If there has been violence, to what extent does the plan contain elements of rehabilitation/reconstruction? If the plan doesn't work, is the plan reversible? Even if the plan does work for this conflict, does it create new conflicts or problems? Is it a good deal? (Galtung & Fischer, 2013, pp. 94–95)

The results of this study are in line with previous studies which concluded that PJ orientations can increase at certain times during conflicts, especially if peace is on the political agenda (Kempf, 2003). In a study that analysed AJE, Press TV, CNN and the BBC's coverage of the Palestinian-Israeli conflict based on PJ, it found that the channels who focused on Peace-Orientated frames were instigated by events and not by journalists' initiatives (Ozohu-Suleiman, 2014). A study that examined Asian media coverage (1973 news stories) of conflicts in India, Pakistan and Sri Lanka showed that PJ frames scored high percentages (51.4%) during peace negotiation and low percentages when peace was not a priority among conflicted parties (37.1%) (Lee, 2010).

A study that analysed the coverage of *Yedioth Aharonot* and *Ha'aretz* newspapers observed that their discourse dramatically altered from WJ to PJ after the signing of the Oslo Accords between then Israeli Prime Minister Yitzhak Rabin and the former head of the Palestinian Authority Yasser Arafat in 1993 (Mandelzis, 2007). Although focusing on "here and now" can actually increase the percentages of PJ frames during certain periods, highlighting events without mentioning their context leaves audiences with a "very narrow slice of the conflict, and therefore a limited understanding of the conflict's root causes and consequences" (Fahmy & Eakin, 2014).

7.7 News Wires

The results of this study show that there is no direct relationship between the extent of dependence on news wires and WJ or PJ framing. Even though 50% of AJA and AJE articles on Bahrain depended entirely on news wires, they recorded more PJ framing than the AJA (38%) and AJE (15.9%) coverage of the Syrian coverage, which relied less on news wires (Table 7.5). These results are not in an agreement with previous studies which showed that reliance on news wires results in high percentages of WJ (Lee, 2010, Lee et al., 2006).

7.8 Conclusion

This chapter argues that WJ frames dominated the AJA and AJE coverage of the second CW attack in Eastern Al-Ghouta more than the Bahraini uprising because of Qatar's heavy involvement in the Syrian conflict. While Qatari officers were part of the PSF deployed in Manama to crack down on protesters, Doha's interests in Damascus are incomparable to Manama's.

This study also found that the high percentage of displaying WJ frames while covering Syria's CW attack can be attributed to the nature of the conflict, which is far more dramatic and intense than the Bahraini one. This is in line with other studies which concluded that the political involvement of media's sponsors (Blasi, 2004; Lee et al. 2006; Fahmy & Eakin, 2014; Shinar, 2009; J. Lynch, 2008) as well as the intensity of the conflict (Wolfsfeld, 1997; Lee, 2010; Galtung & Ruge, 1965, p. 66) can affect the degree of putting PJ orientations into practice.

Table 7.5 The extent of Al-Jazeera's dependence on news wires while covering Bahrain's uprising and Syria's CW attack

Al-Jazeera's dependence on news wires in Bahrain's coverage		
Sources of articles	AJA	AJE
	(80) News stories	(38) News stories
Al-Jazeera only	22 (27.5%)	5 (13.2%)
Al-Jazeera and news wires	18 (22.5%)	14 (36.8%)
News wires only	40 (50%)	19 (50%)
Al-Jazeera's dependence on news wires in Syria's coverage		
Sources of articles	AJA	AJE
	(71) News stories	(82) News stories
Al-Jazeera only	8 (11.3%)	2 (2.4%)
Al-Jazeera and news wires	36 (50.7%)	67 (81.7%)
News wires only	27(38%)	13 (15.9%)

Qatar's foreign policy of backing the Al-Khalifa regime during the 2011 uprising in Bahrain and aiding in bringing down the Al-Assad regime in Syria has manifested in the channels' coverage, especially AJA. The Qatari, "double standard" approach to both conflicts has been translated into AJA and AJE giving more space to the Al-Khalifa regime as well as Syrian opposition groups than Al-Assad regime and Bahraini opposition in their coverage. Moreover, the AJA coverage legitimised a military strike to "protect the Syrian people", while it turned a blind eye to the Saudi troops that were deployed in Manama to quell unarmed protesters. AJA further associated the Syrian conflict with the term "revolution", while similar lexical choices were hardly observed in Bahrain's coverage.

While the AJA and AJE coverage of the Syrian conflict presented more similarities than differences, both channels differ significantly in their coverage of the Bahraini uprising. This study argues that AJA used more WJ framing as well as more polarised, sectarian and demonising language in its coverage of both conflicts. The AJE coverage of Bahrain and Syria on the other hand was more People-Orientated and committed to the standards of professional journalism and objective reporting. These differences, this chapter concludes (along with Chaps. 5 and 6), are caused by targeting different audiences and competitors, employing journalists from different ideologies, practicing different journalism culture and the extent of Qatar's involvement in their editorial policies.

In addition, the empirical results of this study find that the application of PJ frames fluctuated based on certain events and developments on the ground. For instance, the displaying of the Solution-Orientated frames reached their peaks in the AJA and AJE coverage of both conflicts when Kuwait had officially mediated to de-escalate the conflict in Bahrain and when Russia proposed their CW peace deal for Syria. This means that the increase of displaying a certain PJ frame in a certain conflict can more likely be related to an "event" that is reported on, than a "choice" made by journalists. This is consistent with previous studies which found that PJ-Orientated coverage can increase at certain times during conflicts, especially when "peace" is on the top of political agenda (Kempf, 2003; Ozohu-Suleiman, 2014; Lee, 2010; Mandelzis, 2007).

The findings of this study contradict with other studies (Lee, 2010; Lee et al., 2006) which found that the dependence on news wires can increase the practice of WJ. Therefore, the quantitative results demonstrate no relationship between both channels' reliance on news wires and the proportions of PJ frames.

The next chapter dissects the extent of the conformity between Qatar's politics and Al-Jazeera by examining the AJA and AJE coverage of Bahrain's uprising in the periods before and after the 2017 Gulf crisis.

REFERENCES

Al-Nahed, S. (2015). Covering Libya: A framing analysis of Al Jazeera and BBC coverage of the 2011 Libyan uprising and NATO intervention. *Middle East Critique, 24*(3), 251–267.

Al-Najjar, A. (2009). How Arab is Al-Jazeera English? Comparative study of Al-Jazeera Arabic and Al-Jazeera English news channel. *Global Media Journal, 8*(14), 1–35.

Al-Najjar, A. (2011). Contesting patriotism and global journalism ethics in Arab journalism. *Journalism Studies, 12*(6), 747–756.

Ayaad, S. W. (2014). *Qatari Foreign Policy, Al-Jazeera, and Revolution in the Middle East and North Africa* (Doctoral dissertation, Communication, Art & Technology: Communication). Accessed March 24, 2016, from http://summit.sfu.ca/item/14739

Barakat, R. (2011) *New media in the Arab world: A tool for redesigning geopolitical realities* (Master's Thesis, Lebanese American University, Lebanon). Accessed November 11, 2013, from http://laur.lau.edulb:7080/xmlui/handle/10725/1047

Blair, D., & Spencer, R. (2014, September 20). How Qatar is funding the rise of Islamist extremists. *The Telegraph.* Accessed March 14, 2016, from http://www.telegraph.co.uk/news/worldnews/middleeast/qatar/11110931/How-Qatar-is-funding-the-rise-of-Islamist-extremists.html

Bläsi, B. (2004). Peace journalism and the news production process. *Conflict & Communication Online, 3*(1/2), 1–12. Accessed January 4, 2016, from http://www.cco.regener-online.de/2004/pdf_2004/blaesi.pdf

Burweila, A. (2014). How to lose a war: When your allies aid your enemies. *RIEAS.* Accessed November 24, 2015, from http://rieas.gr/images/islamic/ayarieas.pdf

Cottle, S. (2006). *Mediatized conflict: Developments in media and conflict studies.* McGraw-Hill Education.

Dorsey, J. M. (2015). How Qatar is its own worst enemy. *The International Journal of the History of Sport, 32*(3), 422–439.

El-Nawawy, M., & Powers, S. (2008). *Mediating conflict: Al-Jazeera English and the possibility of a conciliatory media.* Figueroa Press.

Fahmy, S., & Al Emad, M. (2011). Al-Jazeera vs Al-Jazeera: A comparison of the network's English and Arabic online coverage of the US/Al Qaeda conflict. *The International Communication Gazette, 73*(3), 216–232.

Fahmy, S., & Eakin, B. (2014). High drama on the high seas Peace versus war journalism framing of an Israeli/Palestinian-related incident. *International Communication Gazette, 76*(1), 86–105.

268 Z. ABDUL-NABI

Fakhri, F. (2011). *Content analysis of how Al-Jazeera English and Arabic channels framed the war on Gaza* (Master's thesis). Retrieved from ProQuest Dissertations and Theses (Accession Order No. 1496764).

Fandy, M. (2007). *(Un)civil war of words: Media and politics in the Arab world.* Praeger Security International.

Ferjani, R. (2010). Religion and television in the Arab world: Towards a communication studies approach. *Middle East Journal of Culture and Communication, 3*(1), 82–100.

Figenschou, T. U. (2010). A voice for the voiceless? A quantitative content analysis of Al Jazeera English's flagship news. *Global Media and Communication, 6*(1), 85–107.

Firdous, T. (2009). *Al Jazeera English presenting a non-western viewpoint and contesting western media dominance during the Gaza crisis* (Master's thesis). Retrieved from ProQuest Dissertations and Theses (Accession Order No. 1507250).

Friedman, B. (2012). Battle for Bahrain: What one uprising meant for the Gulf states and Iran. *World Affairs, 174*(6), 74–84.

Galtung, J., & Ruge, M. H. (1965). The structure of foreign news. *Journal of Peace Research, 2*(1), 64–91.

Galtung, J., & Fischer, D. (2013). *Johan Galtung: Pioneer of peace research.* Springer.

Hackett, R. A. (2006). Is peace journalism possible? Three frameworks for assessing structure and agency in news media. *Conflict & Communication, 5*(2), 1–13. Accessed July 14, 2016, from http://www.cco.regener-online. de/2006_2/pdf/hackett.pdf

Herman, E. S., & Chomsky, N. (2010). *Manufacturing consent: The political economy of the mass media.* Random House eBooks.

Kamrava, M. (2013). *Qatar: Small state, big politics.* Cornell University Press.

Kanaan, W. (2012, February 24). Syria's electronic warriors hit Al Jazeera. *Al-Akhbar English.* Accessed March 12, 2016, from http://english.al-akhbar. com/node/4525

Kempf, W. (2003). Constructive conflict coverage–A social-psychological research and development program. *Conflict & Communication Online, 2*(2), 1–13. Accessed June 22, 2016, from http://cco.regener-online.de/2003_2/ pdf_2003_2/kempf_engl.pdf

Khatib, L. (2013). Qatar's foreign policy: The limits of pragmatism. *International Affairs, 89*(2), 417–431.

Kraidy, M. M. (2014). Media industries in revolutionary times. *Media Industries, 1*(2), 16–21. Accessed January 20, 2016, from http://www.mediaindustries-journal.org/index.php/mij/article/view/45

Kubaisy, F. (2010, May 31). استقالة مذيعات «الجزيرة»: قبول واحدة وترِيّث بشأن البقية. *Assafir Newspaper.* Accessed August 2, 2016, from http://assafir.com/Article/200927

Lee, S. T., Maslog, C. C., & Kim, H. S. (2006). Asian Conflicts and the Iraq War: A comparative framing analysis. *International Communication Gazette, 68*(5–6), 499–518.

Lee, S. T. (2010). Peace journalism: Principles and structural limitations in the news coverage of three conflicts. *Mass Communication and Society, 13*(4), 361–384.

Lister, C. (2016). Profiling Jabhat Al-Nusra. *Brookings Institution*. Accessed January 2, 2017, from https://www.brookings.edu/wp-content/uploads/2016/07/iwr_20160728_profiling_nusra.pdf

Lynch, J. (2008). *Debates in Peace Journalism*. Sydney University Press.

Lynch, M. (2013). *The Arab uprising: The unfinished revolutions of the new Middle East*. Public Affairs.

Lynch, M. (2015). How the media trashed the transitions. *Journal of Democracy, 26*(4), 90–99.

Lynch, M. (2016). *The new Arab wars: Uprisings and anarchy in the Middle East*. Public Affairs.

Mandelzis, L. (2007). Representations of peace in news discourse: Viewpoint and opportunity for Peace Journalism. *Conflict & Communication Online, 6*(4), 1–10. Accessed July 17, 2016, from http://www.cco.regener-online.de/2007_1/pdf/mandelzis.pdf

Miles, H. (2010). *Al-Jazeera: How Arab TV news challenged the world*. Abacus.

Nye, J. S. (2008). Public diplomacy and soft power. *The Annals of the American Academy of Political and Social Science, 616*(1), 94–109.

Ozohu-Suleiman, Y. (2014). War journalism on Israel/Palestine: Does contra-flow really make a difference? *Media, War & Conflict, 7*(1), 85–103.

Pintak, L., & Ginges, J. (2009). Inside the Arab newsroom: Arab journalists evaluate themselves and the competition. *Journalism Studies, 10*(2), 157–177.

Roberts, D. (2015). Is Qatar bringing the Nusra Front in from the cold? *BBC News*. Accessed September 16, 2016, from http://www.bbc.com/news/world-middle-east-31764114

Sengupta, K. (2013, July 26). Homemade grenades and catapults: Introducing the DIY weapons of the Free Syrian Army. *The Independent*. Accessed March 20, 2016, from http://www.independent.co.uk/news/world/middle-east/homemade-grenades-and-catapults-introducing-the-diy-weapons-of-the-free-syrian-army-8732634.html

Sharaf, A. (2013). Al-Jazeera staff resign after "biased" Egypt coverage. *Gulf News*. Accessed March 14, 2016, from http://gulfnews.com/news/mena/egypt/al-jazeera-staff-resign-after-biased-egypt-coverage-1.1206924

Shinar, D. (2009). Can Peace Journalism make progress? The coverage of the 2006 Lebanon War in Canadian and Israeli media. *International Communication Gazette, 71*(6), 451–471.

Ulrichsen, K. C. (2014). *Qatar and the Arab Spring*. Oxford University Press.

Wolfsfeld, G. (1997). *Media and political conflict: News from the Middle East*. Cambridge University Press.

CHAPTER 8

Gulf Crisis (2014–2021): Al-Jazeera's Dramatic Shift from Pro- to Anti-Bahraini Regime

8.1 Introduction

This chapter demonstrates and analyses the quantitative findings of the Al-Jazeera coverage of the Bahraini uprising in three different periods during which ties between Bahrain and Qatar were not stable. The first period starts from March 5, 2014, to November 16, 2014, when Saudi Arabia, the UAE and Bahrain withdrew their ambassadors from Qatar, forming the first unprecedented diplomatic rift between Doha and its neighbours. The second period begins straight after the Gulf states reconciled with Qatar and consequently restored their political ties, from November 17, 2014, to June 4, 2017. The third period starts from June 5, 2017, to September 28, 2021, when Saudi Arabia along with Bahrain, the UAE and Egypt severed diplomatic ties with Qatar, imposing a blockade on the country, in what has been widely known as the "2017 Gulf crisis". This chapter refers to these three periods as "first diplomatic crisis", "non-conflict period" and "second diplomatic crisis".

All online news stories related directly to Bahrain's uprising and published on Al-Jazeera Arabic (AJA) and Al-Jazeera English (AJE) websites were examined based on PJ frames and the extent of their conformity with Qatar's foreign policy (see Chap. 4). From the AJA website, 19 news stories from the first conflict period, 61 news stories from the non-conflict

© The Author(s), under exclusive license to Springer Nature Switzerland AG 2022
Z. Abdul-Nabi, *Al-Jazeera's "Double Standards" in the Arab Spring*, https://doi.org/10.1007/978-3-031-14279-6_8

271

period and 161 news stories from the second conflict period were selected and analysed. From the AJE website, 9 news stories from the first conflict period, 26 news stories from the non-conflict period and 30 news stories from the second conflict period were selected and analysed.

This chapter argues that the deterioration in political relations between the channel's sponsor, Qatar, and the Bahraini regime has transformed the AJA coverage from being pro-Bahraini regime in the non-conflict period in 2014 to pro-protesters during the first and second diplomatic crises. As an illustration, the findings of the AJA coverage show a significant rise in applying the Truth- as well as Solution-Orientated frames during the first and second conflicts.

The AJA empirical data found a sharp increase in reporting on "human rights violations", "torture" and "sexual assaults" committed by the Bahraini regime against the pro-democracy protesters during the 2017 Gulf crisis (second conflict). AJA went further by naming the son of the King, Sheikh Naser Bin Hamad Al-Khalifa, as the "prince of torture" during the same period.

Despite AJA's dramatic shift, its online news stories still recorded lower percentages in applying the Peace/Conflict- and People-Orientated frames. This has resulted in maintaining the "sectarian framing" of the Bahraini uprising. At the same time, however, it has been observed that AJA documentary films presented more attempts to refute the sectarian representation of Bahrain's uprising.

Unlike AJA, the quantitative results of the AJE coverage show that the application of the Truth- and Peace/Conflict-Orientated frames has been relatively high (more than 30%) in all research periods. This consistency has led to producing a mostly "non-sectarian framing" of the Bahraini conflict from March 2011 to September 2021. At the same time, AJE quoted human rights organisations and focused on "violations" and "torture" more frequently during the 2017 crisis.

In a nutshell, this study contends that the AJA coverage of Bahrain's uprising has been in line with Qatar's foreign policy during the conflict periods when relations between Manama and Doha deteriorated. Yet, Qatar's influence on AJE is less intense and less blatantly observed.

8.2 Key Findings

Before analysing and dissecting the findings of AJA's and AJE's coverage of Bahrain's uprising in depth, the following key points summarise the main quantitative results:

- The AJA and AJE coverage of Bahrain's uprising during the first conflict, non-conflict period and second conflict were dominated by War Journalism (WJ) framing.
- AJE's coverage during the three periods of analysis applied PJ frames more than AJA's.
- The application of the PJ framing reached its highest percentages in AJA (18.3%) and AJE (28.4%) coverage during the 2017 Gulf crisis (second conflict).
- The Truth-Orientated frame was the most applied frame in the AJA coverage of Bahrain's uprising. It scored significantly higher percentages during the first and second conflicts (22.8% and 33.5%) than the non-conflict period (8.2%).
- The Peace/Conflict-Orientated frame was the most applied frame in AJE's coverage, recording mostly consistent percentages during all research periods (39.5%, 38.5% and 37.4%).
- The People-Orientated frame was the least presented frame in the AJA and AJE coverage during all research periods, with a slight increase in the application of the frame in AJE news (AJE-N) during the 2017 Gulf crisis (18.3%).
- The reporting on "torture" against protesters has sharply increased from less than 11.5% during the first conflict and non-conflict periods to more than 50% during the 2017 Gulf crisis in both channels' coverage.
- The reporting on "sexual assaults" as a method of the regime's violations against protesters has increased from less than 2% during the first conflict and non-conflict periods to more than 11% during the 2017 Gulf crisis in both channels' coverage.
- Regime sources dominated the coverage of both channels during the first conflict and non-conflict periods (more than 42% in AJA and AJE), whereas human rights organisations were far more quoted than the regime during the 2017 Gulf crisis (more than 67% in AJA and AJE).

- Less than 8% of AJA coverage framed the Bahraini protest movement as an "uprising", whereas more than 23% of AJE coverage framed it as such in all research periods.
- The frequency of framing protesters as "Shia" decreased from nearly 46% in the coverage of both channels during the non-conflict period to less than 13% during the 2017 Gulf crisis.
- None of AJA-N mentioned the deployment of the Peninsula Shield Forces (PSF) during the first conflict and non-conflict periods. Yet more than 90% of the coverage of both channels were critical of the PSF (pro-Qatar) during the 2017 Gulf crisis.
- Dependence on Al-Jazeera network's reporters and editors as the main source of information increased significantly from nearly one third of the coverage in both channels during the first conflict and non-conflict period to more than 52% (in AJA and AJE) during the 2017 Gulf crisis.
- More than one third of the AJA and AJE coverage framed the normalisation deal between Bahrain and Israel as a "betrayal to the Palestinian cause" and more than 78% of the news stories in both channels included "critical accounts" (pro-Qatar) during the first two months of signing the deal.

8.3   Truth Frame in AJA and AJE

8.3.1   AJA: Intensive Focus on "Human Rights Violations" After 2017 Gulf Crisis

The Truth-Orientated frame[1] in the AJA coverage of the Bahraini uprising scored significantly higher percentages during the first (22.8%) and second conflicts (33.5%) compared to the non-conflict period (8.2%) (Table 8.1). During the first Gulf diplomatic crisis in 2014, AJA intensively covered the

---

[1] Analytical criteria of the Truth-Orientated frame:

1. (SFV): Does the article mention the human rights violations committed by the Bahraini security forces or by the regime in general?
2. (PC): Does the article explain the context behind some protesters' involvement in "clashes" with security forces?
3. (DSM): Does the article mention that Shia religious structures and mosques were demolished? Or does the article mention any sectarian acts/abuses committed by the regime and/or its forces?

8 GULF CRISIS (2014–2021): AL-JAZEERA'S DRAMATIC SHIFT... 275

Table 8.1 Percentages of including/mentioning the Truth-Orientated criteria in AJA's coverage of Bahrain's uprising in three research periods, from March 5, 2014, to September 28, 2021

Truth-Orientated frame in AJA	(SFV) Security Forces Violations	(PV) Protesters' Clashes	(DSM) Demolishing Shia Mosques-sectarian acts	Total
First diplomatic crisis: March 5, 2014, to November 16, 2014 (19 news stories)	63.2%	5.3%	0%	22.8%
Non-conflict period: November 17, 2014, to June 4, 2017 (61 news stories)	23%	0%	1.6%	8.2%
Second diplomatic crisis: June 5, 2017, to September 28, 2021 (161 news stories)	90.7%	0.6%	9.3%	33.5%

regime's violations against the protest movement (63.2%) (Table 8.1). When the conflict de-escalated in the period from late 2014 to mid-2017, the reporting on the violations dropped considerably to 23% (Table 8.1). As the conflict escalated again between Qatar and the Gulf states during the 2017 Gulf crisis, the AJA coverage of the violations reached its peak at 90.7% (Table 8.1).

The violations that were heavily reported on by AJA during the conflict periods included arresting activists, subjecting them to torture and unfair trial, revoking their citizenships and deporting them from the country. For example, AJA stated in August 2018:

> The case of this activist [who was arrested] is not unique in Bahrain, where human rights organisations condemn the authorities' stifling of freedom of expression, and the arrest of anyone who speaks out against the government policies and practices. (AJA, August 17, 2018e)

Mentioning of the "human rights violations" criterion can be observed in the AJA headlines more clearly, especially during the 2017 Gulf crisis. For instance, the following headlines state:

Organisations: The noise of Formula 1 hides the groans of prisons in Bahrain. (AJA, March 28, 2019a)

Amnesty speaks about 'the intensification of systemic injustice' in Bahrain. (AJA, February 11, 2021c)

8.3.2 AJE: Consistent Focus on "Human Rights Violations" During All Research Periods

Unlike AJA, AJE's inclusion of the Truth-Orientated frame did not seem to be affected by the political tension between Qatar and Bahrain. For instance, the Truth-Orientated frame scored almost equal percentages during the first conflict (29.6%), non-conflict period (32.1%) and second conflict (37.8%) (Table 8.2). The percentage of the "human rights violations" criterion remained higher than 50% in all analysis periods, with a notable increase during the second conflict (93.3%) (Table 8.2). The inclusion of the "regime's sectarian measures" criterion fluctuated during the research periods, scoring its highest percentages during the 2014 dispute (33.3%) and 2017 Gulf crisis (20%) while slightly decreasing during the non-escalatory period (15.4%).

Table 8.2 Percentages of including/mentioning the Truth-Orientated criteria in AJE's coverage of Bahrain's uprising in three research periods, from March 5, 2014, to September 1, 2021

Truth-Orientated frame in AJE	(SFV) Security forces violations	(PV) Protesters' violence	(DSM) Demolishing Shia mosques-sectarian acts	Total
First diplomatic crisis: March 5, 2014, to November 16, 2014 (9 news stories)	55.5%	0%	33.3%	29.6%
Non-conflict period: November 17, 2014, to June 4, 2017 (26 news stories)	73.1%	7.7%	15.4%	32.1%
Second diplomatic crisis: June 5, 2017, to September 1, 2021 (30 news stories)	93.3%	0%	20%	37.8%

8.3.3 AJA and AJE: Reporting "Protesters' Violence" as a "Fact"

Tables 8.1 and 8.2 show that the majority of the analysed news stories from AJA and AJE covered the regime's allegations that "protesters are involved in 'violent acts' against policemen and civilians" as unchallenged "facts", without providing explanations, reasons or alternative accounts. These alleged acts include participating in "explosions", "clashes with security forces" and "killing policemen".

The study found that both AJA and AJE depended entirely on official statements sent by Bahrain's Ministry of Interior or the state-funded media, Bahrain National Agency (BNA). The channels did not include the perspectives of the protesters, although they were feasibly accessible through their social media accounts.

For instance, during the non-conflict period, on January 15, 2017, AJA published a 215-word news story about the execution of three activists by firing squad for being accused of "killing policemen". The article relied on two sources only, BNA and the Ministry of Interior. Reporting the claims of the Ministry of Interior at face value is better left to what Galtung (2003) calls the "Ministries of Dis-information", instead of doing their work on their behalf. Galtung (2003, p.178) says:

> If a society sees a need for war reporting, better leave it to the ministries of [dis]information, of defence [war], of foreign affairs, etc. Do not corrupt the media by giving the task to them, having them take it on voluntarily, or forcing them into the kind of journalism that the Pentagon did in the Gulf War, following the English model from the Falklands/Malvinas War.

Not countering the allegations made by officials can make journalists "mere conduits" of statements as Shoemaker and Reese (2013, p. 195) put it. Journalists assume that "reporting what people say" is objective whereas including context or fact checking is often seen as being "biased" (Shoemaker & Reese, 2013). Chapters 5 and 6 explain thoroughly how depending only on official accounts can lead to drawing a distorted representation of social reality, justifying violent responses to conflicts and delegitimising marginalised actors.

Moreover, as sources like Bahrain's Ministry of Interior or BNA observe how their statements/allegations are reported, they will—according to Lynch's and McGoldrick's (2005) inference—keep inventing and creating

278   Z. ABDUL-NABI

"facts" that are more likely to be reported again. Lynch and McGoldrick (2005) define this process as a "Feedback Loop" in which journalists—by reporting stories in a certain way—influence the kind of "facts" that are likely to be provided for them in the future. When journalists report these "facts", they provide an incentive to sources/parties to provide similar "facts" on future occasions (Lynch & McGoldrick, 2005).

8.4   AJA and AJE: More Reporting on "Torture" and "Sexual Assaults" After 2017 Crisis

The quantitative results found a sudden rise in the frequency of including the regime's violations and mentioning—at times—those responsible for human rights abuses by name in the AJA coverage during the 2017 Gulf crisis. For instance, in AJA's coverage, reporting on "torture" increased dramatically from 3.3% during the non-conflict period to 52.2% during the 2017 diplomatic crisis. As another example, less than 2% of the AJA coverage during the first conflict and non-conflict periods reported on "sexual assaults" as a method of torture used against activists, yet 11.2% of the coverage focused on the culturally taboo topic during the 2017 crisis (Table 8.3). While the Al-Khalifa royal family had been excluded from

Table 8.3   Frequency of including lexical choices that legitimise the Bahraini protesters in AJA in three research periods, from March 5, 2014, to September 28, 2021

Frequencies of mentioning the following terms in AJA articles:	First diplomatic crisis: March 5, 2014, to November 16, 2014 (19 news stories)	Non-conflict period: November 17, 2014, to June 4, 2017 (61 news stories)	Second diplomatic crisis: June 5, 2017, to September 28, 2021 (161 news stories)
Quelling or crushing protests	2 (10.5%)	6 (9.8%)	59 (36.6%)
Torture of protesters	2 (10.5%)	2 (3.3%)	84 (52.2%)
Sexual assaults/rape/ abuse by the Bahraini regime security forces	0	1 (1.6%)	18 (11.2%)
The role of Sheikh Naser, the son of the King, in the human rights violations	0	0	3 (1.9%)

scrutinisation during the first conflict and non-conflict periods, AJA was critical of the ruling dynasty during the 2017 crisis to an extent that it named the son of the King, Sheikh Naser bin Hamad, as "responsible" of torture in three news stories (Table 8.3).

The following AJA's statements show how the channel covered details of the regime's violations, torture and sexual assaults, attributing the responsibility to the Al-Khalifa royal dynasty directly:

The Bahrain Independent Commission of Inquiry had stated that 'Dr. Al-Singace was subjected to torture after his arrest, including repeated beatings, sexual harassment, being forced to lick the shoes of prison guards, and threatening to rape his wife and daughter'. (AJA, July 30, 2021b)

The deputy [in the Spanish Parliament, Juan Baldovi] said that evidence has emerged that Sheikh Naser [son of the King Hamad] oversaw the arbitrary arrest and torture of protesters, opposition activists, and athletes, after the Bahraini government's violent suppression of the pro-democracy movement in 2011. (AJA, May 6, 2020d)

Moreover, high-ranking individuals such as Sheikh Naser bin Hamad Al Khalifa are still being rewarded for human rights violations rather than being punished for their actions. (AJA, May 6, 2020d)

The deputy Juan Baldovi said that Interior Minister Sheikh Rashid bin Abdullah Al Khalifa 'was not held accountable for the crimes of torture and extrajudicial killings that occurred under his command'. (AJA, July 11, 2020e)

In agreement with AJA, only around 11% of the AJE-N focused on "torture" during the first conflict and non-conflict periods, whereas 60% did so during the 2017 crisis (Table 8.4). Likewise, reporting on "sexual harassments" as a weapon against protesters was not observed at all during the 2014 dispute and reconciliatory periods, yet it recorded 13.3% during the 2017 Gulf crisis (Table 8.4).

This sharp increase in reporting on "torture" and "sexual assaults" in both AJA and AJE during the 2017 Gulf crisis appears to have a clear message from Qatar to the Bahraini regime. The repeating of specific terms in a coverage is called by Machin and Mayr (2012, p.222) "Overlexicalisation". According to this concept, when a word or its synonyms are "over-present" in a text, it implies evidence of an attempt to "over-persuade". It can be argued that the Al-Jazeera network aims to "over-persuade" its audience that the Bahraini regime is an illegitimate government that violates the fundamental human rights of its citizens.

280   Z. ABDUL-NABI

Table 8.4 Frequency of including lexical choices that legitimise the Bahraini protesters in AJE in three research periods, from March 5, 2014, to September 1, 2021

Frequencies of mentioning the following terms in AJE	First diplomatic crisis: March 5, 2014, to November 16, 2014 (9 news stories)	Non-conflict period: November 17, 2014, to June 4, 2017 (26 news stories)	Second diplomatic crisis: June 5, 2017, to September 1, 2021 (30 news stories)
Quelling or crushing protests	5 (55.6%)	13 (50%)	13 (43.3%)
Torture	1 (11.1%)	3 (11.5%)	18 (60%)
Sexual assaults/rape/abuse	0	0	4 (13.3%)
Sheikh Naser	0	0	0

8.5   AJA AND AJE: MORE DEPENDENCE ON HUMAN RIGHTS SOURCES AFTER 2017 GULF CRISIS

The empirical results show very clearly how including human rights organisations and activists as a source of news or quotations has significantly increased after the 2017 Gulf crisis in both channels' coverage.

For instance, Table 8.5 presents that the regime's sources dominated the AJA coverage during the first conflict (42.9%) and non-conflict periods (75.3%); however, human rights activists were the most quoted sources during the 2017 crisis (71%). Similarly, AJE was dominated by official sources during the 2014 dispute (44.4%) and non-conflict period (49.3%), yet human rights activists' quotations prevailed in AJE's coverage (67.8%) during the second conflict (Table 8.6). Ordinary people, victims and un-licenced opposition groups recorded low percentages during all examined periods in AJA and AJE coverage (Tables 8.5 and 8.6).

Table 8.5 Quoted sources in AJA's coverage of Bahrain's uprising in three research periods, from March 5, 2014, to September 28, 2021

Quoted sources in AJA	First diplomatic crisis: March 5, 2014, to November 16, 2014 (19 news stories)	Non-conflict period: November 17, 2014, to June 4, 2017 (61 news stories)	Second diplomatic crisis: June 5, 2017, to September 28, 2021 (161 news stories)
Unauthorised opposition	2 (9.5%)	1 (1.0%)	15 (5%)
Authorised opposition	4 (19%)	7 (7.2%)	10 (3.3%)
Bahraini officials—Bahrain's state media, or representative of Bahraini government	9 (42.9%)	73 (75.3%)	43 (14.3%)
AJ reporter	0	0	3 (1%)
Activists or human rights organisations (HRO)	5 (23.8%)	13 (13.4%)	213 (71%)
Victims/civilians—ordinary people	1 (4.8%)	3 (3.1%)	16 (5.3%)
Total:	21	97	300

Table 8.6 Quoted sources in AJE's coverage of Bahrain's uprising in three research periods, from March 5, 2014, to September 1, 2021

Quoted sources in AJE	First diplomatic crisis: March 5, 2014, to November 16, 2014 (9 news stories)	Non-conflict period: November 17, 2014, to June 4, 2017 (26 news stories)	Second diplomatic crisis June 5, 2017, to September 1, 2021 (30 news stories)
Unauthorised opposition	0	1 (1.4%)	2 (2.3%)
Authorised opposition	6 (33.3%)	4 (5.8%)	1 (1.1%)
Bahraini officials—Bahrain's state media, or representative of Bahraini government	8 (44.4%)	34 (49.3%)	18 (20.7%)
AJ reporter	0	0	0
Activists or human rights organisations (HRO)	4 (22.2%)	28 (40.6%)	59 (67.8%)
Victims/civilians— ordinary people	0	2 (2.9%)	7 (8%)
Total:	18	69	87

8.6 Possible Reasons Behind the Increase of "Human Rights" Coverage

8.6.1 AJA: Delegitimising the Bahraini Regime to Serve Qatar's Interest

Including the Truth-Orientated frame in AJA coverage—reporting on "sexual assaults" against activists, holding the King's son as having "responsibility of torture" and quoting human rights organisations intensively—significantly intensified during the 2017 Gulf crisis. This study argues that the selection of certain frames and facts, distribution of concerns and emphases are techniques applied by media organisations to serve the political agenda of the privileged group (Herman & Chomsky, 2010), in this case, Qatar.

In consistency with the findings of this book, the latest studies that examined AJA coverage of political conflicts that occurred in Saudi Arabia, the UAE and Yemen during the 2017 Gulf crisis found a conformity between the channel's coverage and Qatar's foreign policy (Alshabnan, 2018; Mejalli, 2019; Ajaoud & Elmasry, 2020).

For instance, a quantitative content analysis study that analysed AJA coverage of Saudi Arabia, the UAE and the war on Yemen concluded that the channel focused more frequently on human rights violations against opponents in Saudi Arabia and the UAE after the 2017 diplomatic crisis (Alshabnan, 2018). Furthermore, Alshabnan (2018) found that before the 2017 Gulf crisis, AJA framed the Saudi-led coalition missions in Yemen "positively", whereas it represented the Houthis and the ousted Yemeni president, Ali Abdullah Saleh, "negatively". On the contrary, after the 2017 crisis, the AJA coverage framed the war as a "failure" and "humanitarian disaster" (Alshabnan, 2018).

The findings of another quantitative study that examined AJA coverage of the war on Yemen before and after the 2017 Gulf crisis state that more than 40% of the coverage framed the Saudi military operation in a "positive tone" in 2015, yet only 2.1% framed it as such in 2019 (Mejalli, 2019).

These results are not unexpected, as AJA has a history of operating in a polarised Arab media environment in which news media outlets act as "fully fledged political actors" (Harb, 2019, p.273). For example, a study that analysed the news evening programmes of AJA and the Saudi-funded channel Al-Arabiya found that the AJA coverage framed Qatar as a "victim" that was being attacked by an "oppressor" during the 2017 Gulf crisis (Ajaoud & Elmasry, 2020). Al-Arabiya, on the other hand, depicted Qatar as a "terrorism's sponsor" (Ajaoud & Elmasry, 2020). In addition, the study that utilised framing theory along with quantitative analysis methods stated further that more than 30% of the coverage of both channels gave more space to guests representing their sponsoring countries (Ajaoud & Elmasry, 2020).

In a discourse analysis-based study, Harb (2019) argues that AJA's coverage has been consistent with Qatar's politics which advocates for the Muslim Brotherhood (MB) in the region, while Al-Arabiya's reporting has been in line with Al-Saud's foreign policy, which is openly against the movement.

Another qualitative study that unpacked the coverage of AJA and Al-Arabiya over Qatar's withdrawal from the Organization of Petroleum Exporting Countries (OPEC) in 2018 indicates that their coverage was centred on "safeguarding the position of their funded country as well as their economic interest" (Tartory, 2020, p.12).

Even before the 2017 Gulf crisis, several empirical content analysis studies argued that AJA had already been used by Qatar as a "propaganda tool" to serve its interests, especially after the 2011 Arab Spring uprisings (see Samuel-Azran, 2013; Ayaad, 2014; Al-Nahed, 2015; Abunajela, 2015). As discussed in Chap. 2, Middle East scholars have widely viewed Al-Jazeera as a strategic part of Qatar's diplomacy and foreign policy in the region (Ulrichsen, 2014; Kamrava, 2013; Khatib, 2013; Roberts, 2012).

Interestingly, however, some disagree with this contention as Maziad (2018, p.2) argues that AJA and Qatar's politics in the region "are not identical" and each institution reflects its "own internal logic and enforces external ties". Building his analysis based on the State-in-Society approach, in which the state is not the only monolith player, Maziad (2018) argues that Al-Jazeera's "independence" from Qatar's Foreign Ministry has allowed Islamists to slowly "take it over". Maziad (2018) further infers that the Islamists, mostly foreign born, have increased the Islamic inclination in the Al Jazeera's Mubasher Misr (Live Egypt) and caused political conflict between Qatar and Egypt.

One might argue, however, that AJA's inclination to the MB is already in parallel with Qatar's foreign policy, which has long supported the movement in the region. The first rift and withdrawal of Saudi, Emirati and Bahraini ambassadors from Qatar in 2014 were mainly because of Qatar's support to the MB in Egypt, Hamas in Gaza and Ennahda party in Tunisia (Stephens, 2017). Stephens (2017) says that Qatar has used Al-Jazeera to support these Islamic actors, not the other way around. WikiLeaks revealed that Qatar used Al-Jazeera as part of its politics and deals with Saudi Arabia, as detailed in Chap. 2 (Samuel-Azran, 2013).

Moreover, the argument that the Islamist stuff have hijacked AJA (Maziad, 2018) seems to exaggerate the role of journalists or individuals in determining media content. Shoemaker and Reese (2013, p.166) who coined the "Hierarchy of Influences Model" argue that "decisions are not only made at the whim of the individuals". Shoemaker and Reese (2013, p.166) further explain that the control of governments' policies "exert direct and obvious effects on media" either by restricting it or enabling it to cover certain issues.

8.6.2   AJE: Less Influenced by Qatar's Foreign Policy

The AJE coverage of Bahrain's uprising was consistent in applying the Truth-Orientated frame before and after the 2017 Gulf crisis, albeit it gave more space to human rights organisations during the second conflict. Due to this consistency, this study argues that AJE's tendency to conform with Qatar's politics is less intense than AJA. In partial disagreement with the findings of this research, other studies argued that the AJE coverage has been completely in harmony with Qatar's politics, especially during the 2017 Gulf crisis (Gasim, 2018; Alhendyani, 2019; Kharbach, 2020; Kosárová, 2020).

For instance, a study that examined AJE coverage of the war on Yemen before and after the 2017 Gulf crisis found that the focus on the "humanitarian crisis and civilian casualties" increased after relations deteriorated between Saudi Arabia and Qatar in 2017 (Gasim, 2018). Gasim (2018, p.7) says that AJE has rallied "behind the national flag of Qatar through its selective coverage of the Yemeni crisis". Another study that compared the Saudi-funded channel, Al-Arabiya English (AAE), and AJE coverage of the killing of Jamal Khashoggi in the Saudi Embassy in Turkey in 2018 concluded that both channels reflected the policies of their sponsors and that they were used as "propaganda tools" by Saudi Arabia and Qatar (Alhendyani, 2019). A similar comparative study between the AJE and AAE coverage of the 2017 Gulf crisis found that both channels were "ideologically biased" towards the foreign policies of their sponsors (Kharbach, 2020). However, Kharbach (2020) infers that AJE is less biased and "more accurate" than AAE.

Another comparative study that examined whether the coverage of AJE and AAE reflect the interests of their sponsors while covering the Muslim Summit, held in Kuala Lumpur on December 19, 2019, concluded that both channels have been used as "political instruments" by Qatar and Saudi Arabia. The qualitative study additionally found that AJE and AEE used manipulative techniques such as "ambiguities, half-truths, exaggeration, or omission in order to deliver two very different messages" (Kosárová, 2020, p.104).

8.7   Framing of Saudi Military Intervention and Israeli-Bahraini "Normalisation Deal"

8.7.1   *AJA: Critical Coverage of Saudi Troops After the 2017 Gulf Crisis*

In order to measure the extent of Al-Jazeera's alignment with Qatar's foreign policy more thoroughly, Al-Jazeera's framing of two issues has been examined thoroughly: (1) the Saudi troops deployed in Bahrain to crack down on the 2011 uprising and (2) the normalisation deal signed between Bahrain and Israel in September 2020 (see Chap. 4).

As discussed previously, AJA did not frame the Saudi military deployment in Manama in a negative tone in 2011, as 47.6% of AJA-N and 100% of AJA features (AJA-F) legitimised the presence of the PSF in the country (Chap. 5, Table 5.8). At the time, Qatar had not opposed the Gulf states' consensus and had not refrained from joining the 1500 Saudi troops. However, the results of this study show that, after the 2017 Gulf crisis, 100% of the AJA coverage delegitimised the Saudi military intervention, stating that the troops were deployed to "quell" unarmed protesters (Table 8.7).

The quantitative findings demonstrate that none of the 80 AJA-N, published during the first conflict and non-conflict period, ever mentioned the deployment of the PSF or the role played by Al-Saud in hindering democratic initiatives in Bahrain. Also, only two articles out of 161 posted during the 2017 Gulf crisis stated that the Saudi and Emirati soldiers were deployed to "quell the protest movement" (Table 8.7). This might possibly be due to AJA's tendency to avoid mentioning context and roots of conflicts in its reporting. The study argues that the channel—as discussed previously in Chap. 7—depends more on reporting immediate events

Table 8.7 The framing of the Saudi military intervention in AJA's coverage of Bahrain's uprising in three research periods, from March 5, 2014, to September 28, 2021

Framing of Saudi military presence in AJA	Pro-Bahraini regime narrative—Anti-Qatar PSF were deployed to restore order in the country	Pro-protesters narrative—Pro-Qatar PSF were deployed to crack down on protesters	Objective—Neutral The protesters and the regimes are quoted
First diplomatic crisis: March 5, 2014, to November 16, 2014 (0 out of 19 news stories)	–	–	–
Non-conflict period: November 17, 2014, to June 4, 2017 (0 out 61 news stories)	–	–	–
Second diplomatic crisis: June 5, 2017, to September 28, 2021 (2 out of 161 news stories)	0	2 (100%)	0

(here and now) than historic backgrounds, process, causes and conflict formation.

8.7.2 AJE: Critical Coverage of Saudi Troops Before and After 2017 Gulf Crisis

Unlike AJA, AJE has been systematic in its representation of the Saudi military intervention from the early stages of the uprising in March 2011 to September 2021. As shown in Table 8.8, more than 85.7% of the news stories posted in all research periods stated that the PSF were deployed to "quell the uprising".

Table 8.8 The framing of the Saudi military intervention in AJE's coverage of Bahrain's uprising in three research periods, from March 5, 2014, to September 1, 2021

Framing of Saudi military presence in AJE	Pro-Bahraini regime narrative—Anti-Qatar PSF were deployed to restore order in the country	Pro-protesters narrative—Pro-Qatar PSF were deployed to crack down on protesters	Neutral The protesters and the regimes are quoted
First diplomatic crisis: March 5, 2014, to November 16, 2014 (4 out of 9 news stories)	0	4 (100%)	0
Non-conflict period: November 17, 2014, to June 4, 2017 (7 out of 26 news stories)	0	6 (85.7%)	1 (14.3%)
Second diplomatic crisis: June 5, 2017, to September 1, 2021 (10 out of 30 news stories)	0	9 (90%)	1 (10%)

8.7.3 AJA: Critical Coverage of "Normalisation Deal"

In alignment with Qatar's declared stance towards normalising ties with Israel, the vast majority of the AJA-N (78.8%) posted in September and October 2020 included "critical accounts" of the normalisation deal signed between Bahrain and Israel on September 11, 2020 (Table 8.9).

More than one third of the AJA-N (33.1%) represented the deal as a "betrayal to the Palestinian cause" or a "stab in the back" during the first two months of the coverage (Table 8.10). Moreover, 47.1% of AJA-N labelled it as a "normalisation deal", while only 3.3% referred to it by its formal name, the "Abraham Accord", during the same period (Table 8.10).

Associating the deal repeatedly with the lexical choices, "betrayal", "stab in the back" and "normalisation", can delegitimise the Bahraini

Table 8.9 The extent of critical framing in AJA's coverage of the normalisation deal between Israel and Bahrain

Critical framing of the deal in AJA:	Sep and Oct 2020 52 articles	Nov and Dec 2020 12 articles
Including countering accounts	41 (78.8%)	2 (16.7%)
Not including countering accounts or narratives	11 (21.2%)	10 (83.8%)

Table 8.10 Framing of the normalisation deal signed between Israel and Bahrain in AJA's coverage

Framing US brokered Bahraini-Israeli deal in AJA:	Sep and Oct 2020 52 articles 11/9 to 18/10	Nov and Dec 2020 12 articles 18/11 to 20/12
Peace deal	34 (14%)	2 (13.3%)
Normalisation deal	114 (47.1%)	13 (86.7%)
Crime—partners in crime	6 (2.5%)	0
Betrayal and/or stab in the back/shame	80 (33.1%)	0
Abraham accord	8 (3.3%)	0
Overall:	242	15

regime among the Arabic audience who have always vocally refused signing deals with Israel. This has been witnessed when people took to the streets straight after the declaration of the deal in September 2020 in several capitals such as Manama, Kuwait, Amman, Islamabad, Gaza and the West Bank.

It can be also observed that including "critical accounts" of the deal, as well as framing it as a "betrayal" in AJA-N, decreased notably in the third and fourth months of the coverage (Tables 8.9 and 8.10). This can be attributed to AJA's focus on "here and now", as explored in more detail in Chap. 7.

Although Qatar has had secret trade relations with Israel since the 1990s (as discussed previously in Chap. 2), it has publicly opposed signing a normalisation deal with Tel Aviv. When Bahrain and the UAE signed the normalisation deals with Israel, Qatar's Foreign Minister, Sheikh Mohammed bin Abdulrahman Al-Thani, said "Arab states that establish ties with Israel undermine efforts for Palestinian statehood" (AJA, November 16, 2020c). AJA reported that the Qatari Assistant Foreign Minister, Lulwa Al-Khater, stated that "Qatar confirmed that it will not establish diplomatic relations with Israel before resolving the conflict with the Palestinians" (AJA, September 15, 2020a). AJA reported both statements by the Qatari officials without providing any context or history related to Qatar's relations with Israel. For instance, AJA did not mention as background information that the Qatar Youth Against Normalisation group denounced the participation of an Israeli medical delegation in the World Paediatric Surgery Conference in Doha on November 20, 2019. This particular story had been covered in 2019 but was never mentioned again as context when reporting on Qatar's refusal to the normalisation deals.

While AJA avoids reporting on Qatar's secret ties with Israel, it occasionally and cautiously covers critical voices on the relationship between Doha and Tel-Aviv. Herman and Chomsky (2010) refer to this as "limited autonomy" within media organisations in which professionals' and individuals' values may influence the media content and give some space for dissent and inconvenient facts. However, the "beauty of the [propaganda] system" is that such accounts which show that the system is not "monolithic" are "kept within bounds and at the margins". This allowed dissidence will still not be strong enough to change the domination of the powerful (Herman & Chomsky, 2010).

Interestingly, in May 1996, when the right-wing Benjamin Netanyahu became the prime minister, Israel was allowed to open a trade representation office in Qatar (Miller & Verhoeven, 2020). Qatar was the first Gulf state to establish trade relations with Israel. A year later, Qatar invited Israel to participate in the MENA economic summit in Doha, causing its Arab partners to boycott the conference. Qatar rejected calls to cancel the meeting and insisted that it had the sovereign right to map out its own foreign policy agenda (Miller & Verhoeven, 2020).

Recently, Israel's Regional Cooperation Minister Tzachi Hanegbi hailed Qatar for coordinating closely with the Israeli authorities in 2018 (Miller & Verhoeven, 2020, p.38). According to *The Times of Israel* (2018), Hanegbi said that "Qatar was endeavouring hugely to ensure its aid to the Gaza Strip does not end up as any Hamas force build-up". In August 2020, the same newspaper published a news story titled "Mossad said to ask Qatar to keep funnelling cash to Gaza in de-escalation effort" (Times of Israel, 2020). On December 15, 2021, Al-Monitor published an article stating that Qatar and Israel have secretly signed a "historic diamond trade agreement" (Zaken, 2021). Based on this "secret arrangement", the Qatari government agreed to process Israeli visa requests within five days and permit any Israeli merchant to operate in the diamond and jewellery free trade zone (Zaken, 2021).

None of the reports above were mentioned or covered during the research periods. Excluding such reports, and at the same time emphasising the fact that Doha is against signing normalisation deals, can represent the state as an advocate of the Palestinian cause. J. Lynch and McGoldrick (2005, Location No. 385) say, "How do we decide what [facts] to put in and what to leave out? It's those decisions, above all, that control access to information and communications and, in the process, construct the world around us".

8.7.4 AJE: Critical Coverage of "Normalisation Deals"

More than 90% of the AJE coverage from September to December 2020 quoted critical accounts to the normalisation deal (Table 8.11). Furthermore, the majority of the analysed news stories in AJE represented the deal as a "stab in the back" or "betrayal" to the Palestinian cause during September and October 2020 (45.3%) as well as November and December in the same year (53.8%) (Table 8.12).

Although both AJA and AJE used critical frames and represented the deal as a "betrayal to the Palestinian cause", AJE provided a more in-depth coverage than AJA. For example, AJA depended on reporting quotes, statements and reactive responses over events (here and now), whereas AJE remained "critical" even in the later stages of signing the deal. The English channel equipped readers with context and historic background during the analysed periods. For instance, AJE mentioned in the majority of its news stories, as background, the Arab Peace Initiative that was brokered by Saudi Arabia and endorsed by the Arab League in 2002. According to this initiative, Arab countries can recognise and normalise ties with Israel under the condition of a complete withdrawal from the 1967 occupied Palestinian lands. For example, AJE stated:

Table 8.11 The extent of critical framing in AJE's coverage of the normalisation deal between Israel and Bahrain

Critical framing of the deal in AJE:	Sep and Oct 2020 26 articles	Nov and Dec 2020 10 articles
Including countering accounts	25 (96.2%)	9 (90%)
Not including countering accounts or narratives	1 (3.8%)	1 (10%)

Table 8.12 Framing of the normalisation deal signed between Israel and Bahrain in AJE's coverage

Framing US brokered Bahraini-Israeli deal in AJE:	Sep and Oct 2020 11th Sep to 18th of Oct 26 articles	Nov and Dec 2020 16th of Nov to 5th of Dec 10 articles
Peace deal	6 (6.3%)	0
Normalisation deal	38 (40%)	2 (15.4%)
Crime—partners in crime	3 (3.2%)	0
Betrayal and/or stab in the back/shame	43 (45.3%)	7 (53.8%)
Abraham accord	5 (5.3%)	4 (30.8%)
Overall:	95	13

The Palestinian leadership wants an independent state based on the de facto borders before the 1967 war, in which Israel occupied the West Bank and the Gaza Strip and annexed East Jerusalem. Arab countries have long called for Israel's withdrawal from already illegally occupied land, a just solution for Palestinian refugees and a settlement that leads to the establishment of a viable, independent Palestinian state in exchange for establishing ties with it. (AJE, September 13, 2020a)

Furthermore, unlike AJA, the AJE coverage mentioned the context of Bahrain's uprising and focused on the fact that Bahrainis protested and took to the streets when their regime signed the deal with Israel. For instance, the following statement was mentioned repeatedly during the coverage:

Bahrain, home to the US Navy's Fifth Fleet and a British naval base, has a predominantly Shia population ruled by a Sunni royal family. Arab Spring protests there in 2011 ended with authorities cracking down with the help of Saudi and Emirati forces. (AJE, September 23, 2020b)

AJE, like AJA, avoided mentioning any historic context over Qatar's ties with Israel, when reporting on Doha's stance towards the normalisation agreements.

8.8 Domination of "Al-Jazeera" as the Main Source of News After 2017 Gulf Crisis

The quantitative findings demonstrate that the tendency of AJA's journalists to cover the protest movement increased from 31.2% during the non-conflict period to 52.1% during the 2017 Gulf crisis (Table 8.13).

Interestingly, while none of AJA-N depended on social media accounts as a source of information during the first conflict and non-conflict periods, 22 articles (11.6%) quoted them during the 2017 crisis (Table 8.13).

Like AJA, AJE depended primarily on the channel's reporters (58.1%) as a source of news rather than other news agencies (41.9%) during the 2017 diplomatic crisis (Table 8.14). During the first conflict and non-conflict period, AJE relied heavily on news agencies (71.4% and 61.5%, respectively) more than "Al-Jazeera" as a source of news (28.6% and 38.5%) (Table 8.14). Social media accounts were never relied on as a source of information or news during all research periods.

8.9 AJA and AJE: Peace Frame and Representation of "Protests" and "Protesters"

8.9.1 AJA: Sectarian Framing of Bahrain's Uprising During All Research Periods

Unlike the Truth-Orientated frame, which increased notably during the first and second Gulf crises in 2014 and 2017 (Table 8.1), the Peace/

Table 8.13 News sources in AJA's coverage of Bahrain's uprising in three research periods, from March 5, 2014, to September 28, 2021

News sources in AJA	First diplomatic crisis: March 5, 2014, to November 16, 2014 (19 news stories)	Non-conflict period: November 17, 2014, to June 4, 2017 (61 news stories)	Second diplomatic crisis: June 5, 2017, to September 28, 2021 (161 news stories)
News agencies (AFP, Reuters, Associated Press)	17 (89.5%)	51 (66.2%)	61 (32.1%)
Al-Jazeera	2 (10.5%)	24 (31.2%)	99 (52.1%)
Social media, websites	0	0	22 (11.6%)
International journalism	0	0	3 (1.6%)
Human rights organisations	0	2 (2.6%)	5 (2.6%)
Overall:	19	77	190

8 GULF CRISIS (2014–2021): AL-JAZEERA'S DRAMATIC SHIFT... 293

Table 8.14 News sources in AJE's coverage of Bahrain's uprising in three research periods, from March 5, 2014, to September 1, 2021

News sources in AJE	First diplomatic crisis: March 5, 2014, to November 16, 2014 (9 news stories)	Non-conflict period: November 17, 2014, to June 4, 2017 (26 news stories)	Second diplomatic crisis: June 5, 2017, to September 1, 2021 (30 news stories)
News agencies (AFP, Reuters, Associated Press) Note: 2 were without sources	5 (71.4%)	16 (61.5%)	18 (41.9%)
Al-Jazeera	2 (28.6%)	10 (38.5%)	25 (58.1%)
Social media, websites	0	0	0
International journalism	0	0	0
Human rights organisations	0	0	0
Overall	7	26	43

Conflict-Orientated frame[2] recorded low percentages in all research periods in AJA (Table 8.15). During the non-conflict period and 2017 Gulf crisis, the Peace/Conflict-Orientated frame recorded 5.1% and 9.5%, respectively (Table 8.15).

---

[2] Analytical criteria of Peace/Conflict-Orientated frame

1. (HB): Does the article give a historical background about the protest movement in Bahrain?
2. (AS): Does the article mention that the protesters have been inspired by the Arab uprisings/Arab Spring?
3. (SM): Does the article mention that Shias make up the majority of the population?
4. (SD): Does the article mention that the Shias of Bahrain have been discriminated against?
5. (SSU): Does the article mention that the protesters called for unity between Shias and Sunnis from day one of the protests? Or does the article mention that there is no evidence that the protesters are supported by Iran? Or does the article mention that the protesters have "democratic demands"?
6. (US5): Does the article mention that Bahrain is the home of the US Fifth Fleet?
7. (PSF): Does the article mention that 1500 Saudi and 500 Emirati troops have been deployed in Manama?
8. (SIR): Does the article mention the context of the rivalry between Saudi Arabia and Iran?
9. (PN): Does the article mention the political naturalisation process? Or does the article mention that the royal family belongs to the Sunni sect?

Table 8.15 Percentages of including/mentioning the Peace/Conflict-Orientated criteria in AJA's coverage of Bahrain's uprising in three research periods, from March 5, 2014, to September 28, 2021

Peace/ Conflict-Orientated frame in AJA	(HB) Historic background	(AS) Arab Spring	(SM) Shia majority	(SD) Shia discrimination	(SSU) Unity and democracy	(US5) US 5TH fleet	(PSF) Peninsula Shield Force	(SIR) Saudi-Iranian rivalry	(PN) Sunni rulers	(Total) Peace/ Conflict frame
First diplomatic crisis: March 5, 2014, to November 16, 2014 (19 news stories)	84.2%	5.3%	0%	0%	52.6%	10.5%	0%	0%	0%	17%
Non-conflict period: November 17, 2014, to June 4, 2017 (61 news stories)	24.6%	1.6%	0%	0%	18%	1.6%	0%	0%	0%	5.1%
Second diplomatic crisis: June 5, 2017, to September 28, 2021 (161 news stories)	37.9%	12.4%	1.9%	6.2%	19.3%	2.5%	3.1%	0%	1.9%	9.5%

The study, therefore, concludes that the 2017 Gulf crisis has had no significant impact on the implementation of the Peace/Conflict-Orientated frame.

Table 8.15 shows that the coverage hardly mentioned the fact that the majority Shias have been ruled by the Sunni minority, the Al-Khalifa dynasty, and that they have been discriminated against. Moreover, a limited number of articles mentioned the fact that the protesters' demands are not sectarian (Table 8.15). As argued in Chap. 5, not including these criteria/facts has led to promoting the Al-Khalifa's narrative that the conflict in Bahrain is a result of a Shia-Sunni division, not a pro-democracy movement.

For instance, in the following news story, AJA portrayed the conflict as "sectarian tension", without including any context, historic background or explanation:

> On Thursday, the Bahraini authorities summoned five Shia clerics in a campaign to pursue those they consider to be inciting <u>sectarian tensions</u> in the country. (AJA, June 23, 2016a)

The statement above shows how "presuppositions" like the term "sectarian tension" are represented as incontestable facts. Machin and Mayr (2012, p.133) define "presuppositions" as "one skilful way by which authors are able to imply meanings without overtly stating them, or present things as taken for granted and stable when in fact they may be contestable and ideological".

Herman and Chomsky (2010) argue that if stories are written in a convincing way, without being countered by alternative accounts, they turned quickly into "truth". As a result, any dissenting opinions would later be faced with "an already established popular belief" (Herman & Chomsky, 2010).

At this stage of analysis, AJA's inclination to use sectarian language is not considered surprising, especially in the Bahraini and Syrian conflicts (see Chaps. 5, 6 and 7). Harb (2019, p.283) analysed the discourse of the AJA's controversial programme, the Opposite Direction, and found that "a clear pattern of hate speech is presented as the norm" in the show. Harb (2019, p.289–290) cited some examples of sectarian hate speech raised by hosted speakers and presenter, such as "Alawites are scum", "an octopus that should be killed" and "May God not forgive anyone who forgives the Alawite of Syria".

AJA's consistency in framing the Bahraini conflict as "sectarian" has been accompanied with the lack of representing it as an "uprising" or a "revolution" during all research periods (Table 8.16). Also, less than 9% of the AJA coverage associated the protest movement with "democracy" during the conflict and non-conflict periods (Table 8.16). While the escalation of the Gulf crises seems to have had little impact on the conflict framing, the findings show a slight increase in representing the protests as "peaceful" during the first and second conflicts (9.4% and 8.9%) compared to the non-conflict period (1.3%) (Table 8.16).

Although AJA-N has maintained its overall sectarian framing of Bahrain's protest movement, the empirical results found that associating "protesters" with their "Shia" sect decreased from 46.5% during the non-conflict period to 12.6% during the 2017 Gulf crisis (Table 8.17).

This monograph observes that AJA's documentaries have included more in-depth analysis than the examined news stories. They have refuted the regime's sectarian narrative and given more space to alternative and marginalised accounts. For instance, two out of six documentaries produced from June 2017 to September 2021 have countered the sectarian framing thoroughly. The "Playing with Fire" documentary film included both Sunni and Shia voices, stating that the regime has used sectarianism as a tool to delegitimise the pro-democracy movement. Mohammad Al-Buflasa, a Sunni political activist who has been in exile after being arrested for participating in the 2011 uprising, blamed King Hamad

Table 8.16 Framing of Bahrain's conflict in AJA's coverage in three research periods, from March 5, 2014, to September 28, 2021

Framing of Bahrain's conflict in AJA	First diplomatic crisis: March 5, 2014, to November 16, 2014 (19 news stories)	Non-conflict period: November 17, 2014, to June 4, 2017 (61 news stories)	Second diplomatic crisis: June 5, 2017, to September 28, 2021 (161 news stories)
Uprising	0	5 (6.6)	15 (7.8%)
Revolution	0	2 (2.6%)	2 (1%)
Conflict	0	0	0
Crisis, unrest, turmoil	9 (17%)	12 (15.8%)	26 (13.5%)
Protests	36 (67.9%)	51 (67.1%)	116 (60.4%)
Peaceful protests	5 (9.4%)	1 (1.3%)	17 (8.9%)
Pro-democracy or anti government	3 (5.7%)	5 (6.6%)	16 (8.3%)
Total:	53	76	192

8 GULF CRISIS (2014–2021): AL-JAZEERA'S DRAMATIC SHIFT... 297

Table 8.17 Framing of the protesters in AJA's coverage of Bahrain's uprising in three research periods, from March 5, 2014, to September 28, 2021

Framing of the protesters in AJA	First diplomatic crisis: March 5, 2014, to November 16, 2014 (19 news stories)	Non-conflict period: November 17, 2014, to June 4, 2017 (61 news stories)	Second diplomatic crisis: June 5, 2017, to September 28, 2021 (161 news stories)
Protesters, opposition, opponents, demonstrators	47 (95.9%)	53 (53.5%)	228 (80%)
Pro-democracy or anti-government protesters	0	0	3 (1.1%)
Shia protesters, Shia-led protests, Shia opposition	2 (4.1%)	46 (46.5%)	36 (12.6%)
Peaceful protesters	0	0	18 (6.3%)
Revolutionaries	0	0	0
Total:	49	99	285

directly for "using sectarianism" to maintain his power. He said in the documentary:

> The King of Bahrain wanted to create this [sectarian] conflict, or to preoccupy the Shia community with the Sunni [make them busy] community, with sectarian differences, so he can run away from [his] national responsibilities towards the people. The royal court supports the Sunni political associations, Salafists and Muslim Brotherhood. They [the royal family] appoint a Salafi minister here and a Brotherhood minister there. (AJA, July 14, 2019b)

Furthermore, in the documentary the AJA journalist asked a former Shia member of parliament representing Al-Wefaq opposition group, Jawad Fairooz, if the "country is faced with a sectarian battel". Fairooz replied that the authorities used sectarianism to exert their power. Fairooz further said that when he was an MP, he—along with others—had proposed a bill, advocating for the release of Al-Qaeda member, Mohammad Salah, from Saudi Arabia in 2004. Salah said in a leaked video, aired by the documentary, that he agreed to assassinate Shia activists in 2003 under "the King's directives". Such documentaries—which have worsened the relations between Bahrain and Qatar—started coming to the surface straight after the 2017 Gulf crisis.

8.9.2 AJE: Less Sectarian Framing of Bahrain's Uprising During All Research Periods

The displaying of the Peace/Conflict-Orientated frame in the AJE coverage of Bahrain's uprising has remained consistent during all research periods. It scored significant percentages during the 2014 conflict (39.5%), non-conflict period (38.5%) and 2017 Gulf crisis (37.4%) (Table 8.18). In other words, from 2014 to 2021, more than one third of the AJE coverage included the history and background of the pro-democracy movement, local and international context as well as the demographic aspects of the protesters and ruling dynasty (Table 8.18). Therefore, it can be inferred that the escalation between Qatar and its neighbours during the 2014 and 2017 crises did not affect the application of the Peace/Conflict-orientated frame in the AJE coverage.

Significant percentages of AJE-N mentioned the fact that Shias make up the majority of the population during the first conflict (33.3%), non-conflict period (50%) and second conflict (43.3%). Similarly, more than 40% of AJE-N during all research periods included the fact that these Shias have been ruled by a Sunni minority and that their demands have not been sectarian orientated (Table 8.18). These frequent inclusions of the criteria of the Peace/Conflict-Orientated frame have resulted in portraying the conflict—to a significant extent—as a pro-democracy movement triggered by the lack of freedom and political reforms. As explained thoroughly in Chap. 5, AJE's application of the Peace/Conflict-Orientated criteria has resulted in a less sectarian framing of Bahrain's uprising.

The following statement from AJE demonstrates how the inclusion of Peace/Conflict-Orientated criteria can result in a more accurate representation of the conflict:

> Bahrain has been in turmoil since a 2011 uprising (1) backed by majority Shia Muslims (2) demanding greater rights from the Sunni-led monarchy (3). The government crushed the protests with the help of its Sunni Arab Gulf allies (5) suspicious of Iran and opposed to growing Shia influence in the region. (6) Bahrain hosts the US Navy's 5th Fleet (7). (AJE, June 21, 2016c)

The paragraph above shows that the Peace/Conflict-Orientated frame is applicable even in hard news, which depends heavily on conventional events and "here and now" routine. For instance, this 53-word paragraph includes seven criteria (numbered and underlined in the text) of the

Table 8.18 Percentages of including/mentioning the Peace/Conflict-Orientated criteria in AJE's coverage of Bahrain's uprising in three research periods, from March 5, 2014, to September 1, 2021

Peace/ Conflict-Orientated frame in AJE	(HB) Historic background	(AS) Arab Spring	(SM) Shia majority	(SD) Shia discrimination	(SSU) Unity and democracy	(US5) US 5TH fleet	(PSF) Peninsula Shield Force	(SIR) Saudi-Iranian rivalry	(PN) Sunni rulers	(Total) Peace/ Conflict frame
First diplomatic crisis: March 5, 2014, to November 16, 2014 (9 news stories)	77.8%	33.3%	33.3%	11.1%	66.6%	33.3%	44.4%	0%	55.6%	39.5%
Non-conflict period: November 17, 2014, to June 4, 2017 (26 news stories)	76.9%	7.7%	50%	26.9%	61.5%	23.1%	34.6%	7.7%	57.7%	38.5%
Second diplomatic crisis: June 5, 2017, to September 1, 2021 (30 news stories)	80%	40%	43.3%	10%	40%	23.3%	40%	20%	40%	37.4%

Peace/Conflict frame. In contrast, a study that examined the AJE coverage of the battle of Raqqa attributed the lack of focusing on structural violence and PJ frames to the nature of political hard news (Guta, 2019). Other studies also found that it is more challenging to apply the PJ orientations in news than other genres (Kempf, 2006; Lee, 2010). The results of this chapter, however, show that it is still possible to apply the PJ frames in hard news.

Along with its non-sectarian framing, significant percentages of AJE coverage legitimised the protest movement by representing it as an "uprising" during the 2014 dispute (27.9%), non-conflict period (23.5%) and 2017 Gulf crisis (32%) (Table 8.19).

More than 50% of the AJE coverage referred to the uprisings as mere "protesters" from 2014 to 2021 (Table 8.20). At the same time, less than 7% of the coverage during all research periods associated the protesters with "democracy" (Table 8.20). Also, during the first conflict and non-conflict periods, high proportions of AJE (60% and 46.1%) connected the protesters with their sects, whereas only 11.7% described them as "Shias" after the 2017 Gulf crisis (Table 8.20).

Table 8.19 Framing of Bahrain's conflict in AJE's coverage in three research periods, from March 5, 2014, to September 1, 2021

Framing of Bahrain's conflict in AJE	First diplomatic crisis: March 5, 2014, to November 16, 2014 (9 news stories)	Non-conflict period: November 17, 2014, to June 4, 2017 (26 news stories)	Second diplomatic crisis: June 5, 2017, to September 1, 2021 (30 news stories)
Uprising	12 (27.9%)	20 (23.5%)	32 (32%)
Revolution	0	1 (1.2%)	2 (2%)
Conflict	0	0	0
Crisis, unrest, turmoil	6 (14%)	18 (21.2%)	14 (14%)
Protests	18 (41.9%)	39 (45.9%)	35 (35%)
Peaceful protests	1 (2.3%)	1 (1.2%)	4 (4%)
Pro-democracy or anti-government	6 (14%)	6 (7.1%)	13 (13%)
Total:	43	85	100

Table 8.20 Framing of the protesters in AJE's coverage of Bahrain's uprising in three research periods, from March 5, 2014, to September 1, 2021

Framing of the protesters in AJE	First diplomatic crisis: March 5, 2014, to November 16, 2014 (9 news stories)	Non-conflict period: November 17, 2014, to June 4, 2017 (26 news stories)	Second diplomatic crisis: June 5, 2017, to September 1, 2021 (30 news stories)
Protesters, opposition, opponents, demonstrators	10 (33.3%)	53 (52%)	77 (81.9%)
Pro-democracy or anti-government protesters	2 (6.7%)	0 (0%)	3 (3.2%)
Shia protesters, Shia-led protests, Shia opposition	18 (60%)	47 (46.1%)	11 (11.7%)
Peaceful protesters	0 (0%)	2 (1.9%)	3 (3.2%)
Revolutionaries	0 (0%)	0 (0%)	0 (0%)
Total:	30	102	94

8.10   AJA and AJE: Limited Application of People Frame

Similar to the limitedness of applying the Peace-Orientated frame in AJA, the criteria of the People-Orientated frame[3] were hardly applied during the 2014 dispute (2.6%), non-conflict period (1.6%) and 2017 Gulf crisis (4.7%) (Table 8.21).

AJE's application of the People-Orientated frame was limited during the 2014 dispute (3.7%) and non-conflict period (1.9%). However, displaying of the frame increased slightly during the 2017 Gulf crisis period (18.3%) (Table 8.22). Therefore, the results of this chapter are not very consistent with previous studies which argue that AJE has the tendency to give voice to the voiceless (Daoud, 2019; Al-Najjar, 2009; El-Nawawy & Powers, 2008; Firdous, 2009; Figenschou, 2011).

---

[3] Analytical criteria of the People-Orientated frame

1. (VV): Does the article give voice to civilians, ordinary people or victims?
2. (SC): Does the article mention the suffering that the crackdown caused?

302   Z. ABDUL-NABI

Table 8.21 Percentages of including/mentioning the People-Orientated criteria in AJA's coverage of Bahrain's uprising in three periods from March 5, 2014, to September 28, 2021

People frame in AJA	(VV) Voice of voiceless	(SC) Suffering caused by the crackdown	Total
First diplomatic crisis: March 5, 2014, to November 16, 2014 (19 news stories)	0%	5.3%	2.6%
Non-conflict period: November 17, 2014, to June 4, 2017 (61 news stories)	0%	3.3%	1.6%
Second diplomatic crisis: June 5, 2017, to September 28, 2021 (161 news stories)	0.6%	8.7%	4.7%

Table 8.22 Percentages of including/mentioning the People-Orientated criteria in AJE's coverage of Bahrain's uprising in three periods from March 5, 2014, to September 1, 2021

People frame in AJE	(VV) Voice of voiceless	(SC) Suffering caused by the crackdown	Total
First diplomatic crisis: March 5, 2014, to November 16, 2014 (9 news stories)	0%	11.11%	3.7%
Non-conflict period: November 17, 2014, to June 4, 2017 (26 news stories)	0%	3.8%	1.9%
Second diplomatic crisis: June 5, 2017, to September 1, 2021 (30 news stories)	10%	26.7%	18.3%

8.11 AJA and AJE: Increase in Solution Frame After the 2017 Gulf Crisis

While the Solution-Orientated frame[4] scored less than 11% in AJA coverage during the first conflict and non-conflict periods, more than one quarter of AJA coverage (25.5%) applied the frame during the Gulf crisis (Table 8.23). This significant increase can be attributed to the increase in quoting human rights activists (71%) (see Table 8.5) during the same period.

The application of the Solution-Orientated frame in AJE recorded higher percentages during the first conflict in 2014 (33.3%) and second conflict in 2017 (20%) compared to the non-conflict period (9.6%) (Table 8.24). Like AJA, the increase of the Solution-Orientated frame in AJE coverage during the 2017 Gulf crisis might have been caused by the

Table 8.23 Percentage of including/mentioning the Solution-Orientated criteria in AJA's coverage of Bahrain's uprising in three periods from March 5, 2014, to September 28, 2021

Solution frame in AJA	ISA Implications of sectarian and violation acts	PS Possible solutions	Total
First diplomatic crisis: March 5, 2014, to November 16, 2014 (19 news stories)	0%	21.1%	10.5%
Non-conflict period: November 17, 2014, to June 4, 2017 (61 news stories)	13.1%	0%	6.6%
Second diplomatic crisis: June 5, 2017, to September 28, 2021 (161 news stories)	5.6%	45.3%	25.5%

[4] Analytical criteria of the Solution-Orientated frame:

1. (ISA): Does the article mention the implications of the regime's violations and sectarian crackdown/measures?
2. (PS): Does the article give any possible solution/initiative from any source to break the deadlock and de-escalate the conflict?

304 Z. ABDUL-NABI

Table 8.24 Percentages of including/mentioning the Solution-Orientated criteria in AJE's coverage of Bahrain's uprising in three periods from March 5, 2014, to September 1, 2021

Solution frame in AJE	ISA Implications of sectarian and violation acts	PS Possible solutions	Total
First diplomatic crisis: March 5, 2014, to November 16, 2014 (9 news stories)	44.4%	22.2%	33.3%
Non-conflict period: November 17, 2014, to June 4, 2017 (26 news stories)	19.2%	0%	9.6%
Second diplomatic crisis: June 5, 2017, to September 1, 2021 (30 news stories)	16.7%	23.3%	20%

increase in quoting human rights activists (67.8%) during the same period (Table 8.6). The quoted human rights activists tended to suggest resolutions and demanded that the international community put pressure on the Bahraini regime. For instance, in the following news story, human rights organisations "urge Biden to shift US policy towards Bahrain". AJE stated:

> The letter [sent by human rights groups] also called on Biden, who is due to be sworn in next month, to restore human rights conditions on any arms sales or military support to Bahrain, and to consider the US's willingness to relocate the Fifth Fleet should Bahrain continue to violate the human rights of its citizens. The signatories recommended Biden's administration to work on securing the release of all imprisoned political opposition figures, and to ensure that victims of Bahrain's government abuses receive compensation and justice. (AJE, December 16, 2020c)

While reporting such statements gives "opportunities for society at large to consider and value non-violent responses to conflict" (J. Lynch & McGoldrick, 2005, p. 5), they still lack "creativity" which can—according to Galtung (2003, p.177)—transform conflicts. Galtung (2003) explains that PJ adopts a "high road" approach in which conflict is seen as a challenge and an "opportunity for human progress". This means that instead

8.12 Overall Peace Journalism Framing in AJA and AJE

The Truth- and Solution-Orientated frames were the most applied frames in the AJA coverage of Bahrain's uprising, reaching their peak during the 2017 Gulf crisis (33.5% and 25.5%, respectively) (Table 8.25). This study argues that the increase in displaying both frames during the 2017 conflict can be attributed to the condensed focus on human rights violations committed by the Bahraini regime against the protesters. This focus has been triggered—this study contends—by the deterioration of political ties between Qatar and its neighbours.

The Truth- as well as Peace/Conflict-Orientated frames have been applied consistently, scoring similar percentages in AJE's coverage of Bahrain' surprising during the three research periods (Table 8.26). On the other hand, the application of the Solution-Orientated and People-Orientated frames increased significantly from 9.6% and 1.9% during the non-conflict period to 20% and 18.3%, respectively, during the Gulf crisis (Table 8.26).

Table 8.25 Percentages of PJ frames in AJA's coverage of Bahrain's uprising in three periods from March 5, 2014, to September 28, 2021

PJ frames in AJA	Peace frame	Truth frame	Solution frame	People frame	Total
First diplomatic crisis: March 5, 2014, to November 16, 2014 (19 news stories)	17%	22.8%	10.5%	2.6%	13.2%
Non-conflict period: November 17, 2014, to June 4, 2017 (61 news stories)	5.1%	8.2%	6.6%	1.6%	5.4%
Second diplomatic crisis: June 5, 2017, to September 28, 2021 (161 news stories)	9.5%	33.5%	25.5%	4.7%	18.3%

Table 8.26 Percentages of Peace Journalism frames in AJE's coverage of Bahrain's uprising in three periods from March 5, 2014, to September 1, 2021

Peace Journalism frames in AJE	Peace frame	Truth frame	Solution frame	People frame	Total
First diplomatic crisis: March 5, 2014, to November 16, 2014 (9 news stories)	39.5%	29.6%	33.3%	3.7%	26.5%
Non-conflict period: November 17, 2014, to June 4, 2017 (26 news stories)	38.5%	32.1%	9.6%	1.9%	20.5%
Second diplomatic crisis: June 5, 2017, to September 1, 2021 (30 news stories)	37.4%	37.8%	20%	18.3%	28.4%

8.13 Conclusion

The empirical results found that AJA's coverage of Bahrain's uprising was reserved and became entirely pro-Bahraini regime when Bahrain and Qatar were on good terms in 2011 (see Chap. 5). When the ties deteriorated between the two countries, especially during the 2017 Gulf crisis in which Saudi Arabia along with Bahrain, the UAE and Egypt imposed a blockade on Qatar, AJA coverage became highly critical of the Al-Khalifa ruling dynasty, siding blatantly with the pro-democracy movement in the country.

This fundamental shift has been manifested in the increase of the Truth-Orientated frame and reporting on the regime's human rights violations against protesters. AJA went further by attributing the responsibility of torture to Sheikh Naser Bin Hamad Al-Khalifa, the son of King Hamad. AJA has also recorded a sharp increase in quoting human rights organisations, coinciding with a notable decrease in quoting Bahraini regime sources. In parallel with Qatar's critical position towards formally normalising relations with Israel, AJA has represented the normalisation deal between Bahrain and Israel, signed in September 2020, as a "betrayal" and "stab in the back of Palestinians".

AJA's dramatic shift from one side to another can be understood through what Wolfsfeld (2013) calls "politics first". According to this approach, media coverage can be better comprehended when taking into consideration the political environment surrounding it. When the political environment between Qatar and its neighbours has negatively changed during the 2017 crisis, AJA has changed its coverage of Bahrain's uprising accordingly. As a result of AJA coverage, the relations between Bahrain and Qatar have not recovered, even after Saudi Arabia reconciled with Qatar at the Al-Ula summit on January 4, 2021. This is in line with the Politics-Media-Politics (PMP) model that views the role of the media in politics as a "cycle" in which "variations" in a political environment can lead to "variations" in media coverage (Wolfsfeld, 2013, p.2). This can, in return, result in more "variations" in the political environment (Wolfsfeld, 2013, p.2).

AJA's shift in its coverage on Bahrain has been observed in the channel's coverage of other conflicts as well. For instance, quantitative content analysis studies found that AJA framed the war on Yemen and the Saudi-led coalition in a "positive tone" before the 2017 Gulf crisis, yet they were framed in a "negative tone" after the crisis (Alshabnan, 2018; Mejalli, 2019). The empirical results of other studies also found that AJA coverage during the 2017 Gulf crisis has sided with Qatar against Saudi Arabia while reporting on issues related to both countries (Ajaoud & Elmasry, 2020; Tartory, 2020, p.12).

While AJA has strongly focused on the regime's direct violence (Truth-Orientated frame), it has neglected the structural and cultural violence committed against protesters (Peace/Conflict-Orientated frame). Reporting on violations or "direct violence" is not enough if the aim is to convey a better understanding of the conflict. A PJ approach would give thorough attention to the discrimination of the majority Shia (structural violence). It would also openly discuss the "cultural violence" defined by Galtung and Fischer (2013, p.44) as "any aspect of a culture that can be used to legitimise violence in its direct or structural form". In Bahrain's case, it could be the regime's prejudice that Shias cannot be trusted or granted any power because they are "loyal to Iran". A PJ coverage would further initiate reporting on the implications that direct, structural and cultural violence can cause. For instance, Galtung and Fischer (2013, p.42) explain that direct and structural violence lead to "collective trauma", as they both deprive people of needs, which can make the deprived react by "direct violence... violence breads violence".

Although, AJA's documentaries countered the sectarian narrative of the Al-Khalifa regime and included the voices of the voiceless, such reporting remains still very limited and scattered. What if AJA journalists were aware or trained of applying the PJ orientations? What if they were more reflective and critical of their own coverage? Tiripelli (2016) has touched on journalists' reflexiveness by arguing that "external restrictions" are not the only obstacle towards applying PJ. Tiripelli (2016) who compared the narratives and beliefs of peace promoters and journalists covering the Israeli-Palestinian conflict found that media workers lack "critical engagement" with the political effects of their narratives, as well as media routines and professional principles.

In relation to AJE, the empirical findings show that it quoted human rights organisations and mentioned "torture" and "sexual assaults" more frequently during the 2017 Gulf crisis than the non-escalation periods. Besides, the application of the People- as well as Solution-Orientated frames notably increased in the AJE coverage during the second conflict. However, unlike AJA, the inclusion of the Truth-Orientated frame in AJE coverage has been relatively high and consistent during all research periods. Also, while AJA coverage has hardly mentioned the criteria of the Peace/Conflict-Orientated frame, AJE has applied them before and after the 2017 crisis nearly equally. This has resulted in producing a non-sectarian framing and more accurate representation of Bahrain's protest movement. AJE has also been consistent in framing the pro-democracy movement in the country as a legitimate "uprising" before and after the 2017 Gulf crisis. Still more, unlike AJA, AJE did not shy away from being critical to the military Saudi intervention in Manama before and after the deterioration of the ties between Qatar and Bahrain. Finally, while AJA depends on its coverage on the developments of "here and now", AJE has framed the normalisation deal as a "betrayal" even after the first two months of signing it.

Therefore, this study concludes that AJE coverage of Bahrain's uprising has been mostly consistent from 2011 until the last research period in September 2021. The dramatic political shift in the ties between Doha and Manama has not created a similar shift in AJE coverage. This might be because that AJE has already been critical and inclined towards PJ since the early stages of the conflict. The results of this study therefore do not strongly agree with other research which concluded that Qatar has systematically used AJE as a "political instrument" and "propaganda tool" to promote its foreign policy (Gasim, 2018; Alhendyani, 2019; Kharbach, 2020; Kosárová, 2020).

While researchers tried to explain the difference between AJA and AJE by comparing the content of both channels utilising quantitative and qualitative content analysis methods (Fakhri, 2011; Al-Nahed, 2015; Fahmy & Al-Emad, 2011), Barkho (2019) investigated to what extent both channels' commitment to a Code of Ethics and internal guidelines play a role in shaping their news content. Barkho (2019) found that the absence of written guidelines in AJA has resulted in more control and self-censorship among its staff and encouraged the use of less objective, "expressive and eloquent language". At the same time, however, AJE's adherence to a written guidelines that include instructions on "what to say and what not to say"—as one journalist puts it—resulted in the adoption of normative language and measured expressions (Barkho, 2019, p.94). Committing to such guidelines—one might infer—can save the channel from drastically changing its approach to conflicts. The differences between AJA and AJE can also be attributed to—as discussed in Chaps. 5, 6 and 7—AJE's commitment to conventional, objective reporting style, degrees of Qatar's involvement as well as the variations in their journalists, audiences and competitors.

References

Abunajela, M. A. (2015). *Al-Jazeera (Arabic) satellite television: A platform for the Muslim Brotherhood in Egypt.* [PhD thesis, the University of Bedfordshire]. https://uobrep.openrepository.com/handle/10547/601085

Ajaoud, S., & Elmasry, M. H. (2020). When news is the crisis: Al Jazeera and Al Arabiya framing of the 2017 Gulf conflict. *Global Media and Communication, 16*(2), 227–242.

Al-Nahed, S. (2015). Covering Libya: A framing analysis of Al Jazeera and BBC coverage of the 2011 Libyan uprising and NATO intervention. *Middle East Critique, 24*(3), 251–267.

Al-Najjar A (2009) How Arab is Al-Jazeera English? Comparative study of Al-Jazeera Arabic and Al-Jazeera English news channel. *Global Media Journal, 8*(14), 1–35.

Alhendyani, A. (2019). *The cost of truth in a world of politics: How Al-Jazeera and Al-Arabiya are influenced by Qatar and Saudi Arabia.* [Master's thesis, California State University]. https://scholarworks.calstate.edu/downloads/t722hd103

Alshabnan, A. (2018). The politicization of Arab Gulf media outlets in the Gulf crisis: A content analysis. *Global Media Journal, 16*(30), 1–6.

310   Z. ABDUL-NABI

Ayaad, S. W. (2014). *Qatari Foreign Policy, Al-Jazeera, and Revolution in the Middle East and North Africa* (Doctoral dissertation, Communication, Art & Technology: Communication). http://summit.sfu.ca/item/14739

Barkho, L. (2019). Editorial politics and practices. In H. B. Sadig (Ed.), *Al Jazeera in the Gulf and in the World* (pp. 67–98). Palgrave Macmillan.

Daoud, A. (2019). *Giving a voice to the voiceless: A comparative study of Al Jazeera English and Al Jazeera Arabic coverage of the Syrian refugee crisis* [Masters dissertation, Auckland University of Technology]. http://orapp.aut.ac.nz/handle/10292/12551

El-Nawawy, M. & Powers, S. (2008). *Mediating conflict: Al-Jazeera English and the possibility of a conciliatory media*. Los Angeles, CA: Figueroa Press.

Fahmy, S. & Al Emad, M. (2011). Al-Jazeera vs Al-Jazeera: a comparison of the network's English and Arabic online coverage of the US/Al Qaeda conflict. *The International Communication Gazette, 73*(3), 216–232.

Fakhri, F. (2011). *Content analysis of how Al -Jazeera English and Arabic channels framed the war on Gaza* (Master's thesis). Retrieved from ProQuest Dissertations and Theses.

Figenschou, T. U. (2011). The south is talking back: With a white face and a British accent – editorial dilemmas in Al Jazeera English. *Journalism 13*(3), 354–370.

Firdous, T. (2009). *Al Jazeera English presenting a non-western viewpoint and contesting western media dominance during the Gaza crisis* (Master's thesis). Retrieved from ProQuest Dissertations and Theses.

Galtung, J. (2003). Peace Journalism. *Media Asia, 30*(3), 177–180.

Galtung, J., & Fischer, D. (2013). *Johan Galtung: Pioneer of peace research*. Springer.

Gasim, G. (2018). The Qatari crisis and Al Jazeera's coverage of the war in Yemen. *Arab Media & Society, 25*, 1–9.

Guta, H. A. (2019). Al Jazeera: Non-violence and Peace Journalism. In H. B. Sadig (Ed.), *Al Jazeera in the Gulf and in the world* (pp. 191–220). Palgrave Macmillan.

Harb, Z. (2019). Covering regional conflicts in Arab News: Political loyalties and hate speech. In M. Kelly, H. Footitt, & M. Salama-Carr (Eds.), *The Palgrave handbook of languages and conflict* (pp. 273–293). Palgrave Macmillan.

Herman, E. S., & Chomsky, N. (2010). *Manufacturing consent: The political economy of the mass media*. Random House eBooks.

Kamrava, M. (2013). *Qatar: Small state, big politics*. New York & London: Cornell University Press.

Kempf, W. (2006). *Acceptance and impact of de-escalation-oriented conflict coverage*. Diskussionsbeiträge der Projektgruppe Friedensforschung Konstanz, Nr. 60. Berline: Regener.

Kharbach, M. (2020). Understanding the ideological construction of the Gulf crisis in Arab media discourse: A critical discourse analytic study of the headlines of Al Arabiya English and Al Jazeera English. *Discourse & Communication, 14*(5), 447–465.

Khatib, L. (2013). Qatar's foreign policy: the limits of pragmatism. *International Affairs, 89*(2), 417–431.

Kosárová, D. (2020). Al Jazeera and Al Arabiya: Understanding media bias. *Politické vedy, 23*(4), 87–108.

Lee, S. T. (2010). Peace journalism: Principles and structural limitations in the news coverage of three conflicts. *Mass Communication and Society, 13*(4), 361–384.

Lynch, J., & McGoldrick, A. (2005). *Peace journalism.* Hawthorn Press.

Machin, D., & Mayr, A. (2012). *How to do critical discourse analysis: A multi-modal introduction.* SAGE Publications.

Maziad, M. (2018). Qatar in Egypt: The politics of Al Jazeera. *Journalism, 22*(4), 1067–1087.

Mejalli, W. H. A. (2019). *Analyzing Al-Jazeera Arabic online news articles during the development of war in Yemen.* [Master's Thesis, University of Oslo]. https://www.duo.uio.no/handle/10852/70323

Miller, R., & Verhoeven, H. (2020). Overcoming smallness: Qatar, the United Arab Emirates and strategic realignment in the Gulf. *International Politics, 57*(1), 1–20.

Roberts, D. (2012). Understanding Qatar's foreign policy objectives. *Mediterranean Politics, 17*(2), 233–239.

Samuel-Azran, T. (2013). Al-Jazeera, Qatar, and new tactics in state-sponsored media diplomacy. *American Behavioral Scientist, 57*(9), 1293–1311.

Shoemaker, P. J., & Reese, S. D. (2013). *Mediating the message in the 21st century: A media sociology perspective.* Routledge.

Stephens, M. (2017). Why key Arab countries have cut ties with Qatar—and what Trump had to do with it. In N. Anayiss (Ed.), *The Qatar Crisis* (pp. 12–13). Project on Middle East political science.

Tartory, R. (2020). Critical discourse analysis of online publications ideology: A case of middle Eastern online publications. *SAGE Open, 10*(3). https://doi.org/10.1177/215824402094147

Times of Israel staff. (2018, March 19). *Israeli minister: Qatar making true effort to stop Gaza aid from boosting Hamas.* Times of Israel. https://www.timesofisrael.com/israeli-minister-qatar-making-true-effort-to-stop-gaza-aid-from-boosting-hamas/

Times of Israel staff. (2020, August 14). *Mossad said to ask Qatar to keep funneling cash to Gaza in deescalation effort.* Times of Israel. https://www.timesofisrael.com/mossad-said-to-asks-qatar-to-keep-funneling-cash-to-gaza-in-deescalation-effort/

Tiripelli, G. (2016). *Media and peace in the Middle East: The role of journalism in Israel-Palestine.* Palgrave Macmillan.

312   Z. ABDUL-NABI

Ulrichsen, K. C. (2014). *Qatar and the Arab Spring*. Oxford: Oxford University Press.

Wolfsfeld, G. (2013). The politics-media-politics principle: Towards a more comprehensive approach to political communication. In *APSA 2013 Annual Meeting Paper, American Political Science Association 2013 Annual Meeting, Chicago, Illinois* (pp. 1–33).

Zaken, D. (2021, December 15). Qatar, Israel reach agreement on diamond trade. *Al-Monitor.* https://www.al-monitor.com/originals/2021/12/qatar-israel-reach-agreement-diamond-trade#ixzz7FZNMnhSp

AL-JAZEERA ARABIC ARTICLES:

Al-Jazeera Arabic. (2018e, August 17). إنذار أممي حول زنازين البحري ..نبيل رجب وآخرون. https://www.aljazeera.net/news/reportsandinterviews/2018/8/17/%d9%86%d8%a8%d9%8a%d9%84-d8%b1%d8%ac%d8%a8-%d9%88%d8%a2%d8%ae%d8%b1%d9%88%d9%86-%d8%a5%d9%86%d8%b0%d8%a7%d8%b1-%d8%a3%d9%85%d9%85%d9%8a-%d8%ad%d9%88%d9%84-%d8%b2%d9%86d8%a7%d8%b2%d9%8a%d9%86

Al-Jazeera Arabic. (2019a, March 28). يخفي أنات السجون منظمات بالبحرين: ضجيج الفورميال. https://www.aljazeera.net/news/humanrights/2019/3/28/%-D8%A7%D9%84%D9%81%D9%88%D8%B1%D9%85%D9%8A%D9%84%D8%A7-%D9%8A%D8%AE%D9%81%D9%89-%D8%A7%D9%86%D8%A7%D8%AA-%D8%A7%D9%84%D8%B3%D8%AC%D9%88%D9%86-%D8%A8%D8%A7%D9%84%D8%A8%D8%AD%D8%B1%D9%8A%D9%86

Al-Jazeera Arabic. (2019b, July 14). الالعبون بالنار وما خفي أعظم. https://www.youtube.com/watch?v=BptzscpcCBQ

Al-Jazeera Arabic. (2020a, September 15). ال تطبيع مع اسرائيل قبل حل الصراع مع الفلسطينيين :قطر. https://www.aljazeera.net/news/politics/2020/9/15/%D9%82%D8%B7%D8%B1-%D9%84%D8%A7-%D8%AA%D8%B7%D8%A8%D9%8A%D8%B9-%D9%85%D8%B9-%D8%A5%D8%B3%D8%B1%D8%A7%D8%A6%D9%8A%D9%84-%D9%82%D8%A8%D9%84-%D8%AD%D9%84-%D8%A7%D9%84%D8%B5%D8%B1%D8%A7%D8%B9

Al-Jazeera Arabic. (2020c, November 16). وزير خارجية قطر: اتفاقية ابراهام ال تتالءم مع سياستنا اننا ال تقدم أي. أفق إلنهاء الحتالل. https://www.aljazeera.net/news/2021/10/13/%D9%88%D8%B2%D9%8A%D8%B1-%D8%AE%D8%A7%D8%B1%D8%AC%D9%8A%D8%A9-%D9%82%D8%B7%D8%B1-%D8%A7%D8%AA%D9%81%D8%A7%D9%82%D9%8A%D8%A9-%D8%A3%D8%A8%D8%B1%D8%A7%D9%87%D8%A7%D9%85-%D9%84%D8%A7

Al-Jazeera Arabic. (2020d, May 6). برلماني اسباني يسائل حكومة بالده عما فعلته إزاء الوضع الحقوقي المريع البحرين. https://www.aljazeera.net/news/humanrights/2020/5/6/%d8%a7%d9%84%d8%a8%d8%ad%d8%b1%d9%8a%d9%86-%d9%88%d8%b6%d8%b9-

%d8%ad%d9%82%d9%88%d9%82-%d8%a7%d9%84%d8%a5%d9%86%d8%b3%d8%a7%d9%86-%d9%85%d8%b1%d9%8a%d8%b9-%d8%a7%d8%b3%d8%a8%d8%a7%d9%86%d9%8a%d8%a7

Al-Jazeera Arabic. (2020e, July 11). محكومين بالإعدام. فلق أوربي من إهال محكة الإستئناف بالبحرين أدلة تشير إلى تعذيب.
https://www.aljazeera.net/news/humanrights/2020/7/11/%d9%82%d9%84%d9%82-%d8%a3%d9%88%d8%b1%d9%88%d8%a8%d9%8a-%d9%85%d9%86-%d8%a5%d9%87%d9%85%d8%a7%d9%84-%d9%85%d8%ad%d9%83%d9%85%d8%a9-%d8%a7%d9%84%d8%a7%d8%b3%d8%aa%d8%a6%d9%86%d8%a7%d9%81

Al-Jazeera Arabic. (2021b, July 30). منظمة حقوقية تطالب بالإفراج عن السنكيس المضرب عن الطعام 16على سوء المعاملة احتجا. https://www.aljazeera.net/news/humanrights/2021/7/30/16-%d9%85%d9%86%d8%b8%d9%85%d8%a9-%d8%ad%d9%82%d9%88%d9%82%d9%8a%d8%a9-%d8%aa%d8%b7%d8%a7%d9%84%d8%a8-%d8%a7%d9%84%d8%a8%d8%ad%d8%b1%d9%8a%d9%86-%d8%a8%d8%a7%d9%84%d8%a5%d9%81%d8%b1%d8%a7%d8%ac

Al-Jazeera Arabic. (2021c, February 11). أمنستي تتحدث عن "اشتداد وطأة الظلم المنهج" في البحرين.
https://www.aljazeera.net/news/humanrights/2021/2/11/%D8%A3%D9%85%D9%86%D8%B3%D8%AA%D9%8A-%D8%AA%D8%AD%D8%AF%D8%AB-%D8%B9%D9%86-%D8%A7%D8%B4%D8%AA%D8%AF%D8%A7%D8%AF-%D9%88%D8%B7%D8%A3%D8%A9-%D8%A7%D9%84%D8%B8%D9%84%D9%85

AL-JAZEERA ENGLISH ARTICLES:

Al-Jazeera English. (2016a, May 30). *Bahrain ramps up opposition chief Ali Salman's sentence.* https://www.aljazeera.com/news/2016/5/30/bahrain-ramps-up-opposition-chief-ali-salmans-sentence

Al-Jazeera English. (2016c, June 21). *Bahrain strips sheikh Isa Qassim of nationality.* https://www.aljazeera.com/news/2016/6/21/bahrain-strips-sheikh-isa-qassim-of-nationality

Al-Jazeera English. (2020a, September 13). *What is behind Bahrain's normalisation deal with Israel.* https://www.aljazeera.com/news/2020/9/13/what-is-behind-bahrains-normalisation-deal-with-israel-2

Al-Jazeera English. (2020b, September 23). *First direct flight from Israel lands in Bahrain.* https://www.aljazeera.com/economy/2020/9/23/first-direct-flight-from-israel-lands-in-bahrain-flightradar24

Al-Jazeera English. (2020c, December 16). *Rights groups urge Biden to shift US policy towards Bahrain.* https://www.aljazeera.com/news/2020/12/16/letter-urges-joe-biden-to-reconsider-foreign-policy-on-bahrain

CHAPTER 9

Conclusion

9.1 Introduction

This monograph has examined a total of 713 online articles from the AJA and AJE coverage of Bahrain's uprising (2011–2021) and Syria's second chemical weapons (CW) attack (2013). The articles were selected from the AJA and AJE websites and examined based on the PJ model (PJM), framing theory and quantitative as well as qualitative content analysis methods.

The articles of Al-Jazeera's coverage of Bahrain's uprising were collected and analysed from two periods: the Saudi military intervention from March 14 to June 1, 2011 (Chap. 5), and the periods before and after the 2017 Gulf crisis from March 5, 2014, to September 28, 2021 (Chap. 8). The data of the second CW attack was examined and collected from August 21 to September 14, 2013 (Chap. 6).

The 12 questions stated in Chap. 1, and explained thoroughly in Chap. 4, aimed at measuring the extent of the inclusion and exclusion of PJ and WJ framing in the AJA and AJE coverage of Bahrain's uprising from 2011 to 2021 and the second CW attack in Syria in 2013. It also explored how political developments and environments have impacted on the presence and absence of PJ frames in both conflicts. The study analysed the framing of Bahrain's and Syria's conflicts, quoted sources and the extent of

© The Author(s), under exclusive license to Springer Nature Switzerland AG 2022
Z. Abdul-Nabi, *Al-Jazeera's "Double Standards" in the Arab Spring*,
https://doi.org/10.1007/978-3-031-14279-6_9

316   Z. ABDUL-NABI

Al-Jazeera's dependence on news wires. The monograph also examined the frequency of using certain lexical choices that affected the representations of both conflicts. Most importantly, the degree of agreement between Qatar's politics and Al-Jazeera's framing of the Bahraini and Syrian conflicts was analysed based on comparative and quantitative tools.

This concluding chapter presents a summary of the main empirical as well as analytical findings, followed by the limitations of the study and suggestions for future research.

9.2   Quantitative Findings

- WJ dominated the AJA and AJE coverage of all analysed conflicts. Yet significant percentages of PJ framing, starting from 5.4% to 34.7%, were applied in the coverage of all conflicts.
- AJE coverage of all analysed conflicts displayed PJ framing more than AJA.
- AJE's coverage of Bahrain's uprising during the 2017 Gulf crisis recorded the highest percentage (28.4%) of displaying PJ framing in the news stories of all analysed conflicts.
- AJA's coverage of Bahrain's uprising during the non-conflict period (from late 2014 to mid-2017) recorded the lowest percentage (5.4%) of displaying PJ framing in the news stories of all analysed conflicts.
- PJ framing was significantly displayed in AJE's features more than its news on Bahrain's and Syria's conflicts. However, the percentages of PJ frames in the AJA news and features (AJA-N&F) were recorded as nearly equivalent in both conflicts.
- Qatar's allies recorded the majority of the quoted sources in the AJA and AJE news of all analysed conflicts, except for both channels' coverage of Bahrain's uprising during the 2017 Gulf crisis, as this coverage was dominated by human rights sources.
- AJA's and AJE's coverage of all analysed conflicts were dominated by pro-Qatar framing, except for AJE's coverage of 2011 Bahrain's uprising.
- AJA used more sectarian, emotive and demonising language than AJE in all analysed conflicts.
- High percentages of AJA-N&F framed the Syrian conflict as a "revolution" (20% and 32%), whereas the same term was hardly ever men-

tioned in Bahrain's uprising in the periods from 2011 to 2021 (less than 2%).

- High percentages of the coverage of both channels associated Bahraini protesters with their Shia sect, while far lower percentages associated them with "democracy" or "peaceful-ness" in all analysed news, starting from 2011 to 2021.
- The percentages of PJ frames have been affected directly by developments (here and now media routines) on the ground in the AJA and AJE coverage of all analysed conflicts.

9.3 ANALYTICAL FINDINGS

The results of this book are consistent with previous studies that found that despite the domination of WJ in media coverage, PJ orientations can be still significantly displayed (Lacasse & Forster, 2012; Ross, 2009; Hackett & Schroeder, 2009; Ozohu-Suleiman, 2014; Shinar, 2009; Lee & Maslog, 2005; Lee et al., 2006a, 2006b; Lee, 2010). This monograph, however, is among very few studies that have taken the quantitative findings to another level by exploring the implications of the exclusion of PJ frames in the representation of conflicts (see J. Lynch & McGoldrick, 2005; J. Lynch, 2006; Ottosen, 2010; Nohrstedt & Ottosen, 2015).

9.3.1 Implications of Not Including PJ Frames in 2011 Bahrain's Uprising Coverage

The analysis of the empirical findings concludes that the lack of displaying the Peace-, Truth-, People- and Solutions-Oriented frames in the AJA coverage of Bahrain's uprising during the Saudi military intervention in 2011 led to representing the pro-democracy protests as a "sectarian conflict" and thus delegitimising it. The sectarian framing has not only promoted the propaganda of the Al-Khalifa regime but has also undermined the protesters who have been associated with their "Shia" identity far more than "democracy", human rights and the Arab Spring uprisings. For example, the AJA coverage of the protests in 2011 barely showed the three prevailing scenes in the uprising: Bahrain's national flags surrounding the Pearl Roundabout, protesters carrying flowers as a symbol of adopting peaceful means and the slogans of Shia-Sunni unity.

In addition, not practicing "reflexivity", depending on official sources and marginalising the voice of the Bahraini protesters in the AJA coverage of the uprising in 2011 have facilitated passing "claims" as "facts" and vice versa. For instance, the allegations that the protesters had been financed and militarised by Iran and Hezbollah were represented as unchallenged "facts". On the other hand, "facts" (like torture) which were documented by the Bahrain Independent Commission of Inquiry (BICI) (2011) were reported as mere "claims". The following abuses—as an illustration—were downplayed as allegations: discrimination against the Shia majority, death under torture and destruction of Shia places of worships.

On the contrary, AJE's moderate implementation of PJ frames and critical framing of the Saudi military intervention have made its coverage of the 2011 uprising—to a significant extent—resistant to the sectarian narrative and propaganda of the Gulf Cooperation Council (GCC) and Al-Khalifa regime. The award-winning documentary film *Shouting in the Dark* (which greatly applied the PJ frames) shows how giving space to historical contexts and marginalised accounts can represent a more accurate narrative of conflicts and protect media outlets from officials' manipulation.

9.3.2 Implications of Not Including PJ Frames in the Al-Ghouta CW Attack Coverage

The domination of WJ orientations in the AJA and AJE coverage of the Al-Ghouta CW attack in Syria has resulted in omitting vital facts, context and historical background. For instance, both AJA and AJE hardly mentioned during the research period that the regime's soldiers were among those who died from previous CW attacks. In addition, both channels avoided pointing the finger at the Al-Qaeda-affiliated group—Al-Nusra Front, which had known access to CW and had already committed war crimes in Alawite and Christian villages. These exclusions, this book argues, have narrowed down the suspects to one perpetrator (the Al-Assad regime) and thus legitimised military action against Syria.

Similar to the AJA coverage of the Bahraini conflict, not applying "reflexivity" in the Al-Ghouta attack coverage has aided in misrepresenting the Syrian conflict. This has made both AJA and AJE coverage of Syria vulnerable to propaganda, distortions and officials' claims. This study observes that a significant number of allegations were reported without being countered by alternative narratives. These claims relate to US "intelligence information", the location of the launching point of the rockets that hit Eastern Al-Ghouta and the number of victims killed in the attack.

9.3.3 Double Standard Coverage of Bahrain's (2011) and Syria's (2013) Conflicts

This study infers that the overall coverage of Bahrain's uprising during the Saudi military intervention in 2011 (apart from AJE) and the Al-Ghouta CW attack in 2013 is in line with Qatar's double standard policy in Bahrain and Syria at the time.

Qatar's alliance with the Bahraini regime and Syrian opposition had been reflected in the overall coverage by Al-Jazeera at the beginning of the Arab Spring. The network, especially AJA, legitimised the Al-Khalifa regime in Bahrain and delegitimised Al-Assad's in Syria. This had manifested through giving more space to the Bahraini regime's officials over protesters, as well as giving more space to the Syrian opposition over the Al-Assad regime in the news stories of both channels. AJA also hardly framed the overwhelmingly peaceful protests in Manama as a "revolution", yet, at the same time, the same channel used the term significantly in referring to the Syrian conflict in 2013, in which the Al-Assad regime and opposition groups were fully armed and involved in fierce civil war.

Despite the fact that several media scholars, as well as Middle East scholars, criticised Al-Jazeera's imbalanced coverage of the uprisings in Bahrain and Syria during the so-called Arab Spring (Barakat, 2011; M. Lynch, 2013a, 2015, 2016; Kraidy, 2014; Ayaad, 2014; Khatib, 2013; Ulrichsen, 2014; Kamrava, 2013), this is the first quantitative study that proved the dual standards in both coverages.

Therefore, this monograph argues that the coverage by Al-Jazeera, especially AJA, has lost its role as an effective public diplomacy tool to Qatar and turned into a propaganda instrument and mouthpiece of Qatar's foreign policy during the 2011 Bahraini uprising and Syria's second CW attack.

9.3.4 Al-Jazeera After 2017 Gulf Crisis: Legitimisation of Bahrain's Uprising

When the political ties between Bahrain and Qatar deteriorated in 2014, followed by a more significant crisis in 2017, the AJA coverage of Bahrain's uprising became notably critical to the Al-Khalifa regime. In other words, the shift in Qatar's foreign policy from 2014 to 2021 has been followed by a similar shift in Al-Jazeera's coverage. Although AJA has maintained its sectarian framing of the Bahraini conflict, it applied the

Truth-Orientated frame intensively, quoted human rights activists more frequently and detailed the violations committed by the Al-Khalifa regime. These abuses, including "torture" and "sexual assaults" against protesters, were covered more thoroughly and systematically by AJA and AJE during the 2017 Gulf crisis compared to previous periods. AJA, which had avoided naming and holding the members of the Al-Khalifa ruling family responsible for violations in 2011, did not shy away from doing so after the 2017 diplomatic conflict. AJA attributed the responsibility of torturing activists and arresting athletes to the son of the King, Sheikh Naser Bin Hamad Al-Khalifa. Therefore, the variation of Qatar's politics towards the Bahraini regime was followed by a variation in the AJA coverage.

Unlike AJA, AJE's coverage of Bahrain's conflict has been mostly consistent from 2011 to 2021, during both escalation and de-escalation periods. The dramatic shift in the relations between Qatar and Bahrain has not resulted in a similar shift in the AJE coverage. For instance, although AJE quoted more human rights organisations and focused more on the violations committed by the Bahraini regime after the escalation between Qatar and Bahrain, its application of Truth- as well as Peace/Conflict-Orientated frames has been consistent before and after the 2017 crisis. The study concludes that AJE is less affected by Qatar's foreign policy when Qatar is not heavily involved in the conflict.

9.3.5   AJA and AJE: Similarities and Differences

Unlike the majority of the existing research (Kraidy, 2008; Fakhri, 2011; Fahmy & Al-Emad, 2011; Al-Nahed, 2015), this study found major differences between the coverage of AJA and AJE, especially in their coverage of the Bahraini uprising. These differences are mainly related to the extent of using sectarian as well as emotive language, degree of conformity to Qatar's politics and commitment to the standards of journalistic writing and objective reporting.

The study also concludes that AJE applied PJ frames in all analysed conflicts more than AJA. This, to some extent, agrees with other research that found that AJE has a tendency to give voice to the voiceless (Firdous, 2009; El-Nawawy & Powers, 2008; Al-Najjar, 2009; Figenschou, 2010; Daoud, 2019).

This study argues that Qatar's influence on AJA has dramatically shifted its coverage from pro- to anti-Bahraini regime during the 2014 and 2017 diplomatic crises. This is consistent with the latest studies that analysed the

AJA coverage of conflicts after the 2017 Gulf crisis and found that the channel promoted Qatar's foreign policy and its agenda (Alshabnan, 2018; Mejalli, 2019; Ajaoud & Elmasry, 2020).

At the same time, this study argues that the AJE coverage of Bahrain's uprising before and after the 2017 Gulf crisis has been consistent. The quantitative findings of this study therefore are not in line with other research which found that Qatar has significantly used AJE as a "political instrument" and "propaganda tool" to promote its politics in the region especially when Saudi Arabia is involved in the conflict being covered (Gasim, 2018; Alhendyani, 2019; Kharbach, 2020; Kosárová, 2020).

This book argues that the differences between both channels' coverage of the Bahraini and Syrian conflicts can be attributed to six reasons: (1) different ideologies of journalists, (2) different target audiences, (3) different competitors, (4) journalism culture, (5) absence (in AJA) or presence (in AJE) of internal written guidelines and (6) different degrees of intervention from the Qataris.

9.3.6 Factors Behind Inclusion and Exclusion of PJ Frames

As WJ frames dominated the Syrian coverage more than the coverage on Bahrain, this study agrees with other studies that the percentages of including and excluding PJ frames can be attributed to the proximity as well as intensity of the conflict (Wolfsfeld, 1997; Lee, 2010; Galtung & Ruge, 1965, p. 66) and the degree of the media owners' involvement in conflicts (Lee et al., 2006b; Fahmy and Eakin, 2014; Shinar, 2009; J. Lynch, 2008).

Additionally, in line with previous research, this study found that PJ frames can increase or decrease during certain times and developments in conflicts (Kempf, 2003; Ozohu-Suleiman, 2014; Lee, 2010; Mandelzis, 2007). It also argues that the percentages of applying PJ in features and documentary films are higher than news stories. This is in parallel with other studies that state that the "type of genre affect the proportion of PJ in media coverage (Kempf, 2006; Lee et al., 2006b; Lee, 2010).

Since the monograph found differences of PJ percentages in AJA and AJE in all analysed conflicts, it is concluded that the language and journalism culture of the media, the ideologies of journalists and target audience can affect, positively or negatively, the applying of the PJ frame.

9.4 Suggestions and Limitations

As the "structure is the message", Tehranian (2002) suggests pluralising the ownership of the media or what he calls "media pluralism" in order to practise PJ. Tehranian (2002) also proposes establishing a "World Media Development Bank" (beginning as a UN agency), to fund disadvantaged communities and hence balance the flow of information.

Blasi (2004) says that both academics and journalists should design a strategy to overcome the obstacles that hinder the implementation of PJ. Blasi (2004) suggests the following to increase the application of PJ: (1) developing a guideline for "constructive conflict reporting", (2) raising questions about real freedom of press, (3) advocating independent media ownership and structure, (4) encouraging media workers to be "dissenters" and (5) training reporters and journalists about Peace-Orientated coverage and social psychology. More specifically, Blasi (2004) suggests that journalists covering conflicts should gain three types of competencies: (1) journalistic skills and ability to investigate and write an interesting story under tight deadlines, (2) theoretical knowledge about types of conflicts and methods of resolution and (3) specific knowledge of political/economic contexts, actors, interests, goals and history of conflicts that journalists are supposed to cover. Kempf (2003) advises trainers of PJ to trust journalists' ability and creativity and focus on "learning by doing".

Media and PJ scholars have still not reached a final conclusion about the effectiveness of journalists in changing media content (as discussed in Chaps. 3, 5, 6, 7 and 8). This study has proved that there is a limited opportunity for journalists to practise "scattered opposition". This is not strong enough however, to challenge the editorial policy or change the overall representation of a media outlet (see Chap. 5). J. Lynch (2013b) says that there is a need to measure to what extent training journalists (on the basis of PJ) can affect the content of traditional media.

J. Lynch (2007) calls for a campaign to change the media through the media or advocating what he calls "media activism". Hackett (2011) says that there are three types of media reformers that mobilise to change media content: (1) media researchers, (2) journalists and (3) marginalised social movements.

Since information is no longer controlled by the mainstream and state media, activists and protesters in Bahrain and Syria have notably conveyed their voices through social media during their uprisings. A survey found that 85% of Bahrainis depended on Twitter—to different degrees—to follow the developments of the uprising in 2011 (Al-Sayed, 2016). The study further shows that 58% of Twitter's users have increased their exposure to the website after the pro-democracy movement in the country (Al-Sayed, 2016). Al-Sayed (2016) observes that 73% of elites (political and human rights activists) used formal Arabic and not Bahraini dialect in their tweets in order to publicise violations and convey what was happening to Arabic media outlets and audience.

Hussain Radhi, a Bahraini human rights activist, stated in an interview that Bahraini activists used Twitter, Facebook and YouTube to reach the mainstream media (personal communication, February 27, 2017). Radhi says that Bahrainis were creative in using social media and that they were "protesting online in virtual marches" in which "people tweet at the same time and use the same hashtag about a certain issue" (personal communication, February 27, 2017). Radhi explains that during the first years of the uprising, activists frequently promoted these kinds of campaigns, targeting (emailing/contacting/messaging/inboxing/tweeting) international media outlets and human rights organisations.

Radhi (who was targeted and constantly watched by the Ministry of Interior for his activities before fleeing to Switzerland) further says:

> As there was no media coverage on Bahrain, we [activists] were trying to attract media to report on what was going on in the country. We were contacting journalists, international media outlets and human rights organisations through social media. If a foreign reporter comes to Bahrain and covers the uprising, we would initiate a 'Thank You Campaign' to that journalist. We would bombard their social media accounts with 'Thank you messages.' Many activists in Bahrain contact foreign reporters, coordinate their visit to Bahrain 'as tourists,' take them [while they are undercover] to where protests are, organise their interviews with protesters and families of victims. We risk and put our lives on the line by doing that. Had it not been for the activists, you wouldn't have seen the likes of the Shouting in the Dark documentary film. (personal communication, February 27, 2017)

Likewise, in Syria, Andén-Papadopoulos and Pantti (2013) found that Syrian activists in diaspora have been effectively using social media to act as "brokers" between protesters on the ground and international media outlets. Andén-Papadopoulos and Pantti (2013) conclude that the experience of Syrian activists with foreign media outlets has increased their ability and awareness of media professional routines and measures.

In addition to their efforts to convey the voices of the marginalised to the mainstream media, both Bahraini and Syrian activists and journalists founded their own online newspapers and radios or what media scholarship calls "alternative media". In Bahrain, well-known journalists who were sacked and lost their positions after participating in the uprising in 2011 founded an online newspaper called *Bahrain Mirror*. In Syria, a group of young, independent journalists in diaspora founded SouriaLi online radio in which they broadcast shows and programmes full of raw stories about Syrian people and their daily life, the implications of conflict, poverty, food prices, drama, music, culture and sarcasm. Iyad Kallas, the programme manager of SouriaLi Radio, says in an interview conducted for this research:

> Creating SouriaLi came as a result of the need for an independent media industry in Syria. It came to reflect sincere voices with no censorship in the face of state-run and ideologized or agenda-powered or even affiliated national and international media outlets. It was also founded to provide Syrians with a platform for free speech and access to information. Our focus is not to speak about the Syrians, but with the Syrians. Our main audience is the Syrians themselves, while non-Syrians are a secondary target for us. We do face a lot of challenges, for three main reasons. First, the majority of funds dedicated for Syria go to humanitarian aid—apart from militarisation funds of course. Second, the logistical difficulties and the virtual model on which we built SouriaLi. Third, the fact that we are not politically affiliated. (personal communication, March 8, 2017)

Therefore, several studies can be conducted about the effectiveness of (1) journalists' training, (2) alternative media and (3) human rights activism in increasing PJ content in the mainstream media. Furthermore, studies can be conducted over the extent of the acceptance of PJ orientations among Arab journalists. It would also be significantly beneficial to measure the responses of Arab audiences to PJ and WJ framing especially in polarised areas in which the audience is significantly divided. The second step after this research should be examining whether PJ-Orientated coverage is capable of encouraging Bahraini as well as Syria audiences to consider "non-violent" responses to the conflicts in their countries.

The results of this study are limited as they focus only on the online content of both channels. The sectarian inclination, emotive language and selectivity of AJA—for instance—can be observed more blatantly in the channel's live shows and programmes. The argument of this study could have been stronger if it compared Al-Jazeera's coverage of Bahrain's uprising with the uprisings in Syria, Yemen, Egypt, Tunisia and Libya's in terms of framing, placement, frequency and prominence.

Since this study argues that AJA adopted a sectarian discourse in Bahrain and Syria, further research can be explored about the effects of such sectarian framing on audiences from different sects and affiliations. More specifically, quantitative and qualitative content analysis methods, framing theory and the PJM can be utilised to examine Al-Jazeera's representations of Sunni and Shia armed groups in the region and to what extent sectarian framing can escalate the Sunni-Shia division in the Middle East. There is a need to measure how audiences perceive the credibility of Al-Jazeera after the Arab Spring in several Arab countries.

REFERENCES

Ajaoud, S., & Elmasry, M. H. (2020). When news is the crisis: Al Jazeera and Al Arabiya framing of the 2017 Gulf conflict. *Global Media and Communication, 16*(2), 227–242.

Alhendyani, A. (2019). *The cost of truth in a world of politics: How Al-Jazeera and Al-Arabiya are influenced by Qatar and Saudi Arabia* (Master's thesis, California State University). https://scholarworks.calstate.edu/downloads/t722hd103

Al-Nahed, S. (2015). Covering Libya: A framing analysis of Al Jazeera and BBC coverage of the 2011 Libyan uprising and NATO intervention. *Middle East Critique, 24*(3), 251–267.

Al-Najjar, A. (2009). How Arab is Al-Jazeera English? Comparative study of Al-Jazeera Arabic and Al-Jazeera English news channel. *Global Media Journal, 8*(14), 1–35.

Al-Sayed, B. (2016). *Social media framing of Bahrain's protest movement and its impacts on audience: Twitter as a model* (Doctoral Thesis, Lebanese University).

Alshabnan, A. (2018). The politicization of Arab Gulf media outlets in the Gulf crisis: A content analysis. *Global Media Journal, 16*(30), 1–6.

Andén-Papadopoulos, K., & Pantti, M. (2013). The media work of Syrian diaspora activists: Brokering between the protest and mainstream media. *International Journal of Communication, 7*, 2185–2206.

Ayaad, S. W. (2014). *Qatari Foreign Policy, Al-Jazeera, and Revolution in the Middle East and North Africa* (Doctoral dissertation, Communication, Art & Technology: Communication). Accessed March 24, 2016, from http://summit.sfu.ca/item/14739

Bahrain Independent Commission of Inquiry. (2011). *Report of the Bahrain Independent Commission of Inquiry.* Manama: Bahrain Independent Commission of Inquiry.

326   Z. ABDUL-NABI

Barakat, R. (2011). *New media in the Arab world: A tool for redesigning geopolitical realities* (Master's Thesis, Lebanese American University, Lebanon). Accessed November11, 2013, from http://laur.lau.edulb:7080/xmlui/handle/10725/1047

Bläsi, B. (2004). Peace journalism and the news production process. *Conflict & Communication Online, 3*(1/2), 1–12. Accessed January 4, 2016, from http://www.cco.regener-online.de/2004/pdf_2004/blaesi.pdf

Daoud, A. (2019). *Giving a voice to the voiceless: A comparative study of Al Jazeera English and Al Jazeera Arabic coverage of the Syrian refugee crisis* (Masters dissertation, Auckland University of Technology). http://orapp.aut.ac.nz/handle/10292/12551

El-Nawawy, M., & Powers, S. (2008). *Mediating conflict: Al-Jazeera English and the possibility of a conciliatory media.* Figueroa Press.

Fahmy, S., & Al Emad, M. (2011). Al-Jazeera vs Al-Jazeera: a comparison of the network's English and Arabic online coverage of the US/Al Qaeda conflict. *The International Communication Gazette, 73*(3), 216–232.

Fahmy, S., & Eakin, B. (2014). High drama on the high seas Peace versus war journalism framing of an Israeli/Palestinian-related incident. *International Communication Gazette, 76*(1), 86–105.

Fakhri, F. (2011). *Content analysis of how Al -Jazeera English and Arabic channels framed the war on Gaza* (Master's thesis). Retrieved from ProQuest Dissertations and Theses.

Figenschou, T. U. (2010). A voice for the voiceless? A quantitative content analysis of Al Jazeera English's flagship news. *Global Media and Communication, 6*(1), 85–107.

Firdous, T. (2009). *Al Jazeera English presenting a non-western viewpoint and contesting western media dominance during the Gaza crisis* (Master's thesis). Retrieved from ProQuest Dissertations and Theses (Accession Order No. 1507250).

Galtung, J., & Ruge, M. H. (1965). The structure of foreign news. *Journal of Peace Research, 2*(1), 64–91.

Gasim, G. (2018). The Qatari crisis and Al Jazeera's coverage of the war in Yemen. *Arab Media & Society, 25* (N/A), 1–9.

Hackett, R. A. (2011). New vistas for peace journalism: Alternative media and communication rights. In I. S. Shaw, J. Lynch & R. A. Hackett, (Eds.), *Expanding peace journalism: Comparative and critical approaches* (pp. 35–69). Sydney: Sydney University Press.

Hackett, R. A., & Schroeder, B. (2009). Does anybody practice Peace Journalism? A cross-national comparison of press coverage of the Afghanistan and Israeli–Hezbollah wars. *Peace and Policy, 13*(1), 26–47.

Kamrava, M. (2013). *Qatar: Small state, big politics.* Cornell University Press.

Kempf, W. (2003). Constructive conflict coverage–A social-psychological research and development program. *Conflict & Communication Online, 2*(2), 1–13. Accessed June 22, 2016, from http://cco.regener-online.de/2003_2/pdf_2003_2/kempf_engl.pdf

Kempf, W. (2006). Acceptance and impact of de-escalation-oriented conflict coverage. Diskussionsbeiträge der Projektgruppe Friedensforschung Konstanz, Nr. 60. Berline: Regener. Accessed June 25, 2016, from https://kops.unikonstanz.de/bitstream/handle/123456789/10452/60.pdf?sequence=1

Kharbach, M. (2020). Understanding the ideological construction of the Gulf crisis in Arab media discourse: A critical discourse analytic study of the headlines of Al Arabiya English and Al Jazeera English. *Discourse & Communication, 14*(5), 447–465.

Khatib, L. (2013). Qatar's foreign policy: The limits of pragmatism. *International Affairs, 89*(2), 417–431.

Kosárová, D. (2020). Al Jazeera and Al Arabiya: Understanding media bias. *Politické vedy, 23*(4), 87–108.

Kraidy, M. M. (2008). *Al-Jazeera and Al-Jazeera English: A Comparative institutional analysis*. Woodrow Wilson International Center for Scholars, pp. 23–30. Accessed July 30, 2012, from http://repository.upenn.edu/cgi/viewcontent.cgi?article=1282&context=asc_papers

Kraidy, M. M. (2014). Media industries in revolutionary times. *Media Industries, 1*(2), 16–21. Accessed January 20, 2016, from http://www.mediaindustriesjournal.org/index.php/mij/article/view/45

Lacasse, K., & Forster, L. (2012). The war next door: Peace journalism in US local and distant newspapers' coverage of Mexico. *Media, War & Conflict, 5*(3), 223–237.

Lee, S. T. (2010). Peace journalism: Principles and structural limitations in the news coverage of three conflicts. *Mass Communication and Society, 13*(4), 361–384.

Lee, S. T. & Maslog, C. C. (2005). War or peace journalism? Asian newspaper coverage of conflicts. *Journal of Communication, 55*(2), 311–329.

Lee, S. T., Maslog, C. C., & Kim, H. S. (2006a). Framing analysis of a conflict: How newspapers in five Asian countries covered the Iraq War. *Asian Journal of Communication, 16*(1), 19–39.

Lee, S. T., Maslog, C. C., & Kim, H. S. (2006b). Asian Conflicts and the Iraq War: A comparative framing analysis. *International Communication Gazette, 68*(5–6), 499–518.

Lynch, J., & McGoldrick, A. (2005). War and Peace Journalism in the holy land. *Social Alternatives, 24*(1), 11–15.

Lynch, J. (2006). What's so great about Peace Journalism. *Global Media Journal, Mediterranean Edition, 1*(1), 74–87.

Lynch, J. (2007). Peace journalism and its discontents. *Conflict and Communication Online*, 6(2), 1–13. Accessed June 3, 2013, from http://www.cco.regener-online.de/2007_2/pdf/lynch.pdf

Lynch, J. (2008). *Debates in Peace Journalism*. Sydney: Sydney University Press.

Lynch, J. (2013a). Is Peace Journalism feasible? Pointers for research and media development. *Ethical Space: The International Journal of Communication Ethics*, 10(2/3), 15–24.

Lynch, M. (2013b). *The Arab uprising: The unfinished revolutions of the new Middle East*. Public Affairs.

Lynch, M. (2015). How the media trashed the transitions. *Journal of Democracy*, 26(4), 90–99.

Lynch, M. (2016). *The new Arab wars: Uprisings and anarchy in the Middle East*. Public Affairs.

Mandelzis, L. (2007). Representations of peace in news discourse: Viewpoint and opportunity for Peace Journalism. *Conflict & Communication Online*, 6(4), 1–10. Accessed July 17, 2016, from http://www.cco.regener-online.de/2007_1/pdf/mandelzis.pdf

Mejalli, W. H. A. (2019). *Analyzing Al-Jazeera Arabic online news articles during the development of war in Yemen* (Master's Thesis, University of Oslo). https://www.duo.uio.no/handle/10852/70323

Nohrstedt, S. A., & Ottosen, R. (2015). Peace journalism: A proposition for conceptual and methodological improvements. *Global Media and Communication*, 11(3), 219–235.

Ottosen, R. (2010). The war in Afghanistan and Peace Journalism in practice. *Media, War & Conflict*, 3(3), 261–278.

Ozohu-Suleiman, Y. (2014). War journalism on Israel/Palestine: Does contra-flow really make a difference? *Media, War & Conflict*, 7(1), 85–103.

Ross, S. D. (2009). A Summer's pastime: Strategic construction of the 2006 war in Lebanon. In S. D. Ross & M. Tehranian (Eds.), *Peace journalism in times of war* (pp. 59–78). Transaction Publishers.

Shinar, D. (2009). Can Peace Journalism make progress? The coverage of the 2006 Lebanon War in Canadian and Israeli media. *International Communication Gazette*, 71(6), 451–471.

Tehranian, M. (2002). Peace Journalism negotiating global media ethics. *The Harvard International Journal of Press/Politics*, 7(2), 58–83.

Ulrichsen, K. C. (2014). *Qatar and the Arab Spring*. Oxford University Press.

Wolfsfeld, G. (1997). *Media and political conflict: News from the Middle East*. Cambridge University Press.

INDEX

A
Advocacy, 54, 72–75
Al-Ghouta, 3, 8, 9, 18
Al-Ghouta chemical weapons attack, 91, 95, 97, 98, 117–124, 126, 135, 136
Al-Jazeera, 1–18, 25–46, 91, 94, 95, 107, 108, 119, 133, 134, 136, 143, 145, 157, 164, 165, 171, 175, 176, 180, 191, 195, 198, 199, 205–209, 212–214, 216, 222, 223, 225, 231, 233, 238, 239, 249–267, 271–309, 315, 316, 319–320, 325
Arab Spring, 1, 2, 4, 6, 15, 16, 25–46, 107, 109, 144, 149, 152, 156, 180, 181, 206, 222, 251, 283, 291, 317, 319, 325
Arab uprisings, 44

B
Bahrain uprising/Bahrain's uprising, 3–6, 17, 91, 94, 95, 97, 98, 101–109, 114, 115, 143–182, 249–251, 254, 255, 265–267, 271–276, 281, 283–287, 291–308, 315–321, 323, 325
Blockade, 271, 306

C
Chemical weapons, 3, 4, 7–9, 17, 18
Chemical weapons attack, 191–202, 205, 209, 222, 225–227, 230–232, 239
Content analysis, 91, 132, 134–136

D
Diplomacy, 27, 36–41
Double standard, 45, 249–267

F
Framing theory, 2, 10, 12, 13, 17, 91, 92, 94, 136, 143–146, 148, 155, 166, 167, 169, 177, 182, 191–194, 222–223, 234, 273, 274, 283, 285–301, 305–306

© The Author(s), under exclusive license to Springer Nature Switzerland AG 2022
Z. Abdul-Nabi, *Al-Jazeera's "Double Standards" in the Arab Spring*, https://doi.org/10.1007/978-3-031-14279-6

330 INDEX

H
Here and now, 250, 259–264
Human Rights Journalism
(HRJ), 62

M
Media structure, 76–79

N
News values, 54, 55, 75, 78, 82

O
Objectivity, 54, 68–72, 81, 83

P
Peace Journalism (PJ), 1–18, 92–96,
98–101, 175–178, 191, 193–195,
198, 204, 229, 231–234, 238,
239, 249–253, 256, 259–266,
271, 273, 300, 304–308,
315–318, 320–322, 324
Peace Journalism Model (PJM),
53–85
Propaganda, 41–44, 55, 64, 71–72,
76–78, 82–84, 144, 148, 149,
152, 160, 163, 164, 171, 173,
177, 181, 192, 196, 216, 229,
230, 238, 254–256

Q
Qatar's foreign policy/Qatari foreign
policy, 2, 4, 6, 9, 15, 16, 18, 31,
37, 38, 41, 42, 44, 45, 166, 178,
207, 253–256, 266, 271, 272,
282–285, 319–321
Quantitative, 91, 132, 134–136

S
Sectarian, 143–182
Sectarianism, 149, 155, 157–158,
181, 238
Sexual assaults, 272, 273, 278–279,
282, 308
Sheikh Nasser bin Hamad, 272, 279,
296, 306
Syria chemical weapons attack,
249–251, 254, 262, 265, 266,
315, 318, 319
Syria civil war, 191–239

T
Torture, 272, 273, 275, 278–279,
306, 308
2014 Gulf dispute, 271–309
2017 Gulf crisis, 2–4, 15, 18, 271–309

V
Violations, 272–279, 282, 305–307